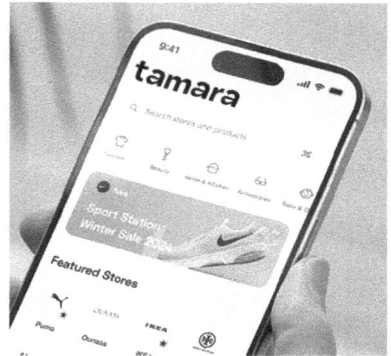

"*Scaleup Arabia* is a definitive guide to navigating the messy middle—when startups must evolve from hustle to structure, and speed to scale."

—**DAVID COHEN**, Founder and Chairman of Techstars, and author of *Do More Faster*

"In a region racing toward digital transformation, *Scaleup Arabia* captures the heart of innovation in action."

—**TIM DRAPER**, Founder at Draper Associates and DFJ

"*Scaleup Arabia* makes a powerful case for why MENA is no longer a frontier—but a global force in innovation and entrepreneurship."

—**CHRISTOPHER M. SCHROEDER**, Co-Founder of Next Billion Ventures, Advisor and Network Partner at Village Global, and author of *Startup Rising*

"After reading the first three chapters of *Scaleup Arabia*, I was astonished by the depth of insight into the thinking, inspiration, and mindset of the region's most daring and brilliant entrepreneurs. This book is a must-read for anyone determined to transform what they do, how they do it, and why they do it in an increasingly entrepreneurial world. I wholeheartedly recommend it."

—**MICHAEL E. GERBER**, Creator of *The E-Myth* and author of *The E-Myth* books

"*Scaleup Arabia* proves that emerging markets like MENA aren't playing catch-up—they're writing their own rulebooks."

—**VERNE HARNISH**, Founder of the Entrepreneurs' Organization (EO) and author of *Scaling Up (Rockefeller Habits 2.0)*

"*Scaleup Arabia* highlights the builders who are reprogramming what's possible across technology, logistics, fintech, and more."

—**STRAUSS ZELNICK**, Chairman & CEO of Take-Two Interactive and Founder & Managing Partner of Zelnick Media Capital

"A vital contribution to global entrepreneurship literature—*Scaleup Arabia* is rooted in MENA, but packed with lessons for the entire global entrepreneurial ecosystem."

—**JONATHAN ORTMANS**, President of Global Entrepreneurship Network

"*Scaleup Arabia* feels like a conversation with 15 of the best founders in the region—raw, real, and incredibly useful."

—**ANKUR WARIKOO**, Entrepreneur, 4× Bestselling Author (including *Build an Epic Career*), and one of India's leading voices on startup growth

SCALEUP ARABIA

JOURNEYS
& LESSONS
FROM TOP
FOUNDERS
& LEADERS
DRIVING
GROWTH
IN MENA

AMIR HEGAZI

TRANSFORMENA
PUBLISHING

TRANSFORMENA
PUBLISHING

Ordering information: Special discounts are available on quantity purchases by governments, NGOs, schools, companies, associations, and others. For details, contact the publisher at www.CapitalDemocracy.com.

Bibliographic Information: Hegazi, Amir. Scaleup Arabia.

Hardcover ISBN: 978-1-0684760-0-6

Paperback ISBN: 978-1-0684760-1-3

E-book ISBN: 978-1-0684760-2-0

Categories:

1. Business & Money, International 2. Business & Money, Entrepreneurship 3. Business & Money, Management

First Edition

Cover design by Hasdho
Interior design by www.meadencreative.com

www.CapitalDemocracy.com

To the next generation of MENA entrepreneurs—
may you always scaleup to new heights of greatness.

CONTENTS

INTRODUCTION

The Journey to *Scaleup Arabia*

When I first set out to write *Startup Arabia* in 2017, my goal was simple but deeply personal: to share the untold stories driving entrepreneurship in the Middle East and North Africa region (MENA). At the time, the region's startup ecosystem was still in its infancy, yet I had witnessed incredible progress firsthand, particularly during my tenure at Souq.com, where I helped launch and manage its marketplace division. The Amazon acquisition of Souq.com in March 2017 marked a major milestone for the ecosystem, a proof that bold ideas and relentless execution could drive real impact.

That experience inspired me to surface the story of Souq.com and other pioneers shaping the regional landscape. *Startup Arabia* was born out of my desire to spotlight the extraordinary founders who defied the odds, challenged cultural norms, and launched businesses that were not only successful but also transformative. The response to the book was humbling—it resonated with thousands of aspiring and current entrepreneurs, investors, policymakers, and ecosystem builders across the region and beyond. The book went on to become an Amazon international bestseller and was selected among "the best startup innovation books of all time" by BookAuthority, the leading entity curating and ranking the best books in various categories based on recommendations from thought leaders, industry professionals, and public mentions. It became clear that *Startup Arabia* wasn't just a book; it was a catalyst for conversation and action, a call to dreamers to take charge of their destinies.

But the story didn't end there.

The Evolution of MENA's Startup Ecosystem

In the years that followed, I immersed myself deeper into the region's emerging startup ecosystem. The launch of my second book, *Ecosystem Arabia*, was a natural next step, an opportunity to widen the lens and examine the broader forces shaping entrepreneurship in the region. Drawing insights from my interactions with hundreds of founders, investors, educators, and policymakers both in the region and globally, I sought to create a practical blueprint for fostering innovation and growth in MENA and beyond, especially in emerging markets.

The success of *Ecosystem Arabia* highlighted an important truth: building a thriving entrepreneurial ecosystem is a collective effort. Success requires visionary policies, bold investors, and founders who turn inspiration into action. The MENA region, fueled by initiatives like Saudi Arabia's Vision 2030 and the UAE's pro-startup reforms, was rapidly transforming. Funding levels skyrocketed, accelerators and incubators flourished, and a new generation of entrepreneurs began to dream bigger and bolder.

Through my work mentoring founders and advising ministers and policymakers over the years, I saw the incredible strides the region had made and was fortunate to partake in. I also saw the challenges that persisted firsthand, particularly in the journey from startup to scaleup. Launching a company was hard enough, but scaling it—navigating regulatory hurdles, securing growth capital, building resilient teams, expanding regionally and internationally—was an entirely different beast. This realization planted the seeds for *Scaleup Arabia*.

The Inspiration Behind *Scaleup Arabia*

Scaleup Arabia, being the sequel to *Startup Arabia*, is my response to the next phase of MENA's entrepreneurial evolution. While *Startup Arabia* captured the spirit of starting and building, this book focuses on scaling—on the challenges, strategies, and lessons of taking more mature companies in more mature regional startup landscape to the next level.

Introduction

In writing this book, I reflected on my own experiences helping launch and scale Souq.com marketplace and other companies I co-founded or helped scale to acquisition and IPOs; as well as my firsthand observations of hundreds of other regional and international startups I closely worked with while navigating similar journeys.

Stories of Grit, Growth, and Transformation

Scaleup Arabia dives into the diverse, insightful, and inspiring journeys of top MENA entrepreneurs as they tackle the complex realities of scaling. From fintech startups disrupting payment systems in Saudi Arabia to e-commerce platforms expanding across North Africa to innovative healthcare providers reinventing patient care, the stories in *Scaleup Arabia* reflect the extraordinary diversity of the region's ecosystem.

I've also highlighted diverse types of entrepreneurs—different geographies, industries, and stages of growth—all united by their determination to drive growth and impact. After all, scaling is not a one-size-fits-all journey, hence I ensured this book reflects this reality and the varied paths to sustainable growth as much as possible.

These remarkable founders and business leaders are tackling local challenges with solutions that resonate globally. They are navigating uncertain regulations, leveraging cultural nuances, and building companies that can thrive regionally and beyond. Their stories provide not only inspiration but also practical lessons for navigating the messy, exhilarating process of scaling a business.

Through this book, I aim to shine a light on their journeys and offer actionable lessons for anyone looking to grow a business in one of the world's most dynamic and challenging regions. Whether you're a founder, an investor, a policymaker, or simply someone passionate about entrepreneurship and innovation, *Scaleup Arabia* provides a front-row seat to the evolution of MENA's startup landscape as told from the very same leaders at its forefront.

A Call to Dream Bigger and Bolder

My "shot-for-the-moon" aim for this book is to awaken dreamers across the region and inspire them not to abandon their aspirations in the name of "being realistic." Quite the contrary: I hope they will embrace the challenges, think bigger, and act bolder. There is hidden power in such pursuit. Whenever you set out to pursue a dream—or search for one—you are already a success. Failure stems only from inaction.

To every dreamer and builder reading this: you owe it to yourself to tap into your full potential and never hold back. I hope you find value in the pages ahead and apply the lessons within to your own journey. Together, we can continue to build a brighter, more innovative future for MENA and beyond.

I would very much enjoy hearing from you. I hope you find value in the following pages and commit to apply whatever lessons you may learn.

—**AMIR HEGAZI**
April, 2025
London, UK

TOMASO RODRIGUEZ

Delivering connections, not just orders

CEO of TALABAT

Dubai, UAE

https://corporate.talabat.com

TOMASO RODRIGUEZ has been the Chief Executive Officer (CEO) of talabat since September 2019. Under his leadership, talabat has solidified its position as the leading on-demand delivery platform in the Middle East and North Africa (MENA) region, operating in countries such as Kuwait, Bahrain, the United Arab Emirates, Oman, Qatar, Jordan, Egypt, and Iraq.

Before joining talabat, Tomaso held significant roles in the food delivery industry. At Grab, a prominent Southeast Asian super-app, he served as the Head of GrabFood, where he expanded the food delivery business from a single city to 250 cities within 18 months. Prior to that, he was Head of UberEATS Regional Operations for the Asia-Pacific region, overseeing the platform's growth across multiple markets.

Tomaso's entrepreneurial journey began in 2008 when he founded AgencyManagement, a web and mobile software company focused on collecting and analyzing consumer engagement data. The company was later acquired by a major consumer goods firm. In addition to his role at talabat, Tomaso has been a member of the Board of Directors of Bin Ghati Development Company since January 2024.

Tomaso's tenure at talabat has been marked by significant growth and innovation. He emphasizes an "experience first" approach, ensuring that products and services are designed with stakeholders in mind. This philosophy is reflected in talabat's continuous efforts to enhance user experience and operational efficiency.

His leadership style is characterized by a hands-on approach and a commitment to understanding all facets of the business. For instance, Tomaso made headlines for working as a delivery rider to gain firsthand insight into the challenges faced by frontline staff. Tomaso Rodriguez's strategic vision and leadership continue to drive talabat's expansion and success in the competitive food delivery industry.

TALABAT, founded in 2004 in Kuwait, has grown into the leading on-demand delivery platform in the Middle East and North Africa (MENA) region. Operating in the United Arab Emirates, Kuwait, Qatar, Bahrain, Egypt, Oman, Jordan, and Iraq, it provides customers with a seamless and convenient way to order food, groceries, and other essential products from a vast network of restaurants and retailers.

In its early years, talabat quickly gained traction in Kuwait's food delivery market. By 2009, its success attracted investor interest, leading to an exit when the company was acquired by Jabbar Internet Group—the same firm behind the success of Maktoob, which was later acquired by Yahoo! This acquisition marked a turning point, providing talabat with the resources and strategic vision needed for regional expansion.

Following this transition, talabat continued its upward trajectory, expanding its footprint across the GCC. The company changed hands again in 2015 when Rocket Internet acquired it for $170 million, marking one of the biggest exits in the region's tech ecosystem at the time. In 2015, talabat became part of Delivery Hero's global portfolio, a move that propelled its expansion into new markets and solidified its leadership in online food delivery.

Over the years, talabat has diversified beyond food delivery. The launch of talabat Mart introduced quick-commerce grocery delivery, promising delivery in under 30 minutes. The company also expanded into convenience retail, offering pharmaceuticals, flowers, and other essential products. Leveraging data-driven personalization and real-time tracking, talabat has optimized its platform to enhance customer experience and streamline operations.

By 2024, talabat serves over six million active users each month and partners with more than 65,000 restaurants and retailers. With a logistics network powered by over 119,000 riders, the company ensures fast and reliable deliveries across the region. Despite multiple ownership changes, talabat has maintained its dominance in the MENA on-demand delivery market, continuously evolving through technological innovation and strategic expansion.

Tell us a bit about yourself and your background.

Thank you, Amir. I'll take a trip down memory lane.

I was born in a small town in Italy called Padova, which has a population of around 200,000 and is near Venice. It's also a university city, with tens of thousands of students flocking in every year. It's a great place to be when you're young.

A fun fact about this part of Italy is that the economy is overwhelmingly made up of small and medium-sized enterprises (SMEs)—99.99% of businesses, to be precise. When I was studying, I was always fascinated by marketing, even though I trained as an engineer. I actually thought I would become a marketer.

After university, I applied for many roles at companies like Unilever, Procter & Gamble, and Coca-Cola—but I got rejected everywhere. I even applied for a Procter & Gamble position in the Dominican Republic and got rejected.

At the same time, during university, I worked small jobs, including as a waiter. I also observed market researchers interviewing customers about their habits and the products they used. That led a friend and me, in 2009, to come up with an idea for an iPhone app that would digitize this process—essentially automating customer interviews and insights collection.

The company did quite well. Today, the idea seems obvious—just replacing paper-based surveys with a digital solution—but in 2009, when the iPhone 3GS had just come out, it was groundbreaking. However, I knew nothing about venture capital or raising funds to grow a business. Coming from an SME-driven environment, I assumed entrepreneurs had to rely solely on their own capital.

I made every possible mistake when launching the startup. One major one was that we didn't have money for legal support, so I asked a friend who had just graduated from law school to draft our contract. We landed a huge client, but the contract was so poorly written that, a few years later, they sued us, claiming our company was actually theirs. Technically, they were right. We had to negotiate and ultimately sell the company back to them for peanuts. I jokingly say I had an exit, but it was a terrible one.

After that, I pursued an MBA and joined a venture capital firm in Italy called 360 Capital Partners. They invest in European tech startups, with funds in France and Italy. It was an eye-opening experience—meeting hundreds of entrepreneurs and learning how venture capital works, how startups scale, and how funding rounds are structured.

Venture capital firms meet hundreds of startups each year but invest in maybe 10. Every meeting felt like a clash of perspectives, with founders pitching ideas they believed would change the world. My job was to determine whether each was one of the rare startups worth investing in. That exposure to different ways of thinking was invaluable.

While working in VC, I was approached by Uber in 2012, when they were launching in Europe. Back then, Uber was a small startup—$10 million in the bank and about 100 employees globally. They only offered black car services—no UberX or other products yet.

At the time, I was conducting due diligence on a French Uber competitor, Chauffeur Privé, so I knew everything about the space. That gave me an edge in the interview process, and I was hired to launch Uber in Italy. I built the ridesharing business, eventually becoming General Manager for Italy and Greece.

In 2015, Uber was launching Uber Eats and needed someone to manage regional operations for Asia. I applied, as I had always wanted to work outside Europe and experience different geographies and cultures. I moved to Asia and launched Uber Eats across 13 countries, including India, Southeast Asia, Japan, Australia, and New Zealand.

The experience was incredible. I learned how business operates differently in Asia compared to Europe. Then, in 2018, Grab acquired Uber's Southeast Asia business. Grab didn't have a food delivery vertical at the time but wanted one.

A challenge arose because, while Uber Eats had a substantial business in Southeast Asia, Grab had no tech infrastructure to support food delivery after the merger. We made a last-minute deal with

DoorDash—back then, a tiny company in the U.S.—to white-label their app for Southeast Asia. It was a clunky process, full of bugs, but we managed to keep the business running while building Grab's own food delivery product. Eventually, we launched GrabFood, scaled it to 250 cities across six countries, and built it into a major player in the region.

In 2019, Delivery Hero approached me about becoming CEO of talabat. talabat was already an incredible company—one of the oldest food delivery platforms in the world, founded in 2004. It had strong brand loyalty and massive potential, but there were areas where we could significantly boost performance.

I was also drawn to the Middle East—a region I had never been to but found exciting. And here we are, five years later—that's where I am today.

What were talabat's strengths and challenges when you joined?

When I joined talabat, one of the first things I realized was how incredibly strong the foundations were. The team and the previous founders had built something very solid. Coming from Uber and Grab, I was used to an environment where you were building the house while also laying the foundation, constantly having to reinforce things to keep them from shaking. talabat, on the other hand, was already a very commercially strong company. The number of orders was steady, customer cohorts were growing well, and the business had a lot of stability.

At the same time, there were clear areas where things could improve. The company was much more commercially driven than tech-driven. A small but telling detail was that the tech team, which consisted of only 20 people, was working out of a basement in Kuwait and was called the "IT team." Fast forward to today, and we have 540 people in product and tech, based in Dubai and Cairo, coming from all over the world—Asia, the U.S., and Europe. But back then, it was difficult to attract top tech talent with that kind of setup. We needed to open up the company to operate more like an international tech-driven business, both to improve our capabilities and to build a strong employer brand that could attract the best people.

———

66 We needed to open up the company to operate more like an international tech-driven business, both to improve our capabilities and to build a strong employer brand that could attract the best people.

———

Operationally, one of the biggest challenges was that talabat was structured as a marketplace, or what we call a "3P" model, where restaurants managed their own deliveries. This created a poor customer experience because people couldn't track their orders, and delivery times were highly inconsistent—sometimes food arrived in 20 minutes, other times it took over an hour. That was one of the most pressing issues to fix in order to improve the overall business. We started working proactively to scale our own delivery fleet, shifting talabat towards a model where we controlled the entire delivery experience. Over time, we moved close to 100% own-delivery, which made a massive difference. As the experience improved, customers started ordering more frequently, and engagement on the platform increased significantly. That shift was one of the biggest drivers of growth.

In your first few months at talabat, what were the biggest challenges and opportunities you tackled?

One of the advantages of coming in as a new CEO is that you don't have any pre-existing biases, relationships, or legacy attachments within the company. That makes it easier to evaluate things objectively and make tough decisions when necessary. It's not about having any special skill; it's just that having a fresh perspective allows you to make changes more decisively.

———

> ONE OF THE ADVANTAGES OF COMING IN AS A NEW CEO IS THAT YOU DON'T HAVE ANY PRE-EXISTING BIASES, RELATIONSHIPS, OR LEGACY ATTACHMENTS WITHIN THE COMPANY. THAT MAKES IT EASIER TO EVALUATE THINGS OBJECTIVELY AND MAKE TOUGH DECISIONS WHEN NECESSARY.

———

There were a few key areas that needed immediate attention. One of the first was the leadership structure. Many people had been with the company for a long time, had grown into leadership roles, and had played a key role in talabat's success. But as the company scaled, in some cases, it outgrew certain leaders. That created a difficult situation because these were people who had been part of talabat for 10 years or more. Making changes wasn't easy, but at the same time, if we didn't, we wouldn't be able to attract top talent to work for them. Leadership at scale needs to inspire, and if the next generation of talent doesn't see that in their managers, they won't want to work for them. That was a crucial aspect of taking the company to the next level.

Another major focus was the shift to own-delivery. The existing marketplace model created too much inconsistency, and customers needed a more reliable experience. Scaling our own fleet was a big operational challenge, but it was necessary. Once we started controlling deliveries, the platform experience improved dramatically, and customers responded by increasing their order frequency. That transformation helped accelerate the business.

Beyond food delivery, we also had to think about how the company should evolve in a rapidly changing industry. Being just a food delivery platform was no longer enough. We started identifying synergies between food and other convenience-driven services, which led us to invest in grocery delivery towards the end of 2019. That's when we launched talabat Mart, our network of dark stores operating 24/7 with deliveries in under 20 minutes. What started as a way to deliver essentials quickly soon scaled into a full offering, catering not just to urgent needs but also to weekly and monthly grocery shopping. At the same time, we built our grocery marketplace, enabling traditional retailers to sell through talabat's platform.

The reason grocery delivery made so much sense was that we already had a fleet on the ground. The same couriers who delivered food could also deliver groceries, making the overall system more efficient. On top of that, we realized that customers who valued convenience in food delivery were likely to want the same for groceries. The results proved that assumption right—customers who ordered from multiple verticals, rather than just food, were significantly more loyal and engaged with the platform at a much higher frequency.

Beyond these strategic shifts, another key focus was transforming talabat into a truly tech-driven company. The company had always been strong commercially, but it needed to evolve into a product-led organization. That meant not just scaling the tech team but also changing the internal culture to think about the business from a product and innovation standpoint rather than purely a sales-driven one.

All of these changes—strengthening leadership, shifting to own-delivery, expanding into grocery and retail, and becoming a tech-first company—were big bets that shaped talabat's transformation.

How did you navigate leadership changes as talabat scaled and ensure the company attracted top talent?

When it comes to the team, I touched on this earlier, but it was really about the heritage of a lot of people who had been with the company for many years. Over time, though, the company had outgrown some of them, and it became necessary to make changes. If you want to attract the best talent from Silicon Valley, Singapore, China, Europe, or anywhere else, you need leaders who stand out—people that others want to work for. Leadership isn't just about experience; it's about inspiring teams and setting a high standard.

———

> LEADERSHIP ISN'T JUST ABOUT EXPERIENCE; IT'S ABOUT INSPIRING TEAMS AND SETTING A HIGH STANDARD.

———

I believe that one of the most crucial responsibilities of a CEO in a scaling company is ensuring that leadership evolves with the business. Sometimes, personal relationships can make those decisions more difficult, especially for founders who built the company alongside their early team members. Even when they recognize that the company has outgrown certain leaders, it's incredibly hard for them to make those changes. I completely respect and understand that. But at a certain point, it becomes inevitable.

Today, I can confidently say that the team I have at talabat is the strongest I've ever worked with in my career. I lean on them completely and trust them fully. They are truly exceptional leaders, and that makes all the difference in scaling the company.

Let's revisit the restructuring—how did you decide at scale who stays and who to replace?

It's a combination of many factors, but one of the most important things I look for is whether people can truly work as a team and support each other. The CEO's role is to ensure that the entire organization moves in the same direction. That's why I spend an outsized amount of time on building OKRs—and I know that in many companies, this process is dreaded. But for me, it's absolutely crucial.

I like to approach it by working closely with my team to align on the company's top priorities. Right now, we have 11 key priorities, though in the past it has been seven or eight. Each team then figures out how they can contribute to those priorities. If they have extra capacity, they can take on additional initiatives, but the focus must always be on those core objectives first. It's an extremely difficult and sometimes painful process because aligning an entire organization around a set of priorities is hard. But when you have leaders who collaborate well, who set aside their individual goals in favor of what's best for the company as a whole, that's when real progress happens. It's about putting ego aside and working toward the greater good. That's the kind of leadership we need.

How do you set and track OKRs across teams while ensuring alignment and accountability?

This might sound crazy, but we reset OKRs every six months, and the process of defining them takes two to three months. On the surface, it seems like an incredible amount of time, but I believe it's the most valuable time spent in the organization.

For each of the 11 priorities, we create a task force. Each task force consists of my six-person executive team along with the relevant leaders from across the company who are essential for that particular initiative. These groups usually have around 10 or 11 people, and every member has clear objectives they are responsible for driving forward.

As we work toward those objectives, we often uncover things we didn't know before. For example, when we first launched grocery delivery, our goal was simply to build and grow a grocery business. But as we progressed, we discovered that when a food customer starts ordering groceries as well, their total order frequency jumps from 3.8 orders a month to 13. And interestingly, most of those additional orders are actually on food, not just groceries.

That insight completely changed how we thought about grocery delivery. It wasn't just about building a new vertical—it was about turning food customers into multi-vertical customers, which made them significantly more loyal and valuable. Because of this discovery, we adjusted our OKRs to focus on increasing multi-vertical adoption rather than just growing grocery orders.

This is why our OKRs are not set in a purely top-down manner. While my executive team and I make the final decisions, the process is highly bottom-up, driven by real insights from our teams and task forces. As we learn more, our objectives evolve. This approach keeps us agile, ensures we focus on the highest-impact areas, and allows us to adjust quickly as we discover new opportunities.

Could you dive more into the other key areas of scaling you focused on.

I think own-delivery was an obvious priority. It was clear that controlling operations was going to be a game changer. If you were ordering from talabat in 2019 or 2020, you would have seen the massive complaints about customer support and delivery quality. The biggest issue behind that was the fact that we weren't managing what happened between the restaurant receiving the order and the customer getting their food.

If you looked at customer support data at the time, the vast majority of inquiries were people asking, "Where is my order?" That was the number one pain point. The problem was that we had no way of accurately predicting delivery times because restaurants were managing their own fleets. We had no insight into how many couriers a restaurant had available at any given moment, how many were already out making deliveries, or even how long a specific restaurant typically took to prepare an order. That meant customers could sometimes receive their food in 20 minutes, but other times it could take an hour and a half, with no consistency or predictability.

To fix this, we started experimenting by building a small fleet and handling deliveries for certain restaurants ourselves. Another issue was that many restaurants didn't have their own fleet at all. Without our own delivery network, we were limiting the number of restaurants that could even operate on the platform. And when you're building a marketplace, the most important factor is selection—the more choices you offer customers, the stronger the platform becomes.

———

> WHEN YOU'RE BUILDING A MARKETPLACE, THE MOST IMPORTANT FACTOR IS SELECTION—THE MORE CHOICES YOU OFFER CUSTOMERS, THE STRONGER THE PLATFORM BECOMES. WITHOUT OUR OWN DELIVERY NETWORK, WE WERE LIMITING THE NUMBER OF RESTAURANTS THAT COULD EVEN OPERATE ON THE PLATFORM.

———

Once we started delivering with our own fleet, the impact was immediate. Customers could now track their orders in real time, see exactly where their food was, and know how long it would take to arrive. As a result, customer support inquiries about order status dropped by about 70%. That alone was a huge improvement in the experience.

Beyond that, by managing our own fleet, we could start optimizing delivery times using data. We tracked when riders arrived at a restaurant, how long they waited before picking up an order, and how much time it took them to reach each delivery location. The more data we gathered, the more accurate our algorithms became, which allowed us to continuously improve delivery time predictions.

We also began optimizing fleet utilization, making sure we had the right number of riders available at the right times. We could adjust dynamically, increasing rider numbers on weekends and during peak hours while scaling back during off-peak times. Managing a single large fleet became far more efficient than having hundreds or thousands of smaller, independently managed restaurant fleets. Not only did this improve service quality, but it also reduced costs, allowing us to offer delivery to restaurants at a much more competitive rate than if they were to manage it themselves.

As we scaled this model, every new insight reinforced that we were making the right decision. Over time, we transitioned nearly 100% of our business to own-delivery, fundamentally transforming the talabat experience.

Was there another area you had to tackle to further scale?

The next major focus was technology—building a real tech-driven company. The early phases of a business like this require a massive commercial push. You need to convince restaurants to join the platform, and that was rightly the full focus of talabat's original founders and leadership. They did an incredible job at that, and by the time I joined, the foundations of the business were very strong.

But as we started evolving into a multi-vertical company, building our own fleet, and competing with global players like Uber Eats and Deliveroo, it became clear that technology had to become a much bigger priority. We needed stronger engineering capabilities to optimize logistics, refine our algorithms, and compete at a higher level.

———

" WE NEEDED STRONGER ENGINEERING CAPABILITIES TO OPTIMIZE LOGISTICS, REFINE OUR ALGORITHMS, AND COMPETE AT A HIGHER LEVEL.

———

Back then, we had just 20 people in tech, working out of a basement in Kuwait, and they were referred to as the "IT team." That setup made it impossible to attract top engineering talent. Imagine trying to recruit a Silicon Valley engineer and telling them to move to Kuwait to work in a basement for the "IT team." It just wasn't going to happen.

The first step was revamping our employer branding. We moved our headquarters from Kuwait to Dubai, which was a significant decision. Initially, there was some resistance from teams who wanted to remain in Kuwait, but we couldn't afford to be split between two headquarters. The entire leadership team had to be in one place. We committed to making Dubai the new tech hub, and we invested in creating a workspace that would attract world-class talent.

When I first joined, we were operating out of a single business tower in Business Bay, all on one floor. As we started expanding, we had to add more floors, but we couldn't get adjacent spaces. At one point, we had teams working across seven or eight different floors—one on the 15th floor, another on the 23rd, another on the 35th. Even though everyone was technically in the same building, people were still relying on Zoom meetings to communicate, which completely defeated the purpose of having an office.

Eventually, we moved to a new headquarters with just three massive floors, allowing for true collaboration. I've always been very vocal about the importance of in-person work. I'm well known—whether positively or negatively—for my five-day office policy. I believe that if you want to build a great company, people need to be together, working side by side, sharing ideas, and building a shared vision. Work shouldn't feel like just a set of tasks—it should feel like you're creating something meaningful. That sense of connection and purpose is what drives innovation and high performance.

Fast forward to today, and we now have 87 nationalities in our Dubai office, with talent coming from some of the world's biggest tech companies and most competitive markets. We've built an incredibly diverse and high-performing team, and I'm extremely proud of where we are today.

We've been recognized as a great place to work for three or four years in a row now, and in terms of culture, I don't want to say it myself because I don't want to toot my own horn. But if you ask anyone inside or outside talabat, I think they'll tell you that our culture is really a defining factor in how we do business.

What is your take on how does in-person work compare to remote?

It's a few things, really. One is exactly what you said—those spontaneous coffee break conversations, the moments where you run into someone in the pantry and bounce ideas off each other. That kind of interaction just doesn't happen remotely.

The second part is something I've observed so many times in remote settings. Let's say I'm in a Zoom meeting, and I see someone on the call. I can tell by looking at their eyes that they're half-distracted, probably multitasking. Maybe they have another window open, making a wire transfer, ordering something online, or even placing their talabat order for food. I can see that I don't have their full attention, and that's frustrating. Or maybe I'm on a Zoom call, and in the background, their kids are jumping on the bed, or suddenly they have to pause the conversation because a delivery just arrived. These things happen in 99% of remote meetings, and over time, they erode the connection between people. Instead of fostering collaboration, it starts to feel like we're just completing tasks rather than working together as a team.

Before COVID, there was a tradition at talabat where a big group of employees would meet every Friday at 6 PM for food and drinks. It started small but kept growing, and at some point, you'd find 200 or 300 talabat employees in the same spot every Friday night. The place even started reserving an entire section for us because they knew we'd be there. Then COVID happened, and that culture disappeared. Even after restrictions were lifted, people didn't naturally return to those gatherings. It took more than a year for that tradition to come back, but now it's happening again, and every Friday, talabat employees are back in the same place, spending time together.

It's not about making people "loyal" to the company—it's about making work enjoyable. It's about feeling like you're part of something bigger than just a job. When people enjoy the time they spend with their colleagues and feel a sense of purpose in what they're doing, they're naturally more engaged and motivated. That's why I believe having people in the office together is so important.

———

> IT'S NOT ABOUT MAKING PEOPLE 'LOYAL' TO THE COMPANY—IT'S ABOUT MAKING WORK ENJOYABLE. IT'S ABOUT FEELING LIKE YOU'RE PART OF SOMETHING BIGGER THAN JUST A JOB.

———

As a company scales, how do you maintain its culture while avoiding common pitfalls and reinforcing best practices?

That's a really interesting question. There are a few key elements to it.

One of the biggest challenges when companies grow is that, at some point, you need to start building specialized departments. Say, for example, you start opening cloud kitchens and dark stores, and suddenly, you need a real estate department. The instinct in many companies is to go out and hire the best real estate professional from the top firm in the industry. That sounds like a great idea, but it comes with a risk.

Someone coming from a major real estate firm is used to being in a central, highly respected role within that organization. They probably had direct access to the CEO, managed a massive P&L, and were one of the most important people in their company. Then they move to a company like ours, where real estate is important, but it's not the core business. Suddenly, their role feels smaller in comparison. And when people feel like their job is smaller than it used to be, they tend to become territorial. Instead of focusing on how their department can best support the company, they start trying to expand their influence—pushing to control other areas, adding unnecessary layers of complexity, and creating silos.

This is why hiring the right people for the job is so important. We need people who are low-ego, who understand that the company's priorities come before any individual department's priorities. When leaders show that they're aligned with company-wide goals, not just their own KPIs, that's when things work best.

We have zero tolerance for bureaucracy, excessive red tape, or overcomplicating things. Of course, as a CEO, I can't always be aware of every little process happening across the company. That's why we have systems in place, like a whistleblower hotline, where employees can report issues they believe shouldn't be happening. We also have internal feedback channels for what we call "broken experiences," which could be anything from inefficiencies in internal processes to problems that customers or partners are facing. By constantly gathering feedback from employees, we try to catch and correct problems before they start affecting culture negatively.

So, feedback is something we actively push, and I think culturally, it's not as common in this region as it is in U.S. companies. That's why we've made a big effort to encourage it across all levels of the organization. We don't just gather feedback from customers—we also regularly ask for input from riders, partners, and internal teams.

I personally hold monthly connects with my team, and one of the standard sections in these meetings is where I ask them for feedback on what I could have done differently in the past month. I want to know what's working, what's not, and where I can improve.

The reason I care about this so much is because of something I learned early in my career. When I was at Uber, I had a lot of disagreements with my boss. It got to a point where I went to her boss to report all the issues I had with her. And I'll never forget what he told me. He said, "You know, when you point a finger at someone, three fingers are pointing back at you."

That moment completely changed my perspective. Instead of blaming my boss for everything, I started thinking about what I could do differently. I decided to sit down with her and ask, "Why are we not aligned? What can I do better?" That conversation changed everything. We ended up working incredibly well together after that. It was a lesson in the power of feedback and self-reflection, and it's something I've carried with me ever since.

When expanding into diverse markets, how do you balance speed with operational efficiency?

It really comes down to two approaches to business, and I'm sure based on your experience, you've seen this as well. On one side, you have international companies like Uber or Amazon, where the strategy is to develop one core product and roll it out across multiple markets with only minor customizations. About 80% of the product remains the same everywhere. Then, on the other side, you have hyper-localized companies that focus on a single geography or region, customizing their offering to an extreme degree to fit the specific needs of that market.

There's evidence supporting both strategies, and in different contexts, one might work better than the other. For us, we've leaned more toward the localized approach, and that has worked quite well. A good example is how we captured a large share of the Arab-speaking community in the region early on because, for a long time, talabat was the only platform available in Arabic. Eventually, competitors caught up and launched Arabic versions of their apps, but being first gave us a strong advantage.

Another example is cash payments in Egypt. We recognized early on that cash was crucial in that market, so we ensured that we enabled cash payments across all our markets. Even today, we continue to support cash, despite the industry trend toward digital payments. We've built strong operational processes around cash collection, allowing us to maintain efficiency while still offering the option that many customers prefer. Some competitors decided to remove cash entirely, but we've seen that even customers who have credit cards or digital wallets often prefer to pay in cash for various reasons.

At the same time, we've also made mistakes when over-localizing. One example is Egypt, where I personally got the strategy wrong. We assumed that in Egypt, customer experience would be less important than affordability. We thought that as long as we focused on providing cheaper prices and discounts, we could deprioritize operational excellence. That assumption turned out to be incorrect. For several years, we struggled to grow the market because we were too focused on affordability and not enough on quality. It was only when our MD in Egypt, Hadeer, really started prioritizing customer experience and improving our operations that we saw significant growth. That was a clear lesson that even in price-sensitive markets, reliability and service quality remain critical.

———

"We assumed that in Egypt, customer experience would be less important than affordability. We thought that as long as we focused on providing cheaper prices and discounts, we could deprioritize operational excellence. That assumption turned out to be incorrect. Even in price-sensitive markets, reliability and service quality remain critical.

———

So, while a localized approach has worked well for us, the key is finding the right balance between localization and scalability. Some aspects of the food delivery business can be more centralized, where you optimize logistics and operations across multiple markets. But for newer business lines, such as our Dine-Out business—where we offer restaurant discounts for customers who dine in—we took a completely independent, local-first approach. This business operates with full autonomy, no centralization, and no complex corporate structure— just pure commercial execution on the ground.

We did something similar with grocery delivery when we first launched. At the beginning, our grocery delivery operated as a fully standalone business, with its own P&L, leadership, and teams, completely independent from the rest of talabat. There were no direct interactions with other teams. Over time, as the business matured, we started integrating it more regionally. But in the early stages, keeping it separate allowed it to grow faster without unnecessary constraints. If you overcomplicate a new business within a large, established organization, you risk slowing it down and preventing it from reaching its full potential.

Is it better to start standalone and centralize later, or is it more about striking the right balance between the two?

It's exactly that—you have to strike the right balance. There's always going to be tension between the local teams, who will argue that everything needs to be hyper-localized, and the regional teams, who will push for full centralization. The regional perspective is often, "Why should every country have its own marketing strategy? Why not centralize rider and customer incentives? Why run separate campaigns for each market?"

But the reality is that both sides have valid points. The key is knowing when to centralize and when to keep things local.

When it comes to efficiencies, I focus on ones that actually increase output, not just reduce costs. For example, if three people are handling something locally, and I centralize it into one regional role, the only way that makes sense is if that one person performs better than the three people combined. If centralization leads to a stronger outcome, then it's worth doing.

But if you centralize just to cut costs, you often end up losing efficiency. Sometimes what happens is that you remove local teams, hire one person at the regional level (often in Dubai, where salaries are higher), and then they immediately start building their own team to manage all the markets. So in the end, you haven't actually reduced costs—you've just moved them. Worse, if that one regional person is less effective than the original local teams, the whole structure suffers.

So, my rule is simple: Centralization should only happen if it actually makes the business stronger. If centralization only saves money but leads to worse outcomes, it's a bad decision.

———

> CENTRALIZATION SHOULD ONLY HAPPEN IF IT ACTUALLY MAKES THE BUSINESS STRONGER. IF CENTRALIZATION ONLY SAVES MONEY BUT LEADS TO WORSE OUTCOMES, IT'S A BAD DECISION.

———

How do you decide when and where to expand—opt for an easier market or a bigger opportunity?

That's a great question, and it's one of the hardest decisions in scaling a business. Expand too early, and you risk stretching your resources too thin. Expand too late, and you risk losing first-mover advantage.

The right approach depends on a few factors. First, you have to assess market dynamics. UAE and Saudi, for example, have strong digital adoption, high purchasing power, and a relatively developed infrastructure for last-mile delivery. If that's your home market, then expanding into Qatar makes a lot of sense because it shares similar characteristics. It's a smaller market, but execution-wise, it's relatively straightforward.

On the other hand, Egypt is a massive market, but it comes with infrastructure and payment challenges. So the decision to expand there isn't just about "Is there demand?" but also about "Can we execute effectively?" If your business model relies on digital payments and seamless logistics, Egypt might be a much harder play initially.

Investor pressure can also influence these decisions. Many investors push for rapid expansion, especially into high-population markets, but moving too fast can kill a company if the core operations aren't stable enough to support growth. I've seen companies rush into new markets before they had the operational discipline to manage multiple geographies, and it ended up hurting them.

The key is finding the right moment—when your home market is strong enough, when you have a repeatable playbook, and when you can execute well in the new market without destabilizing your core business. That's how you scale successfully rather than just expanding for the sake of it.

How do you decide between entering new markets and deepening existing ones, and what factors influence that choice?

That's the million-dollar question, and the answer really depends on several factors. Competition plays a big role—if you're the first to do something in a market where the model is unproven, then the priority should be proving that the model works before expanding. On the other hand, if you're replicating a model that has already been successful elsewhere, you might be able to scale faster because there's a level of validation.

Market size is another critical factor. Many entrepreneurs feel the need to expand into new geographies as soon as they see initial traction, but in reality, they may already be operating in a market so large that they could spend years going deeper without needing to expand elsewhere. Some of the most successful businesses in the world have chosen to focus on strengthening their position in a single market rather than spreading themselves too thin.

A great example of this is Kaspi in Kazakhstan. They operate in a country with a population of around 20 million, which has a relatively low GDP per capita compared to GCC markets. Despite that, they generated $1.8 billion in net income this year without expanding beyond Kazakhstan. They started with retail, then moved into e-commerce. When the economy faced challenges, they acquired a bank and started offering credit to customers. That led them into payments and fintech, building an entire ecosystem of services that are now deeply interconnected.

What they proved is that you can build an incredibly successful business by going deeper rather than wider. Had they chosen to expand e-commerce into multiple new markets before strengthening their core business, they might still be losing money and dealing with intense competition. Instead, because they built such a strong ecosystem in Kazakhstan, they now have a near-monopoly, making them very difficult to challenge.

This is why expansion decisions should always be strategic. If a company is operating in a massive market, the smartest move might be to double down on penetration instead of launching elsewhere. Expanding should never be done just for the sake of expansion—it has to be an educated decision about where every dollar of investment will generate the best long-term return.

A good example from our own experience is Saudi Arabia. talabat operates in eight markets, but not in Saudi, which is the largest market in the GCC. Investors have often asked why we haven't expanded there. But when you break down the data, it becomes clear that even without entering Saudi Arabia, we have enormous growth potential in our existing markets.

If you take the addressable population of the countries we operate in, removing people under 15 or over 64, and you calculate food orders per capita, our customers order about 0.42 times per month on talabat. But people eat about 90 times per month. That means we have 200X headroom for growth just by increasing frequency within our current markets. Entering a new market wouldn't change the total addressable market of food delivery—it would just add new complexity. The biggest opportunity still lies in increasing engagement with the customers we already have.

What are the biggest mistakes founders make when scaling, and how can they avoid them?

One of the biggest mistakes is overstretching and burning too much capital too quickly. Many founders base their decisions on Excel projections that predict perfect unit economics five years down the road, but they don't focus enough on the realistic path to get there. There's often a rush to scale at all costs, sometimes due to investor pressure, and companies end up chasing growth without focusing on profitability. The result is businesses that grow fast but are completely dependent on discounts and subsidies to maintain demand. The moment they try to optimize their P&L, they realize that much of the demand wasn't organic—it was just being bought. Scaling a business means balancing growth and unit economics at the same time, not treating them as separate goals.

———

> MANY FOUNDERS... TRY TO OPTIMIZE THEIR P&L, THEY REALIZE THAT MUCH OF THE DEMAND WASN'T ORGANIC—IT WAS JUST BEING BOUGHT. SCALING A BUSINESS MEANS BALANCING GROWTH AND UNIT ECONOMICS AT THE SAME TIME, NOT TREATING THEM AS SEPARATE GOALS.

———

Another mistake is focusing on marketing before fixing products and operations. The correct sequence should always be product first, operations second, marketing last. A great product with decent operations can still succeed even without heavy marketing. But if a product is bad, no amount of marketing can save it in the long run. Founders sometimes push too hard on marketing before their product is strong enough to retain customers naturally. That leads to high churn, wasted spending, and a weaker brand reputation.

———

> " A GREAT PRODUCT WITH DECENT OPERATIONS CAN STILL SUCCEED EVEN WITHOUT HEAVY MARKETING. BUT IF A PRODUCT IS BAD, NO AMOUNT OF MARKETING CAN SAVE IT IN THE LONG RUN. FOUNDERS SOMETIMES PUSH TOO HARD ON MARKETING BEFORE THEIR PRODUCT IS STRONG ENOUGH TO RETAIN CUSTOMERS NATURALLY. THAT LEADS TO HIGH CHURN, WASTED SPENDING, AND A WEAKER BRAND REPUTATION.

———

Timing also plays a crucial role in expansion. Many startups launch into new countries too soon, thinking that adding markets automatically means adding revenue. Expansion should be about ROI, not just optics. Just because a company can enter a new geography doesn't mean it should—especially if its home market is still far from saturated. Founders need to ask themselves tough questions about whether the investment in a new market will generate better returns than continuing to scale within the existing one. Scaling successfully isn't just about growing fast—it's about growing smart and knowing when to go deeper and when to go wider.

How should a founder's leadership evolve as the company scales, and how can they avoid the pitfalls of being overly hands-on?

This is a really interesting challenge, and it's something I've had to work on myself. One of the biggest shifts a founder or leader has to make as the company grows is moving away from being overly action-biased. In the early days, being highly reactive and fast-moving is a strength—you see an opportunity, identify a problem, or come up with an idea, and without too much analysis, you just go for it. You pull a team together, make things happen quickly, and iterate along the way.

At the startup stage, that approach can be incredibly effective. But as the company scales, that same behavior can become disruptive. When a CEO constantly introduces new priorities without clear alignment, it throws off teams that are already working on structured roadmaps. People start feeling like priorities are changing every day, and it creates frustration, especially for leaders who are trying to set long-term plans.

Another problem with moving too quickly is that many of the things that feel urgent in the moment are actually not urgent at all. Just because an issue has come to your attention doesn't mean it needs to be fixed immediately. When you operate that way, you risk derailing the company's focus by acting on things that aren't properly ranked against other, more strategic priorities.

The other big risk is making major decisions without enough data. I've seen situations where we skipped proper research and A/B testing, and it ended up costing the business significantly. A simple example would be rolling out a new feature on the homepage, only to later realize that it negatively impacted advertising revenue or changed vendor visibility in a way that hurt the core business. If you don't test and analyze properly, you might assume an idea is a guaranteed win, but in reality, it could have unintended consequences.

Early in my time at talabat, I actually got direct feedback from a team member who told me, "We can't work like this because you're firing at the same speed and intensity on every single cylinder, and we don't know what's actually a priority." That was a wake-up call. As a CEO, part of the job is not just identifying opportunities, but filtering them—taking the 200 potential things that could be done and clearly defining the 10 most critical ones. If everything is a priority, then nothing is a priority.

———

“ As a CEO, part of the job is not just identifying opportunities, but filtering them—taking the 200 potential things that could be done and clearly defining the 10 most critical ones. If everything is a priority, then nothing is a priority.

———

At the startup stage, this isn't as big of an issue because you might only have 10 priorities in total, and you can focus on all of them. But in a larger company, the number of possible initiatives grows to 100, 200, even 300, and it's impossible to tackle everything. The hardest but most important skill at this stage is forcing yourself to slow down, be more structured in decision-making, and make sure the company's focus stays razor-sharp on the most impactful areas.

What key differences have you noticed between working in Europe and globally versus the Middle East and North Africa?

There's been a lot of discussion around regulation in Europe recently, and I've personally experienced the challenges firsthand while working there. For Uber, Europe was always an extremely tough region when it came to regulations. In Italy, for example, there were some regulations around the ride-sharing industry that I honestly can't describe as anything other than unreasonable. One example is the rule for black cars—limos—that required drivers to return to their garage after every trip before they could pick up another customer. There's absolutely no practical reason for this rule other than to protect the existing taxi industry and the incumbents who wanted to block competition.

The frustrating part was that even when everyone agreed that the regulation was outdated and inefficient, changing it was nearly impossible. We spent three years working with policymakers across different political parties to develop a proposal that would remove these unnecessary restrictions. Just when we were about to have the bill discussed in Parliament, taxi drivers in Milan went on strike, and overnight, the bill was withdrawn. No one spoke about it again. That experience really showed me how difficult it is to change regulations in Europe, no matter how outdated or illogical they are.

The difference in the Middle East and even Asia is that there's a much more collaborative approach between regulators and the private sector. That doesn't mean companies always get the outcomes they want, but there is at least an open dialogue. There's a real sense that the public and private sectors are working together to find solutions that make sense for both sides.

One of the biggest advantages in this region is the ease of doing business. The relationship between businesses and regulators tends to be more pragmatic. Governments here want businesses to succeed because they see them as contributors to economic growth and innovation. In Europe, you don't always feel that.

Another big difference is how grey areas are handled. In Europe, if there's any regulatory uncertainty, the first response is often a fine. There's very little room for discussion or adaptation. In the Middle East and Asia, regulators tend to observe how new industries evolve before making quick judgments. Many startups today are operating in uncharted territories, where regulations haven't yet been clearly defined. Instead of shutting them down immediately, regulators often try to understand the business first and then work on shaping the right regulatory framework over time.

Can you talk a bit about the current state of talabat, and what exciting initiatives are ahead?

Sure. I can give you a picture of where we are today, and hopefully, by the time this book is out, we'll be even bigger and better. talabat has been around for 20 years, yet we're still growing at an extremely fast pace.

Right now, we operate in eight countries across the GCC, Egypt, Jordan, and Iraq. In 2024, we're managing around $7.4 billion in GMV, and we're still growing at double-digit rates. Last year, we saw 23% growth in GMV and 32% growth in revenue, so the momentum is still strong.

Profitability is also a key strength. We're generating around half a billion dollars in adjusted EBITDA, which puts us in a great position to keep investing in innovation and expansion. The opportunities ahead are massive.

In food delivery, despite how many riders you see on the road, the reality is that we're still just scratching the surface. There is ample room for growth, even without expanding into new geographies.

Grocery delivery is another area that's expanding at a rapid pace. In 2024 alone, our grocery business grew 47%, even though it already accounts for more than $1.5 billion in GMV—about 25% of our total business. What's exciting is that we're still only about 1% of the total offline grocery market, which means there's an enormous opportunity to convert more customers from offline to online shopping.

The shift from offline to online grocery shopping is happening fast because the convenience factor is even greater than in food delivery. With food, you save time by not having to cook, but with groceries, you save even more time—you don't have to go to the store, pick items, pack them, load them into your car, drive home, and carry them inside. With talabat, all of that happens in minutes.

———

> " THE SHIFT FROM OFFLINE TO ONLINE GROCERY SHOPPING IS HAPPENING FAST BECAUSE THE CONVENIENCE FACTOR IS EVEN GREATER THAN IN FOOD DELIVERY.

———

Beyond food and grocery, we're also expanding into fintech. We've launched co-branded credit cards, as well as a post-paid product, which are both performing well. The idea is to build an ecosystem that makes our platform even more valuable to customers. Our subscription program, talabat Pro (T-Pro), is another key part of that strategy. It offers free delivery, exclusive discounts, and other benefits, making it an attractive option for high-frequency customers.

We're not just growing vertically in our core business areas—we're creating an interconnected ecosystem where different services reinforce each other. The goal is to go deeper and build an even stronger foundation that enhances customer loyalty and long-term growth.

———

> WE'RE NOT JUST GROWING VERTICALLY IN OUR CORE BUSINESS AREAS—WE'RE CREATING AN INTERCONNECTED ECOSYSTEM WHERE DIFFERENT SERVICES REINFORCE EACH OTHER. THE GOAL IS TO GO DEEPER AND BUILD AN EVEN STRONGER FOUNDATION THAT ENHANCES CUSTOMER LOYALTY AND LONG-TERM GROWTH.

———

Any final thoughts or anything we haven't covered?

We've covered a lot, and it's been a great discussion. The main thing I'd emphasize is that we're still just at the beginning. Even though we've been around for 20 years, there's so much untapped potential in food, groceries, and digital services in the region.

The Middle East and North Africa are going through a massive digital transformation, and talabat is playing a key role in that shift. The way people order food, shop for groceries, and manage their payments is evolving, and we're focused on being at the forefront of that change.

It's an exciting time, and I think the next few years will be about deepening our impact, expanding in the most strategic way, and continuing to build an ecosystem that makes life easier for our stakeholders.

––––––

ABDULMAJEED ALSUKHAN

Shop now, pay later, stress-free

Founder and CEO of TAMARA

tamara

Riyadh, Saudi Arabia

www.tamara.co

ABDULMAJEED ALSUKHAN is a prominent Saudi entrepreneur, best known as the CEO and Co-Founder of Tamara, the leading fintech platform in Saudi Arabia and the wider GCC region. Under his leadership, Tamara achieved a historic milestone in December 2023, becoming the Kingdom's first homegrown fintech unicorn by securing $340 million in a Series C equity funding round.

This funding round was co-led by SNB Capital and Sanabil Investments, a wholly owned company by the Public Investment Fund (PIF), with participation from Shorooq Partners, Pinnacle Capital, Impulse, and other investors. Previous backers such as Coatue, Endeavor Catalyst, and Checkout.com also contributed. This investment marked one of the largest in a fintech company in the region. Additionally, in November 2023, Tamara secured a debt financing deal, upsizing its warehouse facility to $400 million, led by Goldman Sachs and Shorooq Partners.

Before launching Tamara, Alsukhan co-founded Habli in 2017, a Saudi-based logistics provider for grocery delivery, which was later acquired by Nana in the same year. He then played a key role in the development of Nana, which went on to become Saudi Arabia's largest digital grocery shopping platform, securing over $80 million in funding.

Tamara, founded in late 2020 alongside Turki Bin Zarah and Abdulmohsen Al Babtain, quickly became a market leader in Buy Now, Pay Later (BNPL) services. It was also one of the first companies granted a BNPL license by the Saudi Central Bank (SAMA). As of 2024, Tamara has expanded its operations across Saudi Arabia (KSA), the UAE, and Kuwait, serving over 10 million users and partnering with more than 30,000 merchants. The company has also reported a sixfold increase in annual run-rate revenue in under two years.

Alsukhan holds a Bachelor of Arts in Financial Economics from California State University and a Master of Arts in Economic Policy from Boston University. His strong academic foundation in economics and finance has been instrumental in shaping his strategic decisions within the fintech industry.

TAMARA is a leading fintech company in the MENA region, revolutionizing digital payments through innovative and consumer-friendly financial solutions. Established in late 2020 in Riyadh, Saudi Arabia, Tamara was founded by Abdulmajeed Alsukhan, Turki Bin Zarah, and Abdulmohsen Al Babtain with a vision to transform the way people shop, pay, and bank. The company quickly emerged as a pioneer in the Buy Now, Pay Later (BNPL) space, allowing shoppers to split their payments interest-free and without hidden fees, both online and in-store. By enabling more flexible transactions, Tamara enhances consumer purchasing power while also helping merchants increase sales and customer engagement.

Since its inception, Tamara has expanded rapidly across the Gulf Cooperation Council (GCC) region, operating in Saudi Arabia, the UAE, and Kuwait, with additional offices in Germany and Vietnam. The company serves major global and regional brands such as SHEIN, Jarir, Noon, IKEA, eXtra, and Farfetch, as well as thousands of small and medium-sized enterprises (SMEs). These partnerships have allowed Tamara to become an integral part of the digital shopping experience in the Middle East.

Tamara's growth has been supported by record-breaking investments, making it Saudi Arabia's first fintech unicorn. In 2021, the company secured $110 million in a Series A funding round led by Checkout.com, setting a new benchmark for fintech investments in the region. In December 2023, Tamara achieved another milestone by raising $340 million in a Series C funding round, co-led by SNB Capital and Sanabil Investments, a subsidiary of the Public Investment Fund (PIF). Other investors in this round included Shorooq Partners, Pinnacle Capital, Impulse, Coatue, Endeavor Catalyst, and Checkout. com. In total, the company has raised $500 million in equity funding and secured over $400 million in debt financing, including a warehouse facility led by Goldman Sachs and Shorooq Partners.

Tamara has also gained regulatory approval from the Saudi Central Bank (SAMA), which granted it a license to provide BNPL and consumer finance services in March 2025. This approval places Tamara among the Kingdom's 65 licensed lending companies, demonstrating its compliance with financial regulations and commitment to responsible lending practices. This move aligns with Saudi Arabia's Vision 2030 strategy, which aims to expand financial inclusion and support digital transformation.

In addition to its core BNPL services, Tamara is expanding its financial ecosystem through strategic partnerships. In February 2025, the company partnered with Mastercard to introduce split payment options in the UAE, enhancing access to flexible payments across the region. Additionally, in November 2024, Tamara teamed up with Network International to expand its services into the Middle East and Africa (MEA), broadening its reach beyond the GCC. These collaborations position Tamara as a key player in the future of digital finance, paving the way for more innovative and inclusive payment solutions.

Tamara's impact on the regional fintech landscape has been widely recognized. In 2024, it was named one of Saudi Arabia's top 10 tech startups by LinkedIn, reflecting its rapid expansion and strong influence in the financial sector. The company's BNPL model has also addressed key consumer concerns, particularly in reducing reliance on cash on delivery—a dominant payment method in the region. By offering transparent and Sharia-compliant financial solutions, Tamara has helped many local businesses thrive, boosting e-commerce growth and driving digital adoption.

———

Tell us a bit about yourself and your background.

I was born in Riyadh in April 1988 and spent my entire life there. I attended a middle-class private school until high school. Academically, I wasn't the top honor student, but I was always a good student—usually in the A- to B+ range. I was the kind of student who did just enough work before exams to get good grades. But beyond academics, I was very active in sports. Football was my passion, and I was the captain of my class team. I spent a lot of time outdoors with friends, being involved in various activities in the neighborhood and beyond.

After graduating from high school, I moved to the United States to pursue my studies. I initially chose computer engineering because I was certain that technology would change the world. At that time, it wasn't yet transforming everything, but for those paying attention, it was clear that it soon would. Everything was going to be reimagined and rebuilt through technology. But as I progressed through my studies, I realized that while computer science was important, it wasn't what intrigued me the most. I took some economics classes, and that was when things really started to click for me.

What inspired you to switch from computer engineering to economics?

I wanted to understand why some economies thrived while others struggled, why economic phenomena occurred, why prices behaved the way they did, and why monopolies formed. It felt like economics was the foundation needed to understand and address the challenges of our region. We come from a part of the world that has resources and potential, yet we lag behind in many ways. I didn't think the problem was rooted in science, physics, or chemistry—it felt more structural, an issue of economic foundations and how societies were organized to be productive. That realization pushed me to switch my major to economics, and I graduated with a degree in the field.

I was so fascinated by economics that I wanted to continue in academia. I pursued a master's degree and planned to go for a PhD, thinking I would become an economist. At that time, entrepreneurship never even crossed my mind. I wasn't someone who dreamed of building businesses; I was driven by a desire to make a change in the world, starting with my region. Economics seemed like the best path to achieve that.

But one of the great things about being young is that you don't always know exactly who you are or what you're best suited for, and along the way, you learn. Through my master's studies, I realized academia wasn't for me. It became clear that I wouldn't be able to create the kind of change I wanted if I stayed in that world. I was reading newspapers, following global business trends, and observing what was happening in tech, and I started seeing that the people shaping the world weren't just economists or academics.

At that point, I started thinking about impact in a structured way. I asked myself, who leaves the biggest mark on humanity? To me, it was clear that scientists were at the top—people who change fundamental concepts, like physicists who discover gravity or quantum mechanics, or researchers who make breakthroughs that shift how we understand the world. The second group was politicians, those who shape nations and the course of history. And then, as I looked deeper, I realized the third most impactful group was entrepreneurs.

Entrepreneurs like Steve Jobs, John D. Rockefeller, Elon Musk, Jeff Bezos, and even regional figures like Samih Sawiris and others have shaped not just their communities but the world at large. That realization changed everything for me.

Were there any key realizations that led you to shift your focus from academia to entrepreneurship?

While finishing my master's, I came to a difficult conclusion. I wasn't going to be a scientist—I simply wasn't smart enough to revolutionize an entire field like physics or medicine. And even if I pursued economics to the highest level, I would likely just be another professor teaching at a university, rather than fundamentally changing the field itself. That, to me, felt like a low-impact career. There's nothing wrong with being a professor, but for someone seeking to create large-scale change, it didn't seem like the right path.

So I started paying closer attention to entrepreneurs, what they built, and how they thought. One of the biggest discoveries for me at that time was the difference between traditional business in our region and the kind of businesses being built in the U.S. In the Middle East, business had always been about trade. People bought and sold goods, secured contracts, and built commercial structures around existing markets. That never excited me because it didn't feel like it truly created something new.

But living in the U.S., I saw a different model—people were not just trading, they were creating. They were inventing products and services from scratch, developing completely new ideas, and then throwing all their energy into making them a reality. That was a completely different way of thinking about business, and it fascinated me. I had always viewed business through the lens of buying, selling, or executing contracts, but I came to realize that the biggest and most impactful businesses were built out of nothing. That realization was what ultimately pulled me into the world of entrepreneurship.

Looking back, what would you say was your main driver in pursuing an entrepreneurial path?

I saw that if I wanted to create meaningful and lasting change—real impact—entrepreneurship was one of the most effective ways to do it. Instead of just studying how economies function, I could build something that directly contributes to the economy. It was a complete shift in how I saw my role in the world.

———

I SAW THAT IF I WANTED TO CREATE MEANINGFUL AND LASTING CHANGE—REAL IMPACT—ENTREPRENEURSHIP WAS ONE OF THE MOST EFFECTIVE WAYS TO DO IT.

———

I started digging deep into the skill sets of these entrepreneurs and realized that they weren't just traders or traditional businessmen. They called themselves entrepreneurs, and I wanted to understand what set them apart. What I discovered was that they were visionaries— people who were intellectually driven, highly motivated, and deeply committed to transforming the world. They weren't just running businesses; they were shaping industries, changing the way people lived, and thinking on a completely different level. They were individuals I could relate to because they shared a desire to see the world not as it is, but as it could be.

As I reflected on this, I realized that I, too, had that same instinct. I had always looked at the world and asked how things could be different, how they could be improved for future generations. That's the message these entrepreneurs were sending, and it resonated deeply with me. I began to study them more closely. Being a visionary was one thing, but I wanted to understand what else made them successful.

One of the biggest insights I gained was that they were incredible storytellers. They could articulate a vision so clearly and compellingly that people would rally behind them. They weren't just talking; they were backing up their ideas with real numbers, detailed business models, and well-researched strategies. They also knew how to build teams. They understood that success wasn't just about having a great idea—it was about surrounding yourself with the right people to execute it.

I started reading everything I could about how they built their companies. I studied Jeff Bezos and how he made his early decisions. I looked into other entrepreneurs and the challenges they overcame. At the same time, I was looking around and seeing so many problems in our region that needed solutions. That was during my master's degree, and I came very close to dropping out because I realized I no longer wanted to be in academia. But somehow, I decided to stick with it, and I completed my master's degree at Boston University in Economic Policy.

When I returned to Saudi Arabia, I was still uncertain about what to do next. I considered going into investment as an alternative to academia, so I took the CFA Level 1 exam. While I was figuring out my next steps, I was diagnosed with Hodgkin's lymphoma. At 25 years old, it was a shocking moment. It was also a difficult time because I was already late in starting my career compared to my peers. Most of my friends had started working at 22 or 23, and I hadn't even entered the workforce yet. That made the diagnosis feel like even more of a setback. But I have always believed that every challenge comes with a positive outcome.

Going through cancer must have been a life-changing experience. In what ways did it change your perspective?

The experience of battling cancer completely changed my perspective on risk. Before my cancer diagnosis, I had always thought of risk as something to be minimized. But through that experience, I realized that risk is an unavoidable part of life.

———

66 BEFORE MY CANCER DIAGNOSIS, I HAD ALWAYS THOUGHT OF RISK AS SOMETHING TO BE MINIMIZED. BUT THROUGH THAT EXPERIENCE, I REALIZED THAT RISK IS AN UNAVOIDABLE PART OF LIFE.

———

I also realized that you can try to protect yourself as much as you can, but at the end of the day, things will happen as they are meant to. What you receive in life is what you deserve, and no amount of playing it safe can change that.

The day I was diagnosed, I went home in complete shock. For 30 minutes, I sat alone, processing the news. I didn't tell anyone because I've always preferred to face big moments alone first. But after those 30 minutes, I made a decision. I still felt fine, so I decided to act like I was fine. I put on my running shoes and went for a 10K run. That run became a defining moment for me—I decided that as long as I felt normal, I would continue to live normally. That mindset carried me through my treatment, and by 2015, I had gone through a full year of recovery and remission.

That year reinforced something important for me: risk is always present and avoiding it doesn't make life better. In fact, the best way to live is to embrace risk because that's where the greatest rewards come from. In a strange way, cancer was a blessing. It rewired how I saw the world and gave me a level of fearlessness I didn't have before.

In early 2016, I got my first job at the Central Bank of Saudi Arabia, working in the investment team. At the time, PIF was not yet structured as we know it today, so SAMA's investment team was managing nearly $700 billion in reserves. It was considered the place to be if you wanted to work in investment. But even though it was an incredible opportunity, I had already changed. After my experience with cancer and after reading so much about entrepreneurship, I saw the world differently.

At SAMA, I realized that while I was working at a great institution, my impact would always be limited. I could have a successful career, rise through the ranks, and do well for myself, but would I be able to change my region or make a global impact? The answer was no. That realization led me to start seriously considering leaving my job to build something.

Making that decision wasn't easy. I studied how others had made similar choices. I saw that people who succeeded in building great companies never did it as a side project. They didn't hedge their bets or wait for the perfect moment. They went all in. In the Middle East, a lot of people try to start businesses while keeping their full-time jobs, thinking they'll see if it works before committing. But when I read about how the most successful companies were built, I realized none of them started that way. If you don't have the conviction to go all in, you'll probably never succeed.

That's when I came across Jeff Bezos' regret minimization theory. The idea is simple: imagine yourself at 80 years old, looking back on your life, and make decisions that minimize the regrets you might have. Most regrets come not from things we did, but from things we didn't do. That framework helped me decide. If I stayed in my job, I would always wonder what would have happened if I had taken the leap. But if I left to build something and it didn't work, I could live with that because at least I had tried.

That decision to leave was one of the biggest of my life, but it was also the right one. It set me on the path to creating something meaningful, rather than just being another person in a system.

What were some of the early challenges you faced after taking that leap of faith, and how did you navigate them?

I decided that if I wanted to make an impact, I had to go all in. The only way to minimize my regrets was to take the leap, fully commit, and give myself the best chance of making it work. I knew it wouldn't be easy, and I knew it would be a long journey, but I was ready. In 2016, just six months after starting my first job, I made the decision to leave. It was a complete shock to my family, my friends, and my colleagues. To them, it made no sense—I had just returned home, I had no income, no financial backing, and I was walking away from stability without a clear plan. But to me, it was the only logical step forward.

I had been doing my research on what makes an idea worth pursuing. I knew that to go after something, you needed high conviction. If you don't truly believe in your idea, it's impossible to push through the inevitable challenges. Timing was just as important. If the timing was right, you couldn't afford to miss the window because opportunities disappear quickly. You can't just wait six months and expect the same chance to be there—it will be gone.

My first idea was a delivery app. At the time, women in Saudi Arabia weren't driving, and when I returned home after living in the U.S. for eight years, I saw firsthand what a burden this was. It affected everyone—women, men, families—and I wanted to create a solution that gave people the freedom to simply open an app and get things delivered. The iPhone was becoming widely adopted, and apps were starting to take off. In 2016, food delivery, ride-hailing, and e-commerce were still in their early stages in the region, but it was obvious that this was the beginning of something big. I was certain the timing was right.

I built a financial model and analyzed companies like DoorDash, Deliveroo, and others that were starting to gain traction in different markets. Their growth validated that there was something here. The timing was right, I had conviction, and I had a business model. But to make it work, I needed two critical things—capital and a strong team. I quickly realized that neither was going to be easy to find.

What were the biggest challenges startup ecosystem in Saudi Arabia at that time, and how did it impact your first venture?

In 2016, Saudi Arabia had no real VC ecosystem. I decided to test my idea anyway. I bought three bikes, added delivery boxes, and built a simple HTML page with a dropdown menu listing neighborhood shops. I printed A4 flyers and distributed them everywhere, marketing the service directly in my community. Orders started coming in immediately—it was clear there was product-market fit.

However, without funding, it was impossible to scale. I started looking for investors, but I found that traditional funding sources in the region weren't designed for startups. Every potential investor I spoke to was from a family business background. They didn't understand venture investing. They wanted a majority stake—offering $100,000 in exchange for 70% of my company. That wasn't an investment; it was a buyout.

Hiring was just as challenging. Nobody wanted to join a startup with no funding. People were only interested in working part-time or on the side. It became clear that without the right financial backing and a strong team, the business wouldn't be able to grow.

Because I had taken the risk and jumped into the market early, I was able to join a company that had already raised some funding and had built a team. They acquired my business, and I joined them as a CFO and co-founder. This turned out to be a pivotal learning experience. I got to see firsthand how fundraising worked, how to structure deals, and how to build a strong team.

What did you learn from this experience?

One of my biggest lessons from that period was that while some people can bootstrap their companies—especially in SaaS businesses where capital requirements are lower—many startups need external funding to scale. And in order to raise money, you need credibility. That's why second-time entrepreneurs are often much more successful. They already have the credentials to attract investors and talent.

At that time, I realized that when you have a great idea and the ability to execute, but no one can validate it yet, you end up in a chicken-and-egg situation. Do you build credibility first, or do you push forward and hope to prove yourself along the way? That's why I always encourage people to join a startup before launching their own. Even as an early employee, you gain the experience and credibility that will make fundraising and team-building much easier when the time comes to start your own venture.

I joined that company in November 2017—about a year and a half after launching my first startup, which ultimately didn't scale because I couldn't secure funding. But by then, the startup ecosystem in Saudi Arabia was beginning to take shape. Vision 2030 was driving massive transformations across all industries, including technology and venture capital. Entrepreneurship was becoming more acceptable, and even encouraged. The shift in mindset was happening fast.

By 2019, Saudi had its first local VC fundraise, and the market was finally evolving to support startups in a meaningful way. The changes that were happening—socially, economically, and technologically— were creating an environment where founders had a real chance to succeed. Timing is everything, and Saudi Arabia's timing for startups had finally arrived.

In late 2018, MEVP led our Series A, followed by STV leading our Series B a year later. During 2019, as part of my role, I was analyzing the strategic positioning of the business. At the time, we were operating as a marketplace but were considering a pivot to a dark store model. Grocery tech had always been in search of the right business model, and we were trying to figure out the best approach. It wasn't a clear-cut decision, but we knew that moving from a marketplace to a dark store meant smaller fulfillment centers in every neighborhood, enabling quick deliveries with a limited selection of SKUs.

As I evaluated the competitive landscape, it became clear that our main competitors were not large grocery chains but rather the small neighborhood baqalas. These stores had two major advantages. First, they had proximity—they were located right next to customers, something we could compete with using logistics. Second, they had something more subtle but equally powerful: the daftar, or ledger system. Over time, as customers frequented their local baqala, store owners would develop a sense of trust and informally underwrite them. They recognized customers' cars, knew their families, saw them at the mosque, and eventually extended a line of credit that allowed them to shop and settle their bills at the end of the month.

I found this fascinating and started digging deeper. It wasn't just baqalas that operated this way—barbershops, plumbers, laundries, and many other small businesses used the same model. I wanted to understand the common thread. What enabled all these businesses to offer this informal credit?

What would you say were the gaps in the financial system led you to see an opportunity in consumer credit?

The answer boiled down to two key factors. First, they had access to customer data. These businesses knew their customers personally and had repetitive interactions with them, allowing them to make informed decisions about who to trust. Second, they had full control over the decision-making process. The store owner was also the cashier and the one offering credit, so they could make quick, flexible underwriting decisions based on their understanding of the customer.

That was when I realized that technology could solve this problem at scale. Instead of relying on fragmented, local knowledge, we could create a system where data is centralized, and a technology-driven approach determines creditworthiness. If implemented correctly, this model could break geographical barriers, allowing customers to access credit at any store rather than being limited to the handful of places where shop owners knew them personally.

———

> THAT WAS WHEN I REALIZED THAT TECHNOLOGY COULD SOLVE THIS PROBLEM AT SCALE.

———

What were the biggest challenges in trying to formalize an informal credit system and turn it into a scalable opportunity?

As I thought more about this, I kept asking myself why this hadn't already been solved. This was a widespread need. Every developing market faced the same challenge—millions of people lacked access to structured credit, yet informal credit systems existed everywhere. I started looking at how developed markets had addressed this problem.

In the U.S., for example, I had never encountered anything like the informal credit system we had in our region. Instead, they had a highly developed credit card infrastructure. The credit card essentially functioned as an unsecured credit line, allowing consumers to buy now and settle payments later, just as customers did at a baqala.

I then started digging deeper into why credit cards had not scaled the same way in our region. The answer was clear—banks in developing markets had fallen behind. They didn't have strong underwriting capabilities and had little understanding of unsecured lending. In developed economies, banks extend credit cards based on predictive models, behavioral data, and structured risk assessments. In our region, banks were still relying on outdated, manual methods, requiring extensive documentation and promissory notes to issue even small credit lines.

This inefficiency created a massive gap in the financial ecosystem. Banks were too comfortable with their high-margin, low-risk secured lending businesses. Mortgage loans were backed by homes, auto loans were backed by cars, and even personal loans required some form of collateral. But unsecured lending—the ability to extend credit without physical assets—was virtually non-existent. Credit cards existed but were only accessible to a small percentage of the population due to restrictive underwriting practices.

That realization was a turning point. It became clear that there was an opportunity to bring structured, scalable, and technology-driven credit solutions to the region. Instead of waiting for traditional banks to evolve, fintech could step in to fill the gap.

How did identifying this problem influence your approach?

This shift in thinking reinforced something I had believed throughout my journey—building a successful business starts with solving a real problem. It's not about chasing trends, seeking independence, or following a passion without purpose. The best businesses emerge from identifying inefficiencies, even when people don't explicitly recognize them as problems.

People might not have been saying, "I need a better credit system," but they were experiencing the pain of not having access to credit. That's the key. As Henry Ford once said, "If I had asked people what they wanted, they would have said faster horses." Innovation isn't about asking people what they want; it's about understanding their needs at a fundamental level and building the solution they don't yet know they need.

Realizing the scale of this problem made it impossible to ignore. Millions of people in our region needed access to credit, but the traditional banking infrastructure wasn't equipped to serve them. The question was no longer whether this was an opportunity—it was how to execute it at scale.

I started digging deeper into how to approach my go-to-market strategy, researching similar business models and studying what was happening globally. This is how I first came across the concept of Buy Now, Pay Later (BNPL). It immediately struck me as a formalized version of the informal ledger system used by small businesses in our region. As I continued exploring, I realized that BNPL companies were gaining momentum worldwide, confirming that this was more than just a local phenomenon—it was a massive global trend.

One of the key lessons I learned through this process was that businesses aren't built in isolation. You don't come up with an idea in a vacuum. Instead, the smartest way to start is by building from where others have left off. You don't begin from scratch; you take the existing progress and push it further. That's what I did—I studied how BNPL was evolving globally, looked at how other founders were structuring their companies, and analyzed what was working and what wasn't. That's when I realized that this was much bigger than grocery tech, much bigger than any single sector.

I informed my co-founders at my existing company that I would be transitioning out in the next six to nine months. This was a difficult decision, both professionally and personally. Leaving a company is never easy, especially when you're deeply involved in building it. But timing is everything, and I knew this was my moment. Timing is the single most important factor in the success of any startup. Yes, execution, team, and market fit matter, but timing trumps all of them.

I had seen this firsthand with my first startup in food delivery. The timing was right, but I wasn't financially prepared—I didn't have the personal savings or the funding necessary to scale. The opportunity was there, but I couldn't capitalize on it. That was a different problem, but the lesson was clear: when the timing is right, you can't hesitate.

When I started researching BNPL, I realized it was now or never. The market conditions, consumer behavior, and regulatory landscape were all aligning in a way that made this the perfect time to launch. However, I was still in my current company, helping build a product and managing responsibilities. I had to balance transitioning out while preparing to launch something entirely new. These are the moments where tough decisions have to be made. You have to take risks, even when they seem overwhelming.

How did you recognize that BNPL was the right opportunity and how did you decide to pursue?

By September 2019, I had started putting together a white paper outlining the business model and regulatory requirements. While working on it, I realized that one of the biggest advantages in Saudi Arabia at the time was the Central Bank's sandbox environment. This initiative allowed fintech startups to test new ideas with minimal capital requirements. The financial sector had historically been closed off to new entrants, but the sandbox changed everything. Without it, launching a fintech company in Saudi Arabia would have been nearly impossible. This was yet another sign that the timing was perfect.

By November 2019, BNPL was starting to gain traction in the region. In Dubai, our main competitor, Tabby, announced their first funding round, led by major VC firms. Other players were popping up—former Afterpay executives and other fintech veterans were launching companies across different markets. The race had already begun. I knew that getting in late could mean missing the opportunity altogether.

This was a difficult moment. I was still working at my existing company, fulfilling commitments, but I also knew I needed to move fast.

The decision to leave wasn't easy. The market was heating up, competition was emerging, and there was no guarantee that the region had enough venture capital to sustain multiple major players. Historically, in this part of the world, we tend to see one dominant local player and maybe one global competitor in any given sector. Would there be room for more?

But despite the risks, I had conviction. This was going to be our market. We were going to build something great. I officially started assembling the team, reaching out to people I had met in previous ventures. This is where my earlier experiences paid off—without my time at my first startup and my role at Nana, I wouldn't have been able to build the right team so quickly. When I first spoke to my co-founder, Turki, about the idea, he wouldn't have joined me if I hadn't already built something before. The first engineers we hired were willing to take the risk because they had seen that I had experience, that I had raised money before, and that I wasn't just another person with an idea.

Did your previous experience help your ability to attract top talent and secure investment for Tamara?

Certainly, it did. Building credentials is essential. You don't necessarily have to be a serial entrepreneur, but having a track record helps tremendously. Even if you're not a founder, joining a startup early can give you the experience and credibility to start your own company later. If someone joins Tamara today and in a few years decides to launch their own venture, they will have a much higher chance of success because they've seen firsthand how a startup operates. They will have the right connections, understand the challenges, and know how to navigate the ups and downs of building a company.

We officially wrote our first line of code in February 2020. The team was fully remote—one person in Dubai, one in Germany, and one in Saudi Arabia. Then, COVID-19 hit.

The pandemic changed everything. The world went into lockdown, and suddenly, digital adoption skyrocketed. It was a paradigm shift. Everything moved online overnight, and while COVID was devastating globally, it accelerated the adoption of digital solutions, including fintech. In many ways, COVID acted like steroids for tech companies—everyone was at home, working online, shopping online, and looking for digital financial solutions. This gave us a massive boost.

Just like with my experience with cancer, I've learned that even when something looks like a disaster, there's always an opportunity within it. COVID seemed like a crisis, but for us, it was the perfect time to scale. We doubled down, moved faster, and capitalized on the shift toward digital payments.

> " COVID SEEMED LIKE A CRISIS, BUT FOR US, IT WAS THE
> PERFECT TIME TO SCALE. WE DOUBLED DOWN, MOVED
> FASTER, AND CAPITALIZED ON THE SHIFT TOWARD
> DIGITAL PAYMENTS.

How did COVID-19 impact digital adoption in Saudi, and how did it shape Tamara's early growth strategy?

That period was a whirlwind. We had the right market, the right timing, and the right team. Now, we just had to execute.

Some people, when faced with uncertainty or crisis, choose to hold onto what they already have. We all had jobs at the time, and it would have been easy to say, "This isn't the right moment. There's a global crisis. Let's just stick to our careers and wait for things to stabilize." Instead, we doubled down, recognizing that this shift to digital was actually an opportunity. We were already building something digital, and we understood that this moment could accelerate adoption rather than hinder it. The rest, as they say, is history.

From there, we moved quickly to build our Minimum Viable Product (MVP). In fact, by July 2020, our MVP was fully built in-house. We were incredibly fast. However, finding a merchant willing to go live was a challenge. We had one early merchant who, while not a major player, was good enough for us to launch with. But just as we were about to finalize the integration, internal conflicts within their company led their CEO—whom we had never met—to deprioritize our service. They decided it wasn't a focus for them, and they never took us live.

That was a stumbling block, but we kept searching. Eventually, we found other merchants and officially went live on September 27, 2020, which became Tamara's birthday. The initial product was basic—something that, looking back, we'd probably be embarrassed by today.

But that's an important lesson. Many smart people delay launching because they want their product to be perfect. While there are cases, especially in B2B, where a slow, meticulous approach is necessary to ensure the product meets enterprise requirements, in our case, speed mattered more than perfection. We prioritized getting to market quickly, knowing that execution and iteration would be key to success.

What would you say was the most important factor in making that initial launch successful despite those early setbacks?

Tamara was built to solve a very specific problem—people in the region lacked access to a seamless, widely accepted line of credit. We wanted to create a solution that allowed consumers to pay later, wherever they shopped, without friction. One way to achieve that would have been to issue a credit card. However, launching a credit card in our part of the world came with immense regulatory and capital requirements. We simply couldn't afford it, and there was no way anyone would fund such an ambitious idea at that stage.

Instead, we chose a different approach. Rather than issuing physical credit cards, we built our own network and APIs, integrating directly with merchants, particularly online, to provide a BNPL payment option at checkout—similar to how PayPal operates. This model had a huge advantage in terms of distribution. Instead of spending massive amounts of money acquiring individual customers, we leveraged merchants as distribution partners. The merchant integrated Tamara at checkout, displayed it on their website, and promoted it to customers, allowing us to reach users at the point of purchase.

One of the key lessons I've learned is that while product is important, distribution is everything. This is why large players keep getting larger—regardless of whether their product is the best. They use their distribution advantage to get in front of customers first. If a superior product emerges, they simply replicate it and use their reach to dominate.

———

> ❝ ONE OF THE KEY LESSONS I'VE LEARNED IS THAT WHILE PRODUCT IS IMPORTANT, DISTRIBUTION IS EVERYTHING.

———

For us, the B2B2C model was phenomenal. When merchants adopted Tamara, they promoted it as a payment option, making it visible to all their customers. The pitch was simple: "You don't have to pay the full price today; you can pay in installments." This wasn't just beneficial for customers—it also helped merchants increase their average order value (AOV) and conversion rates. This created a three-way win. The merchant won by increasing sales, the customer won by gaining flexibility in payments, and Tamara won by earning a cut from transactions.

When did you realize this model could scale rapidly, and what major bottlenecks did you face in that regard?

Once we went live with our first merchants, a network effect kicked in. Merchants started telling other merchants, customers started asking for Tamara at more stores, and adoption began accelerating. While we had to do heavy sales early on—strategically targeting category leaders and getting them live—eventually, the flywheel started spinning. More merchants brought in more customers, and more customers brought in more merchants.

But there was one major challenge—funding. In a business like ours, acquiring merchants and customers is just one part of the equation. The real challenge is financing the transactions. BNPL is a capital-intensive business. Unlike SaaS or e-commerce, where you generate revenue directly from operations, we had to lend money to consumers while waiting for repayments. This meant we needed external funding, specifically debt financing, to scale.

When we launched Tamara, there was no clear path for securing this kind of funding in the region. Traditional banks weren't set up to provide capital to fintech startups, and regional investors were unfamiliar with this type of asset class. If we couldn't secure the necessary funding, we would be forced to limit growth, potentially losing momentum and market share.

Given this, how did you navigate this funding gap and position Tamara to attract financing?

At the time, I didn't know exactly how we were going to fund the business. But I knew one thing: globally, others had figured it out. If BNPL companies in mature markets were securing funding, there had to be a way for us to do the same. The key was momentum—if we could demonstrate traction, we could attract global investors to the region.

This required a leap of faith. Without debt financing, Tamara wouldn't have been able to scale. Unlike banks, we didn't have deposits to lend from, so borrowing was essential. The early years were a balancing act—we had to grow fast but not so fast that we outpaced our ability to secure funding. The risk was clear: if we scaled too quickly without sufficient capital, we could choke the business.

To be very honest, luck plays a role in everything. You can have a strong strategy, work hard, and execute flawlessly, but external factors matter. If macroeconomic conditions had been different, or if global investors hadn't been actively seeking opportunities in emerging markets, things might have turned out differently. But we were fortunate—the timing was perfect.

Around the time we were scaling, global investors started paying attention to BNPL, and there was growing interest in alternative lending models. This meant that when we approached international investors, they were already familiar with the space and eager to explore new markets. This allowed us to raise significant amounts of funding in a region where such fundraising had previously been nearly impossible.

Looking back, how important was timing in Tamara's growth?

Timing is critical indeed. Had we started this business in 2016, we likely wouldn't have succeeded. The ecosystem wasn't ready, investor appetite wasn't there, and adoption would have been too slow. Timing is a mix of insight and luck—you need to see where things are headed and take the bet that conditions will align in your favor.

Ultimately, we were able to secure both equity and debt financing, bringing major investors into the region and proving that BNPL could thrive here. That's how Tamara grew into what it is today—a business that not only transformed payments in the region but also helped pave the way for the next generation of fintech companies.

What were other scaleup challenges you faced?

One of the biggest challenges in scaling a company is building a great team. As an entrepreneur, you quickly realize that hiring is one of the most difficult and ongoing challenges. It's not something you solve once—it's an evolving process. There are always competing forces at play. You need to hire high-quality people, but at the same time, you need to move fast. If you're too slow and overly selective, you risk missing key opportunities. On the other hand, if you rush hiring just to fill roles, you might end up with the wrong people, which can be even more costly. Striking that balance is an art.

We often debate whether talent acquisition is more of an art or a science, and the reality is—it's both. No matter how well you plan or structure the hiring process, there's always an element of instinct involved. You have to know when to make a trade-off and when to wait for the right person. The key is to always maintain a high bar and continuously raise it as you scale. Ensuring that you have the best team possible is one of the most critical aspects of leadership because, beyond product-market fit, everything comes down to execution. And execution is all about the team.

What is your approach on hiring?

Many people make the mistake of focusing solely on experience and credentials when hiring. While these factors matter, they don't always determine success. I categorize hiring into three types. First, manpower—people who are there to get things done, move fast, and execute. Second, subject matter experts—people who bring deep knowledge in a specific field. And third, leaders—individuals who can drive a team, create alignment, and maximize the impact of the other two groups.

You don't need subject matter experts in every role. In fact, too many experts can slow you down. What you truly need, especially in the early days, are people with the right attitude and drive. These are the people who are willing to figure things out, push through challenges, and keep going when things get tough. That's why one of our core values today is being fanatical. I look for people who are considered "too much" by others—too serious, too driven, too obsessive about their work. These are the people who don't just see it as a job. They care deeply about what they're building.

It's not always easy to identify these qualities in an interview. Resumes won't tell you who is truly hungry, who has grit, or who will persist when faced with obstacles. That's where the art of hiring comes in. You need to listen to people's stories—understand why they do what they do. Do they have a strong personal reason for being here? Have they demonstrated resilience in their journey? Are they ambitious beyond just having a job?

Talk more about the role alignment plays in team building and driving job performance?

Beyond hiring, one of the biggest challenges in scaling a company is ensuring alignment.

Many people believe that once you hire a great team, you can just set the vision and let them figure it out. That doesn't work. If there isn't someone at the very top constantly driving alignment, teams will naturally drift in different directions. What you want to avoid is having multiple teams, each with their own version of the vision.

After hiring great people, leadership doesn't mean stepping back—it means working even harder to ensure everyone is moving in the right direction. It requires constant reinforcement of the vision, setting clear objectives, and making sure that teams aren't just working hard but working on the right things. Leading by example is crucial. If your team sees that you are putting in the work, they will be more likely to follow.

How you execute alignment depends on the scale of the company. A company with fewer than 100 people requires a different approach than one with 500, and beyond that, the structure must evolve further. But regardless of the phase, maintaining alignment is a constant effort that requires hands-on leadership. It's not about micromanaging—it's about making sure that every part of the company is moving in sync, working towards the same end goal.

Scaling a business isn't just about product, market, or funding. It's about building and leading a team that can execute at the highest level. And if you can figure out how to consistently attract, retain, and align the best people, that's the single biggest driver of success.

———

66 Scaling a business isn't just about product, market, or funding. It's about building and leading a team that can execute at the highest level.

———

Let's dive deeper into team building as foundational for scaling, and related best practices?

Sure. Let's start with hiring. Hiring is mandatory for everyone to participate in—it's not just an HR function. Leaders should be hiring their own teams. I personally hired most of my team by reaching out to people, engaging in conversations, and ensuring I brought in the right talent. I've never hired an executive through a headhunter because, in my experience, it just doesn't work. You need to connect with people, reference them, and convince them to join you. This philosophy cascades throughout the company. If a leader struggles to build a strong team, then that's a leadership issue. True leaders should be able to attract, engage, and convince top talent to join them.

Another key aspect of hiring is investing in youth. While experienced professionals are necessary for their subject matter expertise, it's crucial to develop a structured pipeline for young talent. We've built programs for interns, co-op students, and fresh graduates to identify the best candidates early on. Young professionals can be shaped and influenced by their environment. If they join a mediocre company, they may develop into average employees, but if they are hired by a high-performing company, they have the potential to become top-tier professionals. Of course, this requires patience, as they will make mistakes, but investing in them is fundamental to building a sustainable, high-performing company.

Now, in terms of management, communication and transparency are critical. A culture of openness builds trust, reduces politics—especially at scale—and ensures that everyone is aligned. Transparency is often underrated in this part of the world, but I believe it is essential. Through regular communication channels like all-hands meetings and town halls, we ensure that every team member understands company metrics, objectives, and challenges. This clarity eliminates excuses and empowers people to work towards common goals.

Our philosophy has never been about rigid work schedules. We don't dictate specific working hours because we believe that if you hire highly driven individuals, they will do whatever it takes to get the job done. Instead of micromanaging, we set clear expectations and allow our employees the freedom to execute in their own way.

That ties into our core values. While defining company values can sometimes feel like a corporate cliché, they are only meaningful if actively upheld. For instance, one of our early values was empowerment. We don't tell people exactly how to complete tasks; we simply define what needs to be accomplished and provide the necessary resources. If you give talented people autonomy and ownership, they will deliver results.

Another fundamental value we instilled early on is that the job is never done. This can be uncomfortable for some people who expect moments of pause and celebration. While we do acknowledge achievements, we operate with the mindset that there is always more to accomplish. There is no final destination—just continuous improvement and growth.

Speed is another cornerstone of our culture. We believe in moving fast because, in today's environment, fast is always better than slow. The ability to execute quickly, make rapid decisions, and iterate efficiently is crucial.

As a company grows, it evolves through different phases—scaling from zero to one, then from one to 100, and beyond. Each phase requires different approaches, and some practices that worked early on may no longer be relevant. Likewise, team composition changes, and it's essential to adapt. One key belief we hold is that we are not a family—we are a sports team. This means we always seek the best person for each role, and as the company grows, roles and responsibilities may shift. This mindset allows us to prioritize winning and high performance over sentimental attachment.

As founders and leaders, we've had to make tough decisions, including shifting people into different roles or, in some cases, letting them go when the company needed something different. These transitions are necessary to ensure we always have the right people in the right positions to drive the business forward.

Looking ahead, I believe we are entering a new phase as a company. Each phase brings new challenges, and I'll be happy to share more insights once we navigate this next stage.

What are some of the biggest leadership lessons you've learned while growing the company?

The biggest lesson I learned is that leadership is not static. What worked when we were a small team does not necessarily work at scale. I've had to continuously refine my approach—delegating more, empowering leaders within the company, and focusing on high-impact areas rather than getting caught up in operational details.

Another major lesson is that culture must be actively maintained. It's easy to lose sight of cultural foundations as a company grows, but ensuring that values like transparency, speed, and empowerment remain embedded in the organization is crucial. Leading by example is key. If leadership doesn't embody these values, the team won't either.

Let's shift gears and talk about your future outlook for Tamara.

The future is massive. The world is undergoing a transformation, and AI is at the forefront of this shift. AI is changing everything.

For Tamara, we see ourselves not just as a financial company but as a technology company. We operate in a huge, underserved market of over 400 million people in the region. Now, more than ever, regulators are opening up, creating opportunities for innovators like us to build and expand. Our vision is to establish Tamara as a generational, transformational company that leaves a lasting impact.

We're not just aiming for unicorn or decacorn status—we see this as a $100 billion+ opportunity across MENA and beyond. Too often, companies in this region think locally, but we need to think globally.

———

> WE'RE NOT JUST AIMING FOR UNICORN OR DECACORN STATUS—WE SEE THIS AS A $100 BILLION+ OPPORTUNITY ACROSS MENA AND BEYOND. TOO OFTEN, COMPANIES IN THIS REGION THINK LOCALLY, BUT WE NEED TO THINK GLOBALLY.

———

How do we expand into Africa, Asia, and Europe? That's the level of ambition we should have. Yes, our home market is big enough for initial success, but it's not enough for our long-term aspirations.

How about your thoughts on the region's startup ecosystem?

In terms of the regional startup ecosystem, we are just getting started. Silicon Valley took decades to become what it is today. Our ecosystem only began taking shape about five years ago, and we're now seeing more capital, IPOs, talent, and social acceptance of entrepreneurship. The ambition in the region is growing, and we are becoming a hub for innovation.

What's unique about the GCC is its cosmopolitan nature—it attracts talent from all over the world. This diversity is a major advantage. I hope regulators and policymakers recognize the power of bringing top global talent into this region and implement incentives to attract even more of it. Right now, with some Western economies becoming more isolationist, we have an opportunity to position this region as a global innovation hub.

Historically, the most successful civilizations thrived by embracing diversity and fostering collaboration. If we can create an environment where top minds from around the world feel welcomed and empowered to build here, that will be our greatest strength.

———

> HISTORICALLY, THE MOST SUCCESSFUL CIVILIZATIONS THRIVED BY EMBRACING DIVERSITY AND FOSTERING COLLABORATION. IF WE CAN CREATE AN ENVIRONMENT WHERE TOP MINDS FROM AROUND THE WORLD FEEL WELCOMED AND EMPOWERED TO BUILD HERE, THAT WILL BE OUR GREATEST STRENGTH.

———

Really appreciate the conversation and all the great insights, Majeed.

My pleasure, Amir.

———

MUDASSIR SHEIKHA

Simplifying lives, one ride at a time

Co-Founder and CEO of CAREEM

Ꙅareem

Dubai, UAE

www.careem.com

MUDASSIR SHEIKHA is a Pakistani entrepreneur, tech visionary, and the co-founder and CEO of Careem, the Middle East's leading super app. Born in Karachi, Pakistan, Sheikha's passion for technology, problem-solving, and innovation led him to pursue a Bachelor's degree in Computer Science and Economics from the University of Southern California (USC). He later went on to earn a Master's degree in Computer Science from Stanford University, one of the world's leading institutions for entrepreneurship and innovation.

Sheikha's early career was marked by deep experience in Silicon Valley startups, where he worked on cutting-edge technology projects. He later became an Associate Partner at McKinsey & Company, where he focused on technology and business transformation. This background gave him a strong foundation in business strategy and digital disruption, preparing him for his entrepreneurial journey.

In 2012, Sheikha, alongside Magnus Olsson, co-founded Careem to solve a fundamental problem: the lack of reliable and convenient transportation in the Middle East, North Africa, and South Asia (MENASA). The company started as a corporate car booking service, but quickly pivoted into ride-hailing, where it gained massive popularity, particularly in countries like Saudi Arabia, the UAE, Egypt, and Pakistan. Under Sheikha's leadership, Careem scaled to millions of users, thousands of captains (drivers), and a presence in over 80 cities.

One of Sheikha's biggest achievements came in March 2019, when Uber acquired Careem for $3.1 billion, marking the largest-ever technology acquisition in the Middle East. This milestone established Sheikha as one of the region's most influential tech entrepreneurs. Unlike other acquisitions where the acquired company is absorbed, Uber allowed Careem to retain its brand, leadership, and strategic independence, a testament to Sheikha's ability to negotiate and position Careem as an irreplaceable regional player.

Under Sheikha's leadership, Careem evolved beyond ride-hailing into a multi-service platform, offering Careem Pay (digital payments), Careem Food (food delivery), Careem Shops (e-commerce), and even home cleaning services. In April 2023, Careem took another bold step when e& acquired a majority stake in its Super App business for $400 million, giving the company fresh capital and autonomy to expand its non-ride-hailing services.

Beyond his business achievements, Sheikha has been a strong advocate for entrepreneurship, digital transformation, and social impact in the Middle East. He has championed the need for better urban mobility, digital financial inclusion, and the use of technology to solve everyday challenges. Careem's mission to simplify life in the region is a direct reflection of Sheikha's personal vision.

Sheikha has received numerous accolades, including being named one of the most influential tech entrepreneurs in the MENA region. He has spoken at global forums on the future of mobility, fintech, and the startup ecosystem in emerging markets, highlighting the potential of the Middle East and South Asia as tech hubs.

As of 2024, Mudassir Sheikha continues to lead Careem, now a dominant super app in the region, with a focus on expanding into new services, smart city solutions, and sustainable urban mobility. His journey from a Silicon Valley engineer to the CEO of a multi-billion-dollar company is a testament to the power of innovation, perseverance, and strategic vision. Through his leadership, Careem remains a game-changer in digital services, setting new standards for tech entrepreneurship in the Middle East and beyond.

CAREEM is a Dubai-based technology company that has redefined mobility, digital payments, and urban convenience across the Middle East, North Africa, and South Asia (MENASA) region. Established in 2012 by Mudassir Sheikha and Magnus Olsson, both former McKinsey & Company consultants, Careem started as a ride-hailing service but quickly evolved into a super app offering a diverse range of services, including transportation, food and grocery delivery, digital payments, and even home cleaning services.

The inspiration for Careem came from the founders' experiences with unreliable public transportation in emerging markets. They saw a significant gap in urban mobility solutions and sought to create a seamless, tech-driven platform that could provide reliable, safe, and affordable transport. Starting in Dubai, Careem expanded rapidly to major cities in Saudi Arabia, Egypt, Pakistan, Jordan, and beyond, becoming the region's first homegrown ride-hailing giant.

Careem's journey took a historic turn in March 2019, when Uber acquired the company for $3.1 billion, making it one of the largest-ever technology acquisitions in the Middle East. Under the terms of the deal, Uber continued to operate its own brand in the region, while Careem retained its identity and operations but became a wholly owned subsidiary of Uber. This allowed Careem to expand its services beyond transportation, leveraging Uber's resources while continuing to develop localized solutions for its core markets.

In April 2023, Careem underwent another major transformation, when e& (formerly Etisalat) acquired a 50.03% majority stake in its Super App business for $400 million. This strategic move allowed Careem to operate independently from Uber in non-ride-hailing services, while Uber retained full ownership of its original ride-hailing division. With this investment, Careem accelerated its expansion into fintech, last-mile delivery, and everyday services, positioning itself as the region's leading multi-service platform.

Today, Careem operates in over 80 cities across 14 countries and has millions of users benefiting from its wide array of services. It has also helped create hundreds of thousands of jobs for drivers, known as "Captains," by offering a flexible employment model. Through initiatives such as Careem Pay, a digital wallet that facilitates seamless transactions, and Careem Express, a delivery service for businesses and individuals, the company continues to innovate and adapt to the changing digital economy.

Careem's impact goes beyond business. It has been an advocate for smart cities, sustainable transportation, and digital inclusion in the region. The company has worked on public-private partnerships to improve urban mobility, invest in electric vehicle solutions, and enhance financial access through its fintech arm. By combining technology, convenience, and local expertise, Careem has become more than just a ride-hailing service—it is a super app that improves everyday life in the Middle East and beyond.

———

For new readers, could you briefly share your background and Careem's launch, as we covered in *Startup Arabia*?

Sure, I grew up in Karachi, Pakistan, born into a middle-class family with a small family business—a shop in a commercial part of town that had been passed down to my father and his brothers by their father. My father managed the family business, while my mother was an ambitious student who performed exceptionally well in school. However, she married early, became a housewife, and never got the chance to pursue education beyond high school. My father hadn't studied beyond high school either. They were both humble but ambitious in their own right.

Since my mother never had the opportunity to pursue her dreams despite her ambition, a lot of that drive was entrusted—quite forcefully at times—upon me as the eldest child and later upon my sisters. This translated into my parents making sure we attended the best schools they could afford, which were quite different from the ones attended by children in our neighborhood. They expected us to excel, to be at the top of our classes, or at least as close to the top as possible. At the time, this pressure felt intense, even overwhelming, but in hindsight, I now see how invaluable that upbringing was.

I ended up achieving excellent grades in high school, which earned me a scholarship to the University of Southern California. I initially went there to study economics, but this was around the time the dot-com bubble was forming, so I decided to pursue a double major in economics and computer science. After graduation, I moved to Silicon Valley and joined a startup. At some point, I also completed my master's in computer science from Stanford.

My first startup experience was during the height of the dot-com bubble in 2000, and it ended in failure unfortunately.

How was it like to go through such experience, and how did it shape your approach to building businesses?

It was a roller coaster to say the least. The company had raised a significant amount of funding, aimed for rapid growth, and was built with the intention of flipping it for an IPO. However, the bubble burst, and the entire model collapsed. One of my biggest lessons from that experience was to always "build to last." You can't predict external circumstances, but you can ensure you are building something sustainable with strong foundations. At the same time, working in that fast-paced environment taught me how to be ruthless with limited resources and move quickly—an invaluable lesson for any entrepreneur.

Later, I co-founded a second startup with some of my colleagues from the first venture. While that company didn't take off as we had hoped, we eventually managed to exit with a decent outcome. That period was challenging, but it reinforced the importance of resilience in entrepreneurship.

How did Dubai enter the picture?

At some point, I decided to move to Dubai. My parents were getting older, and as their only son—I have two younger sisters—I wanted to be closer to home. I joined McKinsey as a consultant, initially planning to stay for two years, but that turned into four. The experience was invaluable, teaching me how to solve complex problems and communicate effectively with stakeholders at all levels. It also gave me an excellent introduction to the region, allowing me to build relationships with incredible people—colleagues, clients, and mentors alike.

McKinsey was a crucial stepping stone, but ultimately, my entrepreneurial spirit led me to Magnus and then to co-founding Careem. Reflecting on my journey, I think two things stand out. First, my mother's unwavering belief that we should always strive to be the best version of ourselves shaped much of my drive. Second, my early experience in Silicon Valley, though painful, provided invaluable lessons. You often learn more from failures than from successes, and those early years taught me how to be ambitious, scale fast, build strong teams, and avoid many of the mistakes that can derail a startup.

———

66 YOU OFTEN LEARN MORE FROM FAILURES THAN FROM SUCCESSES, AND THOSE EARLY YEARS TAUGHT ME HOW TO BE AMBITIOUS, SCALE FAST, BUILD STRONG TEAMS, AND AVOID MANY OF THE MISTAKES THAT CAN DERAIL A STARTUP.

———

What was the origin of Careem?

Two key stories define the genesis of Careem. The first and main story is actually that of my co-founder, Magnus, while the second is mine, though it plays a smaller part in the journey.

A year before Careem started, Magnus was at a conference when he suddenly lost his vision. For a few seconds—or maybe just milliseconds—he couldn't see anything. Then, just as suddenly, his vision returned, and everything seemed fine. Though perplexed, he dismissed the incident, attributing it to stress or lack of sleep, and carried on with his life.

A few days later, he mentioned the incident to his father, a doctor in Sweden. His father immediately told him that this wasn't something caused by stress or exhaustion—something more serious could be at play. Magnus underwent testing and scans in the UAE, where he discovered that a vein in his brain had ruptured, causing internal bleeding. That brief period of vision loss had been the result of this rupture. Fortunately, his body had managed to create a new passage for blood flow, which allowed things to return to normal.

However, the doctor warned him that he had been extremely lucky. Any inflammation in the brain could restart the bleeding, and in that case, it could be fatal. The only option was surgery. Magnus was advised to drop everything in his life and seek treatment immediately. He flew to the Cleveland Clinic in the U.S., where the doctors reviewed his case, conducted further tests, and then told him something no 30-year-old expects to hear: "Wrap up your life."

For Magnus, this was a shocking and deeply thought-provoking moment. He started reflecting on his first 30 years and realized that he hadn't done as much as he could have with his time. He made a promise to himself that if he survived, he would come back as "Magnus 2.0"—someone who would build something big and meaningful, something that would leave a lasting legacy.

As we know, Magnus survived. He returned to the UAE, driven by a burning desire to build something impactful. That's when I met him—not for the first time, as we had worked together before as two tech professionals on similar projects—but this time, his mindset was completely different. He shared what he had been through and his determination to create something meaningful.

At that time, I was coming off a project in Pakistan with McKinsey. Without going into details due to confidentiality, my task was to compile a list of potential clients for the firm's early operations in the country. The simplest way to do that was to check the stock exchange for major companies. What I found was shocking: at the time, only one company in Pakistan was worth a billion dollars or more. For a country of that size, this was an eye-opening realization. Having spent years in Silicon Valley, where billion-dollar companies were everywhere, it was staggering to see that Pakistan, with all its potential, had so few large, lasting institutions.

So when Magnus told me he wanted to build something big and meaningful, it resonated deeply with me. I was already grappling with the question: Why don't we build large, lasting companies in our part of the world? His mission aligned perfectly with my own concerns. From there, the next challenge was determining what exactly we should build.

We explored several ideas, and the concept of transportation came from one of our consulting colleagues. He pointed out that transportation was a major challenge across the region—not just for consultants but for assistants, travel teams, and finance teams who had to manage the chaos of arranging transport. Every country had a patchwork of unreliable and unprofessional transportation companies. Drivers didn't always know the locations, language barriers created confusion, and the entire system was inefficient.

That's when I pitched the idea to Magnus: "What if we launched a transportation service?" He gave me a skeptical look and said, "I just got a second chance at life, and you're telling me we should start a transport company to move consultants around? How meaningful is that?"

It wasn't until he saw the impact this idea could have on drivers—whom we later called "captains"—that he became convinced. We realized that we could provide drivers with better, more consistent earnings while treating them with dignity and respect. They weren't just drivers; they were captains, and we aimed to change how they were perceived by society. That's what made it meaningful.

We started as a corporate car service, targeting companies that needed reliable transport for their employees. It wasn't a B2C on-demand service at first. It took us a year to shift toward on-demand rides, and part of that shift was driven by our discovery of Uber. When we learned that Uber was about to launch in the Middle East, we knew we had to adapt. If people could get a car in five minutes, why would they go through a long booking process with us? We realized we had to launch an app and move into on-demand services.

What were the biggest challenges of competing with Uber, and how did you position Careem to scale?

From that point on, everything became a fight for survival. Uber had better technology, more money, and an aggressive expansion strategy. They wanted to dominate, and we had to find a way to compete.

We were bootstrapped, our technology was still in its infancy, and raising funds in the region was extremely difficult. There were very few venture capital firms at the time, and convincing investors to back us wasn't easy.

Another challenge was attracting top talent. Unlike Silicon Valley, where startups were an established career path, in our region, the best talent still preferred to work for multinational corporations or government entities. Getting top-tier professionals to join a startup was not straightforward. We tried to solve this by offering equity and showcasing our wins, but it remained an uphill battle.

Expanding across the region was another massive challenge. The Middle East is incredibly diverse—Dubai is nothing like Cairo, which is nothing like Casablanca, which is nothing like Riyadh. Each market required a different approach, and we had to build local teams led by people who truly understood their respective markets. In many cases, our teams in different countries operated in completely different ways, forcing us to manage the complexity of running multiple versions of the same business.

———

> EACH MARKET REQUIRED A DIFFERENT APPROACH, AND WE HAD TO BUILD LOCAL TEAMS LED BY PEOPLE WHO TRULY UNDERSTOOD THEIR RESPECTIVE MARKETS.

———

Despite all of these challenges, we not only survived but succeeded in competing with Uber. It was a constant battle, but we leveraged our local knowledge, built partnerships that were difficult for a distant competitor to replicate, and executed with relentless focus.

So, those were the early years of Careem. It was a relentless, challenging, but incredibly rewarding journey.

What were the biggest challenges in raising early-stage funding, and what lessons did you learn in that area?

Funding was a challenge, though perhaps less so now than it was back then. We were fortunate to have support early on, but my belief about funding has always been that if you're solving a big problem—one that represents a major opportunity—and you can demonstrate traction, then raising money isn't the hardest part. My advice to founders is simple: find a big problem to solve. Of course, even if the opportunity is massive, you have to start small and prove traction in a way that demonstrates real potential. If you do that well, it's only a matter of time before the right people back you.

Like many startups, we started with our own savings. It's a good signal to investors that you're personally invested. Then, we raised money from friends and family, which gave us enough runway until we secured institutional funding. One of the mistakes we made—and a common one among founders—was becoming too valuation-sensitive. Sometimes, you prioritize investors offering the highest valuation, but that doesn't always mean they are the right partners. We learned the hard way that having the wrong investors on board can create significant problems down the road.

In the Middle East, plenty of capital exists, but not all of it is sophisticated in the way a startup needs. When things are going well, any investor will stand by you. But when challenges arise—as they inevitably do—you need investors who truly understand the risks and can support you through difficult times rather than making them even harder. So my advice is to focus on sophisticated investors who grasp your vision and will stick with you through ups and downs.

At some point, when you become large enough, however, global investors start to take notice. That's when fundraising becomes somewhat easier because your pool of potential investors expands significantly.

What other scaleup challenges did you face during this period?

Talent was also a major challenge at the time. It's a bit easier now than it was back then, but 13-14 years ago, attracting top talent to a startup in the region was incredibly difficult. Imagine trying to convince someone working at a leading investment bank, consulting firm, or tech company to join a tiny startup operating out of a 500-square-foot office, with no proven track record and no clear path to success.

At that time, the only major startup success story in the region was Yahoo's acquisition of Maktoob, which at least provided some precedent, but there were far more examples of failures than successes. That made hiring extremely tough.

One thing that helped was the reason we were building Careem. I had worked at startups before, and startups are often driven by personal ambition—wanting to get rich, achieve fame, or capitalize on the latest trend. But Careem was different. It was born out of Magnus's near-death experience and his desire to leave a meaningful legacy. That was the driving force behind the company, and it shaped everything we did.

Early on, we formalized this mission: to simplify and improve people's lives while building an awesome organization that inspires. The first part—simplifying life—came from the realization that talent in the region often gets bogged down in daily inefficiencies. If we could remove that friction, people would have the time and mental space to dream bigger and achieve more. The second part—building an inspiring organization—stemmed from the widespread lack of confidence in the region. We wanted to prove that big things could emerge from this part of the world.

This mission became a magnet for like-minded individuals. We attracted talented people who were earning half a million dollars elsewhere but were willing to take a pay cut to join Careem because they resonated with our purpose. Many of them are still with the company today, even after the Uber acquisition, because they joined for the right reasons.

What strategies did you implement to attract and retain top talent?

Another key factor in building a strong team was equity. At the time, equity wasn't widely understood or valued in the region—everyone preferred a bit more cash in hand. But we insisted on a generous equity pool, which helped create real ownership and passion. Our philosophy was simple: the more you give, the more it becomes. If employees have meaningful equity, they become deeply invested in the company's success, and that, in turn, increases the value of the equity itself.

At the time of our acquisition by Uber, 17% of Careem was owned by employees outside of the founders. When I meet founders today who are trying to be overly conservative with equity—debating whether they should give 5% or 10%—I always tell them that being too stingy with equity is shortsighted. Being generous with equity pays off in ways you might not expect.

Another hiring strategy that worked well for us was what I call "acqui-hires." In Saudi Arabia, for example, we acquired Anwani in 2015, a company started by Dr. Abdulla Elyas, who became our third co-founder. Anwani was a UAE-based address mapping startup that developed a digital addressing system to improve location accuracy and delivery services. This acquisition helped Careem enhance its mapping and location-based services, making ride-hailing and logistics more efficient.

In Egypt, our entry was through the acquisition of Taxi Sahel, which brought Hadi Shalabi into the team. We did the same in Morocco—though that one wasn't as successful. These acquisitions brought in local entrepreneurs who knew their markets inside out and made Careem's expansion much more effective. Not only did it bring in the right talent, but it also infused our company with an entrepreneurial mindset.

This strategy of partnering with local entrepreneurs helped significantly in geographic expansion. The Middle East is incredibly diverse—Dubai is vastly different from Cairo, which is different from

Casablanca, which is different from Riyadh. Rather than imposing a one-size-fits-all model, we empowered local leaders to adapt the business to their markets. Sometimes, their approaches were entirely different from one another, which created internal complexities, but it was necessary to succeed in such varied markets.

How did Careem approach government regulations, and how did you approach policymakers?

Beyond funding and talent, a major challenge was navigating government regulations. Fifteen years ago, ride-hailing was an entirely new concept in the region, and many countries had deeply entrenched taxi monopolies. In most cases, these companies were owned by large business families or government-affiliated entities, making disruption difficult.

Uber's approach to regulatory challenges was often combative—they would launch first, fight later. But in our part of the world, we knew that wouldn't work. Instead of positioning ourselves as disruptors, we framed Careem as an enabler. In many of these countries, the taxi system was already broken, so we weren't "disrupting" so much as fixing something that wasn't working in the first place.

This approach led us to focus on partnerships rather than confrontation. The best example of this was our joint venture with Dubai's Roads and Transport Authority (RTA) to create Hala, which integrated all of Dubai's taxis onto the Careem platform. This was the first partnership of its kind between a government and a ride-hailing company, and it became incredibly successful. I can't share the exact numbers, but today, a significant percentage of Dubai's taxi rides are booked through Hala.

Instead of fighting regulators, we asked, "How can we work together to create win-win scenarios?" That mindset made all the difference.

So those were some of the biggest challenges we faced—funding, talent, expansion, and regulation. Each came with its own struggles, mistakes, and learnings, but in the end, they shaped how Careem evolved into what it is today.

What were the biggest operational shifts for Careem after being acquired by Uber?

There has been a lot of learning on our side about how Uber operates and how a global technology company functions. One of our biggest realizations was that Silicon Valley tech companies are significantly more tech-first than we were. In many ways, we were a tech company, but we were primarily operations-first. When we encountered a problem, our instinct was to solve it operationally. If the solution worked, only then would we think about making it tech-enabled. Uber, on the other hand, given the scale at which they operate globally, always starts with a tech solution. As you can imagine, that approach is far more scalable and consistent than solving problems purely through operations.

One of our biggest takeaways from Uber was learning how to be more tech-first and how to apply a product-oriented mindset to problem-solving on the ground.

———

66 ONE OF OUR BIGGEST TAKEAWAYS FROM UBER WAS LEARNING HOW TO BE MORE TECH-FIRST AND HOW TO APPLY A PRODUCT-ORIENTED MINDSET TO PROBLEM-SOLVING ON THE GROUND.

———

Let's double-down on how Careem transitioned from an operations-driven to a technology-first company.

Certainly. A clear example of this was how we approached captain (driver) acquisition. Whenever we needed to grow our fleet, we would open what we called Opportunity Centers—small offices across different parts of the city responsible for recruiting captains from those neighborhoods. If we needed more captains quickly, we would push our teams harder, give them higher targets, and send them out to the streets to hire captains manually.

Uber, on the other hand, had a completely different model. Instead of manually hiring captains, they introduced a captain referral program. Whenever they needed more captains, they simply increased referral bonuses and incentivized existing captains to bring in new ones. The entire onboarding process was digital—captains could sign up online, complete training remotely, and get activated without ever visiting a physical location. This dramatically reduced the time and effort required to scale. Seeing this in action was a major learning for us and helped us understand what it truly means to be a global tech platform.

What did Careem learn from Uber, and what did Uber learn from Careem?

While we learned a lot from Uber, they also learned from us. At Careem, we had built a strong reputation for our ability to hustle on the ground, form deep partnerships, and collaborate effectively with key stakeholders in the region. This was an area where we had a distinct advantage over Uber, whose DNA at the time was very different.

How do you think the combination of Careem's local expertise and Uber's global scale were synergistic?

Uber has evolved significantly in recent years, especially under Dara's leadership, but back then, they weren't as partnership-driven as we were. Careem had developed a strong playbook for working with governments, local business leaders, and influential families in the region. That ability to navigate complex regulatory landscapes and build relationships was something Uber learned from us, just as we learned from their tech-first approach. Of course, Uber operates a global business, so they weren't just learning from Careem—they were also absorbing best practices from other parts of the world.

Another key difference was our entrepreneurial mindset. Careem's teams were built differently from Uber's—more flexible, scrappier, and more accustomed to solving problems in real-time on the ground. I often tell my teams that if you can combine Careem's execution strengths with Uber's technology and scale, you create an incredibly formidable player. That's something that started to take shape after the acquisition.

What factors should founders consider when deciding to sell their company, and what did you learn from Careem's acquisition?

Now, when it comes to acquisitions, there are many lessons to take away—knowing when it's the right time to sell, choosing the right acquirer, negotiating the terms, and ensuring a smooth integration while keeping the entrepreneurial spirit of the original company alive.

One of the most important things for founders to understand is timing. When should you sell? The answer isn't straightforward, but it comes down to a few key factors. You have to assess whether selling aligns with your long-term vision, whether you have the resources to continue scaling independently, and whether an acquisition would help you achieve your mission faster and at a greater scale than you could on your own.

Choosing the right acquirer is just as critical. You want a company that aligns with your values, understands your vision, and will support your team and culture post-acquisition. We had discussions with multiple potential acquirers, and while Uber had been our biggest competitor, we recognized that there was a strategic fit. It wasn't just about financials—it was about impact, scalability, and what would be best for our people and the broader ecosystem.

The negotiation phase is where things get tricky. Acquisitions are not just about price; they involve structuring the right deal, defining how much autonomy the acquired company will have, and determining what happens to employees, leadership, and the brand. Every aspect of the business must be considered, from customer experience to internal operations.

After the deal is signed, the real work begins—the integration. One of the biggest challenges is keeping the spirit of the original company alive. When startups get acquired, there's always a risk that they lose their agility and entrepreneurial DNA. In our case, we were very conscious of this. We fought hard to retain Careem's autonomy within Uber and to ensure that our team continued to operate with the same mission-driven mindset.

That's why, post-acquisition, Careem continued running as an independent entity within Uber rather than being fully absorbed into the global structure. That was intentional—it allowed us to keep our startup culture intact while benefiting from Uber's global infrastructure.

What is your advice for any founder considering an acquisition?

My advice would be to deeply understand why you're doing it. If an acquisition won't accelerate your ability to achieve your goals, think twice before selling. Pick the right buyer, not just the highest offer. The highest valuation isn't always the best outcome if the acquiring company doesn't align with your vision. Negotiate beyond price and structure the deal in a way that protects your team, your culture, and your ability to operate effectively post-acquisition. Think about integration from day one and plan how you will maintain your identity and culture within a larger entity.

───────

> IF AN ACQUISITION WON'T ACCELERATE YOUR ABILITY
> TO ACHIEVE YOUR GOALS, THINK TWICE BEFORE
> SELLING. PICK THE RIGHT BUYER, NOT JUST THE
> HIGHEST OFFER. THE HIGHEST VALUATION ISN'T ALWAYS
> THE BEST OUTCOME.

───────

Acquisitions can be transformative, but they need to be approached with a long-term perspective. In our case, we were fortunate that the deal with Uber allowed Careem to retain its essence while leveraging Uber's resources for greater impact. It was a major milestone in our journey and an experience filled with valuable lessons.

There was a lot of learning that came from the acquisition, particularly in understanding how Uber operates as a global technology company. One of the biggest realizations for us was just how much more tech-first companies in Silicon Valley are compared to how we operated. While we considered ourselves a tech company, we were fundamentally operations-first. When we encountered a problem, our instinct was to solve it operationally, and only after proving that the solution worked would we think about making it tech-enabled. Uber, given the scale at which they operate, approaches problems differently. They start with a tech solution from the outset, which makes their processes inherently more scalable and consistent.

Initially, we were skeptical of the acquisition. We had been competing with Uber, and for years they had been trying to outcompete us in the region. The idea of doing a deal with a company that was actively trying to eliminate you didn't sit right at first. Beyond that, we also felt that Careem's purpose was still unfinished. We measured our progress against our vision of simplifying and improving people's lives and realized that most of the region was still underserved. It felt like there was still so much left to do.

The breakthrough happened when Uber's CEO, Dara, assured us that nothing had to change. He told us to keep doing what we were doing, that Uber would simply be a better shareholder than our existing ones. He expressed appreciation for what we had built and promised to support us in continuing our journey. That structure became the best of both worlds. It meant that Careem would continue to operate independently rather than becoming another company that gets acquired, merged, and ultimately disappears. That had already happened twice in the region—first with Maktoob and then with Souq. But Careem is still around, still a strong brand, and still a product that coexists in the market. That was the construct that Dara proposed, and thanks to him and the leadership at Uber, they honored that agreement even through challenges like COVID, which had a huge impact on the ride-hailing industry.

Uber stayed true to their word and allowed Careem to remain independent, giving us the freedom to build beyond ride-hailing. As you probably know, Careem today offers many services beyond transportation, evolving into a broader consumer internet platform. The acquisition wasn't just about preserving what we had built but also about enabling the next phase of our journey.

A couple of other key learnings emerged from the acquisition process. The first was ensuring clear alignment from the top. There has to be open, honest, and transparent alignment on what the future will look like. That could mean anything—from a full integration where the acquired company is absorbed into the parent company, to an arrangement where the company remains independent. Whatever the structure, all parties need to put their cards on the table and be upfront about expectations. Because we did that early on, we were able to find a structure that created a win-win-win. It was a win for the region, a win for Uber, and a win for us as founders and the Careem team. Without that alignment, deals can lead to major issues down the road.

Another key learning was that the negotiation process is not something you can do alone.

Remember, none of us had ever negotiated a deal of this scale before, so we brought in experienced bankers to help structure the deal, navigate the negotiation process, and ensure everything was executed smoothly. It was a long and complex process, but thanks to the expertise of our advisors and our internal team, we managed to see it through to the finish line.

The post-merger integration was another critical phase. Mergers often sound straightforward on paper, but the reality is far more complex. However, we, along with Uber and the Careem teams, developed a comprehensive pre-merger and post-merger plan to ensure a smooth transition. While it wasn't an easy process, it was ultimately a successful one.

———

> IN THE EARLY DAYS, YOU HAVE TO BE A DOER. THERE'S NO OTHER WAY. YOU'RE ON THE GROUND, PUSHING YOURSELF TO GET THINGS DONE, BECAUSE THERE AREN'T ENOUGH PEOPLE IN THE ORGANIZATION TO DELEGATE TASKS TO.

———

How would you say your leadership approach evolved as Careem scaled?

Leadership evolves over time, especially in a fast-growing company. In the early days, you have to be a doer. There's no other way. You're on the ground, pushing yourself to get things done, because there aren't enough people in the organization to delegate tasks to. That hands-on approach is essential in the beginning. But as the company scales, it becomes impossible to do everything yourself. You have to shift from being the one solving problems to being the one building a team that solves problems. One of the most valuable pieces of advice

I received was to focus on solving people, not problems—because if you bring in the right people, they will solve the problems for you. That has been one of my biggest areas of growth, but also one of the biggest challenges.

Another major learning has been taking a longer-term view on things. In the early years, you operate with a strong sense of urgency, trying to be everywhere and do everything at once. But over time, you realize that trying to do too much too quickly often leads to losing focus and ultimately destroying value in the long run. Today, at Careem, we are far more deliberate about what we focus on. We have identified a few core areas that we are deeply committed to, and we are executing on those with discipline rather than spreading ourselves too thin. We now understand that if you build a strong product and take a long-term approach, there's always time to expand into new markets later. There's no need to rush into everything all at once. At the same time, we remain agile and fight the day-to-day battles that need to be fought, but always with a more strategic mindset.

Post-acquisition especially, embracing a more product-driven and tech-first mindset was critical. Uber has influenced us to think differently about how we approach challenges, making us more product-oriented than we were before.

––––––

" IF YOU BUILD A STRONG PRODUCT AND TAKE A LONG-TERM APPROACH, THERE'S ALWAYS TIME TO EXPAND INTO NEW MARKETS LATER. THERE'S NO NEED TO RUSH INTO EVERYTHING ALL AT ONCE.

––––––

Looking back, what is one mistake you made building Careem?

If I had to point to one mistake, it would be around people. Sometimes, you hire people you shouldn't have, and other times, you miss out on hiring people you really needed. Looking back, many of my biggest regrets are tied to hiring decisions—either not acting quickly enough when someone wasn't the right fit, or not bringing in key talent early enough when it could have made a difference. Those decisions have a compounding effect on the company's trajectory, and I wish we had moved faster in some cases.

Thank you, Mudassir. It's been a pleasure hearing about your extraordinary journey and lessons learned.

Thank you, Amir. I hope these experiences help others on their own paths, and I'm excited to see what the next generation of regional entrepreneurs will build.

———

OMAR HAGRASS

Moving freight, driving progress

Founder and CEO of TRELLA

trella

Cairo, Egypt

www.trella.app

OMAR HAGRASS is the co-founder and CEO of Trella, a leading technology platform transforming freight logistics across the Middle East and North Africa (MENA). Founded in 2018, Trella connects shippers with carriers, improving transparency, efficiency, and reliability in an industry that has long remained unchanged. Under Omar's leadership, the company has expanded rapidly, attracting global investors and establishing itself as a key player in the freight tech space.

Before founding Trella, Omar built extensive experience in operations and expansion. He played a crucial role at Uber as the Launch and Expansion Manager for Europe, the Middle East, and Africa (EMEA), where he was responsible for launching UberEATS in major cities like Dubai, Riyadh, Cape Town, Johannesburg, and over 40 locations across the UK. Prior to Uber, he worked as an Investment Banking Analyst at CI Capital, where he specialized in financial modeling and market analysis.

Omar holds a bachelor's degree in Political Economy from the University of Oregon. His expertise in business strategy and market expansion has been instrumental in Trella's success. Under his leadership, Trella raised what was then Egypt's largest seed funding round, securing support from prominent global investors. In 2019, Trella acquired Trukto, further strengthening its market presence, and by 2020, the company expanded operations into Saudi Arabia and Pakistan.

His vision for Trella goes beyond regional expansion. By leveraging technology, real-time data, and AI-driven optimization, Omar aims to digitize freight movement and make logistics more cost-effective and sustainable. His leadership has positioned Trella as a driver of innovation in the logistics industry, empowering carriers with steady, high-quality loads while providing shippers with reliable and cost-efficient solutions.

Recognized as a rising star in Africa's tech ecosystem, Omar is an active voice in industry forums and discussions about the future of logistics in emerging markets. He has also shared insights on business and leadership through platforms like the WAYA Book Club, where he discusses books that have influenced his thinking. His commitment to innovation and efficiency continues to propel Trella forward, with aspirations to expand beyond MENA and redefine freight logistics on a global scale.

———

TRELLA is a technology-driven logistics platform revolutionizing freight transportation across the Middle East and North Africa. Established in 2018 and headquartered in Cairo, Egypt, the company offers a digital marketplace that connects shippers with a vast network of carriers. By providing transparent pricing, reliable availability, and real-time shipment tracking, Trella eliminates inefficiencies in the traditional freight industry and enhances logistics operations for businesses.

Trella operates with an extensive carrier network, boasting over 30,000 carriers across the region. Its platform supports various truck types, including open jumbos, flatbeds, trailers, semi-trailers, and double flatbeds, catering to a diverse range of industries such as FMCGs, manufacturing, agriculture, construction, mining, and retail. The company also plays a critical role in port logistics, serving major hubs like Alexandria, Damietta, and Port Said in Egypt, as well as key routes across Saudi Arabia and the UAE.

The company's impact is evident through its scale and efficiency. In Egypt alone, Trella manages a total freight volume of 130 million tons, facilitated by a carrier network of 20,000 drivers. In Saudi Arabia, Trella serves high-traffic routes like Riyadh to Jeddah and Jeddah to Dammam, with 11,000 carriers transporting 10 million tons of cargo annually. The UAE operation, though smaller in scale, continues to grow, handling 23,000 tons of freight with a network of 800 carriers, covering major logistics corridors such as Dubai to Riyadh, Abu Dhabi to Dammam, and Dubai to Kuwait City.

Trella has attracted top-tier corporate clients, including Amazon, LG, DHL, Maersk, and Arma, underscoring its reputation as a trusted logistics partner. Coca-Cola Manufacturing and Packing Company in Egypt has recognized Trella for its adherence to deadlines and operational efficiency, while major Saudi enterprises such as Ranco & Zamil Concrete Industries have praised the company's ability to optimize complex supply chain operations. In the UAE, logistics leaders like CEVA and Almjadouie have leveraged Trella's expertise to enhance transport efficiency and reduce costs.

Backed by approximately $34.2 million in funding from investors such as Y Combinator, Raed Ventures, and Algebra Ventures, Trella continues to expand its footprint. The company maintains a workforce of nearly 300 employees and reported stable revenues of $19.6 million in 2024. In addition to expanding its core trucking services, Trella is actively investing in digital tools that provide shippers with actionable insights, helping businesses optimize their supply chains and reduce operational inefficiencies.

With its data-driven approach, cutting-edge logistics technology, and commitment to transforming freight operations in emerging markets, Trella is poised to become the leading logistics platform in the MENA region. Its ongoing expansion into the UAE, alongside its strong foothold in Egypt and Saudi Arabia, signals a promising future in reshaping freight mobility and logistics infrastructure in the region.

———

Let's start from the beginning with some background about yourself.

I'm Omar Hagrass, born and raised in Cairo, Egypt. I studied at the Jesuit school, a Catholic school in Cairo. I graduated from high school with an American diploma and a GCSE. My university journey was quite eventful. I initially started studying medicine at Cairo University and Fayoum University, which had a joint program in Australia. A year in, I realized that while I loved the idea of being a doctor and serving people, I wasn't ready to study for 15 years. My father wasn't happy about that, and we agreed that I would pursue engineering instead. I started with architecture, but that didn't work out.

Back then, I was a bit of a troublemaker. My brother and I used to get into a lot of trouble, and my father was skeptical about my future. After architecture didn't work, I tried economics, then journalism. I did OK but not as well as I had hoped or as well as my father had hoped. I had been a strong student in high school, usually graduating with high honors. Eventually, I made a deal with my father: allow me to study abroad for one semester. If I did well, I could continue my education abroad. If I didn't, I would do whatever he wanted without argument.

We struck the deal, and I secured a cultural and sports scholarship at the University of Oregon. In 2011, I traveled abroad, and that experience changed everything for me. I performed well academically and started to understand different cultures, explore my career interests, and develop myself. I returned to Egypt and worked in investment banking.

I usually say there are five milestones that shaped who I am. The first was joining the water polo team at Gezirah Club in Cairo. The second was studying at the University of Oregon. The third was joining Uber as part of the launch team in Cairo, then expanding Uber into multiple cities. The fourth was losing my parents in a car accident at a young age—I was 22 at the time, and it shaped me in ways I never expected. The fifth milestone was founding Trella. More recently, a new milestone has been becoming a father. My daughter was born prematurely at just six months, and we spent the last four months in the ICU. Now, she's finally home, and she's making life so much more meaningful.

I'll start with water polo. As I mentioned, I studied at a Jesuit school, which was very strict—only boys, very disciplined. I was a good student, but joining water polo opened my eyes to a completely different world. From day one, I was addicted to the sport. Water polo is a combination of swimming, endurance, sprinting, wrestling, and boxing, all while trying not to drown. But more than anything, it's about teamwork. Six players in the water, plus a goalkeeper, all working together to win.

Water polo exposed me to new friendships, different cultures, and different ways of thinking. It also taught me perseverance. Building a company has a lot in common with sports—leadership, teamwork, decision-making under pressure. Water polo gave me that foundation.

After water polo, I studied at the University of Oregon. That was another eye-opening experience. When I applied for schools, I intentionally looked at the West Coast. I wanted to be as far away from Egypt as possible—not because I didn't love Egypt, but because I wanted to be on my own. I applied to UCLA, UC Davis, and other schools, but the first acceptance I got was from the University of Oregon. I don't even remember if UCLA accepted me, but I remember that Oregon was farther away and I didn't know anyone there, which made it even more appealing.

I made a pact with my father, traveled to Oregon, and found myself in a completely new world. Different culture, different people, fully independent, figuring everything out on my own. That experience had a huge impact on me. My time in Oregon was about self-discovery. I got into things I had never tried before—wrestling, music, student associations. I joined the International Student Association, the Arab Students Union, started organizing events, and met people from all over the world. I spent a couple of years there, and those were some of the best years of my life. What I cherish most was learning more about myself, reading more, and expanding my perspectives.

A year after I returned to Egypt, I lost my parents in a car accident. I was 22 years old, and that experience changed me forever. Losing them made me grow up instantly. Suddenly, I was responsible for the family, managing the family business, supporting my grandparents, who were deeply affected by it. It forced me to mature, to take on responsibilities, and to think differently about my life and the impact I wanted to have.

A couple of years after that, I got into Uber. Before that, I worked in investment banking at one of the top firms in the region. I got what I needed from the experience, but I never loved it. I always knew it was a stepping stone to something else. When I joined Uber, I was one of the first employees in Cairo, maybe number three or four. I spent a year helping set up and launch Uber in Cairo, developing different products and centralizing customer support.

Nine months later, I moved to Uber Eats, transitioning from ride-hailing to delivery. At that time, Uber Eats had only launched in Toronto and London, and the goal was to expand to 200 cities in less than a year. I joined the launch and expansion team, first launching Uber Eats in Dubai. That was chaotic at first, but after a month, things started running smoothly. From there, I launched Uber Eats in Cape Town, then Riyadh, and then moved to London, where I spent two years launching in cities like Birmingham, Manchester, Liverpool, and Glasgow.

Each launch was different—not just operationally but culturally. The experience of launching in London was nothing like launching in Cape Town or Riyadh. The exposure to different markets, different people, and different ways of working was invaluable. The first day I joined Uber, I remember texting my girlfriend and saying, "I think I found what I want to do for the rest of my life." Operations, managing a marketplace, working with product teams in San Francisco, collaborating with engineers, launching in new geographies—it was exactly what I wanted, and I'll always be grateful for that experience.

During one of my launches, I was in Birmingham, and I texted my colleague at Uber, Al Otros, who is now my co-founder at Trella. I told him, "We've done ride-hailing. We've done delivery. What about moving goods and trucks?" He liked the idea. Over the next few days, we went back and forth discussing different possibilities.

When I flew back to Cairo, we met up and brainstormed ideas. We had three main concepts we were considering: a truck marketplace, a last-mile delivery service, and a grocery delivery platform. We debated the pros and cons of each, analyzing the industry, the challenges, and the opportunities. In the end, we chose trucking because it was the biggest problem—and with big problems come big opportunities. It wasn't a random decision. It came from studying the market, understanding the business, and identifying where we could make the biggest impact.

And just like that, Trella was launched.

Can you walk us through the launch experience and the key steps you took in the early stages?

The early phase of launching a company, that zero-to-one stage, is full of uncertainty. And with uncertainty comes discomfort. If you're not comfortable with ambiguity, the process can be a nightmare. Looking back, I wish I had enjoyed those first couple of years more. They were probably the best years—when the team is small, you're figuring things out, putting things on track, and really thinking through every decision.

When we started, we looked at the landscape. In Egypt, most truck drivers were independent operators who owned their own trucks, typically between one and five. These drivers had three major problems. The first was inconsistent demand—some weeks they had work, some weeks they didn't. The second was accurate pricing—many times, they didn't know if they were getting paid a fair price. The third was payments—getting paid on time was a huge issue. The working capital cycle in trucking is brutal. A truck driver could complete a load and then have to wait anywhere from two to eight weeks to get paid, depending on the type of truck, the type of cargo, and the contracts in place. Expecting independent operators to fund that gap from their own pockets was unrealistic.

So we asked ourselves, how do we solve these problems in a way that will make truck drivers want to stick to our platform? The first thing was to secure demand. We aggressively reached out to businesses that needed trucking services—agriculture providers, FMCG companies, manufacturers. I remember driving from Cairo to a place called 10th of Ramadan, which is an industrial city about two hours away, almost every day for six months straight. I would try to meet as many factory owners and logistics managers as possible.

Sometimes we'd knock on doors and get kicked out. Other times, we'd get welcomed in.

The real breakthrough was signing those first customers. That's when we started to truly understand the business and refine our approach. We launched with the most basic MVP—an Excel sheet and a Google Form. Every day, we would ask manufacturers to fill out the form with the number of trucks they needed and their required destinations. But we quickly realized that most of them didn't want to use a form or any new tool—they wanted to call us or send a WhatsApp message. They'd simply say, "We need ten trucks from Cairo to Alexandria," or "Five trucks from Cairo to Port Said," and that was it. They weren't looking for an app. They just wanted a faster, easier way to do what they were already doing. That insight shaped how we built our platform.

We started by working with small and medium manufacturers. Then, slowly but surely, we landed Coca-Cola. That was a major win. Once you have big names using your platform, momentum builds. By the end of our first year, we were generating a million dollars in GMV per month, just nine or ten months in. Growth was strong, but it also highlighted our biggest challenge—working capital.

As we grew, we needed to unlock financing facilities and venture debt to manage cash flow. Truck drivers needed to be paid on time, but our customers paid on their own schedules, which created a gap we had to bridge. We realized that to solve this, we needed to bring in the right talent. That's when we started looking for a strong CFO. We met Hatem Sabry, who was an AVP at Deutsche Bank between London and Dubai. He joined the company, and within a few months, we started unlocking working capital facilities and venture debt.

Managing working capital was critical because any disruption in payments would immediately affect our truck drivers. If we didn't pay them on time, they would stop using our platform. Consistent demand wasn't enough—we also had to make sure payments were accurate and timely. Slowly but surely, we figured out those pain points and solved them, which helped us build a strong brand in the region.

At the same time, we faced tough competition. Trukker was our biggest competitor, and it felt a lot like the Uber vs. Careem rivalry. We were both fighting for investors, fighting for customers, and fighting to onboard truck drivers. It was a healthy competition that pushed us to move faster. In the end, we won some markets, they won others. Fast forward to today, we're the largest trucking provider in Egypt and expanding our presence in the UAE. That was the journey of launching Trella.

I would define our second and third years as our scaling phase. By then, we were dominating the Egyptian market and expanding into different trucking segments—domestic transport, port logistics, cross-border movements. But that's also when we started opening new markets. I flew to Saudi, which was familiar territory for me because of my experience launching Uber there. I love launching, and I enjoy the process of building something from the ground up. We decided to expand into Saudi, Pakistan, and the UAE, and we launched all three markets within a year and a half.

Scaling, however, came with a lot of challenges and learning experiences. One of the biggest lessons was that you should never launch and scale before the product is ready. That was one of our biggest mistakes. We believed we had to move fast—launch now, figure it out later. Back then, the mindset in the startup world was all about hyper-growth: expand aggressively, fundraise, and optimize profitability later. We followed that playbook, and in some markets, it worked. Saudi, for example, was an instrumental launch for us. But in others, like Pakistan, the timing wasn't right. And in some cases, we expanded prematurely—UAE being a good example.

The problem with launching too soon was that our product and engineering teams weren't ready to fully support new markets. We were still focused on refining our product for Egypt, and that meant our international teams weren't getting the resources they needed. Looking back, I would have been more intentional about our expansion. I still think Saudi was the right move, but we should have been more cautious about some of the others. The only real reason to rush into a market is if competition is aggressively gaining ground and you risk missing the opportunity. Otherwise, the smarter approach is to refine your product first, then scale.

———

> THE ONLY REAL REASON TO RUSH INTO A MARKET IS IF COMPETITION IS AGGRESSIVELY GAINING GROUND AND YOU RISK MISSING THE OPPORTUNITY. OTHERWISE, THE SMARTER APPROACH IS TO REFINE YOUR PRODUCT FIRST, THEN SCALE.

———

What factors influenced your expansion strategy then, and how did competition shape your approach to entering new markets?

I think we were very driven by how our competition was performing. When we were in Saudi, we started seeing a lot of trucking marketplaces emerging in Pakistan. At the same time, our strongest competitor had a solid home base in the UAE. We didn't want to lose UAE because we knew it was a critical cross-border market within the GCC, and we wanted to secure our presence there early. The drive to expand was largely fueled by the ambition to grow quickly and to beat the competition in their home turf.

That aggressive approach is important when building a company. You can't afford to be too laid back. At the same time, there's a balance to strike. With hindsight, we should have asked more critical questions. Was Pakistan as big of a market as the ones we were already in? Could we have grown three or four times more in our existing markets instead of expanding too soon? Could we have skipped Pakistan in the short term and still achieved more revenue growth by deepening our presence in other markets?

Another factor was competition. Just because there are one or two competitors in a market doesn't mean you're automatically going to lose that market. The biggest companies today didn't necessarily invent their industries—Uber didn't invent ride-hailing, Google didn't invent search—but they became global leaders through strategic execution. A competitor entering a market doesn't automatically make them a long-term threat. At the time, we assumed that we had to expand quickly or lose ground, but looking at it now, many of those competitors don't even exist today.

The real learning here is understanding not just whether to launch in a market but also when and how to do it. Expansion is important, but there needs to be a structured, thought-out approach rather than just reacting to external pressures.

The first major lesson was around premature launches—building the product before launching rather than launching first and figuring things out later. The second was about the mindset we had adopted at the time, which was all about growing as fast as possible, gaining market share, and figuring out the P&L later. That worked in an environment where fundraising was flowing and capital was abundant. But then came the war in Ukraine, and everything changed.

It wasn't just us—this was a global issue. As part of the YC community, we had access to insights from other founders and investors. I remember Michael Seibel, the managing partner at YC, sending out a memo warning founders that fundraising was about to become extremely difficult and that companies needed to focus on becoming default alive—meaning, able to sustain themselves without external funding. It was a wake-up call.

The reality is that when you're scaling, it's not easy to suddenly change direction. If you've built a company around hyper-growth, it's hard to pivot overnight. You have to shift the entire company strategy, change internal priorities, realign your roadmap, and communicate a completely new message to investors, both existing and new. Doing all of that in a few months is extremely difficult.

For Egypt specifically, the crisis hit even harder. The war in Ukraine had a direct impact on our economy. Egypt relies heavily on tourism, and the majority of tourists come from Russia. That stream of revenue dried up. At the same time, around 90% of Egypt's wheat imports come from Ukraine, and those shipments stopped, forcing the country to source grain at significantly higher prices. Add to that the rising oil prices, which tripled or quadrupled in just a year, and the entire economy was under strain.

For startups, this made fundraising nearly impossible. Even if an investor was interested in us, they looked at Egypt's macroeconomic situation and said, "We love what you're doing, but there's too much uncertainty right now. Let's wait and talk again in a few months." When your P&L isn't strong—like most startups operating on a growth-first model—you're in an incredibly risky position in those moments.

We had to completely change our strategy. We shifted from growth-at-all-costs to a P&L-driven approach. That meant making hard decisions. We reduced our operational expenses by 70–80% in just one year. Our revenues took a hit—we lost about 30–40% of our revenue in the first six months—but then we started recovering.

One of the toughest decisions we made was exiting Pakistan. We also had to cut certain products and eliminate offerings that weren't core to our business. And then, of course, we had to reduce headcount, which was probably the most difficult part of the entire process. Laying off employees isn't something any founder wants to do, and it's especially hard when you've built a strong team culture. But looking back, those were the right decisions.

At the time, going through it was incredibly painful. But the biggest takeaway from that experience is that as a founder, you need to be in control of your company's destiny as much as possible. If external circumstances shift—whether it's a global crisis, an economic downturn, or something specific to your industry—you need to be able to act immediately and aggressively. If you hesitate or wait too long, you risk losing control.

How should founders balance growth with financial sustainability, especially in volatile markets?

One of the biggest lessons I've learned is to always be fundraising in some capacity. That doesn't mean going out to raise a new round every three to six months, but it does mean ensuring that, no matter what happens, you always have at least 12 to 18 months of runway. If that starts to drop, you need to be proactive—whether it's securing a bridge round, raising a new funding round, or ensuring that your numbers are strong enough to support a compelling narrative for investors. Fundraising should never stop entirely. That was a major learning for us, something we had to adapt to quickly.

Another big learning was around venture debt. In a working capital-heavy business like ours, operating without debt simply isn't an option. But how and when you raise debt is critical. In our case, we raised dollar-denominated debt while 50% of our revenues were coming from Egypt. We weren't properly hedged against currency fluctuations. When Egypt faced a massive devaluation, the dollar went from 15 Egyptian pounds to as high as 75 in the black market, eventually settling around 50. That devaluation put extreme pressure on our P&L. The cost of our debt skyrocketed, making it a major challenge for us.

That experience reinforced the importance of understanding how different types of funding affect a business. Equity fundraising is one thing, but debt is another entirely. Debt investors don't care about your long-term growth; they just want their money back with interest. If anything disrupts that, you're in serious trouble. So one of the biggest challenges we're tackling today is figuring out how to manage that legacy debt we raised years ago and ensure that it enables the business rather than holding it back.

A key part of that process is constantly seeking new sources of capital. Whether through equity or debt, the goal is to lower financing costs over time. Fundraising isn't just about getting money in—it's also about structuring capital in a way that reduces risk and improves efficiency.

Beyond capital, another major learning was around team growth. During the early years, I didn't enjoy the launch phase as much as I should have. But looking back, I see that launching and scaling are two entirely different phases, and with more employees come more complexities.

Scaling the team was exciting at first. Seeing Trella grow, hiring talented people, and giving opportunities to young professionals felt incredibly rewarding. But rapid hiring also brought new challenges. We went from about 100 employees to over 300 or 400 in under two years. While that reflected our growth, it also came with a lot of inefficiencies and misalignment.

When you start a company, you imagine that growth is all upside—you're adding talent, expanding your impact, and increasing productivity. But in reality, it's not that simple. You start dealing with challenges like employee morale, maintaining company culture, and ensuring that new hires are aligned with the company's vision.

One of our biggest mistakes was that while we had a clear vision, we didn't always have a clear strategy on how to achieve it, let alone effectively communicate it. That lack of clarity trickled down to teams. People were working on different initiatives, but not all of them were actually moving us closer to our core objectives. In some cases, teams were tackling two separate problems, and one of those problems wasn't even aligned with our long-term goals. Looking back, I'd say we're much better at this now, but at the time, it was a major challenge.

How did you refine Trella's communication then in order to achieve strategic alignment as the company scaled?

Communication became our top priority. People often take communication for granted, thinking it's just about having all-hands meetings or sending out company updates. But real communication is about alignment—making sure everyone understands who your customer is, what problems you're solving, why you're solving them, and what the ultimate destination looks like.

One mistake companies make is setting an annual strategy, defining OKRs, and then assuming that's enough. In reality, you need to continuously refresh people's understanding of how today's work connects to the bigger vision. Every quarter, every major initiative should tie back to that vision.

Another critical shift was refining our roadmaps. In the early days, our first set of OKRs had something like 75 initiatives. We were a team of just 15 or 20 people at the time, and we had 50+ key results—it was completely unrealistic. We learned that fewer, more targeted objectives lead to better execution. Prioritization is key. Some initiatives, even if they seem important, need to be deprioritized in favor of those with the highest impact and clearest path toward our goals.

A third major realization was that hiring more people doesn't always solve problems. In fact, hiring too quickly created more inefficiencies. We assumed that more problems meant we needed more employees to solve them, but in reality, growing the team too fast made us slower, less aligned, and more complex. Now, we approach hiring more cautiously, focusing on efficiency first.

How do you determine when it's the right time to hire versus making existing team more efficient and resourceful?

I think it's actually a quick answer from my side. You only hire when the absence of that person is actively limiting your ability to grow the company and solve a problem. It's as simple as that. Let's assume you have a team of 10 people, and the company is growing, and people are working super hard and putting in long hours. That does not necessarily mean you need to hire more. In fact, one of the things we've learned is that people don't mind working longer hours as long as they see results.

———

> YOU ONLY HIRE WHEN THE ABSENCE OF THAT PERSON IS ACTIVELY LIMITING YOUR ABILITY TO GROW THE COMPANY AND SOLVE A PROBLEM. IT'S AS SIMPLE AS THAT.

———

One of the problems we encountered was that if those 10 people became 15 and you started taking away some of the responsibility, both groups would actually underproduce. So, back to your question, I would say you only hire when not hiring is actively limiting your growth.

There's a common saying in Silicon Valley: hire slow, fire fast. I'm not sure if hiring slow is always the right advice, but I'm also not convinced that hiring too fast is the best decision either. If you want to hire exceptional talent, you need to sell the vision. People need to join the company excited, knowing that if they do certain things, they will be solving real problems and making a meaningful impact on the business and the ecosystem.

That's something we actually did very well. We didn't struggle to attract the best talent; in fact, we take pride in saying we have one of the strongest teams in the startup ecosystem in this part of the world. Hiring the right people wasn't a challenge because we were very vocal about our vision and where we wanted to go.

The idea that A players hire A players is something we strongly believe in. If you have a very competent founding team, there is no way they will hire people who are less competent than them. If everyone is aligned with a clear vision and purpose, then the company starts moving in sync. That's how you build momentum, and everyone contributes to accelerating that flywheel.

But one of the problems we faced was actually having too many smart people in the room, which created a lot of noise. This ties back to the problem of over-hiring too quickly before having the right foundations in place. Too many voices and perspectives, while valuable in some cases, can slow down decision-making and execution.

That's my experience with hiring. I don't think we had issues attracting exceptional talent. If anything, we had the opposite problem. We scaled too quickly, brought in too many brilliant minds at once, and at times, it made us slower. We are now working on solving that by ensuring that every hire directly contributes to execution and clarity rather than just adding to the discussion.

What hiring mistakes have you made, and what lessons did you learn from them?

If I could go back in time, I would place much more value on character than I initially did. In the past, I prioritized intelligence, sharpness, and strategic thinking, making those qualities about 80% of what I looked for in hiring, with character only accounting for 20%. Now, I would say it should be a 50-50 split between character and skills. Someone who is hardworking, resilient in the face of challenges, and able to push through setbacks is far more valuable in the long run. Of course, intelligence and technical ability are still necessary, but it's about striking the right balance.

We've certainly hired strong résumés that didn't add value, and I believe that was due to two main reasons. The first was character, as I mentioned. The second was that some candidates put more weight on themselves than they actually deserved. One thing to be mindful of is ensuring that new hires understand where they truly stand—not in a discouraging way, but through structured feedback and onboarding.

Onboarding is absolutely critical in determining whether an employee will succeed or fail. That's why we have a structured process to set expectations early. We also implemented what we call F90, which is a first 90-day feedback process for managers after someone joins.

This is a crucial period where we assess their performance, identify areas for improvement, and provide guidance. Beyond that, we have biannual performance reviews where people receive continuous feedback, not just on their work but also on stakeholder management and cultural fit.

Cultural fit is another major factor. Sometimes you hire extremely smart people, but they just don't align with the company's culture. That doesn't mean they're bad employees, and it doesn't mean the company is at fault—it's simply a mismatch. In such cases, it's actually better to part ways early rather than letting it drag on, which can negatively impact the broader team. Having people who are disengaged or misaligned can start affecting those who are engaged and contributing positively. Letting go of employees who aren't a good fit should be done systematically to maintain a strong culture.

How do you identify and empower early employees who evolve into key leadership roles?

One thing that comes to mind is how employees evolve within a company. Some people join early on as regular employees, but over time, they take on a role that's almost like a co-founder. In our case, our head of finance joined within the first few months, and today, I treat him more like a co-founder. There are no major decisions I make without consulting him. At the same time, some of the people who originally joined as co-founders are no longer with the company, even though we remain on very good terms.

This has reinforced for me how crucial it is to be thoughtful when selecting a founding team. But just as importantly, it's about recognizing and enabling the people who might not have been part of that initial group but have since grown into key roles that are even more impactful than those of the original founding team. It's important to make sure they are empowered, that they feel valued, and that their needs are met so they stay motivated and continue driving the company forward.

How has your leadership style evolved as Trella scaled from startup to a regional leader?

If founders don't adapt, their company will either die or they'll get fired by their board—it's as simple as that. Every stage of a company requires a different approach. The launch phase is different from the growth phase, which is different from the scaleup phase. What works in the early days won't work as the company matures.

In the beginning, you're doing everything. You're selling to customers, hiring every single employee, setting up operations, and figuring out product-market fit. But as the company grows, you have to shift from being a hands-on executor to being a people manager. You start hiring leaders who can execute just as well as you, if not better. You have to trust them and empower them to make decisions, rather than trying to do everything yourself.

For me, the learning curve has been steep, but I'm grateful for it. The challenges we've faced at Trella have pushed me to evolve significantly—both personally and professionally. I've learned how to build products at different stages, how to prioritize problems effectively, and how to drive alignment across teams. A lot of it wasn't intuitive. Some things I figured out naturally, but many lessons came through experience—sometimes through mistakes. That's why I'm so appreciative of this journey. It has shaped me in ways I never anticipated.

What's your vision for Trella's long-term future, and what keeps you personally motivated as a founder?

At some point, as a founder, you start thinking about the long-term future of the company. After five or six years, the question becomes, where do you want to take this company? Do you want to take it to an IPO? Do you want to exit? Do you want to keep it private but continue scaling? And on a personal level, what do you want to do as a founder? It becomes a matter of assessing what motivates you and what kind of impact you want to create.

For me, it's always been about impact. I don't want that to stop. If we come to a point where Trella is sold, goes public, or is in the hands of a management team while I step into more of a non-executive role, I don't see myself just sitting back, thinking, "I've made money, so I don't need to work anymore." That's just not how I operate. I actually see myself going straight back into building—starting a second company, then a third, a fourth, a fifth—because as long as I can add value and make an impact, I don't see any reason to stop. That's what drives me.

Making that decision is ultimately about how you want to spend the next five to ten years and what the return on that investment looks like—not just in monetary terms, but in terms of meaningful work and the impact you're making. If I decide to put another five years into Trella, I have to ask myself, what's the return on that investment? And by return, I don't just mean financial returns, but also the scale of impact I can drive. Would I be able to drive more impact by doing something else? Right now, I don't have a final answer to that, but I do know that I want to create an even bigger impact than what we're currently doing at Trella. Trella remains a great medium for achieving that in the next five years. However, if I ever feel that the company is in a position to grow successfully without my daily input, I would absolutely go back to building something new—hopefully something that will one day become the biggest company this region has ever seen, inshallah.

How do you see Egypt's startup ecosystem evolving, and what opportunities excite you most?

Egypt has gone through a lot in the past few years. Looking at the data, the number of startups that emerged in Egypt between 2019 and 2022 was enormous. But then in 2022, 2023, and 2024, that momentum was completely dwarfed. Now, I think we're starting to see an upward shift again, but it's been a rough period. It's unfortunate to see how much the Egyptian ecosystem has suffered.

When you think about building a company, it comes down to three things: the team, the market, and the industry. Can you attract and retain the right talent? Is the market big enough to allow you to scale? And what kind of company are you going to build in that market? When it comes to Egypt, the market size and industry potential have always been strong—assuming political and economic stability. Over the next three to five years, I do see more economic stability, which means we will likely see an upswing in startup activity again.

The one area I remain skeptical about is talent. Egypt has become a net exporter of talent rather than a builder of talent. A lot of smart, ambitious people are leaving the country, which creates a real brain drain. But I came across this quote the other day: "Brain drain is brain gain." It made me think differently about the issue. While many Egyptians are moving abroad to work for leading tech companies— whether at Uber's engineering team in Amsterdam, Booking.com, Deliveroo's product team, or other major global companies—I don't see this as a permanent loss. These people are gaining world-class experience, and many of them will eventually come back wanting to build something in Egypt. So even though it seems like we're losing them now, I believe it's temporary.

I'm optimistic about the Egyptian startup ecosystem, but I do question how many companies can truly scale globally from Egypt. We haven't seen many Egyptian, Saudi, or UAE-based companies reach a global scale. That makes me wonder—if you want to create something with a massive global impact, is Egypt the right place? Probably not. You might need to move to the U.S. or very specific countries in Europe. But if your goal is to build a company that has a direct, immediate impact on Egypt and the region, then Egypt is absolutely the right place to start.

Are Egyptian startups well-positioned to scale across Africa, and if so what's holding them back?

Without a doubt, 100%. But if you actually look at Egyptian startups— including Trella—most of them expanded north into Saudi Arabia rather than south into Africa. Very few, if any, have aggressively moved into African markets. If you ask me, I'd say Africa presents a massive opportunity because it faces many of the same challenges as Egypt. It's where we should be building.

One challenge, however, is funding. Most of the venture capital in this region comes from Saudi Arabia and the UAE. The investors backing Egyptian startups typically want to see them expand into Saudi and the UAE, not into Africa. So as a founder, you're in this position where you know that your product might be a better fit for Africa, but your investors are pushing for expansion into GCC markets. That's the challenge—how do you balance capital availability with solving the real problems that your product is best suited for?

Is Africa an untapped opportunity for Egyptian startups then and how can they effectively expand there?

I completely agree—it's a huge untapped opportunity. A hybrid model where an Egyptian company partners with a local entrepreneur in an African market makes a lot of sense. Egyptian startups have the technology, the operational experience, and the ability to build scalable businesses, while local African partners have the deep market insights and networks needed to execute successfully.

———

" EGYPTIAN STARTUPS HAVE THE TECHNOLOGY, THE OPERATIONAL EXPERIENCE, AND THE ABILITY TO BUILD SCALABLE BUSINESSES, WHILE LOCAL AFRICAN PARTNERS HAVE THE DEEP MARKET INSIGHTS AND NETWORKS NEEDED TO EXECUTE SUCCESSFULLY.

———

I think part of the reason we haven't seen this happen on a large scale yet is that Egyptian founders simply don't have enough visibility into African markets. Unlike Saudi or the UAE, which are well-known expansion targets with strong investor backing, many Egyptian founders just don't know how to navigate Africa. It's not necessarily that these markets are more difficult—many of them actually have greater similarities to Egypt than the GCC does. It's just that the playbook isn't as clear.

I do believe this will change in the future. At some point, founders will start looking beyond the usual expansion routes and recognize that Africa is a massive opportunity. But to really make it work, there needs to be more capital flowing into African markets and more structured partnerships between Egyptian and African entrepreneurs. If that happens, I think we'll see a lot of exciting companies emerge in the space.

I think a lot of founders have been re-evaluating their priorities over the past few years, especially given how difficult the last three years have been. Many of them have had to make tough decisions about whether to focus on Egypt, expand into Africa, or ensure they have enough funding by being in different parts of the world at different times. That has played a role in why we haven't seen more Egyptian startups expanding into Africa.

I do believe we'll see more companies going into African markets in the coming years. Some markets are incredibly challenging—Nigeria, for example, is one of the hardest. I wouldn't say every Egyptian company should immediately launch in Nigeria. However, I would love to see more companies launching in Morocco, Kenya, and even South Africa. South Africa is more mature than most startup ecosystems in Africa, including Egypt, but there are still significant opportunities there.

The past few years were difficult for startups across the region, but I think things will start to shift. We're going to see more companies making moves into Africa, and as the ecosystem stabilizes, more founders will start considering it as a viable expansion market.

Lastly, let's talk about how is AI transforming logistics, and how is Trella leveraging automation to stay ahead in the future?

The term "AI" has been used so frequently that now every company wants to brand itself as an AI company. I get the appeal—there's a certain attraction to labeling yourself that way—but I think we need to be clear about what AI really is. In reality, there will be very few true AI companies in the next decade, and most of them won't come from this region. They're more likely to emerge from China, the U.S., a handful from Europe, and maybe a few from India. I think companies need to be cautious not to overuse the AI label just for the sake of it.

That being said, AI has huge potential to optimize logistics. We're already using AI-powered tools to improve our workflows. For example, previously, collecting proof of deliveries (PODs) was a manual, time-consuming process. It took hours to input all the data into our platform. Now, with AI-driven automation, all we need to do is take a few pictures, and the system transcribes everything instantly. That alone has saved us significant time and reduced human error.

We're not developing core AI models from scratch; instead, we're leveraging existing AI models, such as OpenAI's technology, to optimize our operations. I believe this is where most companies will find value in AI—not in building large-scale foundational models, but in applying AI to improve efficiency and reduce operational overhead.

The impact has been significant. AI has allowed us to do more with fewer people, making our operations leaner and more efficient. No one in the world today is not bullish on AI's potential. In logistics and beyond, AI will continue to reshape industries. However, I want to make sure that we're using AI in a meaningful way rather than just throwing the term around for the sake of hype.

———

NOUREDDINE TAYEBI

One app, endless possibilities

Founder and CEO of YASSIR

Algiers, Algeria

www.yassir.com

NOUREDDINE TAYEBI is a distinguished entrepreneur, investor, and technology leader with a deep passion for innovation and economic development. A native of Algiers, Algeria, he grew up in the vibrant capital, where he developed an early interest in engineering and technology. His academic journey began at École Polytechnique of Algiers, where he earned his Diplôme d'Ingénieur, laying the foundation for a remarkable career at the intersection of engineering, business, and entrepreneurship.

Driven by a desire to expand his expertise, Noureddine pursued graduate studies in the United States, earning a Ph.D. in Engineering from Stanford University. His academic pursuits did not stop there—he also holds three Master's degrees across various disciplines in engineering and management. His deep technical knowledge, combined with strategic business acumen, has positioned him as a leading figure in the global technology landscape.

With a rich and diverse career in Silicon Valley, Noureddine has worked in both corporate and entrepreneurial settings. He held senior positions at Intel, where he contributed to cutting-edge technological advancements. He is also an active Angel Investor, supporting high-tech startups and mentoring entrepreneurs. His passion for fostering innovation led him to become a lead mentor at StartX, the prestigious startup accelerator dedicated to supporting Stanford alumni founders.

After years of working in the world's leading tech hub, Noureddine decided to return to the Maghreb region to drive technological progress and economic transformation. In pursuit of this vision, he founded Yassir, which has since become the most valued tech startup in North Africa. Yassir is a leading super app, providing on-demand services and digital payment solutions across the Maghreb region and expanding into Sub-Saharan Africa. Under his leadership, Yassir has reshaped digital services in the region, empowering millions with seamless access to transportation, delivery, and financial solutions.

Beyond his entrepreneurial success, Noureddine is a prolific innovator, holding over 50 patents and scientific publications. His contributions to technology and business continue to inspire aspiring entrepreneurs and professionals worldwide. Despite his demanding schedule, he remains closely connected to academia and frequently lectures at Stanford University, sharing insights on entrepreneurship, technology, and business strategy.

Through his leadership, mentorship, and investments, Noureddine Tayebi is playing a pivotal role in shaping the future of technology and innovation, bridging the gap between Silicon Valley and emerging markets. His work is a testament to the power of entrepreneurship, innovation, and a global vision for economic progress.

———

YASSIR, founded in 2017 by Noureddine Tayebi and Mahdi Yettou, is a rapidly growing Algerian technology company that has become a major player in the on-demand services sector across the Maghreb region. The company is headquartered in Algiers, Algeria, and has expanded its operations across North Africa, including Morocco and Tunisia, with future plans for growth in Europe and Sub-Saharan Africa. Yassir's flagship product is a super app that integrates a variety of services, such as ride-hailing, food and grocery delivery, and digital financial services.

Yassir's platform has attracted millions of users, particularly in Algeria, where it is now operational in over 45 cities. Its ride-hailing service competes with regional and global players by offering competitive pricing and a reliable network of verified drivers. The food and grocery delivery services cater to a broad range of local restaurants, stores, and supermarkets, providing a convenient option for users to have their meals and essential goods delivered directly to their doorsteps.

One of Yassir's key differentiators is its ability to offer digital financial services, which include mobile payments, saving, and lending features. This service has proven crucial in a region where access to banking can be limited, and digital payments are becoming increasingly popular. The app allows users to seamlessly pay for services, transfer money, and even access loans, creating a more financially inclusive ecosystem.

The company's rapid growth and market expansion have been supported by substantial funding. In 2022, Yassir raised $150 million in Series B funding, led by major investors like Bond, DN Capital, Kleiner Perkins, and Y Combinator. This funding has allowed the company to enhance its service offerings, improve its technology, and expand its presence across multiple countries. With this investment, Yassir has focused on scaling its platform in new markets and refining its user experience.

In 2023, Yassir continued to solidify its brand through strategic partnerships and acquisitions. The company became a sponsor of Paris Saint-Germain (PSG), one of the world's top football clubs, in a move that helped bolster its international recognition. Furthermore, Yassir acquired Flink France, a German rapid delivery platform, marking its entry into the European market. This acquisition, which involved an investment of €500,000 and a commitment of €5 million to refinance operations, enabled Yassir to tap into the competitive European delivery space while preserving over 50% of the 270 jobs at Flink's French operations.

Yassir has also been recognized for its role in contributing to Algeria's economy. In July 2023, the company received the Best Service Exporter Award during the inaugural Exportation Honor Medal ceremony, a prestigious honor given by President Abdelmadjid Tebboune. This recognition is a testament to Yassir's success in driving innovation and expanding its influence beyond Algeria.

Despite its success, Yassir faces challenges in the regulatory landscape. In Algeria, ride-hailing services are not yet legally recognized as a formal business model, which has raised some questions regarding its long-term sustainability within the country. Nonetheless, Yassir has continued to expand its operations and is optimistic about the future of its services, as demand for on-demand services in North Africa and beyond remains strong.

Looking ahead, Yassir is focused on enhancing its super app by introducing new features and services that cater to the growing demands of its user base. The company remains committed to improving its technological infrastructure, expanding its market reach, and empowering entrepreneurs and businesses in emerging markets with its data-driven approach. With the backing of major investors and a strong regional presence, Yassir is well-positioned to become a global leader in the super app ecosystem.

———

Let's start with a bit of background about yourself.

I'm originally from Algeria—that's where I was born and raised. I did all my schooling there. I'm actually the fourth and last child of two amazing parents who are both medical doctors and have instilled in me values that I believe helped me get to where I am today. I attended elementary, middle, and high school in public schools in Algiers. I have a lot of fond memories of enjoying simple things in a way that I think the new generation might not experience. For example, our fun time was playing real football, or soccer, with a ball made of paper and taped with Scotch tape. Just to give you an idea of the kind of things we did as kids.

I've always been diligent in my studies, consistently ranking at the top of my class, graduating from high school, and getting into the best engineering school in Algeria. After five years, I obtained my engineering degree, upon which I decided to leave the country—not permanently, but just to return later. As everyone can guess by now, I chose a different path than most students who graduate from Algerian universities. Often, they pursue further studies or seek jobs, primarily in Europe, particularly France, due to proximity and language. Since most Algerians speak French as a second language, it's the natural choice. However, I decided to go to the U.S., which was quite exceptional back then and still is for people from the region.

To make that happen, I had to learn English because my English was pretty weak at the time. Literally, my knowledge of English consisted of saying simple phrases like "How are you?" and "What's your name?" and making fun of things from songs or pop culture. So

I had to take intensive English classes every night to reach the level necessary to apply to U.S. universities and be admitted.

What motivated me to apply to U.S. universities? First, as we know, American universities are considered among the best in the world. I always had the ambition to seek excellence and push the limits of what's possible, a mindset that goes back to my amazing parents, who instilled that ambition in us. Secondly, I discovered that American universities, especially in engineering and graduate programs, often not only admit students but also fully finance their studies through fellowships, research assistantships, or teaching assistantships.

So, I went through the application process, submitting my applications to several universities. Thanks to my parents, who supported me through this, despite it being a bold and expensive endeavor. For them to believe in me, rather than dismissing it as just a wishful dream, is something highly commendable. In the end, I was not only admitted to many U.S. universities but also awarded scholarships in the form of fellowships, research assistantships, or teaching assistantships. This allowed me to move right after finishing my engineering degree—graduating in June and arriving in the U.S. by July.

I ultimately pursued my studies all the way to a PhD, earning my doctorate from Stanford University, which is considered the birthplace of what we now call Silicon Valley and high-tech entrepreneurship.

What key lessons did Stanford and the broader Silicon Valley ecosystem teach you about entrepreneurship?

The entire experience was just amazing to be honest. It instilled in me not only entrepreneurial values but also a deep understanding of the importance of community.

People often see Silicon Valley as the beacon of high-tech entrepreneurship and assume its success is purely due to money and intelligence. While that is partially true, the real reason is a value system that took a long time to build. That value system is based on paying it forward, helping one another, and the unconscious belief that helping others contributes to one's own success.

Silicon Valley's origins trace back to Stanford University in the 1940s, following the economic recession of that time. As the university gained prestige, its graduates struggled to find jobs in the region, as opportunities were scarce. Many moved to the East Coast. However, the Dean of Engineering at the time, Professor Frederick Terman, convinced the university's board of trustees to start financing companies founded by Stanford alumni. The first batch of such companies included Hewlett-Packard, founded by Bill Hewlett and Dave Packard, both former Stanford students, and Varian Technologies, founded by Russell Varian. For those unfamiliar, Varian invented the vacuum tube, the predecessor of the transistor, which revolutionized computing and enabled many modern technologies.

This created a snowball effect—as these companies gained momentum and succeeded, they helped others. This culture of mutual support continues today in Silicon Valley, where people are committed to giving back to the community, regardless of how busy they are. Over time, this culture naturally attracts both money and top talent.

When people ask why Silicon Valley works while similar attempts in other parts of the world have struggled, despite having financial resources and expertise, the missing ingredient is this deeply embedded value system.

So, as I mentioned, my experience at Stanford was a turning point in both my personal and professional life. It reinforced not only important values but also instilled in me a deep appreciation for entrepreneurship. For those who may not know, Stanford University has had a tremendous impact on high-tech entrepreneurship.

There was a study conducted in 2015—so the numbers are likely even larger today, much larger actually—that showed that former Stanford alumni created over 44,000 companies. As of 2015, these companies employed over six million people and generated over $2.7 trillion in revenue. If that were a country, and you ranked that figure in terms of GDP, it would be the sixth-largest economy in the world, surpassing countries like France. And this is just from one institution. So, just to give you a sense of scale, and considering this was back in 2015, I wouldn't be surprised if these numbers are in the $4 trillion range today.

One example is NVIDIA, whose impact over the last few years has been tremendous, particularly with the chips they've been developing.

In terms of my post-university experience, one might not believe that when I first considered going to the U.S. for graduate school and earning my PhD, my initial goal was actually to become a university professor. However, once I arrived and saw what was happening in Silicon Valley, the entrepreneurial path became the obvious choice for me. There was simply no other path I could see myself taking.

At the same time, I felt that fresh out of grad school, I might not yet have all the necessary tools to take things to the next level. So, before diving into entrepreneurship, I chose to work in big tech. Given my background in electrical and computer engineering, I decided to join Intel—a company we all know as the leader in computer chips, supplying major tech companies as well as everyday computing needs.

It was a unique experience because I joined Intel Labs, a division that operates almost like a startup accelerator. It brings together very bright minds who propose ideas to senior management. If an idea is accepted, it receives internal funding. If it reaches a certain level, it can become a fully developed product or even an independent business unit, depending on its potential.

I was fortunate to see this process all the way through—from the initial idea to commercialization. That experience was invaluable, and I don't think I could have gained that kind of insight anywhere else. At that point, I knew the time was right for me to start my own company.

My first company was based in Silicon Valley and was highly technical. I won't go into details, but it allowed me to build a team from scratch, raise funds, and take things to the next level. A few years later, the company was acquired, marking another incredible learning experience.

One key lesson I'd like to share is the power of networking. People often underestimate it, but your network is everything. It's up to each of us to actively build and nurture our network. There are different ways to do this, and I was fortunate that the Stanford network, along with its strong brand, played a crucial role. It opened many doors for me.

————

> One key lesson i'd like to share is the power of networking. People often underestimate it, but your network is everything. It's up to each of us to actively build and nurture our network.

————

As I mentioned earlier, there is a strong culture of paying it forward in the Stanford community—helping and being helped. Simply being a Stanford alumnus provides an advantage in terms of networking. It helped me significantly in securing warm introductions to investors.

What many people don't realize is that the best way to get funding is through warm introductions for two key reasons. First, if you look at the major VC firms in Silicon Valley, you'll notice that almost none of them provide an email contact on their websites, and very few, if any, respond to cold emails. Instead, they expect deal flow to come through people they know and trust. They even explicitly state that if you can't find someone to make that warm introduction, it suggests you haven't put in the effort to make it happen—which, to them, is an indication that you may not be worth their time.

Second, VCs receive an overwhelming number of pitches, making it nearly impossible to review everything. Warm introductions help filter out the most promising opportunities.

So, if I have one piece of advice, it's to start building your network early—even before college, if possible. If you choose the college path, be intentional about networking and knowing where to go and how to build it. It's an incredibly important foundation for future success.

So, I think that experience of building this company in Silicon Valley was tremendous. There are some anecdotes I can share that really reinforced what I mentioned earlier about paying it forward.

For instance, I remember meeting someone at an event—he actually approached me, and we started chatting. He asked, "What do you do?" and I told him I had just started my company and was in the process of applying for government funding at the time. He genuinely started asking me questions, and before I knew it, he took my phone number and began calling me, sometimes as late as 11:00 PM or even later, saying things like, "I want to introduce you to this person," or "I'm introducing you to this investment firm."

Being originally from the MENA region, I found this quite strange at first. I thought, "Why is this guy doing this? There must be some reason behind it." But over time, we became great friends, and without exaggeration, this person introduced me to at least 20 investment firms, if not more.

One day, I finally asked him, "Why did you help me in the first place?" He never asked for anything in return. His response was simple: "One day, I was in your shoes, and people helped me. So, to me, it was natural to do the same. I saw a lot of potential in you." For him, it was completely genuine and second nature to pay it forward.

Looking back at our region—and when I say "our region," I mean not just the MENA region but also the entire African continent—we don't have this value ingrained in our culture. Instead, there's often an attitude of "If I have something, let me keep it to myself." But that's actually the worst mindset we can have because sharing information, success, and networks only multiplies what we have a thousandfold. This is a value we desperately need to instill in our societies because it's sorely lacking. I still see this gap in our ecosystem to this day.

So, closing this chapter and moving to the next—while I was still running my company, I always had the desire to give back to the region I came from, specifically Algeria. However, since I was busy with my company and my life in the U.S., I started doing this in a passive way—mentoring teams and even funding some that I liked.

But very quickly, I came to a realization: The biggest problem in our region, whether in MENA or Africa, wasn't just bureaucracy or lack of funding, as people often complain. While those are certainly challenges, I saw a much bigger problem—the entrepreneur themselves.

As I interacted with different people, I noticed a lack of values, best practices, and the right mindset. And I realized that no matter how much I contributed through mentoring and other efforts, it wouldn't create the large-scale impact I hoped for.

As I mentioned earlier, I grew up in an environment where we were always encouraged to push the limits of what's possible, to believe that the sky is the limit. So, I came to the conclusion that if I was truly serious about making an impact, I needed to get directly involved. My goal was to build at least one local champion that others could emulate—an entity where people could gain real-world experience, learn, and apply their knowledge.

Because, in my view, the best way to learn is by doing. And hopefully, the entities created by those who go through this experience will achieve even greater success.

One of the key lessons I wanted to instill is that entrepreneurship is never easy. If you're waiting for a red carpet, then you're not an entrepreneur. If you think bureaucracy will stop you, then you're not an entrepreneur. Entrepreneurship is about pushing the limits of what can be done.

———

IF YOU'RE WAITING FOR A RED CARPET, THEN YOU'RE NOT AN ENTREPRENEUR. IF YOU THINK BUREAUCRACY WILL STOP YOU, THEN YOU'RE NOT AN ENTREPRENEUR. ENTREPRENEURSHIP IS ABOUT PUSHING THE LIMITS OF WHAT CAN BE DONE.

———

I love the definition of an entrepreneur given by Reid Hoffman, the founder of LinkedIn: "An entrepreneur is someone who will jump off a cliff and assemble an airplane on the way down." That's exactly what entrepreneurship is.

Every day, you experience extreme highs and lows. Sometimes, within a single hour, you go from being incredibly excited about something to receiving bad news that completely shifts your mood. Resilience and perseverance are critical, and these qualities can be instilled at a young age—through our educational system, parenting, and societal values.

That was the mission behind Yassir—to attempt to build that local champion that others could emulate.

Another key point goes back to ambition. Until recently, in the MENA region, especially in high-tech entrepreneurship, the prevailing mindset was to build a company to a certain level and then seek an acquisition by a big global player. We've seen this happen time and time again. Of course, these acquisitions helped shape the ecosystem, but there was never a strong ambition to build a local champion that could go global and compete on the world stage.

This mindset existed not just among founders but also among investors, who often limited their ambitions to reaching a certain level and then exiting.

With Yassir, we wanted to change that. Our ambition from the very beginning was to create a company that could go global, to build a true industry leader from our region. And I really hope we can make that vision a reality.

That's why I always say that Yassir is more of a mission than just a company. Our values are deeply rooted in that mission.

What steps can we take—at the societal, educational, and business levels—to instill a strong "pay-it-forward" culture?

Certainly, sharing success stories publicly, as you're doing here with this book, helps. Media also play a big role. Additionally, founders need to champion this approach more and more, all of which can help shift the culture over time. But beyond that, as a society, we need to create a value system that embeds these principles as social values and instills them from a very young age.

I'm going to get a bit philosophical here. I mentioned earlier the impact my parents had on me and the values they instilled in me, creating a small value system that perhaps was limited to their children and maybe extended to their immediate circle—family and friends. But imagine if every family did the same, and if the educational system reinforced it. The spread of such a value system at a societal, national, or even regional level could have a tremendous impact.

I'll give you an example from Palo Alto, where Stanford University is located and which is often considered the capital of Silicon Valley and high-tech entrepreneurship. I've seen this firsthand through my kids who have gone to school there.

They have a program that runs from preschool all the way to high school. It's a simple program that costs nothing, yet it lasts six months of every academic year. During this time, each student is paired with someone in the community who has achieved something in their field—it could be an artist, a musician (well, a musician is an artist), a high-tech entrepreneur, or anyone depending on the student's interests.

For a few hours each week, the student and their mentor work on a new project together. Naturally, the complexity of the project depends on whether the student is in preschool or high school. At the end of the six months, all students showcase their work in the Palo Alto Museum, where they present their projects. The entire town comes to visit and celebrate their achievements—not just parents but also older residents and people without children.

As I said, it's a simple program that costs nothing, but the values it instills are profound. It fosters creativity because these kids start learning how to do new things and think outside the box from an early age. It builds ambition because as they interact with their mentors—people who have succeeded in various ways—the students subconsciously see that success is attainable. They think, "If this person has done it, I can do it too." Ambition becomes an ingrained value. Presenting their work helps develop self-confidence, which is a crucial value that is often lacking in our region. People in our region tend to be shy when presenting their work, and when they do, they are often stressed. Learning to confidently showcase their achievements from an early age makes a huge difference. It also reinforces the pay-it-forward mentality. The whole community participates—not just the mentors who guide the students but also the broader society that comes together to celebrate them. Imagine the impact this has on students once they graduate from college. The multiplier effect of such a simple program is enormous.

Unfortunately, these are the kinds of initiatives that are missing in our societies, and we need to push for them.

Now, tying this back to social sciences, engineering, and even anthropology—if we examine what defines culture in a society from an anthropological perspective, it is simply a value system that a person encounters from birth and internalizes as primary capital. This isn't my definition, by the way—it's the formal definition of culture in anthropology. Culture is a value system that a person is born into, which unconsciously shapes their actions within their society.

Do you see where I'm going with this? Our true primary capital is our value system—not money. Of course, money is important, but if we have a strong value system embedded from a young age, it determines how we will impact the society we live in.

This concept ties into a principle from physics—the principle of equilibrium, derived from the second law of thermodynamics. It states that no entity reaches equilibrium until it reaches its minimal energy state. I strongly believe this principle applies to communities, societies, and nations. A society in equilibrium is one where a huge impact can be achieved with minimal effort. A dysfunctional society, on the other hand, requires enormous effort to achieve even a small impact—because it lacks the right value system.

That's the problem we face today in our region. We are not in equilibrium because our value system is misaligned, making progress unnecessarily difficult. And that's what we need to fix.

The good news is that achieving this doesn't require monumental efforts. I always say there are three key ingredients to creating societal impact: knowledge, community involvement, and financial resources. If you lack any of these, it becomes difficult to create a meaningful and lasting impact.

Well, look, from a business point of view, I always tell people, and we see it over and over again—always listen to the market. As companies grow, there's often this subconscious arrogance that creeps in, where we think we know exactly what the market needs. We assume we can develop the perfect product, spending months building it with all the right features, UX, and UI, only to take it to market and realize no one adopts it.

The advice I always give is to launch something as soon as possible, even if it's rudimentary and has a lot of bugs. Start testing quickly because the feedback from customers and partners is what truly allows you to improve the product.

There are specific nuances involved. In our case, the first cycle of our business was something that had been done elsewhere but had local specificities that made it unique. It wasn't just a matter of copying an existing model and expecting it to work. A lot of effort went into adjusting the product, shaping the user experience, and handling practical challenges, such as cash transactions. Once cash is collected, how do you deposit it efficiently while keeping costs low? How do you recoup it completely? These were real issues that required solutions tailored to our environment.

Putting the product in the market as soon as possible and gathering as much learning as possible were essential. Iteration was key because not everything works on the first attempt. The ability to listen and adapt is what ultimately drives success.

From both a marketing and operational perspective, building a strong brand is crucial, and ideally, it should be done quickly. A strong product-market fit makes this process easier. When a product meets an urgent need, people will use it even if it isn't perfect. This is what Y Combinator, the world's largest and most successful accelerator, emphasizes with its philosophy: "Build something people want." Many successful companies like Airbnb, DoorDash, Stripe, and Dropbox came out of YC, and beyond providing credibility, it offers an incredible network and a pay-it-forward culture similar to what I mentioned earlier. They have this core philosophy of building something that people want. Every YC T-shirt even has that phrase printed on it.

> A GREAT PRODUCT-MARKET FIT MAKES EVERYTHING EASIER. WHEN A PRODUCT MEETS AN URGENT NEED, PEOPLE WILL USE IT EVEN IF IT ISN'T PERFECT.

Beyond being an accelerator that helps companies succeed, YC provides a powerful network that opens doors—again reinforcing the pay-it-forward mentality. One of the biggest pitfalls for entrepreneurs is assuming they know what people want without validation. The reality is, the market decides. The sooner you put your product out there, the sooner you'll know whether it's something people truly want.

Even now, as we've grown, we sometimes fall into the same trap—assuming that because we have a strong brand, any new product or feature we introduce will automatically be adopted. But time and time again, we've seen that isn't always the case. We've had many misses, even recently. Every time it happens, we go back to the basics: build something people want, test it as early as possible, and refine it based on user feedback before scaling.

How can startups balance between starting with non-scalable solutions and planning for future scalability?

That´s a great question. I think it´s also important to start with things that may not necessarily scale but have a path to becoming scalable. A good example is how Facebook started. Initially, it was only available on college campuses, and each school had its own server with a unique subdomain—for example, Stanford had stanford.facebook. com, Harvard had harvard.facebook.com, and so on. The reason for this approach was to allow rapid expansion, even though the system itself wasn't scalable in the long run. It gave Facebook the traction it needed before switching to a larger infrastructure.

We applied the same mindset in the early days of Yassir. We made use of cloud credits from Google, Amazon, and Microsoft to minimize costs, which was critical given our need to be frugal. For SMS services, which can be expensive, we built an ad hoc system that leveraged local telecom providers, turning a simple SMS verification process into an efficient and cost-saving OTP system. These small, scrappy decisions helped us scale quickly, reaching millions of users within the first year.

That ability to be resourceful and think outside the box is critical, not just in the early stages but also in shaping the company's culture. It fosters a mindset of frugality and efficiency, which is essential for strong unit economics.

When it comes to fundraising, people often only see the final announcement and assume it was a smooth process. What they don't see is that securing investment usually involves talking to hundreds of funds, with only one or two actually committing. Even after a fund shows interest, it can take months for them to build conviction and move forward.

The most important factor in fundraising is having the right network to facilitate warm introductions. If you don't have that network, you need to actively seek it out. If I know that Amir has a connection to a VC fund, but I don't know Amir personally, I'll do everything I can to get introduced to him, demonstrate my potential, and gain his trust so that he's willing to introduce me to the fund.

Being part of networks like Y Combinator or StartX, which is another major accelerator historically dedicated to Stanford alumni, makes a big difference. These networks provide access to investors and experienced entrepreneurs who have already been through the fundraising process and can offer guidance on what to do—and, more importantly, what not to do.

Perseverance is key. If I had given up every time we were rejected by a fund, we would have stopped within the first month. But it's not just about persistence—it's also about learning. If you keep getting the same feedback from investors, it means something needs to change. Whether it's the pitch, the data, or the vision you're presenting, the ability to listen and adapt is crucial.

So, that's my advice. Keep testing, keep iterating, stay resourceful, build a strong network, and never stop learning from both successes and failures.

Yassir has grown rapidly across multiple markets. can you share some key traction metrics?

We've been growing exponentially year over year. While I can't disclose specific revenue or GMV figures,

I'll give a high-level overview. Today, we have 8 million users across six countries, though some of these markets are smaller or more recent. Our main markets are Algeria, Morocco, and Tunisia, where we operate in over 50 cities. We provide four main products: ride-hailing, food delivery, grocery delivery, and payments. Within each product, we continuously add features to push things to the next level.

Overall, we've been doubling on average every year since we started. In the initial years, the growth rate was even higher. Even at our current scale, we've been able to maintain that level of growth, which has been significant.

Our strategy has been to focus on our core region, extract as much value as possible where the brand is already well known, and where customer acquisition costs are low. Only then do we consider expansion. Many companies fall into the trap of expanding too quickly, thinking that placing a flag in a new market means success. But being in 20 countries doesn't mean much if you're failing in all of them. The key is to develop a strong playbook that can be replicated. And in some cases, it turns out the playbook isn't repeatable across different markets—and that's okay too.

What were the key advantages that allowed Yassir to dominate despite the presence of larger, well-funded players?

There were a few key factors. First, being a first mover is a huge advantage. Many on-demand and fintech services operate as hyperlocal monopolies. Once an incumbent reaches a certain level of growth and penetration, it triggers a network effect. Even if a competitor enters the market with more funding or better capabilities, gaining market share becomes extremely difficult. They have to spend exponentially to gain market share linearly, which makes the economics very challenging. This phenomenon is seen globally, not just in our case.

The second advantage we had was being the only operator offering an ecosystem of services. This created a higher level of stickiness with our customer base. Users come in and find everything they need in one place, so they have no reason to go elsewhere for a single product. The ability to cross-sell and provide incentives across multiple services strengthens this stickiness.

The third advantage, which we didn't initially anticipate but turned out to be incredibly valuable, was the local champion effect. At first, we simply took pride in being a homegrown company and mentioned it in interviews without a specific PR strategy. But it resonated deeply with people. Our users saw that we weren't just selling services but were on a mission to empower local talent and create value.

This had two major benefits. First, it built stronger loyalty among users, who felt they were supporting a local initiative with a bigger purpose. Second, it created goodwill with government officials, who saw us as a local player generating substantial value beyond just providing services. Brain drain is a massive issue in the MENA region, where many of the brightest minds leave for opportunities abroad. The fact that we were creating jobs and becoming the largest employer of software developers in North Africa, while also bringing back talent from abroad, resonated with decision-makers.

This helped us navigate some of the regulatory challenges more effectively. Government officials recognized the value we were adding, which made them more inclined to support us in resolving legal and bureaucratic hurdles. So, in the end, it was a combination of strong execution, product-market fit, first-mover advantage, and some unexpected but fortunate factors that helped us get to where we are today.

How can regulators create an environment that truly enables startup growth in MENA?

A lot has already been done in the countries where we operate, and that progress continues, which is great to see. One positive trend is that policymakers are increasingly involving stakeholders in discussions, creating more dialogue and collaboration.

That said, bureaucracy remains a challenge. Changing laws takes time, and businesses don't always have the luxury of waiting. But there have been meaningful reforms in entrepreneurial laws and tax policies that have made a difference. There's still a long way to go, but at least we're seeing the right momentum.

One thing I wish we had in our region is a regulatory approach similar to what exists in the U.S. When disruptive innovations like PayPal and other payment solutions first emerged, there were no regulations in place. But rather than blocking them, the government allowed them to grow, learning along the way about what needed regulation and what didn't.

In contrast, in many of our markets, there's a tendency to regulate from the start before an industry even exists. Authorities often try to anticipate every possible edge case before drafting regulations, and this process can take years. By the time the regulations are finalized, the startups that could have thrived under them might not even exist anymore.

This approach stifles creativity, innovation, and ultimately, economic progress. However, things are evolving. One promising development is the increasing presence of younger government officials who are more in tune with the needs of the digital economy and are working to shake things up.

Is regulation a timing issue? In the U.S., for instance, startups scale first, then face regulation.

Yes, timing plays a huge role. It doesn't apply to every industry, but in many cases, allowing startups to grow to a certain size before introducing regulation makes sense. Once regulators see the value being created, they are more likely to engage constructively rather than simply impose barriers from the start.

So would you say that founders should be more proactive in educating and collaborating with regulators?

Totally. Thinking that it's the regulator's job to do it on your behalf is completely wrong. I tell every founder I talk to that it's part of your playbook. And it's not something you do only once or twice. If they don't respond to you the second, third, or fourth time, you need to keep knocking on doors and approaching it from different angles. It's your responsibility.

As I said, an entrepreneur is someone who jumps off a cliff and has to build a plane before crashing. If you don't challenge the status quo, you're not an entrepreneur. If you're not pushing the limits, you're not an entrepreneur. This is part of the playbook—you need to do it.

———

> THINKING THAT IT'S THE REGULATOR'S JOB TO DO IT ON YOUR BEHALF IS COMPLETELY WRONG. I TELL EVERYONE I TALK TO THAT IT'S PART OF YOUR PLAYBOOK. AND IT'S NOT SOMETHING YOU DO ONLY ONCE OR TWICE. IF THEY DON'T RESPOND TO YOU THE SECOND, THIRD, OR FOURTH TIME, YOU NEED TO KEEP KNOCKING ON DOORS AND APPROACHING IT FROM DIFFERENT ANGLES. IT'S YOUR RESPONSIBILITY.

———

Does that also mean you could potentially collaborate with others in the ecosystem, even competitors, to advocate change?

Absolutely if it makes sense. It's not always the case, of course. You need to carefully assess the risks of collaborating with potential competitors. Sometimes it works, sometimes it doesn't, but if the alignment is there, it can be beneficial. So in the case of voicing concerns and advocating for change, such collaboration is really a must. I always tell people that the responsibility is on you. Blaming others just shows that you're not the right person for the job.

As I mentioned earlier when discussing equilibrium in a society, in non-equilibrium societies, you put in enormous effort for very little impact. The question is, do you want to be small, or do you want to be big? Do you want to push the limits of what's possible, or do you just settle? If you have ambition, you need to do everything in your power to make things happen.

Going back to the legal side of things, here's an anecdote from within Yassir. The fourth team member to join us was a lawyer. The first three were software developers, but the fourth was a lawyer—who is still with us today as our company lawyer. When he started, he was young, but he had a hustler mentality.

What I loved about him was that in our first interview, he was the kind of person who, when he knew something, he would say, "I know this." But when he didn't know something, he wouldn't pretend—he'd say, "I don't know, but I'll check and come back to you." And when he did check, he wouldn't just come back with an answer. He would say, "Legally, this isn't allowed because there's no law on it. But there's a workaround, a loophole, or an alternative approach we could take to achieve our goal." He had that kind of problem-solving mindset, and he still does. So depending on the business you're in, the legal side can be extremely important as well.

An entrepreneur is someone who makes great things happen from scratch against great odds. If you have that mindset, you expect great challenges, and overcoming them is part of how you make things happen. As opposed to sitting back, complaining, or being passive about it.

Lastly, why did Yassir choose to raise capital primarily from international investors rather than regional VCs?

Initially, I aimed to raise funds locally, believing it was important to keep everything within the region. However, after engaging with regional VC firms, I realized there was still room for growth in terms of investment maturity.

Coming from Silicon Valley, I was accustomed to a certain style of investor relationship—clear, straightforward, and founder-friendly. In contrast, some of the term sheets we encountered in the region had structures that didn't fully align with global best practices.

While there are certainly strong and forward-thinking investors in the MENA and GCC regions, at the time, many deals we came across felt more transactional than truly collaborative. In Silicon Valley, investment terms tend to be clean and streamlined, with a shared understanding that long-term success benefits everyone involved.

That being said, I don't want to generalize—there are undoubtedly visionary investors in the region who support founders in a win-win manner. However, in our case, we found stronger alignment with international investors who shared our vision and recognized the potential of the Algerian market, as well as our ability to execute, at a time when many regional investors did not initially believe in our potential.

Well, you've certainly cleared up this misconception. I'm looking forward to your continued success and more great impact.

Honestly, I always wish I could do more.

———

TARNEEM SAEED

Powering payments, empowering people

Founder and CEO of CASHI

CASHI

Khartoum, Sudan

www.getcashi.com

TARNEEM SAEED, also known as Nina Saeed, is a distinguished entrepreneur and corporate leader, renowned for her pivotal role in revolutionizing Sudan's digital economy. She is the co-founder and Chief Executive Officer (CEO) of Cashi, a burgeoning electronic payment network.

At the age of 14, Saeed left Sudan to pursue her education in Canada. She later attended the London School of Economics and Political Science (LSE), where she earned a law degree and served as the president of the Arabic Society.

Following her graduation, Saeed embarked on a legal career with Allen & Overy, a global law firm operating in over 60 countries. She worked there for four years, gaining valuable experience in corporate law.

In 2014, during a visit to Sudan, Saeed observed a significant gap in the country's digital infrastructure, particularly in accessing information about goods and services. This realization led her, alongside her brother, Tamir, and other friends, to establish Alsoug.com in 2016, as a classified marketplace to facilitate price discovery and buyer-seller interactions. Despite challenges such as limited internet connectivity, Alsoug rapidly evolved into Sudan's leading e-commerce platform, boasting over two million downloads.

Recognizing the need for reliable digital payment solutions, Saeed, the Alsoug founders, and Mostafa Elaghil—who joined the team as CTO and co-founder in late 2017—expanded Alsoug's services by launching Cashi in 2020. Cashi aims to create a highly efficient payment platform to help Sudanese citizens pay their obligations.

In October 2021, Alsoug secured a $5 million investment from Egyptian fintech company Fawry and other tier-one investors. This marked the first foreign venture capital investment in Sudan since the lifting of international sanctions in 2020, underscoring Alsoug's significant role in the nation's economic renaissance.

Saeed is passionate about African consumer markets and is a fervent believer in youth-driven change. She is committed to developing quality mass-market products and services that cater to the evolving needs of Sudanese consumers.

Through her visionary leadership, Tarneem Saeed continues to play a crucial role in transforming Sudan's digital landscape, fostering economic growth, and empowering communities across the nation.

———

CASHI, established in 2020 as a new brand, has rapidly become Sudan's largest merchant-based electronic payment network, serving consumers, merchants, and billers across the nation.

Cashi offers a comprehensive suite of financial services, including bill payments for utilities like electricity, mobile phone credit purchases, and mobile money transactions. These services are accessible through an extensive network of service points located in supermarkets, pharmacies, and kiosks, allowing customers to transact using cash, digital wallets, or bank cards. In addition, Cashi's consumer wallet, MyCashi, provides full financial services to over 1 million consumers across Sudan.

The platform's merchant network is notably expansive, comprising over 60,000 merchants across Sudan. This extensive reach ensures that a wide array of businesses can accept electronic payments and process bill payments, thereby enhancing revenue streams and operational efficiency.

In response to the conflict that erupted in Sudan on April 15, 2023, resulting in widespread displacement and critical humanitarian needs, Cashi played a pivotal role in facilitating multi-purpose cash assistance (MPCA). A pilot project conducted in Khartoum, one of the most conflict-impacted areas, utilized Cashi's omni-payments platform to deliver MPCA to 600 households. This initiative demonstrated the feasibility and effectiveness of using electronic payment networks to provide rapid financial assistance in crisis situations. Since then, Cashi has gone on to deliver humanitarian assistance to tens of thousands of people across Sudan, increasingly in a manner that delivers on long-term financial inclusion to the target communities.

By integrating a vast network of merchants, service points, and consumers, Cashi has significantly contributed to financial inclusion in Sudan. The platform enables individuals, including those in remote or underserved areas, to access essential financial services securely and efficiently. This integration supports local economies by facilitating seamless transactions between consumers and businesses.

Cashi operates on internationally recognized secure technology and holds full licensure from the Central Bank of Sudan as a mobile money financial institution. The platform employs robust encryption methods to protect user data and financial information, ensuring a secure transaction environment for all users.

Cashi's rapid expansion and integration into Sudan's financial ecosystem underscore its critical role in modernizing payment systems and enhancing financial accessibility. Through its extensive merchant network and secure platform, Cashi continues to facilitate efficient financial transactions, contributing to economic stability and growth in Sudan.

––––––

Tell us about yourself and your background.

I was born in Sudan, which is where my father is from. I went to school there in my earlier years, then went to school in Canada for my later years. I read law at the London School of Economics in London and went on to become a corporate lawyer with Allen & Overy LLP. I think that was quite a formative experience because, although my degree was in law and not business, working in a major global law firm instills real discipline and structure.

After a few years in law, I pivoted my career toward the business side. My family is in business, so I had always leaned in that direction. I decided to take a short sabbatical to figure out my next steps. I decided to return to Sudan for a bit—it was only meant to be six months.

I did something completely different in Sudan, working on a project documenting Sudanese artists. I also assisted with the family business, which got me engaged with both Sudanese and Ethiopian consumers. That awakened my interest in consumer behaviour in changing contexts, and I realized the huge potential for development in this region.

What initially brought you back to Sudan, and what made you stay longer than planned?

When I arrived in Sudan, the U.S. sanctions which had been in place on the country for some 20 years were just beginning to be lifted. The country was beginning to open up, and I realised the potential for a startup in this ecosystem. At the time, I still thought I would return to London in the short term, and I therefore approached the idea from an investment perspective. I wondered whether we could find good young entrepreneurs who wanted to build, seed their businesses, and encourage the ecosystem.

Whilst looking at businesses to seed, my brother and I, with some friends, decided to launch a small white-label online classifieds platform, alsoug.com, to test the market. I brought in some young Sudanese to handle basic marketing and ads moderation. The platform grew quite well and saw strong adoption, helping us realize how young and open to technology the merchant and trading communities were. It confirmed my belief that there was huge opportunity in these markets, and I was keen to stay in Sudan for longer to try to build out the platform.

We had young traders using the platform for everything—from real estate to cars, clothing, and even commodities. The population understood the platform's value—it was more targeted and useful than Facebook or WhatsApp groups. About a year after launch, I started looking for developers to take over our white-label platform and build something more robust. Around that time, I met Mostafa Elaghil, who had set up a developer house in Yemen before moving to Cairo. We engaged him and his team to take over the development of Alsoug. Over time, my co-founders and I built a strong relationship with him and decided to bring him in as a full-time CTO and co-founder.

Whilst the classifieds platform was growing rapidly, there was a problem—we couldn't monetize it. That became an instrumental lesson—building a platform with product-market fit (PMF) isn't enough if you can't generate revenue from it.

How did you pivot to solving the revenue generation problem, and what were the key challenges you faced?

Alsoug was growing, but we were getting more concerned with revenue, asking ourselves, how do we make real money off this thing? Growth alone wasn't enough. Fundraising for Sudan was limited. I was mostly doing friends-and-family rounds, and we were being frugal in spending.

We needed a way to monetize, and part of that required enabling digital payments.

What made digital payments a critical next step, and how did you begin tackling it?

When you build a classifieds platform that starts scaling, solving the payments problem is essential—similar to what eBay did with PayPal. You can't scale classifieds revenue if payments rely on people bringing cheques or cash to a single office in Khartoum. So, we put our heads together to come up with solutions.

———

WHEN YOU BUILD A CLASSIFIEDS PLATFORM THAT STARTS SCALING, SOLVING THE PAYMENTS PROBLEM IS ESSENTIAL—SIMILAR TO WHAT EBAY DID WITH PAYPAL. YOU CAN'T SCALE CLASSIFIEDS REVENUE IF PAYMENTS RELY ON PEOPLE BRINGING CHEQUES OR CASH TO A SINGLE OFFICE IN KHARTOUM.

———

When we started, the payment ecosystem in Sudan was very cash-heavy—extremely cash-heavy. However, there was the beginning of growth in digital payments. The banks, particularly the largest retail bank, Bank of Khartoum, were making headway with digital banking apps and with the issuance of local switch-based debit cards to their consumers.

One of the key factors in the growth of digital payments was the government's response to high inflation. The economy was facing severe inflation and currency devaluation. The government was increasingly frustrated with the need to constantly print new banknotes. To address this, the government put pressure on and encouraged banks to create an environment conducive to digital transformation in payments.

What were the earliest foundational steps that helped you build a payments business?

We successfully integrated with Bank of Khartoum's mobile banking application and into the national switch, allowing us to process payments from all local debit cards. To obtain the switch integration, we had applied for our first payments license, best described as a simple PSP (Payment Service Provider) license. This was a pass-through license, meaning we were primarily meant to be card-backed.

As we were trying to better understand digital payments systems, we had a lot to learn, including about the role of Visa and Mastercard, which were just beginning to enter Sudan, and the nuances of Sudan's payment ecosystem. I actively sought out people in the payments industry to share their knowledge and experience. That's when I met two very instrumental individuals.

One of them was Ali Mazandarani, a former partner at Actis, a firm that has done numerous payments deals worldwide. Ali is one of the world's top experts in payments, and I was very lucky to have been introduced to him via an existing shareholder. Interestingly, Ali had visited Sudan once when he was younger, which gave him a small but meaningful connection to the country. Ali played a key role in explaining industry dynamics to me and encouraging our interest in payments as a sector. Most importantly, he introduced me to Ashraf Sabry, the CEO of Fawry.

Ali and Ashraf visited Sudan in early 2020, and following their assessment of the payment ecosystem in the country, concluded that while digital payments were emerging, the space was still very nascent. In particular, no one was tackling the biggest challenge: how to facilitate cash-in and cash-out into the digital ecosystem and how to enable widespread merchant acceptance.

Their feedback was clear. Fawry had successfully solved the same problem in Egypt by thinking bigger. Our ambition of running a small PSP to solve payments for our classifieds platform was too limited. They felt we needed to build a Fawry for Sudan. That realization set us on a new path. We started laying the groundwork for a far bigger payments play, including by raising capital to scale the business.

In retrospect, raising this investment round was one of the most challenging things I've ever undertaken. The process took around a year to close. It wasn't due to a lack of interest. By this time, Sudan had undergone major political changes. The final set of U.S. sanctions was being lifted by the Trump administration. A revolution had taken place. A civilian government had come into power. The country was supposedly transitioning to democracy.

With Sudan opening up, investors were interested. And I believe the fact that our business was a well-structured and transparent business went a long way to swaying potential investors in our favour. Transparency has always been a core part of our company ethos. We spent a lot of time structuring the company in a way that was clean, investable, and legally sound.

We were pulling this investment round together with Fawry as a key investor, but we also needed other investors alongside them. It took about a year, but we finally closed the round. One of the reasons the round took so long was that we were careful in selecting the right investors—those who understood Sudan's market potential, recognized that Sudan was undergoing a transition, and were long-term thinkers who saw beyond short-term instability.

How did political instability and the 2021 coup affect your plans and relationships with investors?

Unfortunately, just two to three weeks after closing the round in the autumn of 2021, there was a coup d'état in Sudan. Despite the coup, however, none of our investors panicked. Everyone remained calm and focused on the long-term vision, and not one investor expressed regret or suggested they wanted their money back.

After securing the investment, we ordered POS devices but faced COVID-related supply chain delays. Ironically, however, COVID accelerated digital payments, with people avoiding cash and using mobile banking more.

We launched our first set of POS devices in spring 2022, by which time the market was already shifting towards digital transactions. By the end of summer 2022, we had fully launched.

What did Sudan's payments landscape look like when you entered the market?

Let me explain the payment ecosystem in Sudan when we launched. There was a national switch, and the central bank was pushing banks to issue more debit cards. The model seemed to follow a bank-led, card-based digital transformation, much like what happened in Egypt. The major banks had launched mobile banking apps. The groundwork for digital payments was there, and people were beginning to adapt to the idea.

Merchants and traders adopted digital payments faster than consumers, which is generally the case, since they need to make larger payments. Handling huge wads of cash is inconvenient, and cheques, which had been prevalent in Sudan for a long time, provided a step toward transitioning from cash to electronic payments. The key issue, however—which we identified along with Ashraf and Ali—was that most of the focus was on issuing debit cards to consumers or getting them to adopt mobile payment apps. There was very little attention on the acceptance side—the merchants. It's one thing for everyone to have a debit card, but if they can only use it at a handful of locations, adoption is going to be very low.

The banks had started rolling out POS devices, but again, these were mostly for bigger merchants in Khartoum, and all were tied to the national switch. Some of the larger banks may have integrated their own POS devices with their internal systems, but most relied on the national switch. Bank-issued POS devices were often unreliable due to poor maintenance and outsourcing, leading to low adoption.

How did you approach rolling out POS devices, and what made that strategy effective?

We used the Fawry model, which is a merchant-led approach. The idea was to empower merchants to act as mini-banks within their neighborhoods, allowing them to accept digital payments from the local people in the area. This is what truly enables financial inclusion and digital transformation.

While we were closing our investment round and importing the POS devices, we were also working on three key areas in the background.

First, we aggressively sought integrations with all the key players in the market. We already had integrations with the national switch, and we focused on direct integration with telcos and banks wherever possible. Any institution ready to be part of the digital payments ecosystem was a potential partner.

Second, we were building the technology itself. We had started as a classifieds platform, so we had technology for that, but nothing remotely close to what was required for a payments business—let alone the complexity of a Fawry-style merchant-based payment ecosystem. Fawry was very helpful during this phase.

Third, we built out our sales and operations teams. This last point was critical and, in many ways, the secret to Cashi's success. Many people assume that building a payments business is easy—you can get white-label technology for most of these products and launch. But without strong sales and operational teams, none of it will work.

On the sales side, we took POS devices directly to merchants, conducted KYC, placed the devices in their stores, collected cash, and helped merchants get banked if needed. We maintained constant engagement—daily visits to ensure merchants were using the devices, offering maintenance, training them on new services, and running point-of-sale marketing. Consumer education was also a key part of this process.

The operational side was just as important. Stability in infrastructure, strong customer service, and market feedback loops were essential. If merchants or consumers had issues, we needed the capacity to respond effectively. That's how we ensured quality and reliability.

When we launched, all of this came together in a way that made our rollout incredibly strong.

———

> STABILITY IN INFRASTRUCTURE, STRONG CUSTOMER SERVICE, AND MARKET FEEDBACK LOOPS WERE ESSENTIAL. IF MERCHANTS OR CONSUMERS HAD ISSUES, WE NEEDED THE CAPACITY TO RESPOND EFFECTIVELY.

———

Why was demand for POS so high, and how did you handle that rapid scaleup?

We started rolling out POS devices in late spring 2022, and the response was overwhelming. This was a defining moment. With the classifieds business, we had clear product-market fit, which was the main factor driving the massive adoption, but the demand for payments was on an entirely different level. We could not distribute

POS devices fast enough. In the beginning, we prioritized shops on main roads and generally applied high turnover requirements, since we had a limited supply of devices, which were expensive. Merchants were complaining on Facebook that they had applied for a Cashi POS and were denied because they didn't meet our high standards. People were even showing up at our office to complain about not getting a POS. The demand was incredible, and this was just in Khartoum—we hadn't even expanded to the provinces yet.

By year one, we deployed more than 5,000 POS devices, validating the market's demand for digital payments. The increased transaction volume benefited multiple stakeholders. More transactions were running through the national switch, telcos were seeing more digital airtime purchases, and banks were witnessing increased engagement with their digital services. The impact on the ecosystem was undeniable. By early April 2023, just a year after launch, we had the largest active POS network in the country. Some other players had shipped large numbers of POS devices before us, including EVD machines, but very few had achieved the level of consistent activity that we did. Our devices had an incredible 90% daily activity rate, which is almost unheard of in payments.

Our second batch of POS had just arrived, and we had just started rolling them out when, in mid-April 2023, war broke out. I think I had mentioned earlier that the coup had already happened, so we had gone through a revolution, followed by a civilian-led government transition to elections, a military coup, and now we were facing a war.

Can you describe the situation in Sudan when the conflict began in 2023?

As a backdrop, at the time of the fall of the Omar Bashir regime (which had ruled Sudan for almost 30 years), Sudan effectively had two standing armies. The national army—the formal military of the state, the Sudanese Armed Forces (SAF)—and another armed group known as the Rapid Support Forces (RSF), which had been set up by the old regime and had grown immensely. Throughout the transition period, the country was constantly navigating the reality that it had two armed groups, both in theory responsible for state security, but also competing for power.

In late 2021, there was a coup d'état, ending the civilian-led transition. Under the civilian-led government, the economy had opened up, investors were starting to come in, and major international institutions like the World Bank and IMF were re-engaging with Sudan. However, after the coup, the country was in a different situation.

It was a strange and volatile situation. In Khartoum, you could literally see two different groups of armed forces on the streets—one belonging to the SAF, the other to the RSF. This became part of everyday life, but nonetheless, the atmosphere was tense. In April 2023, full-scale war broke out between the two sides. The reasons behind the conflict are complex, but from our perspective, what mattered was that the fighting had begun, and it had started right in the middle of the capital city.

Khartoum, a city of almost 10 million people, instantly became a war zone. For Cashi, this was a defining moment. Suddenly, every single team member in Sudan, which was the bulk of our workforce, had to face a tough new world. If you can survive war, you can survive anything. No business challenges compare to the reality of war. It forces you to adapt, to be resourceful, and to operate under extreme pressure. We all went through a baptism of fire.

———

> IF YOU CAN SURVIVE WAR, YOU CAN SURVIVE ANYTHING. NO BUSINESS CHALLENGES COMPARE TO THE REALITY OF WAR. IT FORCES YOU TO ADAPT, TO BE RESOURCEFUL, AND TO OPERATE UNDER EXTREME PRESSURE. WE ALL WENT THROUGH A BAPTISM OF FIRE.

———

Everyone was displaced. Some team members fled to Egypt, others to villages and towns outside the capital, while others left for the UAE or Saudi Arabia. We were suddenly spread across different parts of the world. But at that moment, the situation for Cashi was surreal. While our world was literally falling apart—people fleeing their homes with nothing but a backpack—the business was growing.

That was the craziest part. The demand for digital payments surged because, in moments of extreme insecurity, carrying cash becomes dangerous. Bank branches were completely shut down, the city was in chaos, and people were desperate for alternatives. In those first few days, the growth in Cashi's transactions was unprecedented. With cash inaccessible, digital payments became the only viable option.

Then, something even more unexpected happened. The national payment infrastructure itself got caught up in the war. The central bank building was taken over, and all the physical cash stored there was looted. But the most critical event was the national switch being burned down. Overnight, the entire card payment system ceased to exist. Furthermore, most banks had their physical servers located in their headquarters, all of which were in Khartoum. Many banks lost access to their servers, either because their buildings were occupied or because the servers were destroyed. For a period, it was literally impossible to make any type of payment in Sudan—except on the Cashi network. We were able to operate despite the broader system collapse because, although we were integrated with the national switch, we were not dependent on it. Transactions within our ecosystem could still be processed, even when the larger financial system had come to a halt. Using Cashi, people could still move money across the country, they could still purchase airtime and pay for electricity, and essential payments could still be made.

For a startup that had been operating for barely a year, this was both an incredible and overwhelming moment. There was huge pressure on us to keep the system running. Thankfully, the effort we had put into building a scalable and resilient technology stack paid off. We were able to handle the increased transaction volume and scale rapidly despite the crisis.

Eventually, we lost access to our headquarters, meaning we also lost access to our stored inventory of POS devices. The building itself was in an occupied area, so our ability to distribute new hardware was severely restricted. However, because we had already deployed app-based POS solutions, we could keep expanding without needing physical infrastructure.

At the same time, as our team members fled to different parts of the country, we told them, "Wherever you are, start onboarding merchants. Let's get Cashi running wherever people need it." That's exactly what happened. Despite the displacement, our team continued growing the network across Sudan.

With the entire card system down and no functional bank infrastructure, we were asked if we could launch a consumer wallet to provide another means of transacting. We had already built a consumer wallet—a very basic digital wallet that was originally meant to be card-backed, like MyFawry in Egypt. It had been undergoing testing with the national switch when the war started, and was very bare-bones. It had been tested, but wasn't fully baked and really was not an exemplar consumer payments app. And, of course, it had originally been designed to be backed by a card, meaning users would enter their card details, and the system would pull funds from their bank account. But now, there was no functioning card system, no working core banking systems, and no way to connect new accounts to banks.

We therefore adapted the system to create standalone wallets that operated purely within our ecosystem—and it worked. People needed a solution, and despite its lack of sophistication, our wallet was easy to use, highly stable, and scalable. We saw rapid adoption. We already had the largest merchant network in the country, and now we were onboarding consumers at an unprecedented rate.

This led to even more momentum in digital payments. The entire ecosystem began growing organically. At that point, we had completely transformed into a full dual-sided payments loop.

What was one major lesson from your early days to scaling Cashi?

One of the biggest lessons we learned came from our time in classifieds. It's great to build a business that has product-market fit. It's great to develop technology that gets rapid adoption. But if you can't make money off that technology, you're setting yourself up for a very bad situation. This is especially true in markets like Sudan, Egypt, and many others where fundraising is difficult.

———

> IT'S GREAT TO BUILD A BUSINESS THAT HAS PRODUCT-MARKET FIT. IT'S GREAT TO DEVELOP TECHNOLOGY THAT GETS RAPID ADOPTION. BUT IF YOU CAN'T MAKE MONEY OFF THAT TECHNOLOGY, YOU'RE SETTING YOURSELF UP FOR A VERY BAD SITUATION.

———

If you have a model that depends on constantly raising capital to survive until you reach an enormous scale, it's just not viable. That's why, from day one, we made sure Cashi was generating revenue. Even if we were only taking a tiny fee on each transaction, it was critical that every transaction contributed to covering operational costs. The fees we charged were minimal—low enough to ensure affordability for consumers and merchants—but we made sure they existed. In fact, in some areas, we forced the market to lower prices. For example, when we entered the electricity payments sector, we found that existing providers were charging extortionate fees, so we actively pushed those prices down. But the core principle remained: we were not operating for free.

———

> IF YOU HAVE A MODEL THAT DEPENDS ON CONSTANTLY RAISING CAPITAL TO SURVIVE UNTIL YOU REACH AN ENORMOUS SCALE, IT'S JUST NOT VIABLE.

———

This approach became even more crucial given the instability in Sudan. Especially after the war in Sudan started, we entered a completely different reality where raising money became highly uncertain, if not impossible. That's when it became clear that we had to be self-sufficient, and fast.

Self-sufficiency became a defining part of Cashi's ethos, and not just in terms of finances. It also applied to how we built our technology. When everything in the country collapsed and other companies shut down, we survived and thrived because we had built everything we needed in-house. Even something as simple as SMS delivery—we had built our own capacity for sending messages and weren't dependent on third-party providers. Our POS maintenance, call centers, customer service—everything we considered a core function of the business was kept in-house.

This mindset often led to debates with our product managers. "Why are we building all this tech ourselves? Why reinvent the wheel?" But our experience had shown that relying on external providers was risky. More than once, we had had our account suddenly closed without warning when using a global service provider. When we asked why, they simply said, "You're operating in Sudan," even though there were no sanctions or legal restrictions. It was pure discrimination, and there was nothing we could do about it. That reinforced our belief that if something is core to our business, we must own and control it. I'm not saying every startup should build everything from scratch. My product managers had a valid point—it makes no sense to reinvent the wheel if you don't have to. But I see many startups stitching together various technologies from third-party providers, and I always think, "If this is essential to your business and you don't control it, you're putting yourself in a very vulnerable position."

————

> IF SOMETHING IS CORE TO OUR BUSINESS, WE MUST OWN AND CONTROL IT. I'M NOT SAYING EVERY STARTUP SHOULD BUILD EVERYTHING FROM SCRATCH... BUT IF THIS IS ESSENTIAL TO YOUR BUSINESS AND YOU DON'T CONTROL IT, YOU'RE PUTTING YOURSELF IN A VERY VULNERABLE POSITION.

————

So those were two key lessons: one, don't rely on endless fundraising—make sure your business generates revenue from the start; and two, maintain tight control over critical technology.

The third lesson was about financial discipline. We have always been very strict with costs. We are not a business that burns excessive amounts of money. Of course, now that we've scaled, we are spending more, as you would expect from a company of our size. But since Q2 2024, we've been consistently profitable every quarter. The profits aren't huge, but that's not the point. The point is that we cover our costs comfortably, and we maintain a disciplined approach to working capital, marketing spend, and operations.

————

> WE HAVE ALWAYS BEEN VERY STRICT WITH COSTS. WE ARE NOT A BUSINESS THAT BURNS EXCESSIVE AMOUNTS OF MONEY.

————

Being conservative with money, focusing on revenue generation, and ensuring financial self-sufficiency—those have been the pillars of Cashi's success. After all, we're building a business, not a nonprofit. Yes, we have a significant social impact, particularly in countries like Sudan, but at the end of the day, we need to be commercially sustainable.

There is another key part of the Cashi story: our relationship with the communities where we work. People often ask, "How did you survive all this political turmoil?" The answer is simple: we never looked at Sudan from the top down. Our focus was never on the elite or the rich—it was always on the everyday people, who form the majority of the population.

This approach has given us a much larger market. There's a massive difference between targeting the top 500,000 wealthiest people versus targeting all the approximately 47 million Sudanese. Yes, lower-income consumers may have smaller transaction sizes, but there are far more of them, making it a much more scalable business model.

From the beginning, even when we focused on merchants in Khartoum, we weren't prioritizing high-end businesses. Our ideal merchants were middle-class and lower-middle-class grocery stores, pharmacies, and retail outlets that were integral parts of their communities.

When we built our sales teams, we hired people from those same neighborhoods. That meant there was always a strong connection between our field teams and the merchants they were working with. This approach proved to be invaluable. When the war started, many of our merchants were displaced. Instead of abandoning them, we supported them in restarting their businesses in new locations. This wasn't just about keeping Cashi operational—it was about helping them rebuild their lives.

This deep community integration also meant that our strongest supporters weren't the government or the elite, but ordinary people. Sudan has an incredibly young population that is quick to adopt technology. For many, Cashi represents hope for a better future.

Remember, the country went through a revolution, then it entered a period of uncertainty, and finally, full-scale war. Throughout all of this, Cashi continued growing because we aren't just a financial services company—we want to be part of the social fabric.

People see themselves in brands that represent a better future—something that empowers them to believe tomorrow will be better. Technology and products like ours can serve as an emblem or a symbol of that hope. The way we branded Cashi was very much designed to resonate with that audience. We never wanted to be seen as something big, corporate, or disconnected. Instead, we made it very clear that Cashi was built by young people, for a young population.

We never prioritized older merchants over younger ones. If anything, we had a preference for younger merchants. We were always agnostic to gender, ethnicity, tribe, or socioeconomic status. None of those factors played—or will ever play—a role in our selection process. A good merchant was a good merchant, whether they ran a small kiosk on the side of the road or a larger store.

Because financial inclusion was embedded in the company's ethos from day one, we built very strong connections with local communities. This, in turn, reduced the amount we needed to spend on marketing. Instead of relying heavily on paid promotions, we benefited from word-of-mouth and organic growth. The people around Cashi became our strongest promoters, which helped us weather the turmoil of the time.

———

> INSTEAD OF RELYING HEAVILY ON PAID PROMOTIONS, WE BENEFITED FROM WORD-OF-MOUTH AND ORGANIC GROWTH. THE PEOPLE AROUND CASHI BECAME OUR STRONGEST PROMOTERS.

———

So, one of the most important lessons is understanding who your target audience really is. It may seem instinctive to go after elite segments of the population for short-term gain, but you have to consider who your long-term audience is and how you build a connection with them over time.

What does Cashi look like today, and how have you adapted to new scaleup challenges?

By early 2024, the consumer wallet was live and growing. At this point, a significant portion of the country was under the control of the RSF (Rapid Support Forces). Life for people living in those areas was extremely difficult, and it was challenging for our teams to operate there. While many people had fled into army-held areas or left the country altogether, there were still merchants trying to work in RSF-controlled zones. However, we were struggling to access them and provide support.

To address this, we built and launched another merchant product, called Cashi Lite. Initially designed for these difficult-to-reach areas, it ended up becoming very popular among other merchant categories we hadn't initially considered.

The key difference with Cashi Lite was that it didn't require a sales rep to verify merchants in person. Instead, we built a digital verification mechanism, along with in-app communication features to provide remote support and training. This eliminated the need for face-to-face interaction. As a result, our capacity to scale the merchant network tripled overnight.

Before launching Cashi Lite, we had 29,350 merchants onboarded. Within a few months of its release, we had added another 20,000 merchants. The ease of onboarding made a massive difference.

Meanwhile, the consumer wallet continued to grow. Today, we have around 1.3 million registered users, and the number is growing rapidly every day.

Another major event in 2024 was the cash crisis. During the war, huge amounts of physical banknotes had been looted. On top of that, Sudan's currency devalued by over 400%, leading to spiraling inflation. A small wad of cash that used to buy something substantial now bought almost nothing. Particularly in RSF-held areas, where insecurity was rampant, cash handling became even more dangerous.

At one point, the central bank literally had no physical cash left even to pay government servants. They realized they needed to rapidly digitize the economy. Banks were under immense pressure to enable digital transactions, but many of them still hadn't fully recovered from the destruction of their headquarters and servers. The fall of Khartoum was described as one of the biggest bank robberies in history—every single bank branch in the capital had been looted, servers destroyed, computers taken. The financial system was in total chaos.

The central bank recognized our role in digital payments and financial inclusion and allowed us to apply for a larger license. In the autumn of 2024, Cashi was officially granted a mobile money license, making us a recognized financial institution in Sudan.

This was a huge milestone for us. I have always told the team that this was a testament to everything they had built during the war. It's not easy for a fintech to go from a simple pass-through PSP license to becoming a fully licensed financial institution in just a couple of years. But that's exactly what Cashi has done.

Today, I would say we are probably one of the largest digital payment processors in Sudan, after the Bank of Khartoum, which is of course dominant due to their long history and extensive customer base. However, for us, it is not important who has the largest share of the payments pie. What we take pride in is the contribution we have made to growing the pie by driving financial inclusion across the country—in partnership with all of the other players. We know the market is huge, and we are confident our share will yield a very positive return for our shareholders.

When I look back, the past few years have been incredibly difficult, especially for our team. Many of them have been displaced, and those still in Sudan have had to operate under extreme conditions. Even our engineers outside the country have worked under immense pressure to continuously adapt our technology.

To give you an idea of the challenges we've faced, imagine trying to operate a financial technology business in a country with some of the least reliable electricity and internet connectivity in the world. Every version of every app we release has to be stress-tested under the worst possible conditions.

———

> EVERY VERSION OF EVERY APP WE RELEASE HAS TO BE STRESS-TESTED UNDER THE WORST POSSIBLE CONDITIONS.

———

This requires constant innovation and creativity from the entire team, especially our engineers, who have been absolutely superb. Today, we have a very strong tech stack that has proven itself in terms of robustness, scalability, resilience, and innovation capacity. I believe this leaves us extremely well-positioned for further growth inside and outside of Sudan.

We also invested heavily in 2024 to enhance the consumer application. The first version of the app was basic. Now, it has evolved into what I would confidently say is the best consumer-facing fintech app in Sudan. The improvements align with our core philosophy—we are here to serve, to be part of the community, and to support people through this difficult time while laying the foundation for a better future.

Empowering small businesses has been central to this mission. Many of our product developments are aimed at making life easier for merchants, whether through simplified payroll systems, transaction tracking tools, or other features that enhance business operations. We are constantly asking ourselves if we are truly serving and if we are really meeting the needs of the people.

Many still don't fully understand why Cashi has worked as well as it has. But the answer is simple: our deep connection to the community.

It's not just about having a strong boots-on-the-ground approach, although that remains critical. It's also about fostering two-way communication. We constantly survey users, engage in community discussions, and actively listen to feedback.

———

> IT'S NOT JUST ABOUT HAVING A STRONG BOOTS-ON-THE-GROUND APPROACH, ALTHOUGH THAT REMAINS CRITICAL. IT'S ALSO ABOUT FOSTERING TWO-WAY COMMUNICATION. WE CONSTANTLY SURVEY USERS, ENGAGE IN COMMUNITY DISCUSSIONS, AND ACTIVELY LISTEN TO FEEDBACK.

———

For example, one of our major initiatives in 2025 has been integrating more deeply with more banks to make it easier for users to instantly move money between their bank accounts and Cashi, whether via cash deposits, wallet payments, or other methods. This was a feature directly requested by our community, to which we rushed to respond.

How would you pitch Sudan or North African markets to global investors who are unfamiliar with them?

People often underestimate the size of these markets. Sudan, in particular, has been consistently underestimated, largely due to its history of sanctions, which left the country isolated for decades. Limited trade in and out of the country meant that few people truly understood its economic potential. What many don't realize is that when a country is isolated for such a long period, its economy must become highly resilient and self-sufficient. Internal trade must mature because people have no choice but to find ways to sustain themselves. When the country begins to open up, the potential for growth is enormous.

In Sudan's case, this dynamic created a situation where, despite the challenges, there was a strong, functioning economy beneath the surface. I think this is something that applies to many African markets. A common mistake many investors make is relying solely on official GDP numbers, which are based on government-reported data. The problem is that much of Africa's economy is informal, meaning government statistics often fail to capture the full picture. The data typically reflects only what the government can see, such as revenue collected from taxes or customs, but in reality, large portions of these economies operate outside of those formal structures.

This is why I always feel one can't judge the size of an economy based on what you can read in published reports. I've been to other countries where it was immediately clear that the economy was far more limited in scale. I learned to see this by paying attention to how consumers behave. Coming from a business family with a background in food manufacturing, I was exposed to this way of thinking early on. My father is particularly skilled at reading consumer behavior, and I have been lucky to have had that skill passed down to me. How people shop at supermarkets, how much they spend, what kinds of goods they buy, and how much they save—these small details reveal more about a market's potential than anything you'll find in an economic forecast.

Another major factor investors often overlook is consumer behavior when it comes to technology. Many rely on official mobile penetration numbers, but those figures don't always reflect reality. The best way to gauge digital adoption in a country is to go there and see how people actually use mobile phones. If you walk through a market, how many people are using their phones for transactions? What types of phones are they using? How available are smartphones, and what is the pricing like? These factors provide a much clearer picture of how ready a population is for digital adoption.

What advice would you give to someone returning to Sudan to start a business?

I would say the key is to approach it with patience, humility, and a willingness to learn. It's a completely different environment, but for those who can adapt, the opportunities are immense.

To thrive in a market like Sudan, or really any developing market, you have to be mentally flexible and willing to respect differences. Many people returning from the West, the Gulf, or other developed economies often assume that the way things are done elsewhere is inherently better. While there is truth to that in certain aspects—more developed economies often have more efficient systems—there are also deep cultural and structural differences that cannot simply be overridden.

———

66 TO THRIVE IN A MARKET LIKE SUDAN, OR REALLY ANY DEVELOPING MARKET, YOU HAVE TO BE MENTALLY FLEXIBLE AND WILLING TO RESPECT DIFFERENCES. MANY PEOPLE RETURNING FROM THE WEST... OFTEN ASSUME THAT THE WAY THINGS ARE DONE ELSEWHERE IS INHERENTLY BETTER.

———

For me, it was almost a process of relearning the country after having been away for so long. For example, things move slower in Sudan. I am someone with almost zero patience, and I tend to be rigid with time and scheduling. But in Sudan, meetings don't always start on time. Appointments get pushed. It was frustrating until I realized that the way society is structured places different values on different things.

One of the biggest realizations for me was that, despite all the hardships, people in Sudan seemed to be happier than in many more developed parts of the world. Their lives were undoubtedly harder, yet the strength of family structures, the tight-knit nature of communities, and the general approach to life was different. The pressures of a highly individualistic society were less present. There was a lesson in that. It made me realize that while there were inefficiencies and frustrations in the way business was done, it wasn't just about fixing inefficiencies—it was about understanding why things function the way they do.

Business is often built on personal relationships, and that takes time. People prioritize human connection over rigid efficiency. Once I understood that, I tried to stop fighting it and to start working within that reality.

At the same time, there are core values that I refuse to compromise on. Certain principles are non-negotiable, regardless of where I am operating. Transparency is one of them. From the start, we have been very clear about how we account for things, how we report to shareholders, and how we engage with stakeholders.

Corruption is another red line. We do not pay bribes—ever. Whether it's someone in government or someone in a bank, the answer is always no. We would rather walk away from a deal than compromise on that.

———

" WE DO NOT PAY BRIBES—EVER. WHETHER IT'S SOMEONE IN GOVERNMENT OR SOMEONE IN A BANK, THE ANSWER IS ALWAYS NO. WE WOULD RATHER WALK AWAY FROM A DEAL THAN COMPROMISE ON THAT.

———

There are also broader moral principles that we uphold. Non-discrimination is fundamental to Cashi's ethos. We do not tolerate discrimination based on gender, ethnicity, or social status. Financial inclusion means serving everyone, not just the wealthy or privileged. If a small kiosk on the side of the road needs access to digital payments, they are just as important to us as a major supermarket. These are ethics both Mostafa and I, as founders, were raised with, and we will not allow the business to compromise on them, no matter what societal norms may be in a given place.

What's one key thing founders often overlook when fundraising in emerging markets?

To succeed in underdeveloped markets, entrepreneurs need to approach spending and valuation with a level of realism that differs from more mature ecosystems like in the US. Spending excessively, even when raising from global investors, can be a dangerous trap.

The reality is that fundraising in these markets is significantly harder, and startups need to deliver more to justify the same level of investment. Watching spending carefully, being realistic about valuations, and ensuring revenue generation from day one are all crucial elements of survival.

Managing cash carefully is even more critical in environments with high inflation and currency devaluation, where capital can rapidly lose its value. Founders must be extremely prudent with how they handle capital to avoid unnecessary losses.

What does successful localization look like in markets like Sudan?

Successful localization requires continuous dialogue between the business and its customers. Entrepreneurs must deeply understand who they are building for, how these consumers operate, and what specific pain points they are addressing. This applies not only to product development but also to marketing, trust-building, and overall adoption strategies.

A good example of where mistakes happen is when startups develop features based on internal brainstorming rather than actual customer needs. Many times, a team member—sometimes even the founder—comes up with what seems like a brilliant idea for a feature. The team agrees, builds it, and launches it, only to later realize that the feature is irrelevant to a significant portion of the market.

We have made this mistake enough times ourselves. A better approach is to conduct early research, test a prototype with a small group of users, and observe real-life usage before committing to a full launch. This process helps avoid unnecessary pivots or rushed adjustments after the fact. Over time, Cashi has significantly improved in this regard, ensuring that each major feature goes through rigorous pre-launch research and testing.

Another key lesson is the importance of building a strong local team. One of the reasons Cashi succeeded in Sudan was that much of our core team was Sudanese. Even though some of our senior leadership, including our CTO and key executives, were not Sudanese, we had a deep contingent of local talent. Their insights were invaluable in helping us understand the market and adapt quickly to its realities. A company trying to operate in a country without a strong local team will always struggle to read the nuances of that market.

———

> ONE OF THE REASONS CASHI SUCCEEDED IN SUDAN WAS THAT MUCH OF OUR CORE TEAM WAS SUDANESE. THEIR INSIGHTS WERE INVALUABLE IN HELPING US UNDERSTAND THE MARKET AND ADAPT QUICKLY TO ITS REALITIES.

———

Building trust is a major factor in adoption, especially in markets where digital financial services are relatively new. The reliability of technology plays a crucial role, but even more important is how the company treats its users, particularly when handling their money.

As someone who has personally dealt with the challenges of banking in a post-sanctioned country—facing arbitrary account closures and lack of transparency—I wanted Cashi to operate differently. A fundamental principle has been to always respect that we are custodians of people's money, which means ensuring uninterrupted access to funds.

System downtime is one of the biggest threats to trust in digital finance. If people cannot access their money when they need it, they lose confidence in the platform. Many financial institutions in Sudan have historically made it difficult for people to access their own money, either due to system downtimes, excessive KYC barriers, or general inefficiencies.

Cashi's approach has been the opposite. Maintaining an extremely stable and resilient infrastructure has been a non-negotiable priority—any interruption in service is unacceptable. By ensuring seamless cash-in and cash-out options through a vast network of merchants, customers never have to rely on a single bank branch, which may be closed due to instability.

Interoperability with other financial players has also been a priority, ensuring users can transfer their money freely. Transparency, reliability, and ease of access are what build trust.

What are your thoughts on the Sudanese startup ecosystem?

Sudan's startup ecosystem is very nascent. The barriers to entry are extremely high, and if we hadn't had experienced founders with strong reputations and access to capital, building Cashi would have been significantly harder.

One of the biggest obstacles is simply infrastructure. Electricity and internet penetration are two fundamental issues. If African countries are serious about fostering digital transformation and startup innovation, then their first priority should be ensuring reliable electricity and internet access. Without these two things, rapid technological growth is almost impossible.

Egypt is a useful comparison. The Egyptian government invested heavily in electricity and telecom infrastructure, which created the foundation for digital expansion. It also prioritized education, particularly in areas like software engineering, which helped create a pipeline of local tech talent.

Beyond infrastructure, legal and regulatory barriers can either encourage or stifle startup growth. Sudan, despite its challenges, actually has a relatively straightforward process for setting up a company. Compared to places like Dubai or the UK, it's more time-consuming and expensive, but compared to other African countries, it's quite manageable.

The government also played a role in facilitating fintech growth by offering simple PSP licenses, which allowed startups to enter the market with a low initial regulatory burden. While those licenses didn't allow for much functionality, they gave startups the opportunity to prove product-market fit before making heavier investments. In contrast, some African countries require startups to obtain expensive and onerous licenses before they can even begin operating, which creates a huge financial barrier to entry.

Governments can de-risk startup investments by making it as cheap and easy as possible to start a business and demonstrate viability. Once a startup has proven itself, then more stringent regulations can come into play. This approach allows for a more organic growth path while still ensuring compliance and consumer protection in the long run.

There is also a lot of room for improvement when it comes to tax policy. Like all startups, Cashi faced early-stage losses, but we were never fully able to recover those losses under Sudanese tax law. In theory, the law allows for it, but in practice, the system didn't facilitate it. Offering tax incentives or breaks for startups, particularly in the early years, could make a huge difference.

On a personal level, adapting to Sudan after living in Canada and the UK was a challenge. For expats considering returning to Sudan to build businesses, my biggest advice is to immerse themselves in the local environment and truly understand how things work. It's not enough to have an external perspective or assume that what worked abroad will work in Sudan. Listening to local experts and building relationships with people who have deep, firsthand knowledge of the market is essential.

How should founders navigate regulations in developing markets like Sudan?

I am a big believer in early engagement with government officials and policymakers. It is important to meet regulators early on, introduce yourself, and explain what you are building. If regulators understand your vision, your ethics, and your long-term goals, they are more likely to give you the benefit of the doubt when it comes to navigating grey areas.

If, on the other hand, you operate in secrecy, launch something that appears to be breaking all the rules, and then get caught, you're immediately on the defensive. Regulators will see you as an outsider trying to circumvent the system, rather than a partner in building the economy.

For example, even before the war, we had already approached the regulator in Sudan about creating a new licensing regime for us. The existing merchant license was too narrow and hadn't envisioned an operation at the scale we were building. We proposed a new framework, similar to the merchant aggregator model used in other countries. The regulator saw the logic in our proposal and we began working on it. That type of proactive engagement helps create an environment where fintechs can grow while still respecting regulatory oversight.

Thank you, Tarneem. Your journey is a testament that entrepreneurship can flourish even in unfavorable places.

Thank you for featuring our story.

––––––

MOHAMAD BALLOUT

Scaling hospitality, one restaurant at a time

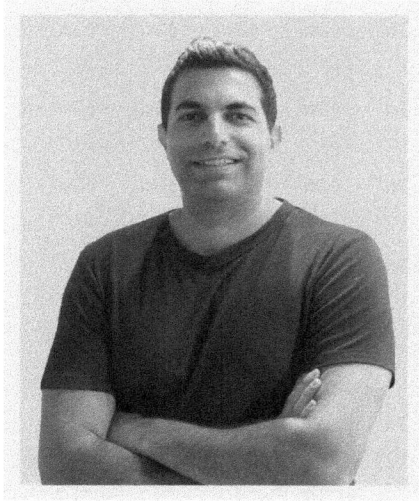

Co-founder and CEO of KITOPI

KITOPI

Dubai, UAE

www.kitopi.com

MOHAMAD BALLOUT is the co-founder and Chief Executive Officer (CEO) of Kitopi, a pioneering tech-powered, multi-brand restaurant platform established in Dubai in January 2018. Under his leadership, Kitopi has rapidly evolved into a leading food and beverage (F&B) ecosystem, operating over 200 outlets across the United Arab Emirates (UAE), Saudi Arabia (KSA), Kuwait, Bahrain, and Qatar, and employing a diverse team of more than 6,000 individuals.

Before founding Kitopi, Ballout co-founded BMB Group in 2007, which has grown to become one of the largest confectionery businesses in the Middle East. His strategic vision and operational expertise were instrumental in expanding BMB's footprint across 32 markets, establishing the first fully automated ethnic sweets manufacturing unit in the region. In 2016, he exited BMB, selling his shares to a private equity firm, and subsequently founded Ripples Capital, focusing on seed-stage investments in tech-enabled ventures.

Ballout's academic credentials include a double major in Mathematics and Economics from the University of Warwick and a Master's in Management from Imperial College London. This strong educational foundation has equipped him with analytical and strategic skills, contributing to his success in the entrepreneurial landscape.

Under Ballout's leadership, Kitopi has achieved significant milestones, including becoming a unicorn in 2021 following a $415 million funding round led by SoftBank's Vision Fund 2. The company's innovative approach integrates technology with culinary arts, offering a Smart Kitchen Operating System (SKOS) that optimizes kitchen operations in real-time, enhancing efficiency and customer satisfaction.

Kitopi's strategic acquisitions have further solidified its market position. Notably, the acquisition of AWJ, a prominent F&B group known for brands like Operation Falafel and Catch 22, marked one of the largest transactions in the region's F&B sector. This move aligns with Ballout's vision to respect and integrate the legacy and culture of acquired entities, fostering a unified organizational ethos.

Ballout's journey exemplifies focus on strategic growth, operational excellence, and market expansion. His ability to blend traditional F&B practices with technological innovation has positioned Kitopi as a leader in the Middle East's F&B industry, contributing to the region's economic development and setting a benchmark for aspiring entrepreneurs.

Fluent in Arabic, English, and French, Ballout's multicultural proficiency enhances his ability to navigate diverse markets and lead a multinational team effectively. His commitment to leveraging digital transformation and business analytics continues to steer Kitopi towards sustained growth and industry leadership.

Mohamad Ballout's visionary leadership and strategic acumen have been pivotal in transforming Kitopi into a trailblazer within the F&B sector, embodying the dynamic spirit of innovation and entrepreneurship that drives the Middle East's economic landscape.

———

KITOPI is the Middle East's largest F&B ecosystem, redefining dining through culinary innovation, technology, and exceptional customer experiences. Founded in Dubai in January 2018, Kitopi has grown to operate 80+ brands over 200 outlets across the UAE, Saudi Arabia, Kuwait, Bahrain, and Qatar. With a team of more than 6,000 employees, the company is committed to creating joy through its diverse range of homegrown and partner brands.

Kitopi pioneers a new operating model by seamlessly integrating multiple brands under one infrastructure, leveraging shared kitchens, centralized supply chains, and cross-brand data intelligence. Through world-class R&D teams and skilled chefs, it crafts exceptional dining experiences that maximize efficiency while elevating hospitality. The company is home to a variety of innovative brands, including Flavor Fields, a concept focused on healthy and mindful eating, and EATOPI, a pioneering platform that empowers emerging homegrown chefs to showcase their most popular dishes. Additionally, Kitopi owns a range of loved brands such as Awani, Catch22, Operation Falafel, Taqado, and Zaroob among many others.

Beyond its regional outlets, Kitopi runs a Global Customer Experience Center in Amman, Jordan as well as an Engineering Hub in Krakow, Poland. These strategic locations support the company's commitment to operational excellence and continuous technological advancement. Technology is at the core of Kitopi's operations, ensuring a seamless and memorable customer journey. At the heart of Kitopi's operations is its proprietary Smart Kitchen Operating System (SKOS), an end-to-end technology ecosystem that powers everything from order processing and kitchen workflows to inventory management and customer insights.

Built to optimize efficiency at scale, SKOS seamlessly integrates with Kitopi's consumer platforms, enabling a frictionless experience across dine-in, delivery, and meal plan services. Its evolution has expanded from managing kitchen operations (SKOS 1.0) to product lifecycle optimization (SKOS 2.0) and, most recently, to customer lifecycle management (SKOS 3.0).

The latest iteration is designed to bring fine-dining-level hospitality to scale in the fast-casual and casual dining space. By embedding AI-driven recommendations, personalized loyalty incentives, and a unified customer profile across all touchpoints, Kitopi is pioneering Connected Hospitality—an approach that bridges operational excellence with elevated guest experiences. This vision ensures that every Kitopi interaction feels seamless, intuitive, and tailored, creating deeper engagement and brand affinity across their 80+ regional brands and 200+ locations.

By continuously innovating and expanding its reach, Kitopi is shaping the future of hospitality in the Middle East, elevating culinary standards, and bringing people together through the magic of food.

———

Give us a bit of background on yourself?

I was born and raised in the UAE, spending the first 18 years of my life here. I come from humble beginnings—my father moved here without even finishing high school. He was one of those people who had to work relentlessly just to give us a shot at a better life. Both my parents worked hard to put us through school, and that shaped a lot of my early mindset.

I saw firsthand what resilience looked like. It wasn't just a word; it was a lived experience. My father, at one point, went completely broke. I was 16 years old when it happened, and watching him go through that struggle left a lasting impact on me. It wasn't just about financial hardship—it was about rebuilding, about finding a way forward when everything seems to collapse around you. That shaped me more than anything else.

I went to college in the UK, thinking I'd end up as a banker. I graduated around 2008–2009—right in the middle of the financial crisis. Decided to go back to Dubai, and that's where my entrepreneurial journey started.

So, with no job prospects in London, I came back to Dubai. My brother, a couple of years older than me, was also figuring out his next move. We started brainstorming ideas, and he came up with one in the confectionery space. It was purely opportunistic—a manufacturer of chocolate ingredients needed a distributor, and he thought, why not us?

At first, I thought it was a terrible idea. But with no job, I gave in. That's how we started our first business. It grew from distributing confectionery ingredients to actually manufacturing them. We built what became the world's largest producer of ethnic sweets. We automated our facility, scaled globally across 32 countries, and eventually sold my stake to private equity in 2016.

Selling wasn't common back then. I barely knew anyone who had exited a business. My brother and I had reinvested everything back into the company, so when private equity firms started approaching us, I had no idea how to even value our business. When I finally realized what it was worth, I decided to sell my entire stake. I was 26 years old, financially free for the first time, and I thought, "Okay, that's it—I'm done."

For about a year, I tried being an investor, but I quickly realized I hated it. I didn't enjoy watching from the sidelines—I missed building. That itch led me back into entrepreneurship. I was about to invest in a food brand when I saw how hard it was for them to scale. Food delivery was growing, but there was no infrastructure to support it. That's where the idea for Kitopi was born. A couple of close friends and I came together, and we decided to build something that solves that problem.

What problem did you identify in the food industry that led to Kitopi?

It all started with the recognition that restaurants couldn't scale in the digital age without eroding their margins. A traditional restaurant doing 100% dine-in business runs on a 20% profit margin. But when food delivery took off, these same restaurants suddenly had two landlords—one physical and one digital. Aggregators were taking 20–30% in commissions, leaving restaurants with little to no profit.

Back in 2018, food delivery was exploding. We believed 60–70% of food consumption would eventually shift online, just as e-commerce had transformed retail. But while the problem was obvious, no one had cracked the solution—so we went all in.

We saw an opportunity not just to solve the margin squeeze but to rethink restaurant operations entirely. Single-location players struggled with underutilized labor and inefficient supply chains, while even large F&B groups ran their brand portfolio in silos, duplicating costs. What if brands could share infrastructure—labor, equipment, and supply chains—while still maintaining their unique identity?

Instead of restaurants expanding physically, we'd scale their brands digitally. By centralizing operations, we could aggregate demand, optimize resources, and extract more margin for everyone. Restaurants would earn royalties while we handled the operational burden.

Kitopi was born from this vision: a smarter, more efficient way for restaurants to scale in the digital age.

We then encountered a critical tech gap on implementation—there was no POS system designed for multi-brand cloud kitchens. No software allowed us to manage multiple restaurant brands from a single kitchen and the tools available to handle delivery orders were at its infancy. So we ultimately decided to build that tech from scratch after struggling with several off the shelf solutions.

In the beginning, ignorance was bliss. If I had fully understood how complex this operating model was, I might never have started. But we took the leap. Originally, there were three co-founders and two angel investors backing us. One of the co-founders dropped out a month before launch, which threw everything into chaos. The initial angel investors ultimately ended up joining us full-time. It was messy, unpredictable, but also incredibly exciting.

There was no playbook. No one else had done this at scale, so we had to figure out everything on our own. We were first movers in this space, globally.

What were the key lessons you learned while scaling Kitopi more than your previous company?

In my first company, I had a great team, but with Kitopi, I realized early on that I needed to bring in the absolute best—an all-star team that could fill in my blind spots and complement my strengths. I was fortunate to assemble an incredible group of people who helped shape the company in areas where I had little experience. That made all the difference.

At the same time, I learned that timing matters. We brought in some corporate professionals too early, thinking they would help us build structure. But in reality, they struggled to adapt to the fast-moving, chaotic nature of an early-stage startup. We needed a more balanced mix—people with corporate backgrounds who understood structure, consultants who could bring analytical problem-solving, entrepreneurial minds who could move fast and embrace uncertainty, and tech-driven individuals who approached challenges differently.

That blend of expertise became our secret sauce, and it's what helped Kitopi scale effectively.

———

> INSTEAD OF PROBLEM-SOLVING LIKE A TRADITIONAL BUSINESS, WE DEVELOPED A MORE STRUCTURED, AMAZON-LIKE APPROACH—ONE THAT EMPHASIZED RAPID EXPERIMENTATION, ITERATIVE LEARNING, AND MAKING DECISIONS BASED ON DATA RATHER THAN GUT INSTINCT.

———

The second major learning was how we approached problem-solving. My co-founder, Sam, played a crucial role in this. Instead of problem-solving like a traditional business, we developed a more structured, Amazon-like approach—one that emphasized rapid experimentation, iterative learning, and making decisions based on data rather than gut instinct. That shift required me to unlearn some old habits and develop new skills. Instead of directing every move, I had to step back and create a culture where the team could think independently, take ownership, and move fast without waiting for perfection.

Sam had built multiple tech startups before, and he brought that DNA into Kitopi. He instilled a culture where we didn't wait until things were perfect to launch—we built, tested, learned, and iterated in real-time. That mindset helped us stay ahead of the curve.

How did Kitopi's evolve as it scaled, and what key strategic decisions shaped its growth?

Kitopi's journey can be broken down into three chapters.

The first chapter was the pure cloud kitchen model, where we were solving the problem of restaurant scalability. While the business model was effective, we quickly realized it wasn't infinitely scalable. That led us to the second phase.

The second chapter was the transition into a tech-enabled, omni-channel, multi-brand restaurant company. At this stage, our technology stack became heavily focused on operational efficiency. We were probably the most advanced player in the space, with a proprietary system that allowed us to optimize every aspect of our operations.

Dur ing this chapter, we also shifted our approach to brands. Initially, we were licensing brands, but we realized that for long-term scalability, we needed to own them. Controlling the supply chain gave us better margins, more synergies, and allowed us to build deeper efficiencies across the business. That's when we made the strategic decision to start acquiring brands instead of just partnering with them.

Another major realization during this phase was around the concept of omni-channel. At first, we assumed the world was moving 100% online, and we built Kitopi with that assumption and neglected the physical dine-in experience. But by 2021, as the post-COVID period settled in, it became clear that consumers still wanted physical dining experiences. We also began to recognize the significance of a physical dine-in store to the customer experience. The best brands would be those that worked well both online and offline. On reflection this is what we feel many cloud kitchen business got wrong or came to realization too late. This insight forced us to rethink our strategy, and we began to focus on becoming more vertically integrated and omni-channel in nature.

This led to a crucial growth decision—should we build brands or buy them? While building brands from scratch is a long, slow process, acquiring great brands and scaling them played to our strengths. So we doubled down on acquiring some of the best brands in the market and expanding them aggressively. The real power came from integrating these brands into a seamless, unified experience—not just to optimize operations, but to enhance the consumer journey. By leveraging data, personalization, and cross-brand synergies, we're creating an F&B

ecosystem that makes discovering and enjoying great food easier, more engaging, and more rewarding. That's the phase we're in now: redefining how consumers experience food through a connected, multi-brand ecosystem

What were the biggest challenges you faced in building Kitopi, and how did you overcome?

One of the biggest challenges we faced was hiring too many people, too fast. Like many fast-growing startups, we thought that more people would mean faster progress. But in reality, efficiency is more important than headcount. We had to go back and reverse some of our hiring decisions, streamline operations, and focus on getting the highest productivity out of a leaner, more agile team. The key lesson here was that throwing people at a problem doesn't necessarily solve it—sometimes it just creates more complexity.

Another major challenge was balancing growth with customer centricity. As a venture-backed company, we had massive expectations to grow at an aggressive pace. But in hindsight, we weren't truly customer-obsessed in the way we thought we were. Growth sometimes came at the expense of customer experience, and that was a painful realization. We had to slow down, fix foundational issues, and rethink our entire approach to customer satisfaction. Looking back, I wish we had prioritized this earlier, even if it meant some short-term slowdowns. In a business like ours—where operational complexity is high and competition is intense—the only way to truly differentiate is by offering the best product and the best experience.

The third challenge was overexpansion. At some point, we got a bit overconfident. We believed that if we could succeed in one city, we could replicate the model anywhere. That led to one of my biggest mistakes—we expanded to three continents in just one year. We stretched ourselves too thin, opened in markets where we hadn't yet "earned the right" to be, and quickly realized that just because something works in one place doesn't mean it will work everywhere.

It was a humbling lesson, and we had to pull back from some markets.

That experience fundamentally changed how we approach expansion today. Now, we ensure that before making any major move, we set clear metrics—cultural, operational, and financial—to determine whether we've truly earned the right to scale. We don't just chase growth for the sake of it anymore. Growth is still important, but never at the expense of customer experience or internal culture.

―――――

66 GROWTH IS STILL IMPORTANT, BUT NEVER AT THE EXPENSE OF CUSTOMER EXPERIENCE OR INTERNAL CULTURE.

―――――

How did you leverage technology to scale Kitopi while keeping its core as a food business?

At its core, Kitopi has always been food company. We're not a software company per se—we don't sell tech, we extensively use technology to enable our business. That's an important distinction. The fundamentals—manufacturing, supply chain, operations—all carried over from my first business. But Kitopi had a whole new layer of complexity.

We had to build significant operational efficiency. We convinced brands to license their online business to us, allowing us to cook for multiple brands from the same kitchen using shared resources. We realized the tech to run this model didn't exist. If we could have bought an off-the-shelf solution, we would have, but it wasn't there. That's when Sam, my co-founder, played a key role in building our engineering team in Poland and they built everything from scratch.

We also wanted to scale fast. I had never raised money in my first business. Everything was bootstrapped. So when we started Kitopi, I wasn't sure—do we go slow and self-fund, or do we raise capital and scale aggressively?

That's when I went to Amir Farha, cofounder of BECO Capital and now running COTU Ventures, for advice. He laid it out for me:

Option one—scale steadily, stay in control, keep it stress-free.

Option two—go big, raise money, move fast, and face intense pressure.

At that point, we had competitors trying to copy us. My co-founders and I sat down and asked ourselves, "What do we want to do?" Without hesitation, we all agreed: we wanted to build something massive, and we wanted to do it fast.

That decision set the tone for everything that followed. And that's the journey we took. We ended up raising a lot of capital and scaling very fast. As you do that, things inevitably break. But one of the most important lessons I learned between my first and second business was the importance of building the right team.

What are your thoughts on startup fundraising in general having gone through quite a bit of yourself?

As startups, we often tend to over-celebrate capital raises. We probably should do less of that. While fundraising is critical because it fuels growth, it is not the milestone itself that defines success. What I learned through this journey is that, depending on the business model, fundraising has to be approached in a very specific way. In a model like ours—where scaling requires significant capital—the focus should be on how to raise the most amount of money in the shortest time possible, rather than getting caught up in negotiations over small valuation differences or dilution. The real way to increase ownership over time is through performance and being awarded more shares as a founder, not by holding out for slightly better terms in early funding rounds. The ability to move faster than the competition made a huge difference for us.

Another key learning from the fundraising journey was the importance of having a strong board. It's not just about assembling a board of impressive names, but about managing that board effectively. A great board isn't just helpful when things are going well. When things are smooth, everyone is clapping, everyone is aligned, and board meetings feel easy. But when things get rough, that's when the right board can make all the difference. A good board will hold you accountable in the right way, push you to think about angles you may not have considered, and help you navigate challenges. At the same time, a board should never be making decisions for the company— that is the job of the CEO and the management team.

This is something I have been very clear about from the beginning. My board's primary decision each year should be one thing: do they want to keep me as CEO, or do they want to replace me? Beyond that, their role is to challenge, consult, and provide perspective (and obviously the right governance oversight)—but not to run the company. The leadership team and I make the final calls, and I believe that is what good governance should look like. As a CEO, you have to be coachable. You have to be open to feedback, willing to listen, and ready to evolve. But you should never outsource your decision-making to a board. That's a line I've always been adamant about maintaining.

This is also why, in fundraising, choosing the right investors matters just as much as securing capital. Some investors want to be deeply involved in operations, sometimes to a level that can slow down the decision-making process. While input is valuable, a CEO has to lead. If you have the choice, always optimize for the right investors. Of course, if you're running out of capital, you take what you need to survive. But if you have the ability to be selective, reference-checking investors is crucial. Throughout my journey, I've had many founders reach out to me, asking about my experience with specific investors. As long as I have direct experience with them, I always share my honest thoughts because this transparency is critical in the founder ecosystem. Every founder should ask questions and learn from others before taking money.

What strategies have helped you run an efficient and successful fundraising process?

Fundraising should be a tightly run process. If I were to break down our playbook, the first rule is to go to market far ahead of when you actually need the money. If you wait until your back is against the wall, you're already at a disadvantage. The best time to raise is when you still have at least 12 months of runway left. Ideally, you start engaging even earlier than that. Investors are highly attuned to a company's financial position, and if they sense desperation, they will negotiate from a position of strength. No one wants to back a company that might run out of cash in a few months.

The second piece is ensuring that the story is crystal clear. One of the challenges we faced early on was that Kitopi's model could be framed in many different ways. Were we a cloud kitchen? A tech company? A logistics platform? A food brand? We had to refine our narrative to ensure our equity story was compelling, precise, and aligned with the long-term vision. Investors need a clear framework for why they should believe in your business and why now is the right time to invest.

Another learning was around working with banks. While we've worked with banks in the past and may continue to do so, I don't believe they are the determining factor in a successful raise. A big bank backing you can add credibility and structure, but ultimately, the fundraising process needs to be founder-led. A bank might improve the process marginally, but it's never the reason you succeed or fail in raising capital.

The process itself varies based on the stage of the company. It can range from a four-week sprint to a 12-week effort. If it takes longer than 12 weeks, there's usually a fundamental issue with the business that needs to be addressed. The way we approached it was to start by engaging only two or three investors for about two weeks, getting an initial pulse on the market appetite. We always wanted feedback early in the process. If the feedback was positive, we kept going. If there were concerns—whether about our unit economics, market choices, or business model clarity—we took that feedback, refined our approach, and re-entered the market stronger.

FOMO (fear of missing out) is a critical part of fundraising. If you're always raising, investors don't feel a sense of urgency. You have to create scarcity. That's why we structured our process to be time-sensitive, approaching targeted investors with a clear deadline. We knew exactly who we wanted to engage, made sure they understood that we were closing within a set timeframe, and ran a disciplined process. That's how we managed to get term sheets within a few weeks and closed most of our early rounds in under eight weeks. Every single one of our first three rounds was closed in less than eight weeks, and we kept that discipline throughout.

Before going to market, our data room was fully prepared. We had every document investors would ask for, every financial detail clear, and every scenario mapped out. From an early stage, two of our angel investors ended up joining full-time—one as our Chief Legal Officer and the other as our CFO and Co-Founder. Having an exceptional legal and finance team early on meant that when investors did due diligence, there were no surprises. They could see that our business was well-structured, our numbers were solid, and we were running a serious operation. That helped build trust.

When we raised our last round, the process was more intensive—the due diligence was far deeper, the check size was much larger, and the scrutiny was higher. But the fundamental approach remained the same: run a tight, structured process with clear timelines, manage investor expectations, and ensure that the company remains in control of the narrative.

What do you think founders often misunderstand about fundraising and scaling a venture-backed business?

Fundraising has been an essential part of Kitopi's journey, but I've learned that raising capital is not the milestone to celebrate. In MENA, and in the broader tech ecosystem, there's an overemphasis on funding rounds—almost as if raising money is an achievement in itself. But capital is just a tool. What matters is how you use it.

From the beginning, we knew that Kitopi would require significant capital to scale. Unlike my first business, which was bootstrapped, Kitopi's model needed investment to build the necessary infrastructure. The challenge was finding the right investors—people who didn't just see Kitopi as a food business, but as an entirely new category. If you take money from investors who don't fully understand your vision, you create friction down the line. We were lucky to attract backers who believed in our long-term strategy.

Each stage of fundraising came with different challenges. In the early rounds, it was about proving the model. Later, it became about demonstrating scalability and operational efficiency. As we matured, the conversation shifted toward profitability and sustainability. Fundraising isn't just about numbers—it's about having the vision, the execution capability, and the resilience to succeed.

If there's one thing I would advise founders, it's to raise money for the right reasons, not just because they can. There's a temptation to raise big rounds because it looks good on paper, but capital can also become a distraction if not deployed correctly. Fundraising is a means to an end, not the end itself. At Kitopi, we've stayed focused on the bigger picture: building a company that transforms the food industry. That's what has kept us grounded, no matter how much capital we've raised.

And the way we talk about it is through a simple example. There was a Forbes article that featured us on the cover, calling Kitopi the "Fastest growing MENA Unicorn" or something along those lines. I can't even remember the exact headline. But what stands out is that we didn't celebrate it and we didn't make it a big deal internally. The reason for that is simple. We would rather be known for building the most customer-centric organization in the world, or the most people-centric organization in the world, than for being the company that raised the most money. That title, that recognition, doesn't drive us. What drives us is something much deeper—our purpose. Kitopi exists to create joyful moments, to satisfy people's appetites, and to bring happiness through food. But to truly bring joy, the experience has to start internally. You can't create joy in the world if the people within your company don't feel a deep sense of belonging, excitement, and purpose. That has become our obsession—how do we build an organization where people are deeply engaged, where they feel like they're part of something much bigger than just another job? That's what matters.

———

> FUNDRAISING IS A MEANS TO AN END, NOT THE END ITSELF. THERE'S A TEMPTATION TO RAISE BIG ROUNDS BECAUSE IT LOOKS GOOD ON PAPER, BUT CAPITAL CAN ALSO BECOME A DISTRACTION IF NOT DEPLOYED CORRECTLY.

———

What is your vision for Kitopi's next phase, and how are you positioning the brand for the future?

Now, fast forward to chapter three in Kitopi's evolution in terms of where we are today and where we're headed next as a business. You can have the best, happiest employees in the world. You can generate the highest profits. You can achieve the best operating metrics. But the reality is, that's not how the world works. At least not from my perspective. At different points in the journey, you have to prioritize different things. The real challenge is making sure that when you do, you don't go so far in one direction that it harms you in the long term.

Sometimes I got that balance right, and sometimes I didn't. What I believe is necessary to increase the chances of getting it right is to stay deeply engaged—listening carefully, being relentlessly curious, and never assuming that you have it all figured out. Curiosity is probably one of the most important qualities any founder can have. It's what keeps you evolving, iterating, and leading effectively as the world around you changes. It's also about surrounding yourself with people who are just as opinionated, who will challenge you, and who will give you the feedback you need, not just what you want to hear. The best teams aren't built on hierarchy; they're built on trust and empowerment, where people feel confident enough to challenge decisions and push for better outcomes.

How do you ensure internal alignment as the company's priorities evolve?

Throughout Kitopi's journey, the focus has constantly shifted. At first, it was all about growth. Then, it became about people. Later, we shifted again to being customer-focused. At another point, profitability became the priority—ensuring we were cash-flow positive and financially sustainable. Then, we returned to focusing on people again, because we realized that to be truly customer-focused and profitable, we first needed to create an organization where people thrive. These shifts are constant, and there is no perfect formula.

One of the biggest realizations we had was that while we understood these trade-offs at a leadership level, the challenge was how to communicate them effectively across the company. Kitopi has over a hundred managers leading teams, and while it's easy for me and my direct leadership team to set expectations, it becomes much harder as you go down the chain. We realized we needed a framework—a set of leadership principles that would act as a guide for decision-making at every level of the company. These principles were designed to help managers understand what to prioritize when faced with a trade-off, ensuring that decisions were aligned with our core values and long-term vision.

Rolling out these leadership principles changed the way we managed complexity. They not only helped leaders across the company make better decisions, but they also gave the entire organization a framework to hold me accountable as well. It became a 360-degree system where everyone in the company understood how and why decisions were being made, which brought clarity and alignment at scale.

So, if chapter one was the cloud kitchen model and chapter two was the evolution into a house of brands, chapter three is about something even bigger. The question we're asking ourselves now is: if we open the curtain and show the world that behind all these incredible brands is Kitopi, is there something more powerful we can unlock?

How is Kitopi evolving beyond cloud kitchens and brand ownership into a fully integrated customer experience?

The journey we're on now is about creating a seamless, magical experience across all our brands, with Kitopi as the underlying brand that customers recognize and trust. But that comes with risk. If a customer has a bad experience with one of our brands, how does that impact the rest? Does it weaken the trust in the entire ecosystem? We've thought deeply about this, and while the risk is real, the upside is massive. If people begin to associate Kitopi with consistently great hospitality, if they see "Powered by Kitopi" and immediately trust that experience, then it creates a powerful flywheel. Customers will be more likely to visit multiple brands within our ecosystem, increasing loyalty and engagement.

To make this work, we're integrating the experience across all touchpoints. While we never want to commoditize the brands—each one should retain its unique identity—we are creating a shared infrastructure that enhances the customer journey. Today, when you walk into a Kitopi-powered location, you can pay with the Kitopi app, earn Kitopi loyalty points, and receive personalized service. We know your preferences—whether you don't eat beef, whether you prefer certain spice levels—and we can tailor your experience accordingly. This level of personalization is what will make Kitopi more than just a group of brands; it will make us a hospitality powerhouse.

Can you share some key metrics today?

In terms of metrics, this year we are on track to generate around $500 million in revenue. We are cash-flow positive, which is an important milestone for us. We operate over 80 brands across five countries in the GCC and processed approximately 40 million orders last year. We're growing at a rate of 25 to 30% annually and currently have over 6,000 employees at Kitopi.

How is Kitopi adapting to the rise of personalized, health-conscious, and hospitality-driven dining trends?

If I focus on the food industry, there are a few major trends we are betting on. The first is that the restaurant and hospitality space is incredibly crowded, and the players who offer the best experiences will win. This has always been true, but it's becoming even more critical. Hospitality is not inherently scalable, but those who figure out how to scale it without losing the magic of great service will dominate the industry. The businesses that can blend high-quality hospitality with scalable operations will have an undeniable advantage.

> HOSPITALITY IS NOT INHERENTLY SCALABLE, BUT THOSE WHO FIGURE OUT HOW TO SCALE IT WITHOUT LOSING THE MAGIC OF GREAT SERVICE WILL DOMINATE THE INDUSTRY.

The second major trend is the shift in how people think about healthy eating. It's no longer just about losing weight. We are at an inflection point where eating healthy is becoming the norm, and people might "cheat" only a couple of times a week rather than seeing healthy eating as an occasional choice. With that shift comes a massive opportunity—making healthy food more affordable, more accessible, and more integrated into everyday life. We're moving beyond the idea of food as just sustenance or a diet tool. More people now see food as medicine, as a way to live longer and healthier. Longevity is no longer just a concept; it's something people are actively pursuing, and food plays a central role in that. The challenge is making nutritious food taste amazing, removing the idea that healthy eating requires a sacrifice. Today, a large portion of our revenue comes from healthier dishes, and we're doubling down on expanding in that space.

The third major trend is personalization. Customers no longer want a one-size-fits-all approach to food. They expect personalized experiences—whether that means meals tailored to their dietary preferences, their health goals, or simply their taste preferences. This ties into the first two trends. As hospitality scales, it needs to remain personal. As healthy eating becomes the norm, it needs to adapt to individual needs. Personalization is at the core of the future of food, and we are working on exciting innovations in this space that we'll be unveiling in the coming months. The idea of walking into any Kitopi-powered restaurant and knowing that the food you're served is optimized for you is something we believe will be a game-changer.

How do trends in food and hospitality differ between the Middle East and other global markets?

The trends are universal, but the Middle East is probably one of the best regions in the world for consumer-facing businesses. The GCC in particular has a unique structure, where labor costs are lower than in many Western markets, which makes the unit economics far more attractive. That dynamic gives businesses here an opportunity to scale in ways that are much harder elsewhere.

So, what's next for Kitopi?

The next phase for Kitopi is about deepening our impact. We're not just scaling for the sake of growth—we're doubling down on innovation, personalization, and customer experience.

We're integrating our technology more seamlessly into the customer journey, ensuring that every Kitopi-powered brand delivers an elevated experience. Whether it's using AI to tailor menu recommendations, optimizing logistics for faster delivery, or enhancing in-store experiences, our focus remains on setting a new standard in hospitality.

We also see immense potential in expanding our healthier food offerings, leveraging data to create meals that align with customers' health goals while still delivering exceptional taste. The future of food isn't just about convenience—it's about enhancing lives.

Ultimately, our mission is to redefine how people experience food. And this is just the beginning.

Thank you, Mo, for sharing your journey. Wishing you and Kitopi continued success.

My pleasure, Amir. Thank you for the conversation.

———

ABDULAZIZ B. AL LOUGHANI

Redefining the gifting experience

Chairman and CEO of FLOWARD

FLOWARD

Riyadh, Saudi Arabia

www.floward.com

ABDULAZIZ B. AL LOUGHANI is the Chairman and CEO of Floward, the preferred online flowers and gifts destination in the MENA region and UK. Abdulaziz is also a Partner at Faith Capital, a venture capital practice that is focused on the MENA region. Abdulaziz is a member of Endeavor, a global network of high-impact entrepreneurs and is the first Kuwaiti to be selected as an Endeavor Entrepreneur.

Previously Abdulaziz was the founding Executive Vice Chairman of the Kuwait National Fund for SMEs Development, a USD 7bn independent public institution responsible for developing the entrepreneurial ecosystem in Kuwait (2013-2017). Prior to this role, he was a co-founder and CEO of Talabat until 2010 and has since then been investing in technology startups and is a member in a number of local and regional entrepreneurial and economical boards/committee/initiatives. Abdulaziz has also previously served as Director at Global Capital Management, the alternative investments arm of Global Investment House "Global", where he has played a major role in managing key investments within the Private Equity Group of Global by handling various assignments on corporate restructuring, business planning, deal structuring, due diligence and managing portfolio companies to exit.

Abdulaziz has served as an executive and member of board on a number of entities in the public sector in Kuwait and the GCC region, as well as companies in the MENA region in the technology, banking, healthcare, manufacturing, consumer finance, food & beverage, and the real estate sectors.

Abdulaziz holds a bachelor's degree – with a double major in Information Systems and E-Commerce from the University of Toledo, and an MBA degree from London Business School.

———

FLOWARD is the leading online flowers and gifting company in the Middle East and the UK. It was founded in 2017, and within five years it expanded its operations to include nine countries.

200

Floward, prides itself on creating a seamless and innovative experience for its customers and making the process of sending flowers and gifts as enjoyable as receiving them.

Floward sources its flowers daily from the best ethical growers and farmers around the world to create one of a kind stunning arrangements and plants that fit every occasion.

The company is known for its flower arrangements, but it also made great partnerships with local and international brands in all its communities to offer its clients a wide range of gifts including chocolate, perfumes, cakes, jewellery, and more.

Operating in around 40 cities in nine countries across the MENA region and London, UK, Floward guarantees same-day delivery across the board through its own refrigerated fleet to ensure that gifts and arrangements arrive fresh to the customer.

———

We covered your journey as Talabat's founder in *Startup Arabia*, but for those unfamiliar, tell us about yourself?

Thank you for having me again, Amir. I was born and raised in Kuwait, and I was fortunate enough to study for short periods abroad during my middle and high school years. More importantly, I pursued my college education in the U.S. Like many Kuwaitis at the time, I initially enrolled in business and finance—a path that seemed logical but, as life would have it, wasn't where I ended up.

Four years later, I graduated with a double major in Information Systems and E-Commerce, which was a fairly new field back then. Despite my education, I returned to Kuwait and found myself in finance, working in private equity. It seemed like all roads lead to finance. It was an unexpected turn, but one that proved invaluable. It gave me a deep understanding of finance and accounting, along with firsthand experience in scaling companies. The discipline, the structure, and the exposure to seasoned mentors in the corporate world helped shape my entrepreneurial mindset.

Beyond Kuwait, I began seeing business from a broader MENA perspective. But as I reflected on my college years, I knew I wanted to do something that merged my interests in finance and e-commerce. That intersection became the foundation of my entrepreneurial journey.

What ultimately pushed you to take the leap into entrepreneurship?

Entrepreneurship was always in my DNA. But my first attempt didn't go as planned—it barely lasted six months. That failure, however, became a stepping stone. I regrouped and soon after joined a team of co-founders at Talabat, which, at the time, was among the earliest online food delivery platforms in the world. I eventually ended up acquiring the business and became CEO.

Early on, we knew that if Talabat was going to succeed, we had to get the fundamentals right. We rebuilt the platform from the ground up, ensuring a seamless user experience. To attract restaurant partners, we leveraged personal networks and offered services for free to major chains, accelerating adoption. To drive demand, we leaned heavily into digital marketing, particularly Google Ads, targeting high-traffic events, and reinvesting our revenues to fuel our next phase of growth. In 2009, we launched the first app version of Talabat on Blackberry as well as started processing online payments, it was truly revolutionary and a great lens to look into the future. The focus was always on building a scalable foundation.

I continued as co-founder & CEO, and in 2010 passed on the baton to my partner, Mohammed Jaffar. Under his leadership, the company scaled aggressively, expanded into new markets, and ultimately caught the attention of Rocket Internet, which acquired Talabat for approximately $170 million—making it the largest tech exit in the Middle East at the time. It was a pivotal moment for the region, proving that homegrown startups could scale and exit at a global level.

After Talabat, you shifted toward venture capital and government-backed initiatives. What motivated that transition?

Indeed, I shifted into venture capital, pursuing my MBA and specializing in VC as an asset class. It was a fascinating shift because I was no longer just building one business—I was now helping many. I also had the opportunity to work with the Kuwaiti government on developing the country's entrepreneurial ecosystem, which was something I deeply cared about. Alongside others, we co-founded The National Fund for Small and Medium Enterprises Development, an institution similar to the U.S. Small Business Administration, offering funding, land access, training, and strategic support to founders. Over four years, we funded over 400 businesses and helped shift the mindset of fresh graduates from seeking jobs to creating jobs. That, for me, was a deeply fulfilling chapter.

But the pull of entrepreneurship never really left me. That's when my partner from Talabat, Mohammed Jaffar, and I started exploring new ideas. We initially launched a private VC practice, but within months, the thought of returning back to hands-on entrepreneurship came back. That's how Floward came into the picture.

Floward has grown into a major player in gifting, but how did the idea first come to you?

I stumbled upon the gifting industry almost by accident. In the Arab world, gifting isn't just a transaction—it's cultural, it's religious, it's ingrained in our way of life. No matter the economic situation, people always find a way to give—a small token of appreciation, sharing food with a neighbor, or sending flowers to mark an occasion. I saw an industry that was massive yet fragmented, without a clear leader.

At first, I was just an investor in a struggling flower business. It wasn't scaling and was seriously struggling. I saw an opportunity to pivot. I approached the investors and proposed a new direction: building a seamless, end-to-end gifting experience.

That's how Floward was born. The name itself blends "flowers" with "ward" (the Arabic word for flowers). From day one, our vision was never just about flowers; it was about revolutionizing gifting. We built Floward as a pure-play e-commerce model—sourcing flowers directly from the best farms around the world, fulfilling orders through our own fullfilment centers, and managing last-mile delivery. This ensured a superior customer experience and long-term scalability.

When you first launched, were people hesitant to buy flowers and gifts online?

The flowers industry already existed, but it was fragmented and inconvenient. There was no market leader, no brand loyalty, and online penetration was low. If I wanted to send a gift to a friend ten years ago, even in a developed market like Dubai or London, my options were limited. I'd have to call a shop, explain what I wanted, and hope they got it right. The florist might say, "I can add a chocolate box and wrap it nicely," but I wouldn't know what it looked like. I wouldn't have control over the selection or presentation. After that I would probably go to a shop and buy a gift, bundle it with the flowers and deliver it to the recipient myself. It was a hassle.

That's why Floward's marketing wasn't about creating demand from scratch—it was about solving an existing pain point. Customers immediately understood the value of what we offered because they had already experienced the problem firsthand. We weren't just selling flowers; we were delivering a seamless and elevated gifting experience.

What were some of the biggest hurdles in launching and growing Floward?

We knew the industry had its challenges. Gifting wasn't as frequent as food delivery, meaning we couldn't rely on high-frequency purchases like we did at Talabat. This meant we had to be extremely strategic in how we scaled.

In 2017, we launched in Kuwait. In 2018, we started seeing strong revenue traction. In 2019, we had a big decision to make: should we expand our product offerings or go after new markets? We ultimately chose to expand into Saudi Arabia. At the time, e-commerce penetration in Saudi was less than 1% of GDP, but with Vision 2030 rapidly transforming infrastructure, logistics, and payments, we saw a major opportunity.

My co-founder, Mohammed Al Arifi, led our expansion into Riyadh and Jeddah. Then, in early 2020, COVID-19 changed everything. While businesses worldwide were shutting down, we saw an unprecedented surge in demand. With brick-and-mortar flower shops closed, we were one of the only players operating on a pure e-commerce model.

Globally, e-commerce was experiencing a seismic shift. In just two months, U.S. e-commerce penetration grew as much as it had in the previous decade. Europe had already been ahead, and though data in MENA was scarce, we could sense the same trajectory.

We made a bold decision. We went to our investors with a clear vision: now was the time to scale aggressively. We executed a playbook based on our Saudi expansion, and in just one year, we went from operating in two cities to 17. By the following year, we were in 34 cities across five countries.

It was a defining moment for Floward. We took a calculated risk, but as the saying goes, "fortune favors the prepared." The results validated our strategy. More importantly, we had investors who believed in our vision, which allowed us to move fast.

Looking back, Floward's success wasn't just about flowers or e-commerce. It was about identifying an industry ready for transformation and executing with precision. The same principles apply to any entrepreneur: find an underserved market, build a strong foundation, and when the moment is right—scale with conviction. Back then, we had only received funding from friends and family. However, later on, we secured our first institutional investment.

I am incredibly grateful to the investors who believed in us during this pivotal moment. Impact 46 was one of them, and they doubled down on us multiple times. The way we navigated COVID-19 forced us to adapt, and in doing so, we turned challenges into opportunities. That decision proved to be highly rewarding in the long run.

As we expanded further, by 2024, we were operating in nine markets, present in nearly 40 cities, and had built a team of over 1,000 dedicated individuals—our superheroes—who played a crucial role in our success along with other leading investors including STV and Aljazira Capital. One of our proudest milestones was when Harvard Business School published a case study on Floward. That moment was a validation of everything we had worked for. It felt much like what you're doing now, Amir, with this book—capturing the journey and insights of the region's entrepreneurs. Around that same time, we recognized the true scale of our operations. In just four years, we had grown into one of the largest e-commerce players in the region.

As we grew, we continued to raise funding and were fortunate to bring on additional investors who supported our vision. However, as we scaled, we encountered an inflection point. Growth had begun to plateau. We were still expanding, but it felt as though we had hit a glass ceiling. That's when we realized that while our approach had worked to launch and skyrocket Floward, scaling a sizeable business required a different mindset and strategy.

Expanding across different markets isn't as simple as just replicating a model. How did you adapt to new regions?

Moving from Kuwait to Saudi—or entering new cities—was not as simple as copy-and-paste. Each market had its own nuances, from consumer behavior to operational challenges and regulatory regimes. One of the most critical factors in our success was partnering with the right local stakeholders. Some of these partners became integral to our operations, even though remote collaboration was initially challenging. There were team members I worked with for over a year through Zoom before meeting them in person. While digital tools helped, I personally prefer working in an office with my partners and effectively practicing the culture we have designed, so that transition was an adjustment in itself.

We followed a structured expansion playbook. Beyond favorable business regulations, two core elements contributed to our success: our team and our business model. Unlike other platforms, we controlled almost every part of our supply chain, except for growing the flowers themselves. Everything else—sourcing, storage, fulfillment, and last-mile delivery—was managed in-house.

So, you made an early decision to control your entire supply chain?

Exactly. Managing our supply chain end-to-end was a game-changer. It became one of our biggest competitive advantages. We had team members in Latin America, Africa, and Europe who helped us source the best flowers at optimal prices and terms. We partnered with airlines for transportation, handled customs clearance, and maintained climate-controlled storage facilities to preserve freshness. Different flowers required different temperature and humidity levels, so we designed specialized refrigeration systems for each type. Our florists were in-house, ensuring that every arrangement met our quality standards before being sent out for delivery.

———

" MANAGING OUR SUPPLY CHAIN END-TO-END WAS A GAME-CHANGER. IT BECAME ONE OF OUR BIGGEST COMPETITIVE ADVANTAGES.

———

On the logistics front, we took a hybrid approach. In some cases, we owned our delivery vehicles; in others, we rented or partnered with third-party providers. However, the one thing we never compromised on was customer experience. When we started, refrigerated delivery vans were almost non-existent in the region. Most logistics providers weren't equipped to transport flowers without damaging them. That's why we built our own delivery infrastructure—so we could ensure quality from start to finish.

This level of control allowed us to offer an unmatched speed, quality, and reliability. No other company in the region could guarantee flower deliveries within an hour—except Floward. It became a key differentiator and reinforced our core mission: providing a seamless and timely gifting experience.

What would you say were the key strategies that helped you build brand loyalty?

Our biggest differentiator was the experience. Marketing was just the final step; the real work was in ensuring that customers loved and trusted our service. Traditional e-commerce focuses on delivering products, but we built something much more—a personalized, curated experience.

We also innovated the sender-recipient model, which wasn't common in the industry at the time. Beyond offering a wide selection, we introduced features that made gifting more meaningful. Customers could record personalized video messages, which were embedded in a QR code printed on the gift card. During COVID-19, when people couldn't see each other in person, this feature became incredibly popular. We also digitized handwritten notes, allowing senders to create a heartfelt message without the constraints of traditional e-commerce.

All of these innovations made Floward the go-to gifting platform in the region. It wasn't just about volume—we saw repeat purchases skyrocket because people genuinely enjoyed the experience. That kind of organic growth fueled our rapid expansion.

How did you go about redefining the gifting experience for customers?

If you wanted to order something online, you'd typically deliver it to a fixed address—your own or someone else's. That meant your gift would arrive in a standard DHL or Aramex box, or some other courier service with your name on it, and it would take a few days to be delivered. We completely changed that. We eliminated the hassle for the sender by automating address collection from the recipient in a seamless way. No one else had ever done this before. There were plenty of online flower and chocolate businesses, but creating a truly integrated gifting experience was unprecedented.

All of these elements helped us become the preferred destination for gifting. It didn´t just drive volumes, we also saw an increase in engagement and repeat purchases, far beyond what we had originally expected, all of which propelled our initial massive growth.

Managing hypergrowth is a challenge for any business. How did you navigate that phase?

The truth is, neither my partners nor I had managed a company at this scale or growth rate before. We didn't fully anticipate what it would take to sustain such rapid growth. As Denzel Washington once said, "When you pray for rain, you gotta deal with the mud too." While it was raining opportunities, we were also navigating through the mud of scaling challenges.

One of the biggest internal hurdles we faced was technical debt. We had built an amazing product, but as we scaled, we started noticing cracks in our infrastructure. At the same time, we saw signs that our hypergrowth was beginning to slow. We had to step back and reassess how to evolve Floward into its next chapter. The journey wasn't just about launching a business anymore—it was about transforming it into a lasting, scalable enterprise.

We also realized that we had built so many features for customers and scaled rapidly, but we had taken shortcuts along the way.

Our infrastructure, architecture, and operational systems needed significant improvements. At the same time, we hadn't applied enough strategic thinking to our product mix. While we had a team dedicated to crafting beautiful bouquets and curating gifts, we had not systematically analyzed our pricing architecture. We weren't carefully measuring SKU distribution across price points, nor were we strategically identifying key occasions to focus on. We lacked a structured approach to determining how deep our collections should be or what percentage of our offerings should fall into different pricing tiers.

At one point, we had 20,000 SKUs and partnerships with 800 different brands, but without a clear methodology. Similarly, customer service from a technological perspective had not received enough attention, and our investment in marketing technology was also insufficient. Recognizing these gaps, we began a process of self-reflection, sought out consultants, and even restructured our C-suite to bring in the right expertise.

How did your leadership team evolve to support scaling from a startup to an enterprise?

Over the past two years, we made three significant additions to our executive team, bringing in seasoned leaders who could help us transition from a fast-growing startup to a sustainable, scalable enterprise. Our organizational structure also evolved. Initially, we operated with a highly decentralized, geography-based model, where local teams had considerable autonomy. However, as we scaled, we realized the need for a functionally structured organization that would drive greater efficiency and alignment.

At the same time, we had to reassess our internal expectations and competencies. Many of our initial assumptions about growth were either inflated or inaccurate. The challenges of scaling required a different skill set than those needed to launch and establish an early-stage business.

> THE CHALLENGES OF SCALING REQUIRED A DIFFERENT SKILL SET THAN THOSE NEEDED TO LAUNCH AND ESTABLISH AN EARLY-STAGE BUSINESS.

Did you make any major strategic shifts for long-term growth?

As we prepared for the next chapter, we prioritized key areas of improvement. First, we tackled our technical debt, ensuring our systems were both agile and stable, with best-in-class security and infrastructure. Operational efficiency became a primary focus, shifting from an aggressive growth-first mindset to one that balanced productivity and optimization.

Marketing also evolved significantly. Initially, our primary focus was digital advertising, but we realized that building a strong brand required much more. We recently launched a new brand slogan: "Unwrap Your Heart" (Arabic: "Min Al Qalb"), reinforcing our mission of creating meaningful gifting experiences.

Marketing today is far more sophisticated, brand-driven, and data-informed. Our operations are structured better, and we now have dedicated teams focused on improving customer experience, resource management, and operational efficiency. We've also started thinking more strategically about the company's lifecycle. Floward is now almost eight years old, and we have both institutional investors and early-stage backers who have supported us from the beginning.

What are your future plans regarding liquidity events like an IPO or acquisition?

As the company matures, we are naturally evaluating potential liquidity events. Investor expectations are increasing, and we are considering options such as an IPO or a trade sale. Given the recent success of regional companies going public, we see this as a strong possibility within the next 12 to 24 months.

For us, an exit is not about stepping away—it's about creating a liquidity event for our shareholders while remaining committed to Floward's long-term vision. We are already operating in nine markets, and there is significant potential for further expansion.

Can you share any non-confidential metrics to illustrate Floward's scale?

A few years ago, we were generating around $95 million in revenue, growing at approximately 4X year over year, with healthy gross margins of around 33%. At that time, we had 600 team members and over 400,000 customers across nine markets: Saudi Arabia, Kuwait, UAE, Qatar, Bahrain, Oman, Egypt, Jordan, and the UK. Our primary categories remain flowers, confectioneries, and health and beauty, and other smaller categories.

Did you say the UK?

Yes, the UK is an adjacent market for us. The majority of our orders originate from the region. For example, if someone in the UK receives an order, it is usually placed by someone in the Middle East. While orders are placed globally, the recipient is often based in the UK.

So the recipient in the UK and are orders also placed in the UK?

That's right—the recipient is in the UK, but the majority of orders are placed from outside the country, primarily from the region. This trend reinforces our approach to market expansion. Rather than focusing on geographic expansion, our priority is strengthening operational efficiency and enhancing the customer experience in our existing markets. We believe there's still significant room for growth by optimizing our current footprint before considering new markets.

What led you to prioritize efficiency over expansion?

We believe that optimizing our existing markets presents the best opportunity for growth right now. There is still significant untapped potential within our current footprint, and refining our experience allows us to maximize value before expanding further.

What were the challenges in transitioning from a geographically-driven structure to a function-driven one?

As companies grow, especially from an early-stage startup, managing that expansion becomes challenging when too many functions are decentralized. In the initial phase, autonomy and local empowerment are necessary, allowing markets to operate with flexibility. However, as we scaled and emphasized brand consistency, we realized that a functional structure was needed to ensure long-term growth.

How did you manage that shift from decentralized to centralized operations?

This transition required significant change management. Many teams were accustomed to making independent decisions based on what they believed was best for their market. Moving to a structured decision-making process, with key gatekeepers ensuring alignment, was a cultural shift.

As a result, we standardized our product offerings, collections, photography, branding, marketing, fulfillment, and customer touchpoints. Implementing this level of centralization took time, and some elements are still evolving. However, as we continue consulting experts and learning from our own scaling experiences, we are increasingly convinced that a centralized approach is the best way forward.

Were there other areas where early-stage strategies became counterproductive as you scaled?

Culture is one of the most critical aspects of scaling. Early on, when you're a small team of five or twenty people working out of a tiny office, culture forms organically. Everyone is aligned, collaborating closely, sometimes even working overnight to get things done. It's an electric atmosphere.

But as you transition into a multinational company, that culture doesn't scale on its own. It has to be intentionally nurtured and embedded into the organization's operations. Culture cannot be left to chance—it must be deliberately designed and reinforced to maintain alignment as the company grows.

Another key lesson is in development. Taking shortcuts always comes back to bite you.

Quick fixes may work temporarily, but when you scale, those same shortcuts create technical debt that eventually must be addressed. Designing systems and experiences with long-term scalability in mind is crucial. Unfortunately, many startups only realize this when they hit a wall.

———

" QUICK FIXES MAY WORK TEMPORARILY, BUT WHEN YOU SCALE, THOSE SAME SHORTCUTS CREATE TECHNICAL DEBT THAT EVENTUALLY MUST BE ADDRESSED.

———

What's your one advice for a founder preparing to scale?

It's crucial to choose the right partners. And by partners, I mean team members as well. These people are your co-founders in spirit, even if they don't hold that formal title. You need an honest and transparent relationship with all stakeholders.

When working with investors, always leave some money on the table to ensure a true win-win relationship. The road to success is never smooth—there will be downturns, and having a financial cushion can make all the difference. Investors are placing their trust in you, and maintaining that trust, even in difficult times, is critical. You want them to feel that their investment is secure and well-managed.

What are the biggest pitfalls founders should avoid when scaling?

One of the biggest mistakes is not fully understanding unit economics. Many founders underestimate the importance of both short-term and long-term unit economics. Strong unit economics ensure resilience— even in tough macroeconomic conditions, companies with solid fundamentals survive, and in favorable conditions, they thrive. A deep understanding of unit economics influences every aspect of your company—from structuring operations to setting up OKRs to building your team. If you truly understand what each function contributes to your overall economic model, you can identify inefficiencies and make the necessary adjustments before they become major issues.

Being a founder, a VC, and being involved with the government, how do you see the evolution of the regional startup ecosystem?

The biggest game changers I've seen—and what I hope to see more of—have shaped my overall perspective on the startup ecosystem. Looking at the past 20 years, I believe we are fortunate to be witnessing this era.

The Arab world is far more connected than it used to be, and inshallah, more peaceful as well. With greater geopolitical stability, we will see even more progress. From a macro perspective, we are in a fortunate position. Much of what has been achieved in the past happened despite immense challenges—fragmented markets, economic barriers, and regulatory complexities. Now, as markets become more interconnected and economies more homogeneous, the opportunities are even greater.

As the total addressable market (TAM) grows, we are seeing increased government support. A decade ago, there were only a handful of accelerators; today, we have a vast network of investors, incubators, and accelerators, many of which now specialize in different stages of the funding cycle.

How has the funding landscape changed for startups in the region?

The funding landscape is significantly better than it was. Today, we have more experienced fund managers who understand the gaps in the asset class and the industry as a whole. Investors today are more mindful of the skill sets required and the value they expect from founders. Founders are also more experienced and are also demanding higher standards of what to expect from investors. This gives me optimism.

The digital economy in the region is growing at an unprecedented rate and will likely continue to do so. Over the next two to five years, I expect e-commerce penetration to grow faster than in most developed markets. Currently, only about 3 to 4% of our economy is online, meaning there is still tremendous potential. I remain bullish on digital commerce and the broader digital economy.

How has the startup ecosystem matured at large?

As you mentioned earlier, some of us now have a few more grey hairs— or, in some cases, no hair at all. I think this reflects the maturity of the founders in the region. More experienced founders are emerging, and this will lead to businesses that operate more strategically rather than focusing solely on exits or liquidity events driven by investor expectations. With this level of maturity, I believe we will see regional startups grow into long-term strategic players in key industries. We are already seeing this shift.

Would you say lack of sufficient growth capital is still a major hurdle for startups looking to scale in the region?

Yes, growth capital remains a challenge. Additionally, we don't see enough strategic investors emerging from the Arab world. Growth capital can certainly help fill that gap. Foreign direct investment (FDI) into the region exists, but it remains very limited. There are legal, TAM and structural reasons for this that must be addressed to attract more international capital.

How do regulatory complexities impact venture investment, particularly from international investors?

One of the key challenges in the region remains our legal and regulatory frameworks. Different countries have vastly different laws, and they are not always venture-friendly or conducive to growth capital investment. If we want to attract more FDI (Foreign Direct Investment), we need to rethink how our legal structures are designed. More harmonized regulations across the region would make investing in the Arab world far more predictable and attractive. Right now, most of the capital entering the region comes in the form of buyouts rather than growth investments.

———

66 IF WE WANT TO ATTRACT MORE FDI (FOREIGN DIRECT INVESTMENT), WE NEED TO RETHINK HOW OUR LEGAL STRUCTURES ARE DESIGNED.

———

Why do many strategic investors prefer acquisitions over growth capital then?

Strategic investors prefer to acquire already-established companies rather than invest in their growth because they want to minimize scalability risk. This is a fundamental issue. I don't see foreign growth capital as a silver bullet solution, but I do believe we will see more buyouts as regional companies scale. As growth capital becomes more accessible, it will help build category-leading companies in the region, which in turn will attract more private equity and strategic investment.

Can governments play a role in supporting growth capital?

Yes, absolutely. Growth capital has evolved, but it has faced ups and downs. Over the past decade, we haven't seen significant growth capital investment in the region, but I am optimistic that this will change in the next phase. The early-stage investments made in regional startups need to be backed by growth capital to help them scale into global or regional powerhouses.

Governments have already played a major role in subsidizing venture capital investment in the region, directly or indirectly. The VC ecosystem in the Middle East has largely developed on the back of strong government support. However, to complete the value chain, there needs to be a greater focus on growth capital. This is an area where governments can step in to provide additional support.

What lessons can be learned from Talabat's and other recent IPOs in the region?

The recent IPOs of regional startups show that companies here can achieve world-class economic models. I have a soft spot for one of them, of course—my old company, Talabat.

One of the region's unique advantages is that we operate with third-world costs but deliver first-world services. This combination enables us to achieve unparalleled unit economics compared to other markets. With strong founders and well-structured businesses, I am confident that more regional champions will emerge in select verticals in the near future, inshallah.

———

  ONE OF THE REGION'S UNIQUE ADVANTAGES IS THAT WE OPERATE WITH THIRD-WORLD COSTS BUT DELIVER FIRST-WORLD SERVICES.

———

On behalf of regional entrepreneurs, thank you for your efforts and contributions to the startup ecosystem in the Arab world.

Thank you again, Amir, for the opportunity to be featured in your book. Your books provide a bird's-eye view of the region's startup evolution, capturing its growth over the years. Keep up the great work.

———

MICHAEL LAHYANI

Revolutionizing real estate classifieds

Founder and CEO of PROPERTY FINDER

Dubai, UAE

www.propertyfinder.com

MICHAEL LAHYANI is the visionary Founder and CEO of Property Finder, a company that revolutionized the real estate landscape in the MENA region. Responsible for launching the region's first real estate classifieds platform in 2007, he has since been instrumental in securing major international investments that have propelled both the company and the broader property market forward.

In 2024, Property Finder secured $90 million in debt financing while executing a strategic buyback of shares from early investor BECO Capital, a move that underscored strong investor confidence. This follows a landmark $120 million investment in 2018 from General Atlantic, a US private equity firm, cementing Property Finder's position as a tech leader and a magnet for global capital.

Michael's leadership is defined by a sharp focus on data, digital transformation, tech, trust and talent in real estate. His influence has earned him a place on Forbes Middle East's Top 100 CEOs and Property Finder's success is studied as a Harvard Business School case study, a testament to its global impact.

A graduate of HEC Lausanne with a bachelor's degree and MBA in finance, Michael was the first entrepreneur from the region selected by Endeavor, a global network of high-impact entrepreneurs. Passionate about fostering the region's startup ecosystem, he actively mentors young founders.

Recognizing his contributions, Michael, a Swiss national, was honoured with the prestigious UAE passport in 2020, a reflection of his lasting impact on the region's business landscape.

––––––

PROPERTY FINDER is building a lighthouse company that is spearheading the region's nascent tech ecosystem, creating an inclusive environment for people – its employees, consumers and partners – to thrive. At its core is a clear and powerful purpose: to change living for good in the region.

It is the #1 destination for home seekers whether buying, renting, or investing in the MENAT region. Established in 2007, the platform connects millions of property seekers with thousands of real estate professionals, shaping the future of real estate through trust, talent, and tech. With 10 million visitors per month and 700,000 homes listed on its platform, it's the most trusted and widely used property portal in the region.

Headquartered in Dubai, UAE, the company operates in a number of key markets, including Riyadh (Saudi Arabia), Cairo (Egypt), Doha (Qatar) and Manama (Bahrain), and maintains a deep understanding of regional real estate trends. This expertise has made the platform the go-to reference for both local and international property seekers.

Beyond this, Property Finder has grown into one of the largest tech employers in MENAT, with more than 600 employees representing over 40 nationalities. Half of its workforce consists of engineers, underscoring the company's strong commitment to cutting-edge technology, data analytics, and continuous innovation. The company attracts top talent and places a strong emphasis on its people and workplace culture, nurturing an environment where employees are encouraged to be their best selves. They are empowered to create, elevate, grow, and care. The team is united by the shared ambition to change living for good in the region.

The company's business model is built around innovative subscription-based services and data-driven solutions. Real estate agents, brokers, and developers use the platform to list properties, providing users with a comprehensive and up-to-date selection of homes for sale, rent and investment. In addition to its core listing services, Property Finder generates revenue through premium advertising, where agencies and developers can enhance the visibility of their properties. The platform also provides valuable market data and analytics tools, offering insights to real estate professionals, investors, and government entities to support data-backed decision-making and improve transparency in the industry.

With a strong focus on digital innovation, Property Finder has developed key services that enhance the real estate experience through websites, mobile applications, and real estate management tools.

They empower real estate professionals with exclusive tools like PF Expert 2.0, ensure best-in class service via SuperAgents, and deliver industry-first Data Insights to support both customers and consumers in their decision making. Its portal leverages AI insights built on more than two decades of industry expertise, ensuring home seekers find their ideal home through a trusted platform. As a consumer-centric organization, its technology is designed to evolve with consumers' and customers' needs and deliver a seamless experience supporting one of life's most important decisions, whether renting, buying or investing.

Under the leadership of Founder and CEO Michael Lahyani, Property Finder continues to expand its influence in the real estate portal space. Supported by a team of industry leaders with expertise in technology, strategy, and real estate, the company remains committed to transforming the property search experience while driving forward the digital evolution of real estate across the MENAT region. With a clear vision and a dedication to innovation, Property Finder is shaping the future of real estate, setting new benchmarks for efficiency, transparency, and accessibility.

———

Can you give us a quick background on your journey?

Sure. It's good to be with you, Amir. My life began in Geneva, Switzerland, in 1980. I grew up in a loving family with my parents and my brother, living on the border of Lake Geneva. I attended international schools, which exposed me to a multicultural environment early on. Sports played a huge role in my life—I was heavily into martial arts and competed nationally in karate. I was always competitive, whether in sports or academics, and I guess now in business.

I studied at HEC Lausanne, just outside Geneva, before deciding to up sticks in my final year and head to UCLA in Los Angeles. That experience was a massive eye-opener for me. Coming from a relatively small city like Geneva, arriving in a place like Los Angeles at 21 years old completely changed my perspective. It made me realize how vast the world really is and how much opportunity there is to explore.

I could have stayed in the U.S., but in the wake of September 11th, the job market had gone quiet. So, I returned to Geneva, where my father—having invested heavily in my education—gently but firmly urged me to put it to good use. While the entrepreneurial itch was already there, I took his advice and stepped into the world of corporate finance. I joined PwC as a consultant, specializing in company valuation and M&A advisory, gaining firsthand experience in the mechanics of business growth and strategy.

How did your first entrepreneurial experience come about?

It didn't take long for me to realize that the corporate world wasn't for me. The rigid structure felt limiting—I wanted to move faster, think bigger, and do more. So, I launched a side hustle—a magazine dedicated to equestrian sports like polo, racing, and show jumping. At the time, I was dating someone deeply involved in the sport, and what started as a passion project quickly became my first real business venture.

Ironically, that magazine is what ultimately led me to Dubai. One day, my uncle, an entrepreneur already living in the city, called me out of the blue. He had just landed a major contract with Nakheel for the piling work on Palm Island and was buzzing with excitement. "You have to come see this place," he said. "The projects here are unbelievable. You'll love it." And just like that, my journey to Dubai began.

Did you know much about Dubai before that call?

Not really. I didn't even know where it was on the map. Inspired by my uncle's call, I decided to visit, and when I arrived, I was completely blown away. The energy of the city reminded me of what people described as the "American Dream" in the '80s and '90s. But this was different—this was the "Dubai Dream." Everyone I met had a story of ambition, success, and relentless optimism. People weren't just welcoming—they were daring me to start a business here.

My uncle took me on a whirlwind tour of sales centers for developers like Dubai Holdings and Emaar. None of their projects were completed yet, but their model displays painted a vision of the future. I looked around and thought: If even a fraction of this gets built, this city is going to be extraordinary.

One night, he took me to the horse races at Nad Al Sheba (now Meydan), where I met Ali Albawardy, the owner of Spinneys supermarket and Desert Palm. He spotted my equestrian magazine and asked, "What's this?" When I told him I was the publisher, he immediately asked where he could get a copy. I explained it was only available in Switzerland. Without missing a beat, he said, "Why don't you launch it here?"

I hadn't even considered it before, but the next day, Ali took me to his polo fields at Desert Palm and made a compelling case—Dubai was the perfect market for equestrian content. When I returned to Switzerland, I pitched the idea to one of my top advertisers, Rolex. Their response? A resounding yes. They were ready to advertise in the Dubai edition, even though it didn't exist yet. That vote of confidence was all I needed to launch Equestrio Arabia in 2004.

For a year, I commuted between Switzerland and Dubai, torn between two worlds. But it quickly became clear—in Switzerland, everything was already built. If you weren't a doctor, lawyer, or banker, your path was set. Dubai, on the other hand, was still being shaped, full of opportunity for those willing to take a risk. I knew immediately that my next business would be in Dubai.

How did you come up with the idea for Property Finder?

At first, I was staying with my uncle in Nad Al Hamar, near Mirdif. However, as I settled into Dubai, I really needed my own place. When I asked around about renting an apartment, the responses shocked me: "Just drive around looking for signs," or "Go into building lobbies and ask the watchman." I was shocked. I thought, "That's how people find homes here?"

A few people mentioned that there was a real estate supplement in Gulf News, so I picked up a copy. I was confronted with 120 pages of listings, without any categorization or obvious search function. Real estate agencies crammed their properties onto full-page ads, each designed differently, with no consistency. If I wanted a two-bedroom on Sheikh Zayed Road, for example, I had to comb through all 120 pages manually. It was a chaotic, frustrating mess.

That frustration became my first major pain point—struggling to find an apartment and not even having a proper medium to search for one.

I kept asking around and searching, but the answers were always the same: "Either drive around, check Gulf News, or let me give you the number of someone who might help." Then that person would give me another number, and then another, creating an endless loop of frustration.

Then it hit me—there was a massive gap in the market. Dubai was booming—Marina, Palm Jumeirah, Downtown Burj Khalifa—all these developments were on the rise, but there was no structured way to buy or rent the properties.

That's when the idea to launch a business with a better user experience was born. I called my best friend from university and asked him if he wanted to join me in the adventure. He suggested conducting a market study to assess if it would be feasible, and the idea snowballed from there.

Our research raised concerns. In 2005, internet penetration in the region was below 40%. In Switzerland, where I was from, real estate classifieds were just emerging online. Could we make a website work in Dubai when internet adoption was still low?

Worse, digital advertising was a foreign concept to real estate agents. "A website? Sure. But you want me to pay for that? I need to see something printed." If I wanted to create a better experience, I had to start offline.

I had experience in publishing, so I decided to launch a real estate magazine. But it had to be structured—not just a chaotic collection of listings. I color-coded Dubai: Downtown was blue, Marina was purple, Jumeirah was green. Each area had a dedicated section in the magazine, making searching effortless. At the front, a large, easy-to-read map helped guide readers. I built a prototype and pitched it to real estate agents. Their response? Overwhelmingly positive. "If you launch this, we're in. We want to advertise." That was all the validation I needed.

But I wanted more than just a magazine. I needed a tech foundation. Instead of manually collecting listings, I asked agencies to upload them digitally. This got them used to inputting listings online, laying the groundwork for a future digital platform.

Now, I had to decide on frequency. "Should it be monthly?" That seemed too slow, as listings would become outdated quickly. "Should it be weekly?" That would be too demanding in terms of printing and distribution. The right balance seemed to be every two weeks.

To ensure a good return, I estimated the number of copies needed. I analyzed population dynamics, the number of properties, and overall demand. I concluded that 70,000 copies every two weeks would generate the necessary traction.

Next, I had to decide what to call it. I wanted a local name, something with an Arabic touch. I liked the word Albab, which means "door" in Arabic. It made sense for a real estate magazine. But Albab. com was already taken.

At the time, when a domain was unavailable, suggestions would pop up: "How about Albab.net? AlbabWorld?" That's when it struck me: "Albab World—it sounds like 'the door to the world,' a mix of Arabic and English." I registered AlbabWorld.com and decided to launch the magazine under that name.

From the start, I envisioned this evolving into an online marketplace. My hope was that people would pick up the magazine, visit the website, and gradually transition to using it digitally. Over time, the magazine would become unnecessary, and I would be able to shift to an entirely digital model.

In November 2005, Albab World hit the stands—70,000 copies, strategically placed in hotels, building entrances, Spinneys supermarkets, and even through door-to-door drops. The response was immediate. Agents saw their phones light up with inquiries and clamored to book space in the next issue. That's how the business took off.

We were gaining traction. But then, we woke the sleeping giant.

What were some of the challenges you faced in those early days?

Finding office space in Dubai back then was incredibly difficult. Commercial space was in short supply. Many residential buildings were being converted into offices. Our first office was in Sheikh Zayed Road's Sheikh Eissa Tower—a two-bedroom apartment that we had turned into a workspace. It felt more like working from someone's home, but it worked for us.

The early days were thrilling. The magazine became a massive success and caught the attention of Gulf News, which quickly recognized that we were capturing market share. Gulf News had exclusivity agreements with advertisers and started calling our clients, warning them that if they advertised with Albab World, they would revoke their discounts and charge full price retroactively.

That was a doomsday moment. One-third of our advertisers panicked and canceled.

This was a real test. I could have walked away. The internet wasn't big enough yet. Gulf News had locked the market. It was impossible to compete. But I had moved to Dubai and put my entire savings into this business. Giving up wasn't an option. Could resilience push us forward?

I firmly believe that entrepreneurship is about resilience. Business is never a straight line. There are ups, downs, and a fair share of luck involved. Hard work and resilience are key, but luck also plays a role.

And as they say, "Luck favors the hardworking."

Just as we were on the verge of shutting down, we received a fax from the Australian consulate.

REA Group, a leading online property portal, was looking to enter the region. They were a publicly listed company and saw potential in what we were building. For me, that was our turning point. If I hadn't kept pushing for a year despite all the setbacks, we wouldn't have been in a position to seize that opportunity. The partnership with REA Group gave us the funding we needed to survive and eventually transition from a print magazine to a fully online real estate marketplace.

Over the years, this resilience has defined Property Finder's journey. We didn't just survive—we found a way to scale despite the odds, turning a simple real estate magazine into the region's leading digital property marketplace.

What were the biggest lessons and strategies that shaped your journey during that period?

There were so many—from resilience and grit to being able to hold your nerve when the chips are down. One lesson that truly stands out for me, and one I want to share with new founders, is to look beyond just funding. Focus on sustainability.

Many entrepreneurs make the mistake of copying businesses simply because they secured funding. Raising a Series A isn't success—it's just the start. The real test is whether a company can scale profitably.

———

MANY ENTREPRENEURS MAKE THE MISTAKE OF COPYING BUSINESSES SIMPLY BECAUSE THEY SECURED FUNDING. RAISING A SERIES A ISN'T SUCCESS—IT'S JUST THE START. THE REAL TEST IS WHETHER A COMPANY CAN SCALE PROFITABLY.

———

Too often, founders chase models that look promising on paper, only to realize years later that the company they emulated shut down due to poor unit economics. Funding alone doesn't validate a business—sustainability does.

And then there's the impact. Scaling isn't just about numbers; it's about the people—customers, users, and the team behind it all. The influence we've had at Property Finder, both in shaping the real estate industry and the lives of the people working here, has been more rewarding than I ever imagined. That's what makes the journey all the more worth it.

How did you assess whether your business could be sustainable in the long term?

I was able to evaluate this early on because REA Group was a publicly listed company. In 2007, REA Group nearly reached $100 million in revenue with 20% profit margins, all while experiencing remarkable growth. According to the latest available data, REA Group's revenue has grown to approximately $1.13 billion USD, with an EBITDA margin of about 55%. This substantial growth underscores the scalability and profitability of their business model, reinforcing the potential for similar success in the Middle East, where the larger population presents a significant opportunity.

When REA Group invested in us, they acquired 51% of the company, as strategic investors prefer a majority stake to consolidate. Beyond the funding, I gained invaluable knowledge from them. I traveled to Australia and observed how they operated their platform, which gave me deep insights into their business model.

The success of this kind of business comes down to a few core factors: it's a B2B subscription model, meaning it generates recurring revenue with high predictability. Additionally, it has high margins because we aren't dealing with inventory or the cost of goods like in e-commerce. Gross margins are around 99%.

That forms a moat around the business, making it incredibly resilient. Given that REA Group built a $100 million business in a country with a population of 25 million at the time—today, this business is worth approximately $19.15 billion—I knew we could replicate that success in the Middle East, where the population was ten times larger. While GDP per capita in the region may not be as high as Australia's, the sheer population size presented a massive opportunity.

I closely followed REA Group as a North Star, tracking their stock and progress. Having a North Star is critical because, during downturns, it helps reaffirm that what you're building is viable. Without that confirmation, pushing through becomes much more difficult.

It was also incredibly fortuitous to have built my business in Dubai, where visionary leadership has created an environment that fosters innovation and success. Here, entrepreneurs are celebrated, and regulators clear the way for growth.

In addition, we've always believed that our success at Property Finder is intrinsically tied to that of our partners—real estate agents and developers. When they thrive, we thrive. That's why we are committed to working exclusively with licensed brokers, ensuring a high level of professionalism and trust in the market. We prioritize quality and transparency, reinforcing the strength of our ecosystem.

This approach has allowed us to build a platform that not only drives business but also elevates the entire real estate industry. When the ecosystem flourishes, it benefits everyone—agents, buyers, sellers, and the broader economy.

What other advice would you give to founders?

If there's one thing I'd tell aspiring entrepreneurs, it's to start young.

I launched my business at 25, and that timing was a massive advantage. The opportunity cost at that age is much lower than when you hit 30 or beyond. By then, many people have commitments— relationships, marriage, children—and a startup demands resilience, long-term focus, and financial sacrifices.

When you're young, you can afford to live frugally. I didn't need a big salary, I was living alone, keeping my expenses low, and reinvesting everything back into the business. Too many founders struggle because they're already accustomed to a certain lifestyle, which adds unnecessary pressure.

Another advantage? Naivety.

Most people think they need years of corporate experience before launching a startup. In reality, structured environments often teach the wrong lessons for entrepreneurship. Corporate life is predictable, whereas startups are pure chaos. If you've spent too much time in a system that rewards caution, you might not understand or have experienced the upside of taking calculated risks. Honestly, if I had known just how difficult this journey would be, I probably wouldn't have started. Only a masochist would knowingly choose this path.

It's far harder than I ever imagined, but the rewards—both financially and personally—have been greater than I expected.

So, if you have an idea, start now. The perfect time will never come, but the younger you are, the more you can afford to take the risk.

> So; if you have an idea, start now. The perfect time will never come, but the younger you are, the more you can afford to take the risk.

If you could go back, what's something you wish you had known?

I often get asked this, and honestly, I don't know if I wish I had known certain things. But one key takeaway is that everything takes three times longer than you expect. If you think you'll reach your goal in five years, it will likely take 15. Building a successful business requires time—far more than most people anticipate.

Let's talk about scaling in different markets. What were some early challenges?

One of the biggest challenges in the early days was educating customers about digital advertising. Back then, digital advertising was viewed with skepticism—similar to how AI is perceived today. It was a new concept, and real estate agents didn't believe in it.

We had to convince agents that online platforms could generate better leads than traditional methods. Buyers researching properties online were more informed and made decisions faster, meaning agents could close deals more efficiently. However, many old-school agents resisted change, so we spent years educating the market.

We decided to raise funding after I bought out REA Group. In 2008–09, during the financial crisis, REA Group wanted us to cut costs and break even. Their solution was to fire 80% of the team, but I was completely against it. I believed in the market and saw an opportunity.

At that time, registered agents needed our support because Gulf News wasn't offering flexible payment terms, and many were breaking their contracts, looking for alternatives. I knew that if we stayed in the market and supported them, we could capture that demand.

However, REA Group had a new CEO and wasn't interested in my strategy. They wanted to cut costs at all costs. So, I proposed an alternative: I told them, "If we're not aligned, why don't you buy me out?" They declined. Then I said, "Well, how about I buy you out?" Surprisingly, they were open to the idea.

We negotiated, and I bought back the company at a much lower price than what they had paid two years earlier—because it was during the crisis.

This was a defining moment for me. I was only 27 years old, negotiating with a major strategic investor. One of the legal loopholes that worked in my favor was that having my name on the UAE trade license meant they couldn't remove me as the general manager without my signature. A local lawyer advised me about this, and it gave me a strong negotiation advantage.

After the buyout, the market rebounded faster than expected. We signed up new real estate agencies, reached profitability, and then decided to raise funds to expand further. Investors kept telling me, "Dubai is too small—you need to scale across the region." That's when we looked at expanding into Qatar—a smaller but viable market where we successfully replicated our business model.

As we grew in confidence again, we decided to open in six markets. Very quickly, we expanded, but that added a lot of complexity to the operation. I don't think we would have survived if we hadn't already been the leading player in the UAE and if we weren't profitable there.

I always tell founders who want to expand into another market— don't do it just to plant a flag. Sure, it's great for internal excitement, PR, and brand visibility, but you really need to ensure that you've maximized growth in your home market first. If your business is still bleeding cash domestically and you rush into multiple new markets, that's a recipe for disaster. Expansion should be sequential and supported by a profitable core business that can fund international growth. Fortunately, the UAE was profitable enough for us, which meant that we could afford to invest a little in other markets.

> *EXPANSION SHOULD BE SEQUENTIAL AND SUPPORTED BY A PROFITABLE CORE BUSINESS THAT CAN FUND INTERNATIONAL GROWTH.*

That said, operating in multiple countries brings a whole new level of complexity—from a product perspective, a management perspective, and a legal and corporate standpoint. The talent required to manage a multi-market operation is very different from what you need for a single-market business.

On that point about expanding into new markets, how do you decide which market to enter next?

A few key factors influence market selection. First, you want to prove that your business model works in another market. That means choosing a market that isn't too different from your home market. For example, expanding from the UAE to Egypt would be a big leap due to the vast differences. Moving into Qatar made sense because it's also an expat-driven market with a high GDP fueled by natural resources.

However, Qatar isn't a game-changer in terms of total addressable market. The move was more about proving that our model could succeed elsewhere. What really mattered to me was whether these markets had an established online portal. I was observing REA Group in Australia, a publicly listed company, and seeing their numbers daily. I realized that owning the number one real estate portal in any given market could be a highly lucrative business on its own.

A major advantage in building a marketplace is being the first mover. That's a massive competitive edge. We were able to enter these markets as the first real estate portal, and even today, it's incredibly difficult for competitors to challenge us in places like Qatar, Bahrain, and Egypt. The first brand that real estate agents adopt and consumers browse becomes deeply entrenched. Disrupting that position would take tens, if not hundreds, of millions of dollars in marketing.

It sounds like you didn't follow a strict scientific approach per se. Was your decision-making more opportunistic?

Yes, we didn't have a rigid formula. We primarily looked for markets where our business model didn't yet exist. We also considered personal preferences—markets we felt comfortable operating in, places that were safe, had reasonable population sizes, and strong GDPs.

Then we assessed whether real estate transactions were happening at scale. We needed to ensure that brokers were consistently earning commissions of 2–3% per transaction. That was crucial because our customers were real estate agents. If brokers in a given market weren't able to charge a percentage-based commission, the pool of revenue we were targeting wouldn't be large enough.

For instance, in Morocco, we found that the real estate industry was dominated by simsars—small independent agents who helped people find apartments for a flat fee, often as low as $50. They weren't collecting a percentage commission, which meant the market wasn't structured in a way that supported our business model. Understanding these nuances was critical.

Did you ever make mistakes in market selection?

In hindsight, we expanded into too many markets too quickly. That meant we had to raise more funding than we initially planned because brand-building in markets like Egypt required significant marketing investment. Eventually, we decided to pull out of Morocco and Lebanon.

Looking back, we should have conducted deeper market studies to analyze how real estate agents transacted, the geopolitical stability, market size, and language dynamics. Morocco and Lebanon had significant differences from our core markets. They included French as a primary language alongside Arabic and English, which added another layer of complexity.

At one point, we were operating in eight markets, but that was too much. You don't need eight markets; you need two or three that perform exceptionally well. So, we chose to double down on Egypt and the UAE, where we built a highly successful business.

> YOU DON'T NEED EIGHT MARKETS; YOU NEED TWO OR THREE THAT PERFORM EXCEPTIONALLY WELL.

Shifting gears to talent. How did your approach to hiring change as your company scaled?

The talent journey is very tricky. In the early stages, we couldn't afford to pay top-tier talent, so we hired people from personal networks—people I trusted, but not necessarily those with the right experience for scale.

The game-changer came in 2019 when we secured a $120 million investment from General Atlantic, a top-tier U.S.-based private equity firm. That investment fundamentally changed the type of talent we could attract.

People working in large global tech companies like Facebook, Google, or Amazon are often hesitant to leave stable jobs to join a startup. Founders, by nature, are a little crazy, and it's risky to work for someone with an unproven business. But when an institutional investor with a strong reputation backs your company, it reassures top-tier talent that your business has governance, funding, and stability.

Before that investment, I struggled to attract executives from these big organizations. Afterward, headhunters could finally get top candidates to take my calls. The executives we hired post-General Atlantic had seen what great looks like. They could quickly identify inefficiencies in our operation and pinpoint what needed to be fixed to scale effectively. As a founder, if I haven't seen what great looks like, I might think something is good when it's actually just okay. Bringing in seasoned executives meant we could elevate the business much faster.

However, hiring talent from large corporations also comes with challenges. They bring experience, but they also come with ingrained habits from their previous organizations. That can sometimes clash with the fast-moving startup culture.

How did you manage that cultural shift as your company grew?

That's one of the hardest aspects of scaling—ensuring that your company culture evolves without losing its core essence. As you grow, you must introduce processes and professional management, but you don't want to become just another corporate entity and lose the agility and passion that made you successful in the first place.

Your culture is something your customers can feel, and it's a big part of what keeps employees motivated. Balancing that while scaling is a challenge, but it's essential if you want to sustain long-term success.

———

"
YOUR CULTURE IS SOMETHING YOUR CUSTOMERS CAN FEEL, AND IT'S A BIG PART OF WHAT MAKES EMPLOYEES MOTIVATED. BALANCING THAT WHILE SCALING IS A CHALLENGE, BUT IT'S ESSENTIAL IF YOU WANT TO SUSTAIN LONG-TERM SUCCESS.

———

You had to reinvent yourself, you couldn't run the business the same as before. Can you talk about that transition?

When you're leading as a founder, especially in the early days before General Atlantic invested, everything was culture-driven. There were very few processes, very little company rhythm, and limited democratization of data across the organization. I had the vision, I knew where we were going, and I called the shots. Everyone was behind me, following that vision.

At some point, you hit a glass ceiling. Your instincts are no longer enough. You need data and expertise in specific fields to continue scaling. That's when you must reinvent yourself. You can't lead an experienced leader the same way you lead an early-stage startup team. I had to work on myself extensively to transition out of that pure founder mode and grow into the role of a full-fledged CEO—someone who manages functional leaders with more expertise in their respective areas than I'll ever have.

As a founder, you must provide these leaders with breathing room. You need to articulate the strategy clearly, ensure they understand the company's direction, and get their full buy-in. Founders are naturally ambitious, but seasoned professionals tend to be more skeptical, so you have to sell them on your vision and make sure they believe in it.

There's no playbook for this transition. I recently took part in a 360-degree feedback review, where I asked my C-level team and board members to give anonymous feedback through a coach. The feedback was insightful—there were a lot of positives, but also many areas where I need to improve. That's one of the most fascinating aspects of leadership—it's a continuous journey of personal growth.

More broadly, what strategies that work well early on in the startup lifecycle can become liabilities as the company scales?

In my experience, one of the biggest reasons founders hit a wall is that they must abandon what once worked in order to evolve. The startup mentality is all about being hyperactive, hustling, and leading from the front. It's about giving direction and pushing forward without worrying too much about how things get done—just making sure they get done.

When you reach 100–150 employees, that approach stops working. You can't stand in front of a large team and say, "Let's just solve this problem—follow me." People need structure. They want to understand the mission, the strategy, and the execution plan. At this stage, you need to define who your customers are, what your mission is, what the key pillars of your strategy are, and how you will measure success.

You have to move from an instinct-driven approach to a structured strategy. And then comes operational excellence—management processes and execution frameworks. Every company has its own approach, so it's more of an art than a science.

Early on, when people ask about your strategy, you can say, "Our strategy is to win." But as you scale, that's no longer enough. You must put everything in writing, define the mission, break it into strategic pillars, outline key initiatives, and set measurable goals.

Some founders, especially those with consulting backgrounds from firms like McKinsey or Bain, might be structured from day one. But I wasn't. I saw a pain point, built a team that believed in the vision, and we pushed forward. However, as we scaled, I realized that I had to slow down and go deeper into execution. We couldn't just keep moving fast—we had to build sustainable processes.

Communication is also everything. When you scale, you bring in highly intellectual individuals who don't just respond to passion and energy. They want to understand the "why" and the "how." You need to over-communicate to a point where you feel like you're repeating yourself constantly. If every employee in the company can't articulate the mission, the strategy, and the core pillars, then alignment is impossible.

It was a huge learning curve for me. I had to transition from being a doer to being a communicator. When you're in startup mode, you can get away with leading by example and just charging ahead. But at scale, it's about making sure everyone is aligned, moving in the same direction, and executing with precision.

———

> I HAD TO TRANSITION FROM BEING A DOER TO BEING A COMMUNICATOR. WHEN YOU'RE IN STARTUP MODE, YOU CAN GET AWAY WITH LEADING BY EXAMPLE AND JUST CHARGING AHEAD. BUT AT SCALE, IT'S ABOUT MAKING SURE EVERYONE IS ALIGNED, MOVING IN THE SAME DIRECTION, AND EXECUTING WITH PRECISION.

———

You also mentioned defining a bigger purpose beyond just business growth. Can you elaborate on that?

Over time, I started asking myself, Why do I keep doing this? Yes, we help people find homes, which is one of the biggest financial and emotional decisions in their lives. But beyond that, I became passionate about proving that world-class tech companies can emerge from the Middle East.

Look at how Spotify put Sweden on the global tech map. Who would have thought the world's leading music streaming service would come from Sweden? Similarly, I believe the Middle East has the potential to produce globally recognized tech giants.

When General Atlantic invested in us, it wasn't just about raising capital. It was about showing global investors that the Middle East is home to innovative, scalable tech companies. If we can prove that, it will open the door for more global investments in the region.

But with that comes responsibility. If GA invests $120 million and we don't create value, they won't invest in the region again. I took that responsibility seriously; we had to prove that we could build a great company and deliver results.

That's why we crafted our company's purpose: *"To change living for good in the region."* It's about improving the real estate experience, but also about elevating the entire tech ecosystem here.

On the topic of investors, can we touch a bit on best practices you've learned about fundraising along the way?

One of the most important things for founders to understand is that they need to be able to quickly and clearly articulate their business model. If you must do an elevator pitch, the best way is to reference a successful company and explain how you're doing the same thing in your region. Ideally, you should be following a proven model with some localized tweaks.

Global investors don't typically want to take on both business model risk and geographic risk at the same time. If they're investing in a new business model, they'll likely do so in their home market, where they have a better understanding. If they're investing abroad, they want to see a model that has already been de-risked elsewhere.

They're not going to travel all the way to Dubai to invest in an unproven model, right?

Indeed. You also need to understand that every type of capital or investment fund has its own identity and specific focus. Some funds are looking for B2B business models, while others focus on consumer models. Some investors prefer early-stage ventures, while others look for mid-stage or late-stage companies. Then, you have funds that operate with different ticket sizes—$5 million, $10 million, $20 million, even $100 million.

I see a lot of founders wasting time pitching to the wrong investors. Just because someone has money doesn't mean they're interested in your business. Founders need to read and understand an investor's thesis. Investors follow specific strategies, and if they've never invested in your business model or in your region, it's unlikely they will start now.

For example, General Atlantic (GA) had never invested in our region before, but they had invested in classified businesses, and I knew they loved that model. That was my entry point. You also don't want to waste time pitching the wrong amount. If you're raising $20 million, don't go to GA because they don't write checks smaller than $50 million. That's a deal-breaker right from the start. Many founders think, "If they can do $50 million, they can do $20 million." No, they can't. Investors have targets and deployment strategies. Learning this early can save you a lot of time.

A great way to navigate this is by having a friend who is a banker or someone experienced in startups who can provide insights. These tips can be invaluable.

What is one thing that early-stage startup founders mis-read about investors?

Investors may love your business model, but at the end of the day, they're taking a big risk on the founder and CEO. When they're investing at the scaleup stage, you're likely not profitable yet or just on the verge of profitability. So, they need to validate who you are.

The hardest thing to assess about someone is their integrity. You can get a glimpse of it when you meet someone, but real confirmation takes time. That's one of the biggest challenges global investors face—not finding businesses, but ensuring those businesses are run by people with the right values.

———

THAT'S ONE OF THE BIGGEST CHALLENGES GLOBAL INVESTORS FACE—NOT FINDING BUSINESSES, BUT ENSURING THOSE BUSINESSES ARE RUN BY PEOPLE WITH THE RIGHT VALUES.

———

Investors don't micromanage how you spend every dollar, but they need to trust that you're making ethical decisions—no shady related-party transactions, no misuse of funds. If someone's moral compass is off, it doesn't matter how good the business is; it won't succeed.

That's why investors take the time to build trust. Trust doesn't come from Zoom calls or boardrooms alone—it comes from spending time together, dining, traveling, and meeting mutual connections. If an investor doesn't know anyone in their network who can vouch for you, it's unlikely they'll take the risk. You might be the best con artist, telling them exactly what they want to hear, so they need external validation.

You've got to remember, investors talk. They'll ask, "Who knows Michael?" They want to hear, "Oh, I've known him for 10 years—great guy, high integrity." Those reference checks can make or break an investment decision.

Most founders who lose deals at the last minute don't realize it's often because something questionable came up in a background check. It's like hiring—if the reference check raises red flags, you might pull the offer.

What about managing relationships with your board?

Founders often raise funds when they're desperate, and in that desperation, they might be tempted to say whatever investors want to hear. I get it—you have to sell. But don't lie. If an investor finds out later that you weren't honest, trust erodes quickly.

Once trust is lost at the board level, it creates toxicity that spreads through management and employees. Look at what happened with Uber and WeWork—issues at the board level trickled down and affected the entire business.

Building trust with investors is crucial, but equally important is choosing the right investors. Some funds are on their first raise, and you don't always know their background.

I remember receiving a term sheet from a fund in an Eastern European country—not known for transparency or governance. The valuation was tempting, better than I had seen before. But I turned it down because I knew that if I took their money, reputable firms like General Atlantic wouldn't invest later. They wouldn't want to sit at the same cap table.

You must think long-term. It's not just about raising money; it's about raising the right money.

Building the right cap table from the outset is crucial. You want investors who understand your business model, your region, or at least something about your market. General Atlantic was patient. They invested in 2018, and by 2019, we didn't hit the budget we promised. Then COVID hit in 2020. So, two years into their investment, we were behind. Luckily, they stayed calm.

Not every investor can stomach the first 18–24 months of an investment not going as planned. But experienced investors understand the J-curve—business performance often dips before improvements take effect. Having patient investors is a huge asset.

Before GA, I had incredible local investors like Danny Farha from BECO Capital, who has been an important part of our progress. Having a reputable local investor is crucial if you want to attract global investors. If you don't, global investors will ask, "Why hasn't any local investor backed you?" That's a red flag.

I also brought in a Swedish investor along the way. My board was always aligned, and I kept them well-informed—not just with the good news, but also with the challenges. Transparency builds trust. If you have trust, you can weather storms together. Without it, every setback becomes a crisis.

What's next for you and Property Finder?

The journey never stops. We're constantly iterating, learning, and refining our strategy. The goal is to build a company that not only succeeds commercially but also leaves a lasting impact on the industry and the region. There's still so much more to do, and that's what keeps me excited every day.

How do you see Property Finder's role in shaping the region's tech landscape?

Property Finder is building a lighthouse company that is spearheading the region's nascent tech ecosystem while furthering the possibilities of a world-class tech company based in the Middle East. This means it is founded on the values of great ambition.

We're creating an inclusive environment where people can thrive—our employees and potential talent, our consumers, our business partners, and our investors. I truly believe we have a unique opportunity with a three-sided marketplace. On one side, we have the customers—the paying agents and developers. On the other side, we have the consumers. And then there is the community, which includes Property Finder employees and stakeholders.

We have the chance to create an ecosystem where these three groups can thrive, and Property Finder can have a meaningful impact on their lives. The culture within Property Finder is deeply rooted in people. When I first came to the Middle East, I realized that people weren't really excited about their jobs. One reason for this was that most available jobs were in companies acting as distributors of global brands. Whether in luxury goods like Cartier and Van Cleef, automotive brands like Aston Martin and Mercedes, fashion, or even restaurants—the headquarters and decision-making powers were elsewhere.

There weren't many locally created brands designed for the people in this region. I wanted to build a company where people could truly thrive, where young professionals would be excited to join, learn from the best, and grow. But you can't learn from the best if the leadership team isn't based in your city.

For example, if you work for Amazon in the Middle East today, much of the strategy comes from Seattle. When Souq was still independent, its leadership team made decisions locally. But once Amazon acquired it, the strategy was no longer set in the UAE—it shifted to Seattle. The same thing happened with Careem after Uber acquired it. While selling to Amazon and Uber were essential exits for the UAE tech ecosystem, it's a shame that the region then lost strategic control of those businesses.

We should be able to keep our local businesses that serve local communities here in Dubai and the UAE. These companies should act as institutions where people can learn, grow, and become the best versions of themselves. Then, they can either start their own businesses or join other companies and bring that knowledge with them. That's why I've brought executives from Microsoft, Amazon, Facebook, and Google into my company. For the first time, leaders from global tech firms joined a local company and started sharing their expertise.

Today, Property Finder operates very much like a Silicon Valley tech company. Our operational rhythm, product management, marketing strategies, and decision-making processes all follow global standards. At the same time, we've cultivated our own unique culture.

My ultimate goal is for Property Finder to outlive its founder. People often ask, "What's your long-term goal for Property Finder?" My answer is simple: I want Property Finder to still be thriving long after I'm gone. That's the hallmark of a truly successful company.

———

"

My ultimate goal is for property finder to outlive its founder. People often ask, "what's your long-term goal for property finder?" My answer is simple: i want property finder to still be thriving long after i'm gone. That's the hallmark of a truly successful company.

———

I want Property Finder to be a company that university students aspire to join after graduation because they know that spending three or four years here will be an invaluable learning experience. If we were to exit to a global strategic buyer that merely turns us into a sales center, we would lose that opportunity.

That's why our purpose is to change living for good in the region. We have the power to transform the way people live and make a lasting impact. I've seen this not just with our employees but also with our customers. When we started, we had 20 or 30 agencies working with us. Today, we have over 6,000 agencies listing properties on Property Finder. Some of these agencies began with one or two agents, and now they have 500 or 600. Many of them say they couldn't survive without Property Finder—it's their lifeline.

We've built an ecosystem where thousands of companies employing hundreds of agents rely on our platform. And then there are the 10 million users who visit Property Finder every month to make better investment decisions, find homes, and make informed choices about renting or buying.

Some people ask how Property Finder is changing living for good in the region. The impact may not be immediate, but over the next 25 to 30 years, I believe the transformation will be undeniable. I may no longer be the CEO by then—maybe I won't even be on the board—but I want Property Finder to be a source of national pride, a company that stands the test of time. That's what I'm working on today—extracting myself from day-to-day operations and institutionalizing the business so it continues to serve the local community for decades to come.

Along the way, we've created significant wealth—not just for shareholders but also for employees. We were the first company in the region to grant equity to employees. When I first drafted our ESOP (Employee Stock Ownership Plan), it was difficult, and our lawyers weren't sure how to structure it. We worked it out, and today, hundreds of current and former employees own equity, and many of them have been able to retire early because of it.

When I run into ex-employees who are now traveling the world or playing golf, it makes me proud. They contributed, created value, and earned their success. That's what I mean when I talk about giving back to the community and changing living for good in the region.

Do you have final advice for founders?

Yes, one more piece of advice—when parting ways with key talent, partners, or any business relationship in general, always make sure they leave on good terms. Especially with ex-staff, never let an employee walk away with a grudge. A detractor can undo the work of 100 promoters. If someone leaves and still speaks highly of your company, that says everything about your culture.

As founders, we're frugal, but the one time to be generous is when letting someone go. That goodwill pays off in the long run.

Thank you, Michael. Maybe you will also will be part of my threequel book if there's ever one—*IPO Arabia*?

Who knows. But thank you, I appreciate your support. Looking forward to seeing how this turns out.

———

HAMDI TABBAA

Breaking barriers in education

Founder and CEO of ABWAAB

abwaab

Amman, Jordan

www.abwaab.com

HAMDI TABBAA is a Jordanian entrepreneur known for his contributions to the technology and education sectors in the Middle East and North Africa (MENA) region. He is the co-founder and CEO of Abwaab, an innovative online learning platform aimed at transforming education for Arabic-speaking students.

He pursued higher education in the United Kingdom, earning a Bachelor of Science in Business Management from King's College London. He later obtained a Master of Science in Real Estate Economics and Finance from the London School of Economics and Political Science (LSE).

After completing his studies in 2009, Hamdi returned to Jordan and started his entrepreneurial journey by establishing Dukkan, a specialty grocery store. This venture was one of the first in Jordan to introduce organized retail at the neighborhood level. Over six years, he expanded the business, reaching over $15 million in revenue before selling it.

In 2015, he joined Uber as the General Manager for the Levant and GCC regions. During his time there, he successfully launched and scaled Uber's operations in Jordan, Lebanon, Qatar, and other MENA countries. One of his major achievements was leading public policy negotiations that resulted in the implementation of the first progressive ride-sharing regulations in Jordan.

Motivated by his passion for education and inspired by the impact of technology during his tenure at Uber, Hamdi co-founded Abwaab in late 2019. The platform provides concept-based video lessons, continuous assessments, and performance-tracking features, allowing secondary school students in the MENA region to learn at their own pace. Abwaab's mission is to make high-quality education more accessible and affordable, addressing the widespread reliance on after-school tutoring in the region.

Shortly after its launch, Abwaab faced the challenges of the COVID-19 pandemic. In response, the company partnered with the Jordanian Ministry of Education to produce and distribute educational content, significantly increasing its reach. Under Hamdi's leadership,

Abwaab has expanded its operations to multiple countries, including Egypt, Iraq, Saudi Arabia, and Pakistan, and has raised substantial funding to support its growth.

His vision for Abwaab is to leverage technology to provide personalized and adaptive learning experiences tailored to each student's needs. He believes that true innovation in education technology is still unfolding and is dedicated to building a platform that enhances learning through curated content and advanced analytics.

Through his entrepreneurial journey, Hamdi Tabbaa continues to shape the future of education in the MENA region, striving to make learning more accessible, engaging, and effective for students across diverse communities.

––––––––

ABWAAB is an online learning platform founded in 2019 and headquartered in Amman, Jordan. It aims to revolutionize education for secondary school students in the Middle East and North Africa by providing short, engaging video lessons, continuous assessments, and performance analytics. The company was co-founded by Hamdi Tabbaa, Sabri Hakim, and Hussein Al-Sarabi. Hamdi Tabbaa, who serves as the CEO, previously worked as the General Manager for Uber in the Levant and GCC regions, where he played a key role in expanding operations and shaping regulatory frameworks. His experience in scaling technology-driven solutions has been fundamental in developing Abwaab's strategy.

Since its launch, Abwaab has raised substantial funding to accelerate its growth. In November 2021, the company secured $20 million in a Series A funding round, bringing its total funding to approximately $27.5 million. Investors in Abwaab include BECO Capital, 4DX Ventures, GSV Ventures, and Watar Partners. As of 2024, the company employs approximately 456 individuals and generates an estimated annual revenue of $75.4 million, with an estimated revenue per employee of $175,000.

The platform offers concept-based video lessons, continuous assessments, and performance analytics that help students track their progress and identify areas that need improvement. These features allow students to learn at their own pace, ensuring a deeper understanding of their subjects. Initially focusing on the Jordanian curriculum, Abwaab has expanded to Egypt, Iraq, Saudi Arabia, and Pakistan. In July 2021, the company acquired Edmatrix, a Pakistani e-learning platform, marking its entry into the South Asian market.

Abwaab seeks to make high-quality education accessible to all students, regardless of their background. By providing an affordable and effective alternative to traditional after-school tutoring, the platform addresses key educational challenges in the region. The company leverages technology to create personalized and adaptive learning experiences that cater to each student's unique needs. With its innovative approach, Abwaab continues to make a significant impact on the education landscape in the MENA region, empowering students to reach their full potential.

———

Tell us a bit about your personal background.

I was born and raised in Amman, where I spent my school years. I jumped between three different schools growing up, and reflecting on that now as an adult, I realize it developed a lot of adaptability and resilience in me. Looking back, I see that it also contributed to me becoming quite extroverted. Changing schools multiple times meant that every time I had to hit the reset button, get used to a new environment, and make new friends altogether.

I was also heavily involved in sports. I played football, basketball, tennis, baseball, swimming, track and field, and handball. I was on both school and club teams for many of these sports, and I think that shaped my personality in many ways. Being part of a team, competing, and learning how to work with different people all played a huge role in my personal growth.

I remember my kids asking me the other day, "Baba, how was life when you were our age? Wasn't it boring without technology?" And I told them it was actually very similar to theirs. I'd come home from school, and almost every day, I had some kind of sports activity. In my teenage years, I played so hard that sometimes I would literally collapse on the floor from exhaustion. My parents would come home and find me sleeping on the living room floor, just trying to regain some energy. I try to instill the same habits in my kids now because I know how much playing sports shaped me—not just physically but in terms of teamwork, discipline, and resilience.

Towards grade 12, I started to realize I was quite an achiever. I had always been ambitious, but in high school, it really started to show, both academically and in sports. I was awarded Athlete of the Year and felt like I was on top of the world, convinced I would cruise through life. I genuinely felt like I was on a rocket ship, soaring.

But then, that rocket ship crashed when I turned 18. I had applied to many top universities in the US and UK, expecting great results. Instead, I was rejected from almost all of them. That was a massive slap in the face—my first real failure.

I ended up studying Business Management at King's College London instead of my initial choice, Accounting and Finance, because I had missed my preferred university offer. For three years, I worked hard, determined to prove myself. Eventually, I graduated with first-class honors and got into LSE—my dream university, the one I hadn't been able to attend for my bachelor's. I felt like I was back on my rocket ship. I was sure I would land the best job in banking. But then, 2008 happened—the credit crunch hit, and banks were shutting down left and right. Suddenly, my dream job was no longer an option. That was another major reality check.

Do you recall your first exposure to entrepreneurship?

I come from a long line of entrepreneurs. My grandfather, father, and great-grandfather were all tradesmen and businessmen in various fields—commodities, automotive, and more. Even my mother is an entrepreneur, running her own business. So, deep down, I always felt drawn to building something of my own.

In high school, I also had a small taste of entrepreneurship when we set up a company as part of our economics class. My classmates nominated me as GM, and I ended up hiring different functions, selling stock, raising capital, and even distributing dividends. That experience gave me a rush. I realized then how much I loved the process of creating and leading something.

After graduating from LSE, I knew the job market wasn't promising, and I had this itch to start something that could create real value. I saw a huge gap in the Jordanian and regional market— organized retail was missing. Everything was still based on small, independent stores and supermarkets. I had seen big chains like Sainsbury's, Tesco, and Waitrose in the UK, and I thought, "I want to bring that concept to Jordan."

So, I went for it. But that journey was filled with challenges— many, many slaps in the face. I often tell my father that my experience was equivalent to getting a Harvard MBA, considering all the lessons I learned. I spent around five to six years trying to build that business, and in the end, I failed.

What were some of the biggest lessons you took away from that failure?

There were many, but a few stand out. First, starting a business without enough capital is extremely tough. I promised myself I wouldn't do that again. Later, when I joined Uber, I saw how well-capitalized they were, and I realized how much more you can achieve when you have the necessary resources.

Second, I was too young and naive, thinking I could own the entire business myself. I didn't want to give away equity, even to key team members. I would walk into investor meetings valuing my company at $100 million when it was essentially nothing at the time. That was a huge mistake. I now understand the importance of sharing the pie because owning a small piece of something big is much better than owning 100% of nothing.

Third, I realized I never wanted to work in a slim-margin business again. The grocery sector had incredibly thin margins, and it was exhausting trying to operate under such conditions. A small dip in sales could completely wreck the business.

Fourth, managing cash flow is critical. I actually got physically robbed during that time, which made me hyper-aware of financial security. Beyond that, I learned not to overspend and to keep a close eye on every dollar.

Another major lesson was the power of focus. When my supermarket business started struggling, I launched a separate distribution business to sell fresh produce and meat to restaurants and hotels. At first, I was excited—I was making deals, growing sales. But I quickly realized I had created a cash flow disaster. I was buying produce in cash, selling on credit, and running out of money to restock essentials in the supermarket. Customers would come in expecting their usual items, find empty shelves, and leave. That drove the business into further decline.

Finally, I learned that businesses shouldn't try to do both B2C and B2B at the same time, at least not in the early stages. They're completely different models, and trying to juggle both before establishing a stable foundation was a big mistake.

Around that time, a friend called and asked if I wanted to join Uber? It's a global tech leader, remote, part-time, and you can still run your business." I weighed it and thought, Why not? High-paying, remote, part-time—I could manage both. Three interviews in three days later, I got the job. And because I wasn't desperate, I came across confident—which worked in my favor during the interviews. I joined Uber as an Operations Manager.

People assume you join Uber and it's this big, fancy company, but I was literally calling drivers one by one from my parents' garden, onboarding them in parking lots—doing all the typical startup grind.

On my first day, I walked into the office expecting a fancy setup—lots of screens, a Silicon Valley-style space. Instead, I found four white walls, two brown desks, and two green chairs—an ugly color combination in a business center we had rented.

I sat alone with my laptop. The silence in the room was killing me. I was used to the buzz of a supermarket—4,500 customers coming in daily, vendors and suppliers walking in and out, the constant problems and challenges, even the sound of the butcher's chopping board from my office upstairs. Now, I was sitting in a completely silent room, and it drove me crazy.

By noon, I got into my car and drove back to the supermarket. At that time, I hadn't told my supermarket team that I had taken the Uber job. What would I say? I'm abandoning you for another job? When I got to the supermarket, my brother Kareem was already managing things. He took over the business while I transitioned to fully focus on Uber.

At Uber, I took it as a personal challenge. I was coming from a failure and wasn't OK with it. I wasn't OK with failing at my supermarket. It took time, but I eventually learned that failure is part of learning. I powered through for four to five years, growing the business from around $10,000 in sales to hundreds of millions by the time I left.

As the business grew, I built a team. By the end, I was Head of Levant and Qatar, managing operations in Jordan, Lebanon, and Qatar. I was also preparing to launch in Kuwait and Iraq, but then the Careem acquisition happened, and they were already operating in those markets, so we didn't pursue them.

What inspired you to start Abwaab?

My time at Uber opened my eyes to the impact of technology on industries. Seeing what happened in ride-sharing, I realized there was a huge opportunity in education. I've always believed that when you're fortunate enough to receive the best education—attending top universities—you have a responsibility to give back to the region. I thought if Uber could create so many jobs and opportunities through technology, imagine what we could do in education.

———

<blockquote>
I THOUGHT IF UBER COULD CREATE SO MANY JOBS AND OPPORTUNITIES THROUGH TECHNOLOGY, IMAGINE WHAT WE COULD DO IN EDUCATION.
</blockquote>

———

I had also taken an online learning course between Uber and Harvard—a strategy and leadership program. It was intense. I'd wake up at 2 AM, dial into class, and interact with students from Brazil to Tokyo. I'd probably crash on the couch for an hour during the four-hour session, but I still got so much out of it. That experience made me realize how powerful online education could be. Also, my grandfather had invested in a university and always told me how profitable it was. So everything aligned—there was potential, it was a lucrative business, and it had a strong mission behind it.

At first, I was lost. Despite having built my own business before, I thought EdTech meant teaching everyone everything. In 2017, I wanted to do something futuristic—AR and VR medical training, a broad online learning platform covering everything from coding to cooking to grade seven math.

But over time, I refined the idea. I realized I needed to solve a specific problem. The Middle East has over 100 million students, and because of weak public and private school infrastructure, after-school tutoring is massive. I saw a gap where we could build the best technology and platform to deliver better learning experiences at better value.

How did you overcome the challenge of having no tech background while launching Abwaab?

The transition wasn't easy at all. First, I had zero tech background. Even though I worked at Uber, I had never worked with a product team, never spoken to an engineer—I had no idea what it took to build a platform. So I made a promise to myself: I wouldn't start unless I found the right technical co-founder. Through my network, I connected with Hassan Sarabi, who became my co-founder and CTO. More importantly, our values and mission aligned, so we decided to build together.

We met frequently at each other's offices. But when the time came for me to resign, Uber refused. They said, "No, Hamdi, you're one of our top performers. We'll send you to a leadership course in San Francisco."

Fast forward a few months, and I was obsessed with the idea of starting my company. I had also started talking to Sabri, my future co-founder, who had been the GM of Careem and a tough competitor. I knew I wanted to build something with him.

We even started running EdTech focus groups while I was still at Uber.

A few months later, after we built further conviction in the attack space, I decided to resign from Uber. The day I resigned was an incredibly tough moment for me. I had twins who were just a few years old and about to enter school, so it wasn't the best time to take a financial hit. I had a stable job with a good income, but the entrepreneurial itch just wouldn't go away. I kept thinking about it, and eventually, I knew I had to take that leap of faith.

What finally pushed you to leave Uber and fully commit to building Abwaab?

In late 2018, early 2019, I stumbled upon your book *Startup Arabia*. I remember ordering it online and diving into it. Even though I worked at Uber, I never felt like I was truly part of the tech ecosystem. I was working for a tech company, but I wasn't building one. Before that, I had only been a founder of a supermarket business.

Your book resonated with me deeply. I remember the first chapter about Samih Toukan, and as a Jordanian, I looked up to him—as did many founders across the region. He was a pioneer in the tech startup space, and reading about his journey made my heart race. I was already contemplating leaving Uber and starting my own business, but I was unsure. Then, I came across his quote: "The riskiest thing in business is not taking any risks."

That was my lightbulb moment. I realized that if I stayed at Uber for another four or five years, I'd have a great salary, and the company liked me—but I'd be risking something even bigger: the chance to pursue what I truly wanted. I knew I'd regret it for the rest of my life if I didn't take action.

So, I resigned. Just like that. After resigning, I found myself alone in the Uber office at King Hussein Business Park, and I cried— loudly—for 45 minutes. My wife called me and asked, "Hamdi, why are you crying?" I told her, "I just resigned from Uber." Of course, we had already discussed it and agreed on it. She simply said, "Hamdi, you already made your decision. Have faith in yourself. Have confidence. You're going to build something great."

From that moment on, I went all in. For the first few months, I ran Abwaab while still transitioning out of Uber, overlapping the two for about three months to get things moving. Then, I went full force into Abwaab.

———

> **"** THAT WAS MY LIGHTBULB MOMENT. I REALIZED THAT IF I STAYED AT UBER FOR ANOTHER FOUR OR FIVE YEARS, I'D HAVE A GREAT SALARY, AND THE COMPANY LIKED ME—BUT I'D BE RISKING SOMETHING EVEN BIGGER: THE CHANCE TO PURSUE WHAT I TRULY WANTED. I KNEW I'D REGRET IT FOR THE REST OF MY LIFE IF I DIDN'T TAKE ACTION.

———

I'm truly touched that *Startup Arabia* helped you navigate such a pivotal moment in your career and finally go for Abwaab.

Indeed, *Startup Arabia* was a great eye opener and quite inspiring at the time.

And here you are, coming full circle, being featured in *Scaleup Arabia*, the sequel—so what was the initial launch like?

We launched very quickly, following a typical Silicon Valley mentality—just get something out there in the market. Initially, it was nothing more than the equivalent of YouTube but for educational content. It was a basic app featuring video lessons covering subjects aligned with the national curriculum. Our goal was to help students excel academically, but at the start, it was just a simple video platform.

We iterated heavily on the product experience and started scaling rapidly. That was a mistake. Six months after launching—right at the peak of COVID—we experienced an explosive growth period. We had secured a contract (actually for free) with the Jordanian government to support students during lockdowns. The team was on a high, adrenaline was pumping, and we raised two rounds of funding within five months, first $2.5 million and then another $5 million. Investors were pouring money into edtech. I was working day and night. While the world was on lockdown, I was leaving my wife and kids to go to the office, thinking, This is working. Let's keep pushing.

By summer 2020, we expanded into Egypt. Then we ran a pilot assessments product in Saudi Arabia the following year. Shortly after, we explored Iraq. We interviewed people there and brought on board someone who had been part of the ride-sharing industry. He had worked with my co-founder Sabri at Careem and had the same mindset.

We launched Iraq and continued scaling without truly finding proper product-market fit, which was a major mistake. But we were growing so fast, it felt impossible to slow down. We even acquired a startup in Pakistan, founded by ex-Uber colleagues. They called me, I liked what they were doing, and I thought, You guys don't have much experience in fundraising or building tech; why don't we acquire you? So we did. They focused on Pakistan, while my CTO and I handled the broader business and tech.

In theory, it made sense at the time. In hindsight, it couldn't have worked. A year later, Sabri and several team members returned from Pakistan and told me, "Hamdi, we need to shut it down." Sabri and I have a relationship built on trust. We competed against each other for years before becoming co-founders, so we respect each other's judgment. He laid out his reasons, and I agreed. We shut down Pakistan, let go of the team, and decided to focus on the markets where we had already expanded: Jordan, Egypt, Iraq, and Saudi Arabia. And for the next two years, we stopped further expansion and focused on finding true product-market fit, strengthening our foundation in these markets.

What mistakes did you make while scaling Abwaab, and how did you correct them?

The first major lesson was to never scale before finding proper product-market fit. When you have it, you feel it—it's not just about data. The best analogy I've heard is that PMF (product-market fit) feels like you're struggling just to keep the lights on because demand is overwhelming.

We scaled too fast, hiring people and expanding aggressively before truly nailing the value of our product. This cost us time and money. Our retention and renewal numbers weren't optimal. Eventually, we had to go back to the drawing board.

This process wasn't easy—it was intense. As co-founders, we sat in rooms, debated, wrote on whiteboards, and asked tough questions. Why is this working? Why isn't this working? We dissected data, ran student interviews, and surveyed parents. One of the most useful tools was the Superhuman Experiment Survey, which helped us analyze customer needs in depth.

We had two major realizations that reshaped our approach. Students need accountability. Education is unique because the buyer, which is the parent, and the user, which is the student, are different people. Most students don't actually want to study unless there's external motivation. That's why we introduced academic coaching as a service—every student now has a coach to guide them.

Students trust teachers more than technology. Initially, we focused on making our product sleek and tech-driven. But we learned that students respond better to real teachers, especially those who have credibility or social media presence. So, we pivoted to make teachers the face of the platform. We validated these insights through experiments across different markets. Once we saw positive results, we doubled down on them.

What would you say are the most critical factors to scaling successfully?

One of the most valuable insights I've come across recently is that to scale successfully, you need two things: product-market fit and product go-to-market fit.

Many founders believe that once they have product-market fit, growth will happen automatically. That's almost never the case. Even TikTok, despite its viral success, had to put in enormous effort to take its product to market.

―――

" ONE OF THE MOST VALUABLE INSIGHTS I'VE COME ACROSS RECENTLY IS THAT TO SCALE SUCCESSFULLY, YOU NEED TWO THINGS: PRODUCT-MARKET FIT AND PRODUCT GO-TO-MARKET FIT.

―――

Scaling isn't just about having a great product—it's about effectively bringing that product to customers. In our case, we started aggressively pursuing product go-to-market fit before achieving product-market fit (PMF). But even then, if I were to share my experience, we learned that taking a product to market requires a well-structured and aggressive approach to sales and marketing.

We started by hiring sales agents who would immediately call students within 24 hours of signing up on a BLOB because intent at that time was still very high. We initially built these sales teams in Jordan, where we aggressively explained the Abwaab offering to students and parents, attempting to convert them. At first, this approach worked. We saw an increase in sales and started replicating it in other markets.

However, we made a few mistakes. We assumed we could continue operating at a central level. Our head of sales, a very strong leader named Surah, was based in Jordan, and we asked her to build and manage sales teams remotely in Egypt, Iraq, and later Saudi Arabia.

What went wrong with this approach?

We quickly realized that in the early days of scaling, local insights are crucial to cracking the customer psyche. If you believe you can operate from a high tower and apply a one-size-fits-all approach across markets, you will miss out on significant local value and fail to resonate with customers.

We learned this the hard way. Sales started to flatten, and our country heads repeatedly told us, "We're missing local insights. Why aren't you empowering us to manage sales locally instead of centralizing everything?"

This led to difficult conversations. Internally, there were political challenges—"Why are you taking this away from me?" "Why am I not being empowered to run sales?" These were tough discussions, and at the time, we weren't sure if we were making the right decisions.

But once we decentralized and allowed local teams to report to their own managers, everything changed. The feedback loop became much faster, and we could experiment more efficiently with pricing, messaging, and marketing strategies. Sales began to take off again.

Then, something interesting happened. In the world of startups and scaleups, we went from a fully centralized sales structure to an entirely decentralized one. We thought we had found the perfect model, but then a new challenge emerged.

What happens when decentralization goes too far?

We had decentralized so aggressively that we lost shared learnings between markets. Each team was reinventing the wheel instead of benefiting from insights generated elsewhere. We lacked consistency in data tracking, which made it difficult to make informed, data-driven decisions.

So, once again, we had to reorganize. This led to another round of difficult conversations—"Why are you taking away some of my autonomy?" "Why are we centralizing again?"

This time, we focused on creating a middle ground—a structure where teams could share knowledge across markets while maintaining their autonomy. We built playbooks, standardized data tracking, and created a culture of replicating successful experiments instead of treating each market as an isolated unit.

I learned this lesson first at Uber and later at Abwab: flexibility in organizational structure is crucial for scaling startups. If your business is growing rapidly, your approach must evolve with it. If you don't adjust your structure to match your growth, you risk dropping the ball.

Now, another major challenge we faced was related to scaling too quickly. If you expand too fast, you essentially outsource finding PMF to the new markets. We made this mistake. By asking our operations and sales teams to scale a product we weren't fully convinced had PMF, we shifted accountability to our local teams—something that was unfair and ineffective.

To fix this, we had to change our approach. Instead of enforcing a central vision, we empowered local teams as intrapreneurs—people who have an entrepreneurial mindset but work within a company. At Uber, I always considered myself an intrapreneur, and we wanted to cultivate that mindset at Abwab.

We encouraged our local teams to run their own product and go-to-market experiments instead of just executing a centrally developed strategy. This required humility from our leadership team.

Founders sometimes assume that just because something worked in one market, it should be replicated in others.

Indeed, but we realized that, in some markets, we needed to work with celebrity teachers—something that wasn't part of our initial strategy. In two of our markets, we experimented with partnering with well-known teachers. Their needs were entirely different from what we had anticipated. They already had a strong following and demanded different product features and marketing support. This meant our usual approach—where product teams conducted experiments and then rolled them out—had to change. We had to listen to these stakeholders and adapt.

Initially, this shift wasn't easy. But we were under pressure to find what would drive the most growth, so we embraced it. We took local learnings and applied them across other markets, fostering a culture of shared knowledge.

How do you balance local autonomy with central strategy?

This required careful stakeholder management. Each market was competing in a healthy way, but we also needed to ensure they learned from one another. I can't claim we've perfected this, but it has shaped Abwab's DNA.

Instead of forcing a rigid, top-down strategy, we've created an environment where local teams have the freedom to innovate. If a local team discovers a successful approach, they receive full support from headquarters, and we champion their learnings so that other markets can benefit. Of course, this depends on the type of company. For highly centralized products—such as B2B SaaS—it might make sense to build everything centrally and distribute it outward. But for consumer businesses, where being close to the customer is key, value creation determines success.

No matter how good your marketing or sales tactics are, if your product isn't delivering value, customers won't buy it. That's why our approach shifted from "let's sell this product everywhere" to "let's empower teams to create value in their markets." Now, reflecting on it, I think this is one of the most important lessons we learned during our scaling journey.

What about marketing during rapid scaling?

Going back to when we were expanding quickly into multiple markets—Egypt, Saudi Arabia, Iraq—we made another big mistake, which is we over-invested in marketing without ensuring strong fundamentals.

At the time, we had raised nearly $20 million within 18 months of our seed round, so we felt the pressure to scale aggressively. We assumed that pouring money into sales and marketing was the best way to drive growth.

This led us to a common startup pitfall, which is over-reliance on paid performance marketing, especially on Google and Meta (Facebook). I recently read a statistic that suggests 30–40% of global ad spend is wasted. That stuck with me, because I saw firsthand how easily that waste can happen.

We spent heavily on Google Ads. Initially, it produced results—we generated millions of student signups. But over time, the return on investment began to plateau. We realized that simply pouring money into ads wasn't sustainable.

Obviously, many businesses rely heavily on cloud services and other essential tools, which is a legitimate reason to invest in digital channels. But when companies overspend on marketing before focusing on two crucial aspects—first, delivering clear value to customers to drive word of mouth, and second, acquiring customers through smart, tactical grassroots efforts—they end up burning a lot of money.

We made this mistake. We believed performance marketing would be a silver bullet, but it wasn't. We fell into the trap of trying to do too many things at once instead of focusing on building a clear, efficient growth flywheel.

Jeff Bezos talks a lot about this concept: a company doesn't need multiple flywheels—just one that works. I've read multiple books that echo this. And it made me reflect on our own approach.

I recently came across an article where someone claimed to have saved Uber $35 million by cutting down on performance marketing spend. I shared it with my team immediately to reinforce a key point: we need to focus on qualified, high-value leads rather than casting an overly wide net. Because if your net is too big, you might end up catching nothing substantial.

We learned this firsthand at Aboab, and since then, we've shifted our approach. We're now focused on acquiring customers in a way that allows us to scale sustainably—by building something valuable enough that people talk about it, and by growing deliberately instead of reactively.

> WE FELL INTO THE TRAP OF TRYING TO DO TOO MANY THINGS AT ONCE, THINKING GOOGLE ADS WOULD BE A SILVER BULLET, BUT IT WASN'T.

Of course, for competitive reasons, there are some strategies we can't publicly share, but in essence, success starts with going where your customers are. If you're an ed-tech product, your students might be in schools, and their parents might be in digital or offline spaces relevant to their children's education. If you provide genuine value to them, they will find their way to you organically through word of mouth.

What were your experiences with scaling to and localizing to different markets?

In terms of product experience, human behavior is generally consistent across markets. If you can create a product that delivers value to customers in one country, you can often replicate it in others. However, education is unique in that some governments intervene more than others, which affects how the private sector can operate.

For example, Saudi Arabia has strong government-backed education platforms that don't exist in other markets, creating different competitive dynamics. Still, from a product perspective, global tech companies like Netflix and Uber have shown that scalability is possible with the right approach.

The biggest challenge in scaling regionally is understanding how to communicate with stakeholders in each market. Competing with Careem for several years taught me this firsthand. Careem had an exceptional ability to localize—it spoke the language of each country so well that people genuinely believed it was a local brand. I've done informal surveys where people assumed Careem was from their own country, whether Egypt, Saudi Arabia, or Jordan.

Uber, in contrast, had a more standardized and global tone that made it feel less connected to local audiences. That experience inspired me to ensure that my next company would prioritize localization.

At Abwaab, we make sure to build a strong local presence in every market, with local marketing teams, teachers, and dialects. We tailor our content to local exam schedules, holidays, and even cultural inside jokes. The biggest validation of our approach came when someone recently told me they thought Abwaab was a local brand from their country. That's when you know you've done localization right.

What are some of the challenges around convincing parents and students to use your services?

Two key thoughts come to mind. First, in today's world, younger generations are increasingly accustomed to instant gratification. Attention spans are shortening, and people expect immediate rewards—whether it's consuming short-form videos, ordering food that arrives in minutes, or engaging with apps designed to provide instant feedback. Education, by contrast, is the opposite. It requires long-term effort before results become visible. In many cases, real benefits only emerge decades later, when students enter their careers and realize the impact of their learning.

For those in the education and edtech sectors, this presents a challenge: how do you keep students engaged when the rewards aren't immediate? Companies like Duolingo have done a great job incorporating gamification through streaks and instant feedback, which helps bridge the gap in human psychology. But ultimately, the true reward of education comes much later.

The second challenge is convincing parents and students that valuable learning experiences don't always require in-person interaction. Despite the shift to online learning during COVID-19, skepticism remains. People recognize the value of in-person education, and we also understand that transitioning too quickly can be disruptive.

If the goal is to scale rapidly and reach millions of students, a gradual transition is necessary. That's why we've introduced hybrid and blended experiences. Instead of expecting students to fully commit to online learning immediately, we offer a combination: they can come in once a week for in-person testing, mock exams, and discussions, while completing other parts of their education online. This helps them feel the value of in-person learning while maintaining flexibility. Certain activities—like workshops, debates, and high-pressure exams—are better suited for an in-person setting. Meanwhile, individual study and AI-powered personalized learning can be done online. This balanced approach is the direction we're taking.

Looking ahead, what are your future plans?

Our ultimate vision is to become the lifelong learning partner for every student in the Arab region. We want to build trust with students early in their educational journeys, showing them real results. Trust in our platform will come over time, but once established, we believe we can support learners not just in school, but through university and even into their professional careers.

Education doesn't stop after graduation—it's a lifelong process. Whether it's university studies or acquiring professional skills like coding, sales, marketing, or time management, we want to be the go-to platform for continuous learning. If we successfully build this trust, we'll have the data to truly personalize learning for every student, guiding them toward unlocking their full potential.

This is a long journey, and we've learned that focus is key. Scaling into different verticals at the right time is a challenge, but our goal is clear. Even within the K-12 space, hybrid and blended learning are evolving, and we aim to become the largest and most effective learning platform in the region—not by competing directly with schools but by complementing and enhancing traditional education.

Do you see opportunities for collaborations and partnerships with schools and governments?

Yes, absolutely. It's a well-known issue that most curricula today are outdated. Despite ongoing updates, many education systems still rely on traditional, subject-by-subject learning with little emphasis on interdisciplinary skills or real-world applications. Life skills, leadership, and future-oriented education are often missing.

At some point, as we grow and gather more data on student learning behaviors, we aim to collaborate with education ministries to help modernize curricula. Our vision is to create an Abwaab curriculum—a unified learning approach across the Arab region that integrates academic subjects with essential life skills and future job training.

Right now, we're still too small to influence government policies, but once we have a few million learners, those conversations will become possible. We already maintain good relationships with governments, and in the future, we hope to proactively shape education policies.

With schools, the situation is similar. The traditional education system was designed for the industrial revolution, mimicking a production line model where students sit in rows and receive standardized instruction. While some schools are experimenting with new learning models, most still operate in this outdated format.

———

" THE TRADITIONAL EDUCATION SYSTEM WAS DESIGNED FOR THE INDUSTRIAL REVOLUTION, MIMICKING A PRODUCTION LINE MODEL WHERE STUDENTS SIT IN ROWS AND RECEIVE STANDARDIZED INSTRUCTION.

———

Imagine a future where students learn foundational concepts at home, at their own pace, with personalized AI-driven guidance. Then, when they go to school, teachers already have access to data on their progress. Instead of passive lectures, classroom time is used for discussions, interactive problem-solving, and collaboration. This would transform the role of teachers into mentors and facilitators, making education far more effective.

This vision is within reach, and we're excited about the role we can play in shaping the future of learning. School isn't just about sitting in classrooms—it's about running workshops with other students, engaging in interactive activities, and solving problems in a group setting. Why is this important? Because students need to breathe, take a break, go outside, play games, and interact with others. They also need to experience tough situations, manage stakeholders, and take on leadership roles within small groups. I see this happening with my kids at school right now. That's how the setup naturally evolves, and we aim to become a partner to schools to help facilitate this process. Right now, we haven't taken significant steps in this direction because we're still early in our journey. However, I can already see us moving toward this vision.

How do you imagine scaling a business? You might picture a group of people in a high-rise tower, meticulously crafting a master plan for expansion. But in reality, things don't happen that way.

Our first expansion to Egypt happened just six months after launching. It was during Ramadan, in the peak of COVID lockdowns, and we were deep in our project with the government and the Ministry of Education (MoE). I was coming home late from executing that project, which had us working around the clock for three months. That night, I checked my LinkedIn and found a message from a young man named Muhammad. He told me he was passionate about what we were doing and wanted to learn from us.

How did a simple LinkedIn message lead to an entire expansion? I immediately saw an opportunity for rapid expansion into Egypt. I asked Muhammad to jump on a call, and we ended up talking at 10 PM that night. I remember taking the call outside in my garden because my kids were asleep, and the weather was nice. At the end of the call, I asked him to prepare a presentation on how he thought we could approach the Egyptian market.

Just 24 hours later, right after Iftar, I received a well-structured deck from him. I called my co-founder, Sabri, shared the deck, and we quickly agreed to bring Muhammad on board. We tasked him with assembling a team in Egypt to create content tailored to the Egyptian curriculum. Over the next two to three months, he made impressive progress for someone just 20 years old. However, as the operation scaled, we realized we needed someone with more experience to lead such a massive effort.

At that time, Uber Eats was shutting down across the region. The head of operations for Egypt, Zizo, happened to be a colleague and a friend. How do you convince the right people to join your mission? I called him the day after the shutdown was announced, and he told me he had already been following Abwaab and was passionate about our mission. After multiple interviews with him and other candidates, we quickly decided to bring him on board. He took charge of the entire operation, and from there, we built the Egypt business.

Our expansion to Saudi Arabia was inspired by an all-hands meeting, which we've held every Monday morning since we started. In one session, I encouraged the team to suggest any ideas or ask any questions they had.

What happens when you create an open space for ideas? After the meeting, one of our engineers approached me with a question that sparked the idea for a new project. We realized we could explore the Saudi market without immediately setting up a full-fledged operation. Instead, we started by remotely building an assessment bank and opening the product to Saudi users for testing.

To take this further, we asked our regional head of content, who had prior experience in Saudi's content creation space, to lead the mission. Karim relocated to Riyadh to build the team, set up sales operations, onboard the best teachers, establish partnerships, and run product experiments. Fast-forward a few years, and we now have a solid team working around the clock to build Abwaab in Saudi.

What happens when you move too fast? The story of Pakistan was quite different. We might have moved too quickly, but at the time, everything was evolving rapidly, and the EdTech industry was growing fast.

One night, as I was going through my LinkedIn inbox—my usual routine—I saw a message from an ex-Uber colleague, Raja. He was inspired by what we were doing and wanted advice on launching something similar. We exchanged a few messages, but the pace of everything was so intense that we didn't have a proper chat. A few months later, he reached out again, and we finally got on a call.

During that call, I was in our old office with Sabri. I muted the call for a moment and asked Sabri if it was okay to throw out a crazy idea. When I unmuted, I proposed that we acquire Raja's startup— where his team would focus on business development while we handled fundraising and tech development. How do you react when an unexpected opportunity arises? The idea came completely out of left field for Raja, but I asked him to think it over. A few weeks later, we reached an agreement, and we announced our expansion into Pakistan through the acquisition of EdMatrix.

We mobilized the team quickly, recruiting teachers across the board to cover Pakistan's four educational boards, each corresponding to a different province. Our team worked tirelessly on the ground, creating content, and we even signed Pakistan's top cricketer—one of the world's highest-ranked players—as the face of the brand. We went all out.

Our expansion into Oman followed a similar pattern. In 2024, I received a short email—just a subject line and a single sentence in Arabic—that I initially overlooked. Later that night, as I was checking my inbox again, I decided to loop in Omar, who was overseeing our regional expansion.

What happens when you take a second look at something? We met Mizna and immediately liked her. She had built something from scratch in Oman and had gained decent traction, all while pursuing her master's in cybersecurity. She spent time with our team, learning how we operate, and was truly inspired by our work.

We eventually structured an acquisition deal, allowing us to reassess within nine months based on specific milestones. Omar built a strong business team, and they began scaling our operations in Oman. Where do things stand now? It's still early days for us, but we're optimistic.

Reflecting on all of this, I come back to my original point: How does scaling really happen? For us, it wasn't about months of planning in a closed room. It was the result of multiple coincidental moments where we decided to be bold, take risks, and push forward without fear of failure. Sometimes, it only takes one unexpected opportunity to spark something much bigger.

———

" IF THERE'S ONE THING OUR JOURNEY SHOWS, IT'S THAT BUILDING SOMETHING MEANINGFUL ISN'T ABOUT WHERE YOU START—IT'S ABOUT HOW YOU THINK, HOW YOU ADAPT, AND HOW BOLD YOU'RE WILLING TO BE.

———

How do you see the balance between human interaction and AI in education?

I don't think it's a binary choice. Early on, I believed AI would advance so quickly that it would immediately replace teachers. We even structured Abwaab with that mindset at first. Our vision was always to personalize learning based on each student's cognitive abilities, learning pace, and behavior using AI and data.

We are still working toward that vision, but we've realized that AI isn't an "on/off" switch. Instead, it will act as a supplement to human interaction, evolving gradually over time. Right now, every student at Abwaab has an academic advisor or coach, and AI can provide insights into students' learning habits—where they struggle, which lessons they repeat, and their common mistakes in assessments. AI can analyze their natural language interactions with teachers and help tailor the learning experience accordingly.

Today, students still crave human connection, so we use AI to empower our teachers rather than replace them. I envision a spectrum: today, it might be 99% human and 1% AI, but in the future, it could shift to 95% AI and 5% human. There will likely always be a need for some level of human engagement to maintain relatability.

What an amazing journey—from a supermarket operator to a top EdTech, proving that you don't have to be engineer to scale?

Absolutely. If there's one thing our journey shows, it's that building something meaningful isn't about where you start—it's about how you think, how you adapt, and how bold you're willing to be. Tech entrepreneurship isn't reserved for engineers; it's for anyone who can spot a problem, rally the right people, and move fast to solve it. At the end of the day, it's not just about coding—it's about vision, execution, and the willingness to jump into the unknown, even if that means working well past midnight as we're doing now.

I appreciate you staying up late for this interview, Hamdi.

My pleasure. Amir. I hope our story resonates with others and that they find it insightful and inspiring.

———

YARA BURGAN

Hiring, redefined by AI

Founder and CEO of ELEVATUS

ΞLΞV∕ATUS

Amman, Jordan

www.elevatus.io

YARA BURGAN is the Co-Founder and Chief Executive Officer of Elevatus, a pioneering AI-driven recruitment platform transforming the hiring processes of global enterprises. Since its inception in 2019, Elevatus has become the go-to solution for over 150 major companies, including Samsung, RE/MAX, Omantel, Arab Bank, Dr. Suleiman Al-Habib Medical Group, Virgin Mobile, and STC Academy. Under Yara's leadership, Elevatus has helped organizations conduct over 3 million video assessments and successfully recruit thousands of candidates, setting new benchmarks in HR tech innovation.

Yara holds a degree from the University of Toronto's School of Business and Professional Studies and York University's Faculty of Science. Further cementing her expertise in global business and entrepreneurship, she recently completed a certification in "Entrepreneurship in Emerging Economies" from Harvard Business School. Her education in dynamic environments has brought vitality, professionalism, warmth, and a service-driven mindset to her career. Her hands-on experience in leading and working with major organizations has earned her admiration across all her professional roles.

In 2022, Elevatus secured a $10.5 million Series A funding round, co-led by Global Ventures and Wa'ed Ventures, with participation from Jasoor Ventures. This strategic investment fuels the company's expansion, market reach, and product innovation, reinforcing its position as an industry leader. Elevatus' AI-powered solutions—EVA-REC (a comprehensive hiring platform) and EVA-SSESS (a secure video interviewing software)—centralize recruitment processes, making talent acquisition more efficient, cost-effective, and scalable.

Beyond her role at Elevatus, Yara is deeply committed to fostering technology and entrepreneurship to nurture social and economic development, particularly in the Middle East. She actively builds awareness about technology's potential, engages in partnership-building, and consistently seeks new business opportunities.

———

ELEVATUS is an industry-leading AI-powered recruitment platform that has been transforming the hiring landscape since its inception in 2019. Led by CEO Yara Burgan, the company has helped global enterprises streamline their talent acquisition process, centralize recruitment operations, and significantly reduce hiring costs. With an advanced AI-driven approach, Elevatus has facilitated over 3 million video assessments and powered the hiring decisions of more than 150 companies across diverse industries, including Samsung, RE/MAX, Omantel, Arab Bank, Dr. Suleiman Al-Habib Medical Group, Virgin Mobile, and STC Academy.

Elevatus' technology is designed to eliminate inefficiencies in traditional hiring methods, delivering an 80% reduction in time-to-hire, a 96% decrease in hiring costs, and saving recruitment teams 17+ hours per hire. The company's flagship products, EVA-REC and EVA-SSESS, have revolutionized recruitment by automating the entire hiring workflow. EVA-REC, an award-winning AI-driven hiring platform, enables companies to identify and engage top talent five times faster, while EVA-SSESS, an advanced video interviewing solution, has helped businesses conduct thousands of remote interviews, achieving a 90% faster candidate screening process.

Elevatus' impact is evident across industries. A pharmaceutical company utilizing Elevatus' video interviewing software reduced hiring costs by 33% and sped up assessments by 92%. Jordan Kuwait Bank (JKB) leveraged Elevatus to achieve a 3X faster time-to-hire, while an international school adopting its solutions saw a 76% increase in student assessment engagement. Additionally, companies using Elevatus' technology report a 91% improvement in process efficiency and an 87% boost in candidate engagement, enhancing both internal hiring operations and the overall applicant experience.

Recognized as a trailblazer in AI-powered HR solutions, Elevatus has received numerous prestigious awards, including Best AI for HR Services in 2022, Recruitment Category Leader in 2022, and the AI-Powered Hiring Solution of the Year in the UK in 2023. These accolades solidify its reputation as the #1 AI-powered recruiting software, continuously pushing the boundaries of HR technology.

Beyond technology, Elevatus is committed to fostering entrepreneurship and business scalability in the Middle East. By equipping businesses with best-in-class AI recruitment tools, Elevatus is driving economic development and empowering enterprises to hire faster, smarter, and more efficiently in today's competitive talent marketplace.

With a dedicated leadership team and a relentless commitment to innovation, Elevatus is redefining the future of recruitment. By merging artificial intelligence with hiring excellence, the company is setting new industry benchmarks, enabling organizations worldwide to build high-performing, agile teams that thrive in the modern workforce.

Give us some background on yourself.

My story starts with my Jordanian roots, surrounded by warmth, tradition, and family. Then, Toronto became my home—a city full of life. This is where my education, career, and everything fell into place. I come from a small family—just me and my sister. My father, an engineer, instilled a scientific, logical mindset in us, while my mother, had this incredible ability to understand people and could read a room in an instant. Growing up, I learned the importance of balancing logic and empathy, simply by watching them.

Academically, I majored in chemistry and project management. Science and problem-solving always clicked with me, but memorization, not so much. I've always worked and studied at the same time, I took on different jobs at restaurants, coaching at summer camps, then as an assistant at a chemistry lab throughout my university years. That early exposure taught me a lot about people, conflict management, and the value of time.

I've always felt the need to do more and my curiosity kept pushing me forward. During university, I launched a student wellness initiative that aimed to help students adopt a healthier and more balanced lifestyle, despite all the pressure that comes from their studies. Later, I joined the "leadershape" program, which focused on shaping students' core values and key strengths to become future leaders. This program gave me clarity on what my true strengths and weaknesses were, and taught me that in life, you should capitalize on your areas of strength, rather than dwell on your weakness.

By graduation, I landed a job with a Canadian railway company, managing overseas projects. But two and a half years later, life took me back to Jordan. In what was supposed to be a temporary move, turned into a return home and the start to something big.

At 22, with a diverse experience and two degrees under my belt, I expected to find job opportunities easily. I applied to over 80 positions which I knew I was a great fit for, but reality hit hard, four months of job hunting and not a single interview. That frustration led to the birth of Elevatus.

———

" I APPLIED TO OVER 80 POSITIONS WHICH I KNEW I WAS A GREAT FIT FOR, BUT REALITY HIT HARD, FOUR MONTHS OF JOB HUNTING AND NOT A SINGLE INTERVIEW. THAT FRUSTRATION LED TO THE BIRTH OF ELEVATUS.

———

It started with me recording a 30-second video pitch, showcasing my experience beyond what was written in my resume. I submitted my profile to the same job applications with this video attached and interviews started pouring in. In that moment I thought, if this worked for me, it could work for others. Alongside working full-time at HyperPay, I began training job seekers and university students on how to present their key strengths in a short video – known as an elevator pitch. Once I compiled a sizable database of video resumes,

I started sending weekly mailshots to potential employers from every sector, highlighting the top 5 candidates of the week.

Meanwhile, I've connected with many human resources professionals through my outreach and gathered insights about the key challenges they face in their role with the existing legacy solutions implemented. The 30-pages document I put together from these meetings became the blueprint for Elevatus.

Initially, Elevatus was about problem-solving, not business building. We developed a platform, incorporated AI, and transformed video content into a comprehensive solution, aiming to modernize outdated HR systems. In 2019, Elevatus was launched with my co-founder, Yacoub, and a team of talented friends.

Commercialization followed landing our first client, a telecom company. Our product development roadmap was driven by user feedback. Momentum grew, culminating in an EY Startup of the Year nomination, which significantly increased our visibility in the market.

How did you manage to win such an award?

This nomination stemmed, in part, from a viral video we produced featuring a brilliant coder with a disability. He was unable to find a job and the short video allowed him to display his passion and ability to perform to his potential employer. The video ultimately caught the right people's attention, resulting in him receiving many job offers. Especially in a competitive job market like Jordan, this simple tool proved to be very effective and allowed many of our applicants to stand out.

What strategies helped you land your first client, and how did their feedback shape Elevatus early on?

Cold outreach – it took several attempts to secure a meeting with the head of HR at a telecom company. During the in-person meeting, I demonstrated the beta version of our platform and showcased the database of job seekers' video resumes. For every video, we generated a psychometric report using our in-house developed AI algorithm. During the demonstration, the client pointed out one specific profile to verify their psychometric report analysis based on her personal knowledge of the candidate. The accuracy of the results excited her about our technology, and that's how we won our first contract.

It wasn't easy, though. We weren't fully prepared. Our early clients were large enterprises with complex needs and requirements, so we were under a lot of pressure constantly. We've faced many challenges in the early days related to legal contracts, security and compliance requirements, I remember receiving a questionnaire of 120 compliance questions that we didn't fully know how to answer. But thankfully, our early clients were patient and worked with us, not against us.

Landing paying clients was a game-changer, it turned my idea into a real business. Passion is important, but resilience is what helps a startup scale. Setting up the legal structure was the first challenge, then came team building, product development, and funding. Each stage brought its own hurdles.

One of the key challenges we faced was related to our pricing structure. Finding the right business model was crucial for the continuity of the business, it impacted our product development, marketing and sales strategies. Across the MENA region, cultural and economic factors play a huge role in shaping the business model. We tried feature-based pricing but found that clients wanted full access to all features for the best price. Through extensive trail-and-error we find out what works best for us.

Fast forward to today, Elevatus operates across nine different countries and supports over 200 enterprise clients such as Al Habib Medical Group, Omantel, REMAX global, Mediclinic, Redsea global and many government entities.

In the early days, a founder's involvement is crucial. Clients had trusted me and my vision. Even if there were challenges related to the product, they gave us leeway, and we built trust by delivering value, even if it meant providing services to make up for gaps—gaps we filled over time.

———

> IN THE EARLY DAYS, A FOUNDER'S INVOLVEMENT IS CRUCIAL. CLIENTS HAD TRUSTED ME AND MY VISION. EVEN IF THERE WERE CHALLENGES RELATED TO THE PRODUCT, THEY GAVE US LEEWAY, AND WE BUILT TRUST BY DELIVERING VALUE, EVEN IF IT MEANT PROVIDING SERVICES TO MAKE UP FOR GAPS—GAPS WE FILLED OVER TIME.

———

As the product matured, the need to achieve operational excellence became detrimental for scalability. I worked closely with an advisor and tech guru to help me implement the right processes and ensure harmony across departments. We've adhered to the principle of "less is more", maintaining a lean team and focusing on efficiency and automation. Achieving this takes time, investment in the right tools, bringing the right people onboard, and establishing a clear direction in terms of company goals and KPIs.

My co-founder and I always had the mindset that for every complex problem there's a simple solution. And this mindset was reflected in how we approach product design. By simplifying the most complex hiring process among enterprise clients, we offered an agile and adaptable technology that can help organizations scale more efficiently.

Scaling a B2B SaaS enterprise solution can be done in two ways; direct sales and channel partners. Direct sales is important to build client references and mature your revenue engine, while, channel partners can capitalize on their existing client base and acquire a bigger market share through their local market knowledge and shorter sales cycles.

So, we started with direct sales then pivoted into channel partners to scale faster, with 80% of our current revenue is generated through regional and global partners.

Now let's talk about fundraising, HR Tech has never been an attractive domain for investors. The countless rejections I received in the early days were extremely discouraging. However, I focused on the problem at hand, and truly believed in our solution, because I saw the real impact we had on our clients – we were solving a huge challenge that none of the legacy solutions were able to tackle and solve.

To be able to successfully fundraise for Elevatus, I've had to understand the investors mindset and fund mandates. I sought guidance from a founder-turned-VC, who had shared his knowledge and provided guidance on managing our process more efficiently. I adopted a sales approach for fundraising, identifying, qualifying, negotiating, and closing. With a more qualified pipeline of potential investors, the higher the probability of converting and closing a round.

How did you manage to improve your fundraising approach and close investment rounds more efficiently?

During the introduction calls, I started qualifying by asking questions, not just the other way around. I shifted from trying to impress, to looking for the right fit, and ensuring that our goals were aligned. Where it once took me months to secure a lead investor, I later closed a round in a fraction of the time. It's about identifying the right investors, qualifying them and aligning our needs. Until founders do that, they'll struggle.

In my questions, I look to gather information related to their fund mandate, the returns they expect, the investment process, key people involved in decision making, process timeline, and due diligence checklists. I believe asking the right questions leads to better decisions in any process, not just for fundraising.

How is Elevatus evolving, and what role will AI play in the future of recruitment?

Elevatus today is a market leader within the HR Tech industry helping organizations scale by governing and automating their recruitment processes.

Looking ahead, our R&D and Innovation team have been focused on developing algorithms that address specific challenges within the recruitment cycle. But, with the immense domain experience that we've acquired, we will launch something groundbreaking in June, an autonomous AI engine that will run the entire recruitment cycle based on historical behaviour and best practices on a user level. So, everyone will get to enjoy a personalized user experience on the Elevatus platform, while improving their work efficiency by up to 90%. For example, writing a job post, shortlisting candidates, interviewing and assessing them, sending offers, background checks, and generating reports will be fully run by our in-house built AI agent.

Including finding and recruiting talent?

Hiring and team building remain an ongoing challenge. We prioritize cultural fitness alongside skills, and we use our own technology to attract, assess and hire candidates.

Attracting talent is tough for startups without strong branding. We focus on strengthening our brand using our EVABRAND solution which allows any company to build a fully branded career page instantly. We showcase our company's core values and highlight key benefits for job seekers that are interested to apply. Building a strong team requires time, agile processes and a robust company culture. People are motivated by different things, when you can tap into what drives people—be it passion, security, recognition, or a sense of purpose—you position your company to not only meet their needs but also engage them on a deeper level.

Our core team has been with us since day one. If your team believes in the mission and feels they are contributing to something meaningful; they are more likely to be driven and invested in your company's success. In the early days, skills were paramount. Now, cultural fit comes first.

How has Saudi Arabia's business ecosystem supported Elevatus' growth, and what have you learned about doing business there?

Saudi Arabia has really been a game-changer for Elevatus. Launching in 2019 turned out to be perfect timing. A lot of people underestimate how open Saudi's business culture is. You can easily reach decision-makers, pitch your ideas, and have real, meaningful conversations. For any B2B startup, that kind of accessibility is crucial.

Coming from Canada, where everything is pretty direct—sometimes even a little abrupt—Saudi was definitely a culture shock for me. I remember calling a potential client, a VP at a government institute, and jumping straight into business. He laughed and said, "My dearest, connect with people first, then talk business." It was a big shift for me, but honestly, Saudi's culture has been so welcoming and supportive. It's been a huge learning curve, but one I'm grateful for.

The country has evolved so much. Things like compliance, data security, and the growth of large enterprises have really impressed me. For us, that meant more work, but it was inspiring to see how seriously companies were taking their growth and improvement.

Product adoption in Saudi has also skyrocketed. People are way more aware of the importance of technology now and are really excited to leverage it. We've seen a huge jump in adoption rates, which is fantastic for us.

Culturally, Saudi is all about experiences. Whether it's Ramadan gatherings or the traditions of majlis, experiences are what matter most. As tech founders, we really need to focus on offering a great experience, not just a product.

Working in Saudi has been an incredible journey. We've gone from a regional solution to competing with ERP giants like Oracle and SAP on a global scale. The fact that this technology, which started right here, is now being exported to the US and Europe is something I'm super proud of. It's been amazing to see how far we've come, and Saudi has definitely played a huge role in that.

———

> WE'VE GONE FROM A REGIONAL SOLUTION TO
> COMPETING WITH ERP GIANTS LIKE ORACLE AND SAP
> ON A GLOBAL SCALE.

———

What has been your experience as a female founder in KSA and the region?

When it comes to female entrepreneurship, I've found it to be an advantage for me personally. I focused more on sales and business growth rather than getting caught up in the "female founder" conversation. Honestly, I think there's a tendency to put too much focus on gender when it comes to business. If you're passionate, have a clear vision, and focus on execution, that's what really matters.

Sure, there are fewer female founders, but I don't think that's where the attention should lie. At the end of the day, business owners care about the value you bring to the table, not whether you're a man or a woman.

The lack of female founders in the region is definitely a mix of things. Women often carry more family and household responsibilities, which can be a big barrier. But I've met so many amazing female founders who are quietly building successful businesses behind the scenes. They may not always be in the spotlight, but they're doing incredible work.

Personally, moving to Riyadh has been nothing but supportive for me. It's really about mindset. If you believe in what you're doing and focus on executing your vision, success will follow. I like to visualize my goals because that drives my actions and gives me the momentum I need to move forward.

At the end of the day, it's not about gender it's about resilience, courage, and execution. Anyone can move mountains if they choose to. The potential is limitless—it's just about believing in yourself and going for it.

———

> IT'S NOT ABOUT GENDER IT'S ABOUT RESILIENCE, COURAGE, AND EXECUTION. ANYONE CAN MOVE MOUNTAINS IF THEY CHOOSE TO. THE POTENTIAL IS LIMITLESS—IT'S JUST ABOUT BELIEVING IN YOURSELF AND GOING FOR IT.

———

What role have advisors and mentors played in your entrepreneurial journey?

In the B2B enterprise world, the challenges never stop. I was navigating a sea of obstacles, and I needed someone who had already been through the grind and come out on top. That's when I met David Gurle. He was already an expert in the tech domain, having built massive teams and orchestrated the sale of Skype to Microsoft.

I started emailing him, detailing the specific hurdles I was facing. Slowly but surely, he agreed to take me on in an advisory capacity.

During our very first session, I vented about how tough everything seemed. I expected some sympathy, but instead, he calmly told me, "If you think this is hard, you're looking at it wrong. Challenges are part of the process. Challenges weren't something to dread—they were just a natural part of the journey, and they were manageable – with the right mindset."

From there, we focused heavily on operational excellence. David helped me fine-tune my approach, teaching me how to manage things more efficiently and apply best practices that made all the difference.

So, to all the founders out there: seek out advisors who've been through it. Be persistent, ask the tough questions, and always stay open to learning. You'll be amazed at how they can reshape your thinking and push you to the next level.

Great advice indeed. Thank you, Yara.

You're very welcome.

———

MOSTAFA AMIN

From bread to everything, fast

Founder and CEO of BREADFAST

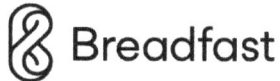

Cairo, Egypt

www.breadfast.com

MOSTAFA AMIN is an Egyptian serial entrepreneur renowned for his significant contributions to the tech and startup ecosystem in Egypt and the broader Middle East. He has co-founded several successful ventures across diverse sectors, including media, machine learning, and e-commerce.

His professional journey reflects a strong foundation in technology and entrepreneurship. His first major entrepreneurial venture was Egyptian Streets, which he co-founded in 2012. Egyptian Streets quickly became one of Egypt's fastest-growing English-language news websites, providing insightful coverage of Egyptian affairs and aiming to present authentic narratives from the region. This venture laid the foundation for his broader interest in digital transformation and business development.

In 2017, recognizing a gap in the market for fresh bread deliveries, Amin co-founded Breadfast. Initially, the startup focused on delivering freshly baked bread to customers' doorsteps every morning through a mobile app. Over time, Breadfast expanded its offerings to include a wide range of grocery items, evolving into a comprehensive online store with over 6,000 products, including electronics and personal hygiene items. The company has achieved significant milestones, such as being accepted into Y Combinator, a prestigious U.S.-based startup accelerator, in 2019. Under Amin's leadership, Breadfast has grown significantly and now serves over 300,000 households in Egypt, offering delivery times as short as 30 minutes. His focus on customer satisfaction and sustainable growth continues to shape Breadfast's expansion and impact, particularly in emerging markets where efficient, tech-driven grocery delivery remains a challenge.

Amin's entrepreneurial achievements have earned him international recognition. He was listed in Forbes' "30 Under 30" Europe list in 2018, highlighting his impact on the media and e-commerce sectors. Additionally, he has been involved with the World Economic Forum as a Global Shaper, reflecting his commitment to driving positive change in society. His influence extends beyond his businesses, as he actively mentors emerging startups in the Middle

East and Europe, offering guidance on entrepreneurship, e-commerce strategies, and leadership skills. His dedication to mentoring young entrepreneurs has contributed to the growth and development of the startup ecosystem in the region.

Beyond his professional endeavors, Amin is also a professional singer, showcasing his diverse talents and interests. His journey exemplifies the spirit of innovation and resilience. Through his various ventures, he has significantly impacted Egypt's digital landscape, providing valuable services and inspiring a new generation of entrepreneurs in the region.

———

BREADFAST is a fast-growing Egyptian online grocery delivery company that has revolutionized the way consumers shop for their daily essentials. Established in 2017 by co-founders Mostafa Amin, Mohamed Habib, and Abdallah Nofal, the company is headquartered in Cairo, Egypt. Initially, Breadfast focused on delivering freshly baked bread and breakfast items to customers' doorsteps each morning, catering to a niche market that prioritized convenience and quality. However, as demand for reliable and efficient grocery delivery services grew, Breadfast expanded its product offerings to include a wide range of grocery items, including fresh produce, dairy products, meats, beverages, snacks, personal care items, and household essentials. Today, it operates as a fully vertically integrated online supermarket, offering over 6,000 stock-keeping units (SKUs) to meet the daily needs of hundreds of thousands of customers.

A defining feature of Breadfast's success is its vertically integrated supply chain, which allows the company to maintain end-to-end control over procurement, storage, and last-mile delivery. By eliminating reliance on third-party logistics providers, Breadfast ensures consistent product quality, freshness, and availability, while also optimizing operational costs. The company employs micro-fulfillment centers strategically located across Cairo and other major cities in Egypt, enabling them to manage inventory efficiently and complete deliveries in as little as 30 to 60 minutes—one of the fastest grocery delivery times in the region.

As a technology-driven company, Breadfast has invested heavily in its mobile app and digital infrastructure, ensuring a seamless shopping experience for users. Customers can browse through thousands of products, schedule deliveries, and track their orders in real time. The company's data analytics and AI-driven inventory management system help optimize stock levels, predict consumer demand, and reduce waste, making the operation both efficient and sustainable.

Breadfast's rapid growth has attracted significant interest from investors and industry leaders. The company has secured multiple rounds of funding from prestigious venture capital firms, including Y Combinator, 500 Global, VNV Global, and Shorooq Partners. These investments have facilitated Breadfast's geographic expansion, improved its supply chain capabilities, and accelerated its technological innovations. In 2021, the company raised $26 million in a Series A funding round, which has been instrumental in supporting its expansion efforts and scaling operations. Since its inception, Breadfast has delivered millions of orders to customers, with its user base growing by over 300% year-over-year in key markets.

Currently, Breadfast employs more than 6,500 employees, spanning roles in technology, logistics, customer service, and marketing. The company's customer retention rates remain high, reflecting strong brand loyalty and satisfaction. It has also expanded beyond Cairo to serve additional Egyptian cities, with plans to expand into other Middle Eastern and African markets. Breadfast is positioning itself to become a regional leader in online grocery delivery, leveraging its expertise in logistics, customer experience, and technology to scale beyond its current footprint.

Breadfast's commitment to innovation and efficiency has set new standards in the e-grocery sector in Egypt. The company will be introducing features such as subscription-based deliveries, allowing customers to receive essential items on a regular schedule without having to place repeat orders manually. Additionally, Breadfast's focus on hyper-local sourcing supports local farmers and suppliers, contributing to the broader economic ecosystem.

Looking ahead, Breadfast aims to continue expanding its services and product offerings, with potential moves into adjacent markets such as instant meals, pharmaceuticals, and non-food consumer goods. By staying ahead of technological trends and maintaining its commitment to quality and customer satisfaction, Breadfast is poised to redefine how people in Egypt and the broader Middle East access their groceries and everyday necessities.

———

Let's get started with a brief background about yourself.

Thank you so much, Amir, for having me. I was born, raised, and am currently based in Cairo, Egypt. Everything about my story and journey comes from Egypt. I studied biomedical engineering, and for a long time, my passion was in neuroscience and radiology engineering.

Interestingly, I took on a pretty crazy challenge—I studied two majors at two different universities simultaneously. My first major was biomedical engineering, and my second was simultaneous translation from English to Arabic. Despite spending five years on each degree, I managed to complete both at the same time. That essentially means I crammed 10 years of study into five years. It was an intense experience that taught me a lot about time management, which has been invaluable in building Breadfast and other ventures.

I think Egypt is a very unique place, and I feel lucky to have been born here. By nature, I love emerging markets and the challenges that come with them. I firmly believe in the future of growth in emerging markets. What makes these markets unique is that the challenges they present are unlike those in well-developed markets like the U.S. or Europe. I always see it as if you're training your mind and body in a gym that is completely different from any other gym you might visit. It builds a mindset where, if you love solving problems, you start to embrace the word "problem" itself. That's what I love about emerging markets.

When you were growing up, did you know you wanted to be an entrepreneur?

Two major things shaped my entrepreneurial ambition. First, I was a Boy Scout for 16 years, which was an incredible experience. Being a Scout teaches you how to take risks and how to push through challenges to reach your goal. No matter the obstacles, you always have to be ready, take responsibility, and lead.

Second, my father was an entrepreneur. He ran a small-to-medium construction business that provided painting materials. I started helping him at his store when I was about five years old. He strongly believed in teaching his children the value of responsibility. I come from a family of five kids—four brothers and one sister—and from a very young age, we were all encouraged to understand the meaning of hard work.

By the time I was eight or nine, my father would leave me in charge of the store while he went to pray at the mosque. Over the years, I began to understand how the business worked. There was cash collection, delivery schedules, logistics, inventory management, and customer service. I was exposed to both B2C sales—where customers would walk in and buy products—and B2B deals, where companies would place large orders.

From the ages of five to 18, I essentially grew up in that store, learning the fundamentals of business: managing a team, handling cash flow, understanding taxation, and even dealing with HR-like situations. I didn't know at the time that these were formal business functions, but I was absorbing everything. For example, I learned about commercial registration and tax ID responsibilities, payroll, and how to handle employee needs—whether it was a team member needing an advance for a family emergency or a worker requiring early payment before a wedding.

Balancing my experience in my father's store with my time in the Boy Scouts gave me a unique perspective. Scouting instilled in me a deep respect for preparation and problem-solving. When we climbed mountains, we had to anticipate potential challenges—ensuring we had enough water, food, and first-aid supplies while keeping our packs light. Leadership was essential. As I got older, I became responsible for younger Scouts, which meant ensuring their safety and well-being. If someone fell sick, it was my job to figure out a solution and communicate with their family. These experiences taught me the importance of responsibility, resilience, and leadership—qualities that are crucial in entrepreneurship.

Another defining moment came during the 2008 global financial crisis. My father's business was doing very well until the crisis hit, and suddenly, everything collapsed. Overnight, we went from being financially stable to struggling. At that point, I had just started university in September 2007, and by 2008, I realized I needed to find another source of income to support my education. I couldn't let my father shoulder all the financial burden alone.

So, I pivoted. I started teaching Arabic to expats in Egypt as a freelance job. I marketed myself to international students and professionals who wanted to learn Arabic. By forming groups and offering lessons, I was able to generate an income to help pay for my studies. This experience taught me not to take anything for granted. Life can change overnight, and you need to be able to adapt.

Between my father's store, the Boy Scouts, and my experience navigating financial struggles, I learned invaluable lessons about business, leadership, and resilience.

Great head start, I can see how these experiences helped shape your development. Any others?

Before launching Breadfast, I went through four failed startups. After graduating, I worked for about six months before realizing academia wasn't for me, despite being the second-highest-ranking student in my class. I wanted to build something of my own—something impactful—so I started experimenting with business ideas.

At one point, I joined a Japanese biomedical devices company in Egypt, expecting an engineering role, only to find myself in sales, meeting doctors and selling ultrasound devices. It wasn't what I wanted. I had envisioned real engineering work, something more technical and innovative. I started researching how to break into R&D in biotech and biomedical fields, but Egypt had few opportunities. Leaving for Europe, China, or the U.S. wasn't an option, so I began looking for other engineering roles outside the biomedical sector.

I applied to a leading multinational petroleum services company, passed four interview rounds, and the final stage required spending two weeks in the field with senior engineers evaluating my skills. I traveled to an offshore site in the desert, where I worked alongside engineers with 15 to 20 years of experience. They were highly paid in USD, but something struck me: their lives revolved around repetitive tasks, running the same analyses, always on call, and constantly away from home. Over time, they had lost their passion and personal lives. Watching them, I knew I didn't want to be in their position decades later.

Two days before the trial period ended, I made my decision. When HR called to officially offer me the job, I immediately declined. The recruiter was shocked. "What do you mean?" she asked. I told her I had decided to pursue something else. The next day, the HR director called personally. "Do you know how many engineers would kill for this job, and you're rejecting it?" His reaction only reinforced my decision. "Thank you for confirming my choice," I replied. "This job isn't for me."

How did your family and peers react when you rejected a stable, well-paying job to pursue entrepreneurship?

They thought I was insane. A petroleum job with a USD salary is a dream for many engineers in Egypt, but I was certain this wasn't the life I wanted. Instead, I co-founded Egyptian Streets, which grew into Egypt's largest independent English-language news outlet. It was my first real experience with fundraising, hiring, and managing a company. In 2012, I raised my first convertible note from a German investor, though many in Egypt didn't understand the concept at the time. While the venture was a success in terms of audience and impact, media monetization was a major challenge. Scaling it meant aligning with investor agendas, which we weren't willing to do. To maintain our independence, we chose not to expand further.

After your early ventures, what key lessons did you take away that influenced your approach to building Breadfast?

After that, I did, in fact, experiment—not just with one, but with three more startups in machine learning, directories, and other fields. They all failed. By 2016, with Egypt facing economic turmoil and severe inflation, I told my wife that I was considering leaving for the U.S. I had always been influenced by Silicon Valley's approach—focusing on scale first and monetization later—but it wasn't working in Egypt. Fundraising was difficult, and people weren't willing to pay for cloud-based solutions. I told her, "Before we make a final decision to leave, I need one last week to think." That week changed everything. I took out a white sheet of paper and asked myself, If I build one final company, what should it look like? What must it get right?

One of the key lessons from my past failures was the importance of a committed founding team. I had learned that talent alone wasn't enough—deep commitment mattered more. Before even settling on an idea, I reached out to two people I trusted, Mohammed and Abdullah. I told them, "I'm starting a company. I don't know what it is yet, and I have no money. But I want to do this with you." They both said yes without hesitation. Convincing people to join you without funding, a product, or a track record of success is rare, and to this day, they remain the most committed partners I've ever worked with.

———

> I'M STARTING A COMPANY. I DON'T KNOW WHAT IT IS
> YET, AND I HAVE NO MONEY. BUT I WANT TO DO THIS
> WITH YOU.

———

The second principle I defined was that whatever we built had to be a tangible product. In emerging markets, people don't trust purely digital solutions. Unlike in the U.S. or Europe, where software-as-a-service (SaaS) models thrive, in Egypt, customers need to physically see what they're paying for. That's why many global tech models fail when applied locally—aggregating a broken supply chain doesn't guarantee a great customer experience.

With these principles in mind, we started meeting every week in 2016. We had no office, no funding—just a belief that we would build something great. That's how the journey to Breadfast began.

How did you arrive at the idea of Breadfast?

That first year was brutal. We went through seven different ideas before Breadfast finally emerged as number seven. All three of us—Mohammed, Abdullah, and I—came from a tech background. Mohammed had built the largest ed-tech platform at the time, Nepham.com, while Abdullah had his own software house. Naturally, we leaned toward software-based ideas like VR, AI, and AR, but each time we evaluated them against our criteria for emerging markets, they failed. They were exciting but not monetizable.

With no full-time jobs and financial responsibilities to meet, we resorted to freelancing—Abdullah built websites, Mohammed took on side projects, and I did the same. Yet, no matter how busy we were, we met every week, determined to figure out what we were going to build. One night, Mohammed and I were having a late dinner at a seafood restaurant in Cairo when the waiter brought out a basket of freshly baked Egyptian bread, still warm. Over the past year, I had trained my brain to identify problems and think of tech-based solutions. I looked at the bread, then at Mohammed, and said, "Freshly baked bread, delivered to your doorstep every morning using a mobile app." He paused, intrigued.

Abdullah, however, was asleep at the time. When I called to wake him up and pitched the idea, his half-asleep response was, "Are you waking me up for a bread company?" I insisted, "No jokes. Let's meet tomorrow to brainstorm this." That night, I knew we had something. The next morning, while driving with my wife, I confidently told her, "I'm starting a new company." She laughed and said, "What's new? You start a new company every quarter." To her, I was the definition of instability—always chasing the next big thing. When I explained the idea, she immediately suggested, "Why not call it Breadfast?" That was it. I stopped the car, searched for the domain name, and found it available—but expensive. Since Egyptians couldn't pay in USD at the time due to credit card restrictions, I called a friend in the U.S. to purchase it for me. I paid him back over six months. With a name, a committed team, and a strong idea, we finally had a clear direction.

What was the initial business model?

Given our tech backgrounds, our first instinct was to create an Uber-like model for bread—an app that simply connected demand with supply. However, I rejected this idea immediately. Instead, I told Abdullah and Mohammed, "We are going to bake the bread ourselves." Their reaction was immediate confusion. "What do you mean? We have zero experience in this industry," Abdullah asked.

I reminded them of what we had learned from our research—reliability in emerging markets is almost nonexistent. If we built our model around aggregating a broken supply chain, we would never be able to deliver a great customer experience. The only way to ensure consistency was to own the supply chain ourselves.

For the next six months, we dedicated ourselves to learning how to bake. I reached out to a friend whose family owned a hospitality group, and he introduced us to a chef from one of their hotels. Through this connection, we developed our first high-quality bread recipes. This hands-on approach laid the foundation for what Breadfast would become.

What was the initial focus of the company?

For the first two years, we focused exclusively on bread, bakery items, and pastries. Initially, we only had three products, and to be honest, they weren't great. But we listened to our customers, refined our recipes, and continuously improved. Three products became six, then seventeen.

Our model revolved around a unique next-morning delivery promise—if you placed an order before midnight, fresh bread would arrive at your doorstep by 5:00 AM. No one else was offering this at scale.

For mothers in Egypt, this was a game-changer. They could wake up, receive fresh bread, and prepare breakfast for their kids before school. As a result, our peak delivery hours became 5:00–7:00 AM, during which we developed a deep emotional connection with our customers.

How did you secure funding when investors were skeptical?

We set out to raise $150K in pre-seed funding, but every investor we approached came from the tech world. When I pitched the idea, their response was always the same: "Why bake your own bread when so many bakeries already exist?" They saw our model as asset-heavy and repeatedly advised us to pivot to a more traditional tech-driven approach.

This experience reinforced an important lesson for me: founders should not let investors dictate their decisions. If you believe in the problem you are solving and the solution you've created, stick to it. Investor advice, while valuable, can sometimes be misleading.

———

" FOUNDERS SHOULD NOT LET INVESTORS DICTATE THEIR DECISIONS. IF YOU BELIEVE IN THE PROBLEM YOU ARE SOLVING AND THE SOLUTION YOU'VE CREATED, STICK TO IT.

———

We started baking in 2017, and over time, I came to realize that what truly fascinated me about emerging markets was their broken supply chains. That's where the real opportunity lay. Unlike developed markets, where infrastructure has been built over decades, in emerging markets, you have to build it yourself.

How did YC play a role in your growth?

We applied to Y Combinator four times before finally getting accepted. Initially, YC struggled to understand our model. In our final interview, they asked, "Why bake your own bread?"

To clarify our vision, we filmed a video showcasing our production process and demonstrated exactly what problem we were solving. The next morning, we received an email: "Congratulations, you got in." That moment changed everything. From that point on, Breadfast was no longer just a bread company—it became Egypt's largest online grocery platform. And this is just the beginning.

How challenging was fundraising in the early days?

It took us six months to raise our first $150K. At that stage, our product portfolio was limited, and expanding into groceries required a cold supply chain—something we didn't yet have. By the end of 2019, we faced a crucial decision: should we invest in refrigerated trucks or build micro-warehouses? This moment marked a pivotal shift in our strategy. We decided to pivot to on-demand delivery, transforming Breadfast from a bakery startup into a full-fledged grocery platform. The response was overwhelming—demand skyrocketed, and we had found our product-market fit.

Can you explain how Breadfast is positioned as a quick commerce company?

Breadfast is a quick commerce company, but we don't follow the 10-minute or 15-minute delivery model because we don't believe in the unit economics of that approach. Instead, we promise our customers a one-hour delivery. Over time, as we improve and enhance our supply chain, we have already managed to reduce delivery times to 30 minutes.

What makes Breadfast unique from a customer perspective is our exclusive selection of products that cater to households' daily needs—from breakfast to lunch and dinner. Customers can find all the ingredients they need to cook their meals. We've also ventured into the coffee supply chain, and today, Breadfast Coffee operates as a consumer-facing outlet. From the same fulfillment points, we deliver hot coffee directly to customers' doorsteps.

Beyond that, we strongly believe in retail, technology, and omnichannel models. Today, Breadfast operates close to 30 specialty coffee locations. Since we already own the bakery and pastry supply chain, coffee became a natural extension. It's a high-retention, high-frequency product with healthy margins. In just eight months, we anticipate that Breadfast Coffee, as a separate vertical, will surpass the largest international coffee brand in Egypt.

What is the broader vision for Breadfast?

The bigger vision for Breadfast revolves around serving household needs. These needs vary from fresh and non-fresh groceries to coffee and even financial services. Our goal is to build a customer experience engine based on trust and relationships. We prioritize the customer first, ensuring that we communicate that trust and expand our services accordingly.

For example, if a customer is already spending money to access certain products, we want to integrate additional services seamlessly into our supply chain. We aim to create a shopping experience where customers can fulfill all their household needs through Breadfast.

From bread to everything—that's our journey. We started with the most basic household staple, fresh bread, and are working toward providing every essential item a household requires.

———

> " FROM BREAD TO EVERYTHING—THAT'S OUR JOURNEY. WE STARTED WITH THE MOST BASIC HOUSEHOLD STAPLE, FRESH BREAD, AND ARE WORKING TOWARD PROVIDING EVERY ESSENTIAL ITEM A HOUSEHOLD REQUIRES.

———

Do you see Breadfast evolving into a super app?

I personally dislike the term "super app" because many operators overuse it. However, the dream is to become one. Rather than labeling ourselves as a super app, we want our customers to recognize us as one organically. Once our customers start referring to Breadfast as their go-to platform for multiple services, that's when we will have earned the title.

The story will be that this so-called super app started with one of the hardest aspects of the supply chain—delivering fresh bread at 5:00 AM in a densely populated city like Cairo. Over time, we expanded our offerings while maintaining our focus on execution and customer experience. We recognize this is a long journey that will take years of refinement and development.

What challenges have you faced, particularly in scaling and fundraising?

Challenges are inevitable, and we could go into much more depth on this. Regarding fundraising, we're proud to have attracted global investors to the region due to Breadfast's traction and execution. Our investors come from the U.S., Europe, UAE, Saudi Arabia, and Egypt, showcasing confidence in our business model.

How do you approach operational efficiency and data-driven decision-making?

Our entire operation revolves around supply chain agility. Many tech companies rely on third-party infrastructure, which can limit decision-making. If you're an aggregator or marketplace, for example, you depend on a supermarket's stock, which can cause fulfillment issues.

Let's say a customer is shopping at a physical store while another orders the same product online. The in-store customer takes the last available unit, and suddenly, the online customer gets a notification that the item is unavailable. This creates frustration. However, by owning our inventory, we can ensure that what customers order is always available and delivered as promised.

There are thousands of similar touchpoints within the supply chain that influence customer experience. One major challenge is waste reduction, particularly in the fresh supply chain. We operate with one of the most efficient waste management systems globally, thanks to our technology and demand forecasting models. Our big data team builds in-house models instead of relying on third-party companies from the Bay Area or Europe. These models help us efficiently manage inventory and reduce waste, benefiting both the environment and our bottom line.

Breadfast also operates one of the most profitable unit economics in the on-demand grocery sector. Many online grocery players struggle to achieve operational profitability, but we reached this milestone two years ago. Now, we are focused on scaling while maintaining efficiency.

What are your plans for market expansion?

We are preparing for international expansion, starting with Saudi Arabia. Our ambition extends to the broader Middle East and Africa. If you ask about long-term plans, an IPO is definitely part of our vision. We want to create a global success story from emerging markets.

The question we ask ourselves is: Why not? If we can build world-class operations, technology, and unit economics, then why not pursue a strong public offering? Our goal is to inspire other entrepreneurs and showcase that global-scale businesses can emerge from our region.

––––––

> IF WE CAN BUILD WORLD-CLASS OPERATIONS, TECHNOLOGY, AND UNIT ECONOMICS, THEN WHY NOT PURSUE A STRONG PUBLIC OFFERING?

––––––

Why did you choose Saudi Arabia as your first expansion market?

Several factors played into our decision. Saudi Arabia has a population of 35 million, mostly local consumers. Unlike some other Gulf countries, there is no language barrier. Additionally, Egypt exports a significant amount of fresh produce to Saudi, which strengthens our supply chain capabilities.

The logistics between Egypt and Saudi Arabia are also favorable—Cairo to Jeddah is just a one-hour and 20-minute flight. Another factor is the large Egyptian expatriate community in Saudi, which numbers around 3.5 million, or roughly 10% of the population.

Saudi Arabia is also actively developing its supply chain infrastructure beyond Riyadh and Jeddah, which presents a great opportunity for us. We see potential in building a competitive advantage in fresh food logistics in the region.

What are your thoughts on the future of the startup ecosystem in the region?

I'm extremely optimistic about the region's growth. We are seeing great success stories emerging from Saudi Arabia, Egypt, and the UAE. If execution continues at the same trajectory, I believe we will see more unicorns and decacorns emerging from MENA in the next five years. While regions like Latin America and Southeast Asia are currently ahead, the Middle East has the talent, market potential, and investor interest to catch up and become a global startup powerhouse.

———

" IF EXECUTION CONTINUES AT THE SAME TRAJECTORY, I BELIEVE WE WILL SEE MORE UNICORNS AND DECACORNS EMERGING FROM MENA IN THE NEXT FIVE YEARS. WHILE REGIONS LIKE LATIN AMERICA AND SOUTHEAST ASIA ARE CURRENTLY AHEAD, THE MIDDLE EAST HAS THE TALENT, MARKET POTENTIAL, AND INVESTOR INTEREST TO CATCH UP AND BECOME A GLOBAL STARTUP POWERHOUSE.

———

The key to success lies in three main factors: attracting global investors, pushing local investors to grow, and developing a strong talent pipeline. We have an abundance of talented individuals, but scalability remains a challenge. The biggest hurdle in the coming years will not be market size or fundraising—it will be talent scalability.

Recruiting the right people and developing them into strong operators will be critical. If we don't address this now, scaling businesses in the future will become significantly more challenging.

Thank you, Mostafa, for your time. Best of luck with Breadfast and all your exciting plans.

Thank you, Amir.

———

ALI HASHEMI

Holistic health, data-driven care

Co-Founder and CEO of META[BOLIC]

meta(b◌lic)
health

Dubai, UAE

www.metabolic.health

ALI HASHEMI doesn't bend to fit the world's expectations—he bends the world to fit his vision. A self-proclaimed "square peg in a round hole," Ali has carved an unusually unconventional path through life, from launching a non-alcoholic nightclub as a Duke undergrad to pioneering healthcare ventures that defy industry norms. Today, as Co-Founder and CEO of meta[bolic], he's tackling the global metabolic health epidemic from Dubai, wielding a hybrid model that fuses human care with cutting-edge technology. His platforms—GluCare.Health and Zone.Health —are rewriting the playbook on metabolic health and healthspan maximization, delivering outcomes that outpace global benchmarks.

Prior to these ventures, Ali founded Amana Healthcare, the Middle East's fastest-growing continuum-of-care hospital platform, which set a new benchmark for post-acute, rehabilitation, and long-term care in the region. Amana Healthcare was acquired by Mubadala Healthcare in 2018, marking one of the largest healthcare mergers and acquisitions in the region.

Ali's expertise extends beyond entrepreneurship. He previously led the Middle East Healthcare Practice at Booz & Company, where he advised governments, investors, and industry leaders on healthcare strategy, digital transformation, and investment trends. Before that, he was part of the Healthcare and Private Equity practices at Bain & Company in New York City, shaping growth strategies for major healthcare players.

Academically, Ali holds an MBA and (almost) a medical degree from McGill University. He earned his B.S.E. with Distinction from Duke University, with a dual major in Biomedical Engineering and Religion, along with a minor in Chemistry. His commitment to education and leadership continues as a member of the Global Advisory Board for Duke University's Fuqua School of Business and as a lecturer for the Duke Global Executive MBA Program.

Ali is deeply passionate about scaling healthcare innovations, building high-impact ventures, and transforming the future of metabolic health. His work exemplifies the resilience, creativity, and forward-thinking leadership that define the MENA startup ecosystem.

Ali's story is a tapestry of resilience, reinvention, and relentless curiosity, woven from an eclectic education at Duke, a bruising detour through medical school expulsions at McGill, a failed startup in his early twenties, and a triumphant rise as a healthcare innovator in the Middle East. What follows is Ali's own voice—raw, reflective, and unflinching—tracing the experiences that shaped him, the failures that forged him, and the data-driven revolution he's igniting.

———

META[BOLIC] is a pioneering healthcare provider based in Dubai, United Arab Emirates, transforming metabolic health management through a hybrid digital therapeutics model. Founded in 2019 initially as a diabetes practice called GluCare.Health, it integrates continuous remote monitoring, artificial intelligence (AI), and personalized in-clinic care to create a proactive, data-driven approach that is redefining chronic disease treatment.

Unlike traditional diabetes care, which relies on episodic visits and delayed interventions, meta[bolic] employs continuous monitoring using wearable devices that track glucose levels, physical activity, sleep and stress patterns in real time. This constant data stream enables its clinical team to provide immediate, personalized interventions, allowing patients to make real-time adjustments to their lifestyle and treatment. AI-powered analytics further enhance this model, helping detect potential health risks before they escalate.

The results of this approach have been transformative. Diabetic patients at GluCare have achieved an average reduction in HbA1c levels of 2.19% within three months, with those starting at higher baseline levels seeing reductions of up to 3.67%. Weight loss has been another key success metric, with participants losing an average of 5.05 kg over the same period. Cardiovascular health indicators have also improved, with reductions in LDL cholesterol and total cholesterol contributing to a significantly lower cardiovascular disease risk.

Engagement has proven to be a critical factor in these outcomes; patients who interacted with meta[bolic]'s digital platform more than 11 times within the three-month period saw the most significant health improvements, demonstrating the power of a connected and data-driven care model.

meta[bolic]'s diabetes platform, GluCare.Health, has gained international recognition for its innovative model. It became the first healthcare provider outside the United States to receive URAC accreditation in Remote Patient Monitoring, a significant milestone highlighting its leadership in digital-first healthcare. It has also received accreditation from ICHOM, as the world's first value-based care provider, a reflection of its commitment to transparency and measurable health outcomes in diabetes care. These accolades further validate GluCare's impact in setting new global standards for chronic disease management.

By merging high-touch clinical care with cutting-edge technology, meta[bolic] has successfully scaled a model that is both efficient and effective, reducing healthcare costs while improving patient outcomes. Its success serves as a blueprint for how startups in the region can leverage technology to build scalable, high-impact healthcare solutions.

As the MENA region positions itself as a global hub for innovation and entrepreneurship, meta[bolic] stands at the forefront of the healthcare revolution. It exemplifies how technology-driven, patient-centric solutions can disrupt traditional industries and create lasting impact.

———

Tell us a bit about yourself and your background.

Look, if there's an overarching theme to my story, it's that I've always been a bit of a square peg in a round hole. Growing up, I was the kid who marched to his own drumbeat—always chasing ideas that didn't quite fit, less out of defiance and more because that's just how my mind worked.

School was where it started showing up. I'd latch onto projects that baffled my teachers—not to stir trouble, but because I couldn't resist poking at the edges of what was possible. That quirk became my compass, guiding me through life's twists.

Growing up, I didn't have some grand plan—I just liked figuring stuff out my way. My parents saw it early; they'd watch me take apart toys (or worse, their appliances) or ramble about some random idea and just let me run with it. That freedom stuck.

By the time I hit high school, I was the kid who'd rather build a weird science project than stick to the textbook labs. In the early years, I candidly didn't have an overflowing social calendar—just wasn't that interested. I was the kid who'd disappear into the basement for days on end and emerge with a functional RC airplane or a fully built-to-scale replica of the Pantheon. I was a bit of a nerd.

Teachers didn't always get it, but they'd let me roll anyway. And I'm sure it was all very odd for my parents as well. If we were testing for such things back then, I'm sure I would have landed somewhere on the neurodivergent spectrum. A superpower, for sure.

That's where I started seeing the world as a puzzle I could tinker with—not just something to fit into.

At what point did this different perspective start to make sense to you?

At Duke as an undergrad, it all started snapping into focus. I couldn't settle for a single lane, so I double-majored in biomedical engineering and religion—two fields with absolutely zero overlap. I'd haul textbooks on circuit design to one lecture and ancient scriptures to the next, my backpack a jumble of wires and theology.

It was a grind, no question—late nights wrestling with equations, early mornings decoding texts—but it fed both halves of me: the analytical tinkerer who loved systems and the restless seeker asking why they mattered. That mash-up taught me to see problems from odd angles, a habit that's stuck with me through every venture.

Duke wasn't just about hitting the books—"work hard, play hard" was the school mantra—it was a place that dared you to do something real. The vibe there was less "memorize this" and more "build it, try it, see what happens." The best professors didn't just lecture; they pushed you to take a swing. That's where I first felt the entrepreneurial itch, even if I didn't have a name for it yet. Those years wired me to question, try things, and keep pushing—stuff I still lean on every day.

But at Duke, it wasn't all smooth sailing. The two degrees meant I'd overload my schedule—engineering labs running late, religion seminars piling on reading—and still find time to mess around with side projects. Friends thought I was nuts, juggling that much, but it felt right. That mix of chaos and curiosity shaped me—taught me I could handle more than I thought, push past the usual, and come out with something worth keeping.

Were you always interested in entrepreneurship, or was there a particular moment that sparked your passion for it?

No, it wasn't part of the plan—entrepreneurship kind of ambushed me. My first taste was in my second year at Duke. The social scene was frat central: loud parties, kegs everywhere, messy—not my speed. My circle of international student friends and I didn't really vibe with it—we wanted a spot that felt like ours, no booze required. So we dreamed up a non-alcoholic nightclub right on campus. We called it The Underground.

Picture this: dim lights, thumping beats, students crammed in, sipping mocktails instead of shots. We pitched it to the university, half-expecting a polite "No thanks." Instead, the Dean of Student Affairs handed us an on-campus restaurant, a decent budget, and a green light. We even swiped the London Underground logo—cheeky, probably illegal, but no one sued for copyright infringement.

Opening night was a rush—nerves on edge, music blasting, the place buzzing. I stood there, soaking it in, thinking, "We pulled this off." That's when it hit: finding a hole in the world and filling it felt alive. That was my spark.

The Underground wasn't just a cool hangout—it showed me what's possible when you've got a team and a mission. My classmates and I made it work because we each brought something unique to the table, all clicking together. Duke's "go for it" attitude fueled the whole thing—gave us room to try something nuts and see it land. I didn't know then that I'd build companies, but I knew I'd never be happy just sitting back as a bystander.

———

> I DIDN'T KNOW THEN I'D BUILD COMPANIES, BUT I KNEW I'D NEVER BE HAPPY JUST SITTING BACK AS A BYSTANDER.

———

It wasn't perfect, mind you. We'd overbook DJs sometimes, or the mocktail menu would flop—too much pineapple one night, not enough fizz the next. But we'd laugh it off, adjust, and keep rolling. That's where I got my first taste of running something—messy, fun, and totally ours.

Looking back, it's wild how much that shaped me—showed me I could take an idea, any idea, and make it real.

How did that entrepreneurial streak keep rolling at Duke?

The Underground wasn't a one-and-done—it kicked off something bigger. By senior year, I wanted to graduate with distinction in biomedical engineering, which basically meant doing a master's-level thesis as an undergrad—no small feat. I went to my favorite professor, Dr. Jim McElhaney—he was also the Dean of Engineering, a real legend—to be my research advisor. I'd taken several of his courses, wild stuff like breaking down the physics of head and neck injuries from motorcycle crashes or slip-and-slide wipeouts. I figured he'd toss me something loud and kinetic, like crash-test dummies or biomechanical chaos.

Instead, he sits me down and goes, "Ali, I want you to design an at-home Pap test for women to screen for cervical cancer."

I'm 20, a college guy who'd barely thought about women's health past a quick bio lecture. My brain's scrambling—Pap tests? At home? What?

But Dr. McElhaney had this look, like he knew it was going to change my life arc, so with some hesitation, I said, "Yeah, sure. Okay."

I spent a year on it—sketching designs, testing materials, imagining how it'd work for a patient. It was gritty—lots of trial and error, late nights in the lab—but we made great progress. Duke and the investors sponsoring the research patented it. It felt like I'd cracked a code, an n of 1 experience.

A few months before I graduated, those same investors cornered me. "Forget med school," they said. "Come build this with us."

I was stunned—me, a startup guy? What did I know? Who cares—I was in. Employee #2.

Employee #1 was a guy they hired to be the CEO, and we were off to the races. We named it GyneConcepts, Inc.—not the smoothest company name—and moved into a biomedical incubator linked to the University of Cincinnati. There I was, 22, setting up preclinical trials with physician-scientists from Duke and Harvard, drafting NIH grant applications, feeling unstoppable.

But the CEO they hired ultimately couldn't raise the cash to get us off the ground. A year in, we folded—my first real flop. It stung deeply. I dusted off my med school applications and headed to McGill, figuring I'd pivot back.

That crash taught me more than I knew then—it was just the warmup. Took me a while to see it as a lesson, not a dead end.

Looking back, what lessons from those early ventures still stick with you?

The Underground and GyneConcepts were the beginning of boot camp—taught me stuff I still lean on. The Underground was all about jumping in. We had no roadmap—booking DJs, mixing drinks, keeping the vibe right—but we figured it out as we went.

GyneConcepts hit harder. It showed me that failure isn't fatal—it's fuel. We had the science dialed—patented tech, top-tier collaborators—but the business side tanked. I learned that cash is king; you can't innovate without capital. It also flagged that there was an entire universe I just did not understand—I didn't speak the language of funding and finance, and I was simply too young and inexperienced to see the CEO's fundraising fumble ahead of time.

Now, I'm ruthless about team fit. At meta[bolic], I build crews that click, surrounding myself with people who outshine me in their lanes. Back then, it was about keeping the dance floor alive or pushing a prototype; now, it's about keeping patients thriving. The stakes are sky-high, but the playbook is rooted in those early days.

Did you expect the same entrepreneurial openness to carry on at McGill?

Oh boy. Yes. Let's fast-forward to McGill, where my square-peg streak slammed into a brick wall.

After the failure of GyneConcepts, I enrolled in the dual MD-MBA program at McGill—medicine and business, my sweet spot. There were only five of us in this brand-new, five-year program. The first year was business school, the rest was medical school, with the second-year MBA curriculum sprinkled in between. Although I was young and really knew nothing about real life, I still enjoyed it—everything was new to me.

In the first year of medical school, I was elected student body president and figured I'd shake things up a bit—mostly to satisfy my own curiosity about life and career. I started bringing in venture capitalists, consultants, and private equity folks to talk to us about alternate career paths beyond the usual doctor training. It was certainly interesting for me, and I thought it'd spark some ideas for my fellow med students stuck on one track.

Well, the Dean wasn't having it. He saw me as a troublemaker, not a trailblazer. I figured there'd be some grumbling—change always stirs the pot—but I didn't see the axe coming. The Dean demanded I "cease and desist" these extracurricular activities and stop distracting my fellow students from the traditional path.

Things escalated from there. I continued as student body president and began to see real issues in the governance model of the Faculty of Medicine that led to some students being unfairly academically penalized for what amounted to purely solvable personal issues. These were structural flaws I felt compelled to take up with the Dean—consequences that detrimentally affected my peers and classmates.

Only thing is, he wasn't having it. Zero interest in engaging, and now I had a brighter red target on my back.

Over time, this turned into a highly contentious relationship with the administration, ultimately leading to me being expelled from medical school—three times. Yes, the same school. And yes, I fought my way back in twice through the university's grievance process. But those three years were extraordinarily difficult.

The first expulsion came as a surprise and knocked the wind out of me. I fought my way back through the grievance process, thinking it was a one-time clash. Then it happened again. And a third time. Each one hit harder—not because I didn't expect friction, but because I couldn't believe they'd go that far over a student who dared to step out of line. My academic performance was excellent; this was about power, not performance. It was a shock every time. It was about control, and they wanted me gone.

In the end, I reached a breaking point and had to accept that I was never going to be a physician. That realization was devastating. Medical training requires obsessive dedication, and when that path was taken away from me—without a Plan B—it was incredibly traumatic.

I talk about this part of my journey a lot now. When I'm invited to speak to students, I don't spend 30 minutes talking about entrepreneurial success—I talk about my failures. I've come to believe that you learn a lot more about someone, especially entrepreneurs, by understanding the challenges they've faced and how they rebounded.

A wise friend once told me, "There are only two types of people in this world: those who have failed and talk about it, and those who don't."

I believe in being someone who talks about it because there's value in sharing those struggles—not just for yourself, but for others who might be on a similar path.

How did you manage to hold it together during those tough years of expulsion and reinstatement?

Those three years were rough—my darkest days. The first expulsion hit like a freight train—everything I'd worked for, gone in an instant. By the third, I was a shell, barely keeping it together. Nights were brutal—lying awake, replaying every clash with the Dean, wondering if I'd screwed myself for good. I was killing it in class, so it didn't make sense—it felt personal, and that gnawed at me.

Looking back, I was naive—thought good intentions and good grades would shield me. Nope. It was a lesson in reading power, not just people.

My friends and family kept me afloat. My parents never flinched—they'd raised me to defy the script, and they had my back. Duke pals would call, crack dark jokes, yank me out of the spiral. I hung on with pure grit and resilience—I wasn't about to let them break me.

Each reinstatement was a war—hours of paperwork, meetings, arguing my case with gritted teeth. I'd win, get back in, redeemed in front of my peers, feel a flicker of hope, then bam—another kick. After the third episode, I'd had enough. I sued McGill—a long, ugly legal battle that ultimately settled out of court.

Letting go of medicine broke me—I had poured my soul into it—but it also opened a new path, one with greater impact than I could have ever imagined at the time. With the passage of time, I came to understand perhaps the greatest lesson of all—the importance of having gratitude for adversity.

———

> WITH THE PASSAGE OF TIME, I CAME TO UNDERSTAND PERHAPS THE GREATEST LESSON OF ALL—THE IMPORTANCE OF HAVING GRATITUDE FOR ADVERSITY.

———

What was the trickiest part of switching from medicine to consulting?

Well, there was a pit stop in Silicon Valley first. After finishing the MBA, I wound up in the Bay Area, helping a family startup in sleep diagnostics. We scaled it to become the largest network of diagnostic sleep centers in Northern California. But I didn't feel ready, candidly. There was a bit of impostor syndrome, and I felt I needed to learn more.

A friend suggested I explore management consulting, so I applied for a job at Bain & Company. They pulled me into their healthcare and private equity team in New York—didn't blink at the expulsions, which was a relief. Guess they saw the chaos as a plus.

Consulting was an entirely different beast. Medicine is slow, meticulous—you hoard and gather data like a detective, piecing together every clue before acting. Bain was the opposite: the 80/20 rule, move fast, nail the big levers. I'd spend hours digging into minutiae, only to hear, "Ali, we don't need the full autopsy—just the headline." It felt sloppy, like skipping steps in a diagnosis. The hardest shift was letting go of that need for all of the information and embracing a hypothesis-driven approach.

I floundered at first—honestly, I was an awful consultant—until I learned to cut through the noise. Medicine had me trained to boil the ocean—patient charts, lab results, every scrap mattered. Consulting was more like, "What's the one thing that moves the needle most?" I'd sit in meetings, itching to dive deeper, while they'd push for first-principles thinking. It took me forever to stop fighting it—probably annoyed a few folks along the way—but I got there. It was like retraining my brain to zoom out, not zoom in, and that shift was a challenge.

What stood out about the entrepreneurial scenes in the U.S. versus the Middle East?

The Middle East was a major adjustment after the U.S. In New York, you're one voice in a sea—expertise gets you a seat, but you're grinding for clout. Here, it's wide open. At Booz, I was briefing ministers on healthcare strategy within months—crazy access, crazy fast. If you have the chops, you can shape big agendas, no waiting in line. No layers of red tape, just raw opportunity.

———

" THE MIDDLE EAST WAS A MAJOR ADJUSTMENT AFTER THE U.S. IN NEW YORK, YOU'RE ONE VOICE IN A SEA— EXPERTISE GETS YOU A SEAT, BUT YOU'RE GRINDING FOR CLOUT. HERE, IT'S WIDE OPEN. AT BOOZ, I WAS BRIEFING MINISTERS ON HEALTHCARE STRATEGY WITHIN MONTHS—CRAZY ACCESS, CRAZY FAST. IF YOU HAVE THE CHOPS, YOU CAN SHAPE BIG AGENDAS, NO WAITING IN LINE. NO LAYERS OF RED TAPE, JUST RAW OPPORTUNITY.

———

Entrepreneurially, it's a different game. The Middle East runs on relationships and vision. Show up with a track record and a big idea, and people listen.

I planned a two-year gig, but meeting my wife here and the region's pull locked me in. It was like a viral vector in medicine—my ideas spread fast, and I couldn't walk away. The pace, the access, the trust—it's a founder's dream if you play it right.

What was the trigger to leave consulting and start Amana Healthcare?

By 2012, consulting was getting stale for me—felt like I was babysitting client relationships, not cracking cases. But as a consultant, you get privileged access to insights and data on the market that you wouldn't otherwise see. Some of that shaped my view on gaps in the market that an entrepreneur could tackle.

I left Booz in mid-2012 to start Amana Healthcare, zeroing in on subacute care—stroke rehab, brain injuries, long-term ICU-level care. The need was glaring: no one owned that space here. But selling it? Man, that was a slog. No one wanted to invest.

Investors balked—hospitals as a startup sounded like an insane idea to anyone who heard the pitch. I'd pitch the upside—half a billion in value over six years—and they'd stare like I'd lost it. Kept hitting the typical walls: "Too slow," "Too risky," "Why bother? Let the big boys do it."

Those early pitches were brutal—hours prepping slides, practicing in my head, only to get blank looks. I'd tweak it, try again, same deal. Took months to crack the code—I had to stop selling numbers and start selling the story.

The breakthrough came when we tied it to something deeper and went after patient capital aligned with our double bottom-line story. A significant portion of this value stemmed from how a particular Quranic verse was interpreted in the healthcare context. The verse states that saving one life is as if you have saved all of humanity, and this principle became deeply embedded in local laws and regulations, mandating that every possible effort be made to preserve human life.

This translated into regulations outlawing DNR (Do Not Resuscitate)—meaning it was prohibited to deliberately pull life support and let go of a patient, even for vegetative, comatose cases. That meant an increasing pile of patients needing long-term care. Many, if not most, of these patients were being sent abroad for this type of care at a cost of multi-millions of dollars per year per patient.

Rather than seeing this as an insurmountable challenge, we saw an opportunity to build specialized ICU-level beds to care for these patients in a more humane and sustainable way. Once we proposed a model of care that would lead the world in terms of quality and outcomes, the government bit.

We entered into a contract with the public insurance fund and built the region's largest network of ICU-level beds in the private sector. We ended up not raising any equity at all but funded the entire company with various forms of debt. By 2018, we flipped it to Mubadala Healthcare in a rare full exit for a founder—and what was, at the time, probably the largest healthcare M&A deal in the region.

With a big exit and big payout on the books, did you think to then retire?

Not at all. The exit afforded my wife and me the freedom to think and be deliberate about what we took on next. I did take a couple of days off, got a haircut, and bought a new pair of shades. That was the celebration. But then, I got back to work.

We wanted to tackle something of scale, consequence, and meaning. And the answer was clear: diabetes and metabolic disease.

In the U.S. alone, healthcare spending is approaching 20% of GDP, and about a quarter of that is directly or indirectly related to metabolic disease. That means close to 5% of total U.S. GDP—an astronomical amount of money—is being allocated to a problem that is largely preventable or manageable. In the GCC, estimates suggest that 15–

20% of the population is diabetic, and over 60–70% is metabolically dysfunctional (including pre-diabetic and obese/overweight). And it's only getting worse.

I teamed up with Dr. Ihsan Al Marzooqi, the former Deputy CEO of Mubadala Healthcare, who had already built an incredible collection of healthcare assets, including the Imperial College London Diabetes Centre, one of the largest groups of diabetes clinics in the region. He and his team had also built Cleveland Clinic Abu Dhabi, Healthpoint Hospital, The National Reference Lab, and several other assets.

We started by asking a first-principles question: Why is metabolic disease so widespread and getting worse, particularly against a backdrop of ever-evolving "inputs" to the healthcare system—tools, tech, drugs, facilities, financing, regulation, education?

All the ingredients that make up the healthcare system have been getting better, but our collective outcomes were only getting worse. It just didn't make any sense to us. Something was missing. And it wasn't just an "app."

We wanted to understand why the healthcare system was failing so badly in this area and what that meant for a potentially transformative business. Instead of jumping straight to solutions, we focused first on defining the problem with absolute clarity. As we dug deeper, we realized that the root of the issue lay in the misaligned incentives that dictate healthcare decision-making.

There's an often-loud cry of complaint that healthcare systems worldwide are broken. That's incorrect. They're working precisely as they were designed to. Just follow the incentives.

———

> " THERE'S AN OFTEN-LOUD CRY OF COMPLAINT THAT
> HEALTHCARE SYSTEMS WORLDWIDE ARE BROKEN. THAT'S
> INCORRECT. THEY'RE WORKING PRECISELY AS THEY
> WERE DESIGNED TO. JUST FOLLOW THE INCENTIVES.

———

The industry operates on a fundamental disconnect: the person consuming healthcare services—the patient—is not the one paying for them. Instead, in many markets, the insurance company or the public payor is the true customer, and this misalignment significantly constrains what can be built and how it can be delivered.

We also realized that the problem wasn't a lack of innovation—it was a lack of agency at a human level. The old system—pop in, grab a script, see you later—wasn't cutting it. We wanted to dig into the why and build something better.

Did you get pushback on your vision?

Oh yes, absolutely.

While most startups in the space were embracing fully digital solutions, we decided to go in the opposite direction, betting on a hybrid model that combined physical clinics with a strong technology backbone.

A year after we launched, our most visible virtual care competitor in the space, Livongo, was acquired by Teladoc for over $18 billion. If we had pitched our hybrid concept to investors at the time, we would have been laughed out of the room.

Everyone was fixated on digital-only solutions because they were scalable, investor-friendly, and avoided the complexities of dealing with insurance companies, payroll for doctors and nurses, and high capital expenditures. Hybrid was clunky in their view—CapEx heavy, messy, and unscalable.

But we had a major advantage—we were self-funded and patient. That allowed us to bypass the usual fundraising hurdles and go straight into building the business we felt made the most sense—the one that would ultimately earn the right to win.

With everyone obsessed with speed, what's your take on patience in building a business?

We didn't sprint. Silicon Valley was churning out digital fixes—Livongo, Virta, Onduo, Verily—all racing to scale. We went slow, piecing together a hybrid model: a 10,000-square-foot clinic in Dubai, tech-packed but human-first.

Self-funding meant no pressure to rush—no VC clock ticking. Our bet on a hybrid care model "earning the right to win" paid off—in our first year, we topped Livongo's best published outcomes by 70%; in our second year, we doubled them in half the time.

Our December 2024 New England Journal of Medicine Catalyst study lays it out: folks in our program dropped HbA1c by 2.19 points in three months, shedding an average of 5 kilos—while the control group barely budged. Patience let us build and test a vision—experiment, screw up, fix it, get it right.

Here's my take: speed's a trap in healthcare. It's a long game—five, seven years to break even, easy. Go slow to go fast—build it solid, then grow when it's locked in. Rush it, and you're doomed; take your time, and you've got a shot.

We spent months tweaking—testing wearables, fiddling with the app—before we hit our stride. Could have started to scale half-baked, but waiting meant we hit the ground running, not stumbling. That's how you last.

What helped you understand the reimbursement and regulatory side of healthcare?

Traditional healthcare is an enormous cash cow. Think of it as the Mississippi River—huge, murky, always moving. The winners don't dig new streams; they tap what's flowing.

At meta[bolic], we lock insurance deals for the basics—labs, consults, diagnostics, meds—because payors know how to pay for these services. The really transformative, fun stuff they resist paying for—wearables, AI, nutritionists, coaches—we fund with profits from our own lab and pharmacy.

It's a hustle: steady money keeps the new ideas alive. We built those in-house setups to keep the margins healthy, so we're not begging for every dime—or worse, dying on the vine.

Even with Amana, our second play, we pitched a rehab hospital with no playbook—zero laws or regulations on the books to govern building the region's first private rehab hospital. We had credibility carried over from our first hospital, so the regulators said, "Okay, let's figure it out."

We co-wrote the rules, regulations, and reimbursement frameworks with them in weeks—open, fast, teamwork. Here, gaps aren't walls; they're chances to build. Years of that taught me what flexes, who to call, and how to push without breaking.

At meta[bolic], we're stretching it again—wearables, remote tweaks—but we pitch it smart: better health, lower costs. Experience makes it click.

Revenue-wise, it's about understanding what's reimbursable and what's not. Insurance loves the known and the predictable—give them that, and you've got a lifeline. We started small at meta[bolic]—one clinic, basic services—then layered on the tech once we had cash coming in.

How did you get comfortable with the risk of putting your own capital to work on an unproven model?

In those early years, we treated our clinic as a laboratory rather than a traditional business. It generated revenue through insurance contracts and patient billing, but we were also burning a substantial amount of cash because much of what we were doing wasn't covered by insurance.

A prime example was continuous glucose monitoring (CGM). Today, CGMs are widely recognized as valuable tools for managing blood sugar, and a wave of startups has tried (and mostly failed) to create direct-to-consumer models around them. But for us, CGMs were a non-negotiable part of our care model from day one.

The problem? Insurance companies only covered them for insulin-dependent diabetics, meaning even most Type 2 diabetics weren't eligible. We didn't let that stop us—we simply covered the cost ourselves. Back then, CGMs were incredibly expensive, costing us upwards of $500 per month per patient.

This willingness to invest in patient outcomes, even at our own expense, set us apart from the competition and allowed us to generate an overwhelming body of evidence demonstrating the effectiveness of our approach. As a result, we quickly gained credibility—not just regionally, but globally—reinforcing our belief that the hybrid model was the right bet.

In the early days, our biggest risk was concentrated in one area, and I recognize that our story is unique and largely not replicable because most founders don't have the ability to self-fund a project of this scale.

But there are some universal lessons that apply, particularly around the idea that an entrepreneur's job is not to take risks recklessly. A very clever friend of mine once pointed out that there's a common perception that entrepreneurs are natural risk-takers, but that's not exactly accurate. Sure, risk is involved, but truly great entrepreneurs are exceptional risk mitigators.

Ali Hashemi

 THERE'S A COMMON PERCEPTION THAT ENTREPRENEURS ARE NATURAL RISK-TAKERS, BUT THAT'S NOT EXACTLY ACCURATE. SURE, RISK IS INVOLVED, BUT TRULY GREAT ENTREPRENEURS ARE EXCEPTIONAL RISK MITIGATORS.

What that means is that they don't just accept risk blindly; they analyze it, quantify it, and most importantly, build ways to mitigate it into their execution strategy. That's what I would call entrepreneurial risk arbitrage.

The key difference between an entrepreneur and an investor is that the entrepreneur is much closer to the risk and has control over the levers of risk mitigation, whereas an investor is looking in from the outside and will always perceive something as riskier than it might actually be.

The gap between an investor's perception of risk and an entrepreneur's ability to mitigate it is where real value creation happens.

For us, that meant rapidly iterating and taking calculated risks by implementing strategies that we knew wouldn't be immediately profitable but would demonstrate clear impact and efficacy. So we started publishing. Over the years, we've averaged about one publication per month, totaling nearly 40 so far.

A couple of months ago, we earned our first feature in the New England Journal of Medicine—a 17-page spread on our model—which, as far as we know, is the first from the Middle East.

Our journey has been shaped by an almost gleeful irreverence toward the existing financial rules of healthcare while maintaining a deep reverence for clinical and academic integrity. It's a delicate balance—knowing which rules to challenge and which must remain intact.

This is one of the biggest hurdles for outsiders trying to innovate in healthcare. Many non-healthcare entrepreneurs, often coming from tech backgrounds, enter the industry with noble intentions and innovative ideas, but they frequently fail because they don't fully grasp the operational and regulatory realities of healthcare.

The blind spots are enormous.

What are key unlocks to being a disruptor in the healthcare space?

Navigating the regulatory space was another major challenge. Healthcare, particularly in the Middle East, is a highly regulated industry. It's possible to hire regulatory experts, but the key is knowing who to hire and when.

If you're building something traditional, regulatory approval is often just a matter of execution. The rules are published, and if you have an experienced operational team, they can guide you through the process. The real challenge arises when you want to do something new—something that doesn't fit neatly into existing regulations. This is where relationships matter.

One advantage we had was a deep understanding of the regulatory landscape and established relationships with the key decision-makers. We knew which conversations regulators would be open to having and how to frame our proposals in a way that made sense to them. My previous experience at Amana Healthcare was invaluable in this regard.

This experience reinforced a crucial lesson—while healthcare is highly regulated, not all regulations are immovable. In areas where established frameworks exist, you must operate within them. But in emerging or undefined spaces, particularly in the Middle East, there is a unique opportunity to collaborate with regulators and influence the development of new policies. This flexibility allows for rapid innovation in ways that are often impossible in more rigid regulatory environments like the U.S. or Europe.

One of the most common mistakes I see founders make when scaling up is amplifying the wrong signals. The most important job of an entrepreneur is to anticipate the future and build for it. However, many founders become overly fixated on short-term trends and misinterpret them as sustainable opportunities.

A prime example is the surge in continuous glucose monitoring (CGM) startups a few years ago. When CGMs entered mainstream conversation, a wave of startups emerged, positioning themselves as metabolic insight platforms. Investors flocked to these companies, believing they were riding a transformative trend. However, most of these businesses failed because they were built around a temporary market enthusiasm rather than a sustainable healthcare need.

The long-term reality of healthcare is that the winning organizations will not be those that offer isolated, point-solution tools. The true winners will be the ones that earn patient trust.

If you own the patient's trust, you own their data. If you own enough data over time, you own the insights. If you own the insights, you can shape interventions. And if you can guide a patient through their healthcare journey in a way that delivers meaningful outcomes, you ultimately control the flow of capital and investment where interests are aligned.

Understanding this changes everything. Rather than building fragmented tools or apps, successful healthcare companies will act as systems integrators—curating best-in-class technologies, continuously enhancing patient engagement, and creating an ecosystem that reinforces trust and long-term relationships.

Entrepreneurs who recognize this will shift away from standalone solutions and toward models that emphasize patient continuity, comprehensive care, and long-term value creation.

How does meta[bolic] use tech and AI to transform health, and what makes it stand out?

meta[bolic] thrives on data—it's our driving force. We don't just offer static solutions; we track them in real time, continuously analyzing what keeps them effective. When new patients join, we equip them with continuous glucose monitors (CGMs), Oura rings, smart scales, and blood pressure cuffs. Every heartbeat, glucose fluctuation, and sleep cycle feeds into our system in real time. It's not a data mess—it's a constantly updating, clear picture of their health.

Our tech stack is custom-built. At its core are our app and patient portal, where users snap photos of their meals, and AI identifies the food, tracks glucose responses, and facilitates real-time chats with coaches. Behind the scenes, we process millions of data points. Over time, our algorithms detect patterns—like a late-night burger disrupting sleep and spiking blood sugar—then flag the insights to our team. Coaches guide behavior, dietitians refine meal plans, sports scientists adjust workouts, and doctors fine-tune medications—all in real time. Our December 2024 NEJM Catalyst study backs this up: patients with 11+ virtual check-ins over 90 days lowered their HbA1c by 2.38 points and lost 6 kilos, while traditional care—just two visits, no tech—barely moved the needle at 0.10 points. The difference is staggering.

AI is our quiet powerhouse, but we've learned to use it wisely. In 2019, I invested in an AI wearable startup, hoping to integrate its technology into GluCare. It promised multi-layered clinical risk scores—cutting-edge in theory but a disaster in practice. The risk scores fluctuated unpredictably—jumping from 20% to 42% between visits—leaving patients panicked and doctors without answers, as none of it was clinically validated. We scrapped it, took the loss, and got smarter. Now, we focus AI only on clinically validated applications—retinopathy screening, coronary calcium scoring, thyroid nodule detection, and fatty liver quantification. These AI-driven diagnostics don't replace specialists but enhance our team's capabilities, helping them prioritize cases that truly need attention.

What sets us apart? We're not just an app slapped onto a clinic or a fancy office with a gimmick. We are a fully integrated hybrid model—seamlessly combining physical and virtual care. Our clinics serve as hubs, offering labs, imaging, and pharmacy services instantly—no waiting a week for results. You walk out with answers and a plan. Between visits, our virtual platform works relentlessly—wearables ping us 24/7, and we respond immediately, coaching and course-correcting before minor issues become major ones. It's continuous, proactive care—not stop-and-start medicine. And the outcomes speak for themselves.

We're obsessed with making this ecosystem work. Each team member gets their own tailored data stream—dietitians monitor glucose spikes from meals, sports scientists track recovery via Oura's heart rate variability, and doctors oversee medication and vitals. We don't drown in data; we harness it effectively. And we're transparent—our 40+ published papers, including our NEJM study, lay it all out. Competitors can chase us, but they have to match our hustle.

This isn't just about diabetes anymore—most of our patients aren't diabetic. They're people who want to stay healthy, optimize performance, and extend their healthspan. That's what drives us.

Technology is deeply embedded in our system. CGMs provide glucose readings every five minutes—delivering hundreds of data points daily. Oura rings track sleep stages, stress levels, and heart rate variability—metrics that doctors rarely see in a standard visit. We built our app to synchronize everything—patients log food, medications, and mood, while AI cross-analyzes it with wearables. If someone's glucose spikes at 2 a.m., we identify the trigger, connect it to a late dinner, and send a real-time nudge: "Ease up on the carbs tonight." That's the loop—data to action, fast.

Our three-month study recorded an average of 15.28 virtual interactions per patient—proving that these small nudges add up. The system learns, adapts, and keeps us ahead.

How do you integrate technology into healthcare without losing the human element?

Patients leave our clinic saying, "I've never had a doctor look me in the eye for ten straight minutes," or "I've never had a doctor take the time to explain my lab results in a way I actually understand." These moments matter far more than any AI-generated score or predictive algorithm.

At the core of our business is the concept of agency. People struggle with their health not because they don't care, but because they don't know what to do. The modern healthcare system provides diagnoses and prescriptions, but it does a poor job of empowering people with actionable knowledge. Most patients leave their doctor's office with only a vague understanding of their condition and no clear sense of what steps to take.

That's where we focus our efforts—giving patients the tools, guidance, and support they need to take control of their own health. It's not about dictating what they should do; it's about enabling them to make informed choices. And ultimately, that's what real healthcare should be about—not just treating disease, but equipping people to live healthier lives.

Looking ahead, I see our mission as not just expanding geographically, but continuing to evolve how we approach healthcare. The real challenge isn't just scaling the business—it's ensuring that as we grow, we never lose sight of the human element that makes our model successful. Expansion isn't just about replication; it's about continuous learning, refining, and improving. That's what keeps this journey exciting, and that's what drives us forward.

In a state of confusion, humans default to what is easy, leading us down a series of poor decisions that, over time, accumulate into larger health issues like obesity and diabetes. One of the fundamental challenges in healthcare is not just providing people with data but transforming that data into meaningful knowledge, actionable insights, and ultimately, real behavioral change. That is what we set out to build—a data and technology platform that empowers both doctors and patients to make better health decisions.

Knowledge on its own is not particularly useful unless it leads to insight. Even insights, while intellectually stimulating, are meaningless unless they translate into concrete actions. The traditional medical model often stops at diagnosis and basic advice. A doctor might tell a patient, "You are prediabetic and need to lose 30 kilos," and consider their job done. But that alone does not equip the patient with the tools or guidance to change their trajectory.

We take it much further. We collect a comprehensive dataset from wearables like Oura rings, tracking sleep, activity, stress, heart rate, and variability. We require patients to log their food intake diligently, integrate continuous glucose monitors to analyze blood sugar fluctuations, and provide connected scales and blood pressure monitors to track other critical health metrics. As new technology emerges, we continue to incorporate additional data sources to refine our understanding. However, data by itself is not enough—it must be translated into actionable strategies.

———

> DATA BY ITSELF IS NOT ENOUGH—IT MUST BE TRANSLATED INTO ACTIONABLE STRATEGIES.

———

Most people already have access to wearable technology but do not use it to its full potential. They are overwhelmed with data but lack the framework to make sense of it. That is where our care team—physicians, nutritionists, lifestyle coaches, behavioral specialists, and trainers—comes in. Each member of the team extracts unique insights from the data and presents them in a way that is clear and immediately applicable.

For example, a nutritionist might notice a correlation between poor sleep and exaggerated blood sugar spikes after consuming a banana. A trainer might identify how stress levels impact physical performance and recovery. By connecting these dots in a personalized and meaningful way, we make it easier for patients to take action. This is what we see as our true product—not just clinical services or technology, but the agency we create for patients to regain control over their health.

What have you learned on your fundraising journey?

On the fundraising side, we've had a unique trajectory in both of our businesses. When I started Amana Healthcare in 2012 with my business partners, my wife and I provided most of the initial funding, which bootstrapped us for the first year. As a former management consultant, I had some savings, but my wife was the real powerhouse. She was the first entrepreneur in our partnership, having successfully built a digital media startup called Fishfayce in 2010.

For nearly two years, I went without a salary, and we relied entirely on my wife's business to sustain us. Those early days were tough— every investor we pitched told us we were crazy for trying to build a hospital as a startup. Not a single institutional investor was willing to back us with equity funding.

After facing repeated rejections, we reassessed our strategy and concluded that the traditional institutional investment path was a dead end. So, we pivoted. Instead of targeting traditional venture capitalists, we focused on successful entrepreneurs and business leaders who were further along in their careers and had a personal interest in healthcare's social impact. While they wanted a return, they were also drawn to the mission of improving healthcare.

Since I wasn't a finance guy bound by conventional thinking, I sat down with a blank sheet of paper and devised a new structure. We ended up raising $20 million over the course of a year through a unique share class that was effectively structured as fully bulleted debt—this was before venture debt was common, before mezzanine financing was available, and before there was even a robust VC ecosystem in our region.

The structure was simple: we created investor shares that were sold at $1 per share, with a contractual obligation to buy them back at $2 per share within a defined timeframe. If we failed to buy back the shares, they would convert into equity at a steep discount. This approach de-risked the investment significantly for our backers, giving them the potential for strong returns while protecting downside. We ended up delivering a 25% IRR to our investors.

This structure also allowed us to be highly capital-efficient. We raised funds in tranches at increasing share prices—early investors paid $1 per share, while later investors paid $1.15, $1.25, and so on. This meant we only raised what we needed at each stage, minimizing dilution and aligning investor incentives.

———

" WE CONCLUDED THAT THE TRADITIONAL INSTITUTIONAL INVESTMENT PATH WAS A DEAD END ... WE CREATED INVESTOR SHARES THAT WERE SOLD AT $1 PER SHARE, WITH A CONTRACTUAL OBLIGATION TO BUY THEM BACK AT $2 PER SHARE WITHIN A DEFINED TIMEFRAME ... THIS STRUCTURE ALSO ALLOWED US TO BE HIGHLY CAPITAL-EFFICIENT.

———

For our second hospital, we secured a $25 million credit facility from Gulf Capital. The team there, including Fidaa Haddad and Walid Cherif, was fantastic to work with. Ultimately, Amana Healthcare became one of the most successful investments in Gulf Capital's credit portfolio. We repaid our investors a year ahead of schedule, and the business thrived.

Interestingly, this type of alternative fundraising is now making a comeback. Several funds have launched models that offer non-dilutive, structured financing, allowing founders to raise capital without permanent equity dilution. While this type of capital can be expensive, it offers a viable alternative to the traditional venture model.

This brings me to a broader point about fundraising. Many early-stage founders instinctively gravitate toward pitching VCs, but they need to take a step back and ask whether that's truly the best path for their business. In healthcare, timelines are long—often much longer than the lifecycle of a typical VC fund. This can create conflicts between investors and founders, particularly when investors have predefined exit timelines that may not align with the optimal growth trajectory of the business.

The first sign of misalignment often comes in the form of relentless pressure for rapid growth. Many VCs need to show returns to their limited partners, so they push for aggressive scaling, sometimes at the expense of long-term sustainability. If we had taken traditional VC funding early on, we likely would have been forced down a path that led to failure. Our ability to go slow initially—to iterate, refine, and find product-market fit—was what ultimately enabled us to go fast later.

———

" THE FIRST SIGN OF MISALIGNMENT OFTEN COMES IN THE FORM OF RELENTLESS PRESSURE FOR RAPID GROWTH. MANY VCS NEED TO SHOW RETURNS TO THEIR LIMITED PARTNERS, SO THEY PUSH FOR AGGRESSIVE SCALING, SOMETIMES AT THE EXPENSE OF LONG-TERM SUSTAINABILITY.

———

The second point of misalignment comes at the exit stage. Healthcare businesses often require longer gestation periods to achieve their full value, but VCs may push for an exit before the timing is right. This pressure can force founders into suboptimal decisions, such as selling too early or scaling in unsustainable ways.

So, what is the alternative? While structured fundraising solutions like the one we used for Amana are one option, the broader lesson is that founders should not automatically default to the traditional VC route. Networking is crucial—building relationships with strategic investors, family offices, and high-net-worth individuals who understand the industry and align with your long-term vision can be a better fit than institutional capital.

Ultimately, the key takeaway is to be deliberate about fundraising choices. Even if a term sheet looks attractive in the short term, founders need to consider the long-term implications. Every decision made today has consequences that play out years down the line. Being consistently good at predicting the future—and structuring your business accordingly—is one of the hardest but most critical aspects of being a founder.

As you reflect on on your own journey, how had your leadership approach evolve?

I've gone through distinct phases of leadership over the years. In the early days, my focus was on launching something new, proving a hypothesis, and demonstrating viability. As we grew, my role shifted toward scaling the organization, hiring the right leadership, and institutionalizing processes. Now, as we expand into new markets, my mindset has evolved again. The focus is no longer just on growth but on learning—understanding how our model adapts to different regulatory environments, payer structures, and cultural contexts.

One of the most important transitions for any founder is recognizing that what worked in the early days won't necessarily work at scale. The skills required to launch a business—scrappiness, speed, and risk-taking—must eventually be complemented by structure, discipline, and long-term strategic thinking. The best entrepreneurs continuously evolve, embracing new challenges and learning from every phase of their journey.

Scaling is a shift—you can't just hustle harder; you have to grow up. As a founder, I was all in—managing patient flows, tweaking the app, and being hands-on with everything. As a CEO, it's about stepping up: hiring people smarter than me, setting the direction, and letting them execute. But I still stay involved—sometimes I sit at meta[bolic]'s front desk, watching how things run—because you can't lead what you don't feel. It's a balance.

———

> SCALING IS A SHIFT—YOU CAN'T JUST HUSTLE HARDER; YOU HAVE TO GROW UP. AS A FOUNDER, I WAS ALL IN— MANAGING PATIENT FLOWS, TWEAKING THE APP, AND BEING HANDS-ON WITH EVERYTHING. AS A CEO, IT'S ABOUT STEPPING UP: HIRING PEOPLE SMARTER THAN ME, SETTING THE DIRECTION, AND LETTING THEM EXECUTE.

———

Grit is essential—things fail, pile up, and you have to move forward. When GyneConcepts tanked, it could have ended me, but instead, it pushed me forward. You need a north star—for us, it's about rewriting metabolic health, one person at a time, on a global scale. And you have to check your ego—I shouldn't be the smartest person in the room; my team should be. I didn't start as Amana's CEO—I brought in someone better suited for the role. Hire talent, empower them, stay real—that's how you scale without breaking.

It hasn't always been smooth. Early on, I struggled with micromanaging—trusting the team took time. Letting go wasn't easy, but now, I lean on my people: engineers who live for data, coaches who connect with patients, and doctors who master the science.

Scaling is messy—I've made bad hires, chased the wrong markets, and had to course-correct. But that's the trick: build a system that runs without you, but never lose the pulse.

What's next for meta[bolic], and how is tech shaping it?

meta[bolic] is still in its early days—we're just getting started. Dubai is our testing ground, where we experiment, iterate, and learn. But our sights are set on bigger markets—the U.S., Europe, and the GCC. Each comes with different regulations, different populations, and different challenges. The question isn't just whether we can replicate our model—it's about adapting it. What needs to bend? What might break? What holds up? The key will be understanding how our hybrid approach—blending physical and virtual care—can evolve within different healthcare systems.

Continuous data is our fuel. We're already tracking millions of live data points from CGMs, Oura rings, and an expanding range of wearables. As these technologies improve, we're diving deeper—extracting more precise insights and pushing the boundaries of personalized health optimization.

The right use of AI will be a game-changer for scaling impact. Right now, each of our health coaches manages 70 patients—but with AI-driven smart nudges, that number could double to 140 while still keeping the human touch intact. We're ramping up our machine learning capabilities—because as patients build their own deep, personal longitudinal datasets, we'll be able to deliver sharper predictions, better habit adjustments, and truly proactive care.

That's the plan—care that stays ahead of the curve.

You've certainly piqued my interest in visiting your clinic and experiencing an assessment firsthand.

You're welcome to visit anytime, Amir.

———

HUSSAM HAMMO

Gaming the Arab world

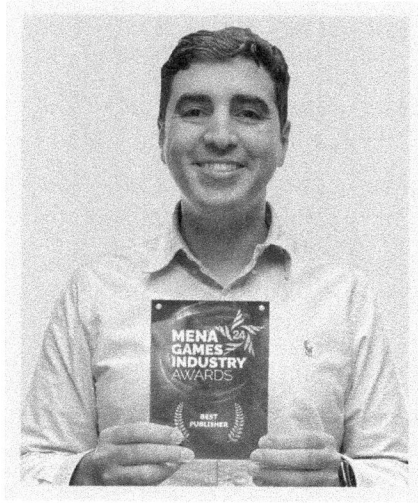

Founder and CEO of TAMATEM GAMES

Amman, Jordan

www.tamatem.co

HUSSAM HAMMO is the driving force behind Tamatem Games, boasts over 17 years of entrepreneurial expertise. His journey with Tamatem began in 2013, driven by a vision to create games that authentically represented the language and culture of the Arab region. A dedicated gamer himself, Hussam recognised the glaring absence of Arabic content in the mobile gaming industry. To address this void, he founded Tamatem Games, focusing on the development of user-friendly games that resonated with their target audience.

Hussam Hammo, a Jordanian entrepreneur, stands as the CEO and Founder of Tamatem Games. His inspiration for launching Tamatem stemmed from the notable scarcity of Arabic games catering to the Arabic-speaking world. Tamatem Games serves as a mobile games publisher, collaborating with international developers to adapt and introduce global games to the Arabic-speaking audience. It has become the foremost mobile games publisher in the MENA market, boasting a portfolio of more than 50 games since its inception in 2013. The company has achieved a remarkable milestone of over 150 million game downloads and maintains 3.5 million daily active users on its top games.

Hussam's journey began in 2006 when he started as a product manager at d1g.com, an interactive portal serving Arab online users. His career continued to evolve as he transitioned to Maktoob.com, an Arabic internet portal and online platform, where he co-founded Faye3.com, one of Maktoob's most popular products, with over 1 million users. In 2009, Yahoo! acquired Maktoob for $175 million. Subsequent to this acquisition, Hussam made a pivotal decision to pursue his dreams as an entrepreneur. In 2009, he co-founded Wizards Productions, a game studio specialising in online browser-based games. Despite the company's success, Hussam eventually decided to close the studio, recognizing the premature state of the gaming industry in the region and opting to explore a different approach in the realm of mobile games. However, Hussam's unwavering belief in the potential of the Arabic mobile games market persisted. In 2013, his innovative idea of localising and publishing international mobile games for the Arabic-speaking market captured the attention of California-based accelerator '500 Startups.' This provided Tamatem with its inaugural acceleration opportunity, leading to its journey of bringing the best Arabic mobile games to the world.

———

TAMATEM GAMES is the leading mobile games publisher in the MENA region, transforming the gaming industry by delivering high-quality, localized content tailored to Arabic-speaking audiences. Since its establishment in 2013, Tamatem has solidified its position as an industry powerhouse, amassing over 350 million downloads, publishing more than 50 successful titles, and engaging 1.5 million monthly active users.

With a deep understanding of the region's cultural and linguistic nuances, Tamatem goes beyond simple translation, fully adapting international games to ensure they resonate with local players. Through strategic partnerships with top global developers, the company provides expert localization, user acquisition, distribution, cross-promotion, monetization, community engagement, digital marketing, and whale management—making it the ultimate gateway for developers looking to succeed in the rapidly growing MENA gaming market.

The demand for Arabic-language content is at an all-time high, driven by a population of over 400 million Arabic speakers and a significant gap in available localized games. MENA is one of the world's most lucrative gaming markets, with an average revenue per paying user (ARPPU) eight times higher than China. Tamatem's expertise in market penetration and cultural adaptation empowers international developers to maximize their success in this high-growth region.

With a team of over 100 professionals and a 110% year-over-year growth rate, Tamatem continues to set industry benchmarks. The company has forged more than 10 strategic partnerships with international studios and has been recognized for its achievements, receiving the prestigious Best Publisher in MENA award at Pocket Gamer Connects 2024. As the MENA gaming industry expands, Tamatem remains at the forefront, committed to shaping the future of Arabic gaming and offering unparalleled opportunities for global developers seeking to thrive in one of the world's most promising markets.

––––––

Give us a bit of background about yourself.

So, I was born and raised in Jordan. I studied computer science at Princess Sumaya University. Before university, I was always passionate about computers and doing something on my own. I had this dream of being a successful entrepreneur, but without really understanding what that meant. I grew up in a tough period, caught between two generations.

During university, I started doing a lot of freelancing—graphic design, coding, and trying to understand how things worked. After graduation, I had the idea of starting a web development company with a friend, but we quickly realized how difficult that would be. I got incredibly lucky by joining a very small startup, and I say lucky because joining a startup instead of a big company allowed me to learn everything about how a business operates.

Can you describe a specific moment or lesson from that startup that had a profound impact on your future as an entrepreneur?

While I was at that startup, the founder, Majid, got excited about creating something similar to Yahoo! at the time. He wanted to compete with Maktoob, and I had the opportunity to witness everything—from fundraising to hiring a team, product development, design, and everything in between. That was an incredibly exciting experience.

I approached my manager with an idea and told him, "I want to become a product manager, and I have a few ideas I'd like to present to you." His response was to focus on my current work because he thought I was too young. But I didn't stop there. I came back to him with a full business plan for a social network. At that time, platforms like Hi5 and MySpace were gaining popularity, and I thought, "Why not create something similar but in Arabic?" I believed that a lot of people in the region would be very interested in using a platform in their own language.

I presented the business plan, but unfortunately, my manager rejected it. He still believed I was too young for such an idea.

How did that rejection impact your mindset at the time?

Luckily, there was an entrepreneurship competition at my university, even though I had already graduated. It was the first version of the competition, and my friend and I decided to apply. Out of 200 applicants, we went through the program and ended up winning first place. That was a significant milestone in my life because it marked the launch of our social network. It was called Faye3, which means hip or cool in Jordanian slang.

Immediately we entered the Queen Rania Entrepreneurship competition in Jordan, which we won. During the competition, when we presented our project, some key figures were in the audience—specifically, Samih Toukan and Hussam Khoury, the founders of Maktoob. They loved what they saw and asked us to join Maktoob as employees. We presented our project to them, and they decided to acquire it.

At the time, I didn't fully understand the implications of selling our project—I was too young and the internet ecosystem was still in its early days. But we decided to sell and move to Maktoob as product managers to transform it into a more social platform. Maktoob was very limited in design—grey-scale and structured—whereas our project was vibrant, colorful, and part of the new Web 2.0 movement.

After joining Maktoob, I worked hard to push this new vision forward. In 2007, the project was rebranded within Maktoob as Ashab (which means friends in Arabic), and it became the largest channel within Maktoob's portfolio, generating over 50 million page views per month. That was a major achievement.

By 2009, I started noticing the rise of online gaming and how much money was being spent on it—especially browser-based games that didn't require downloads. Many of these were only available in English, but one game in Arabic caught my attention.

Maktoob had a payment method called CashU, and I noticed that a significant portion of transactions were coming from Saudi Arabia and the Gulf region. That was my moment of realization: "This could be the next big thing."

My friends and I at Maktoob decided to quit our jobs and start a gaming company called Wizards Productions in 2009. Little did we know that we were quitting at the worst possible time—the financial crisis had just hit.

Two months after we quit, Maktoob was acquired by Yahoo! in what became the largest acquisition in the Arabic internet market.

Looking back, do you think quitting when you did was the right decision, despite missing out on the stock options?

Unfortunately, part of our deal with Maktoob included receiving cash and employee stock options (ESOPs). However, because we had resigned before the acquisition, we didn't meet the three-year vesting period, which meant we forfeited all our stock options. That was a massive financial loss.

Maybe it happened for a reason. We had already started Wizards Productions, raised some money from friends and family, and hired a few engineers to develop the games we wanted. I focused on product and design, while my friend handled the technical work. Month after month, we saw incredible growth, which was very exciting.

We managed to raise around $400,000 through a convertible note from a local VC in Jordan, which helped us scale. But looking back, we lacked experience in running a business. There weren't many resources available online at the time to teach entrepreneurship. Concepts like Minimum Viable Product (MVP) weren't widely understood in 2009 and 2010. We made a lot of mistakes.

One major mistake was getting carried away with unplanned projects. One of our employees pitched an amazing idea—a shooting game that could be played in a browser. He showed us a demo he built over the weekend and convinced us it could be the next big thing.

Initially, we treated it as a side project, but slowly it started consuming more of our resources. Our investors encouraged us to go all in. They told us, "This looks amazing. Drop everything else and focus on this. Don't worry about money—if you complete this project, you'll raise tons of funding and make millions."

That's exactly what we did. We stopped everything that was generating revenue and focused entirely on this project.

The original timeline was six months. It ended up taking a year and a half. We burned through all our cash reserves and finally launched the product, only to realize we still needed more time and resources.

What would you do differently today in terms of balancing innovation and financial sustainability?

When we went back to our investors, they asked for traction and revenue—but we had nothing to show, because we had put everything into development.

Without revenue, no one was willing to give us more money. That led to the company shutting down in 2012. We had to lay off all our employees.

That was one of the hardest lessons of my life. From that experience, I learned the importance of focusing on revenue and profitability at all times. It also taught me that while taking advice from investors, board members, and advisors is important, ultimately, as an entrepreneur, you have to make your own decisions.

—————

> **FROM THAT EXPERIENCE, I LEARNED THE IMPORTANCE OF FOCUSING ON REVENUE AND PROFITABILITY AT ALL TIMES.**

—————

When the company shut down, I lost everything—my savings, my job, my relationships. I went home with nothing, feeling like a 30-year-old entrepreneur who had completely failed.

Family and friends started telling me, "Enough with this nonsense. Just get a real job like everyone else. Why do you insist on being different? Who makes money from gaming anyway?" The cultural perception of failure in the region didn't help either. Unlike in Silicon Valley, where failure is seen as a learning opportunity, here it was seen as the end of the road. Investors who had backed us kept reminding us that they had lost money, even though they were institutional funds.

No one gave me a second chance. No one believed I could stand up again.

How did you find the strength to keep going despite so much external doubt?

Despite everything, I still believed in gaming. I still believed that our failure wasn't due to the market—it was due to poor execution.

During this transition, my co-founder left. I was completely alone—no employees, no money, just a business plan.

I started pitching the plan to investors, but their response was always the same: "Come back when you have traction." Of course, I needed money to build traction, but no one was willing to take that leap with me. That was one of the toughest periods of my life.

After going through that rough period of being jobless, pitching to investors, and facing constant rejection, I applied to an accelerator program in the U.S. called 500 Startups in Silicon Valley. At the time, I thought there was no way they would accept me. They had never invested in the Middle East before, nor had they invested in gaming. I didn't think I had a chance.

One technique I used was leveraging all the investors who had previously rejected me. I reached out to them and asked them to send a recommendation email to 500 Startups, telling them they should at least talk to me. I believe 500 Startups received around 30 to 40 emails from different investors saying, "You must talk to Hussam."

Eventually, someone from 500 Startups called me and said, "We're not particularly interested in what you're doing, but we're very curious to know who the hell you are because everyone seems to want us to meet you."

I had the chance to pitch to them, and they loved it. They said, "Maybe we're wrong for not considering this sooner. We're not sure if this will be successful or not, but you know what? Come and join."

So, in 2013, I traveled to the U.S. and received a $50,000 investment from 500 Startups, only to later find out that $13,000 of that would go toward program fees. That left me with just $37,000 to start my company. But I also needed to rent an apartment, travel, eat, and survive for six months in one of the most expensive places in the world. On top of that, I needed to build a company with this limited amount of money.

I went to Silicon Valley alone, without a product—just a business plan and an idea.

What was the most intimidating part of that experience, and how did you overcome it?

Once I joined the program, all my previous beliefs, shaped by growing up in Jordan, started getting shattered.

One of the biggest lessons I learned was that sharing knowledge with peers is beneficial. Back home, we were always told to keep our ideas and plans to ourselves, fearing that someone might steal them.

But I realized that the more you share, the more help you receive. Competition is not the real threat—stagnation is.

———

" THE MORE YOU SHARE, THE MORE HELP YOU RECEIVE.
COMPETITION IS NOT THE REAL THREAT—STAGNATION IS.

———

Another major realization was that I had underestimated myself. I thought that being in the U.S., surrounded by entrepreneurs who had studied in world-class institutions, I would struggle to compete. I assumed they were all leagues ahead of me. But as the program went on, I realized I was just as good—if not better—than half the people in the room in terms of knowledge and understanding. That was surprising and eye-opening. It also highlighted how much entrepreneurs in the Middle East tend to doubt themselves. Unfortunately, many of us don't believe in our own capabilities as much as we should.

At first, I made a classic mistake—I put all my energy into raising money instead of building the business. Because I was in Silicon Valley, I kept hearing that I should have at least two or three calls per day with investors. So, I started reaching out to investors left and right, but I kept getting rejected for multiple reasons.

First, I was in the gaming industry, which meant I needed niche investors who specifically understood that market. Second, I was from the Middle East, targeting the Middle Eastern market, and most U.S. investors had no understanding of that region. Third, I didn't have a product or traction to show—just an idea.

For the first three months, I chased funding, growing more frustrated with each rejection. I kept thinking about leaving, going back to Jordan, and accepting that I had failed. But I knew deep down that failure wasn't an option. I couldn't be the person who went to Silicon Valley and came back empty-handed.

Then, one investor told me something that changed my entire approach. He said, "Hussam, stop talking to investors. No one will give you money right now. Show us the promise you're making.

How did that piece of advice shape your strategy moving forward?

You still have some money in the bank from 500 Startups—why don't you build what you're claiming to be capable of, instead of expecting us to take the risk for you?"

That struck me. I spent the next week working day and night to develop the first game. I found a freelancer online to handle the coding, while I took care of the design and content. We finished it, launched it, and I started seeing traction. People were downloading and playing the game. I was even generating a little revenue.

At first, the revenue was small—just $200 to $300 in the first month. But because we were starting from zero, the growth looked like a hockey-stick curve. The numbers were increasing day after day, and I was finally able to show investors some results.

Right, so I was able to show traction and revenue that was growing daily. With this data, I went back to investors and said, "Look, with the limited money I had, I was able to achieve this. Imagine what I could do if you invested more."

That pitch landed me my first $25,000 investment from the guy who created Guitar Hero, a massively successful game that was later acquired for around $200 million by Activision. That investment gave me validation and confidence.

After that, there was a demo day for 500 Startups, where I raised another $25,000. Then, during a trip to New York, I secured another $25,000. That momentum showed me that I was truly building a company—I wasn't just chasing a dream.

Around that time, a few Middle Eastern investors also took notice. Three investors each committed $25,000, adding another $75,000 to our funding.

By October 2013, I returned to Jordan with around $200,000 in the company's bank account. That was the real beginning of Tamatem. With this funding, I was able to hire a team.

What were the key qualities you looked for when building your first team, and how did you ensure they shared your vision?

The core vision of the company was to become a mobile game publisher focusing on the Middle Eastern market. The strategy was simple: Arabic-language content was scarce, but the region had one of the highest spending behaviors in the world. If we provided users with the content they wanted, they would engage, enjoy, and ultimately pay for it.

One of the first challenges I faced was credibility. When I reached out to international gaming companies to license their games and localize them in Arabic, their response was, "Who are you? What's your track record?"

That made me realize I needed a different approach. Instead of licensing games immediately, I decided to develop my own small, simple games—things like trivia and quiz games—to build a portfolio. That way, when I pitched to partners later, I would have actual numbers to back me up.

I hired a team of six or seven people and focused on rapid development. We launched a new game every two weeks. By the end of the first year, we had released around 30 games, gained traction, and built credibility.

As we scaled, I continued raising funds to support marketing, hiring talent, and operations. At first, I handled everything alone, but over time, I hired an accountant and other key roles. Eventually, my best friend from university joined to help manage operations.

Between 2014 and 2015, Tamatem truly started taking shape. In 2017, I raised a $1.25 million Series A investment from regional and global investors. Compared to today's standards, that amount would be considered a pre-seed round, but back then, gaming was a tough sector for investors.

In 2019, I raised a $3.5 million extension to our Series A. In 2022, we raised $11 million.

To date, the company has raised $17 million.

Fast forward to today, Tamatem has over 100 employees, with offices in Amman, Abu Dhabi, and Riyadh, as well as operations in Egypt, Iraq, and other markets. We've launched over 100 games through partnerships with companies from the U.S., China, Korea, and beyond.

Our next focus is solving a major challenge in the region: payments. With 70% of the Middle Eastern population unbanked, we launched Tamatem Plus to provide alternative payment solutions, ensuring more users can access in-game purchases.

That's the future of Tamatem—scaling mobile gaming and payments to take the company to the next level.

I believe the learning process started early for me because I had already been in the gaming industry for three or four years before launching Tamatem. So I knew exactly what I was doing and what I wanted to achieve. I also learned a lot from my previous experience—specifically, that you need to start small. You can't just jump in and build the biggest product in the world with limited resources. That was an important lesson.

At the same time, I focused on ensuring profitability or at least breaking even. That was my number one priority.

We focus on multiple aspects when it comes to culturalization. The first is language. We ensure that all text is translated from English to Arabic in a way that is clear, consistent, and written in formal Arabic. We only use traditional Arabic in our games, and we have strict quality control over spelling and grammar.

Arabic, as a language, presents its own challenges for game localization. For example, it is written from right to left, which means the entire UI layout often needs to be adjusted. Arabic text also takes up 25% more space than English, so the code must accommodate that additional spacing.

Another crucial aspect is marketing. All marketing materials must be localized to resonate with the regional audience. This includes social media, advertising, and community engagement. We also provide customer support in Arabic, ensuring that users can communicate with us in their preferred dialects.

Payments are another major factor. Many users don't have credit cards, so we have to provide alternative payment solutions. It's common for players to reach out to us asking if they can pay with cash. Some even approach us with $20 in hand, wanting to purchase in-game items. Adapting to these local payment preferences has been critical to our success.

Beyond that, we've developed internal initiatives to refine our approach. Tamatem Labs, for example, allows us to test new games with thousands of players before officially launching them in the region. We also have Tamatem Academy, which collaborates with universities to host hackathons, training programs, and internships to nurture the next generation of game developers.

I mean in terms of generating revenue and profits from user engagement. What are some best practices around acquiring and retaining users, increasing engagement, and ensuring recurring revenue?

There isn't a single formula for success, but when it comes to user acquisition, one challenge is that there are very few experts in this field within the region. Most of the people who worked with us in this area were homegrown talent—meaning it was their first job in the industry.

We had to invest heavily in training, certifications, and building relationships with social media platforms to optimize our marketing efforts. As you scale, user acquisition becomes increasingly complex. Many people claim to be digital marketing experts, but their budgets are often small—maybe $500 a month. When you're spending half a million dollars per month, it's an entirely different game. Data analysis and performance tracking become critical.

On the product side, monetization plays a crucial role. We were fortunate that, since we primarily localized and published existing games, we didn't have to reinvent monetization strategies. The original developers had already figured out the best monetization models in their markets. Our job was simply to adapt and optimize them for the Arabic-speaking audience.

That said, game design and game economy design are areas where the region still lacks expertise. We don't have many professionals with experience in designing in-game economies and monetization strategies. It's something we continue to learn and refine as we grow.

We aim to be an employer of choice for university students, which is why we actively engage with young talent on social media, LinkedIn, and through events. We tell our story, give interviews, and promote an entrepreneurial mindset among potential hires. Even for those who don't necessarily want to start their own business, we offer an exciting and fun workplace culture.

We take fun very seriously—it's a crucial aspect of our company culture. At the same time, we ensure high productivity levels.

To attract top talent, we rely heavily on referrals. Our existing employees understand the company culture and the type of people who would thrive here, so we encourage them to refer their friends.

We also invest in headhunting and attending industry events and conferences. However, I won't deny that hiring in gaming is a massive challenge. The region has incredible talent, but not in gaming specifically.

Whenever we hire, we make sure that candidates understand the gaming industry, the key metrics, and the market dynamics. It's not easy, but it's essential for our long-term success.

I think we've already talked a lot about the lessons I've learned from my own experience—what I did wrong and how I would approach things differently today. But if I could add one more point, it would be that chasing investments is not an achievement in itself.

Building a successful company should always come first. If you have the opportunity to grow your company without raising money, then don't raise money. Fundraising is a massive hassle, it's time-consuming, and it's incredibly stressful. If you can build a profitable company from the start—one that doesn't need fancy offices or expensive hires—it will be much better for you as an entrepreneur.

Another crucial point is managing relationships with investors. Entrepreneurs often think that investors have the upper hand simply because they have the money. But that's not the case. The entrepreneur has the upper hand. Investors should be seeking you, not the other way around. You're taking their money to make them more money—it's a mutually beneficial relationship, not a one-sided power dynamic.

It ties into what I just mentioned—investors can easily give advice, but I would say don't ask for advice. Ask for shared experiences.

Instead of saying, "Tell me what I should do," ask, "Have you faced this situation before? What did you do?"

> "
> INSTEAD OF SAYING, 'TELL ME WHAT I SHOULD DO,' ASK, 'HAVE YOU FACED THIS SITUATION BEFORE? WHAT DID YOU DO?'

When you ask for advice, you often get generic responses that may not fit your specific situation. And if things go wrong, you end up blaming the person who gave you that advice. But when you ask for shared experiences, you get real-world insights that allow you to make better-informed decisions.

I'm part of Entrepreneurs' Organization (EO), and one of the key concepts of EO is to never give direct advice. In EO, we share experiences instead. We have forum settings where a group of entrepreneurs discuss their top 5% challenges—the issues they don't talk about with anyone else. It could be family problems, struggles with a spouse, children, or business-related dilemmas.

Imagine sharing a personal challenge, and someone immediately tells you, "You should absolutely do this." That's terrible advice.

Instead, the right approach is for someone to say, "I had a similar situation. This is what I did, and this was the outcome." Then it's up to you to read between the lines, think critically, and make the best decision for your situation.

I'd say this is important for both entrepreneurs and investors.

What are your thoughts on the future of gaming in the MENA region?

Sure. From my perspective, the future of gaming in the region looks very promising.

The Middle East has been putting a lot of effort into growing its gaming industry. Saudi Arabia, in particular, has been doing incredible work in promoting gaming on a global scale. They've made massive acquisitions in recent years, which has put the region on the map.

One of the biggest challenges I used to face was that whenever I spoke to investors or other gaming companies, their first reaction was: "The Middle East? Where is that? Do people even play games there?"

Today, I don't hear those questions anymore. Now, everyone wants to invest in the Middle East and in Saudi Arabia. Everyone wants to be part of the programs and initiatives happening here. That's an incredible shift.

Abu Dhabi is also doing a great job in supporting the gaming industry. We moved our operations to Abu Dhabi last year, and now we have a significant presence there. If you visit Yas Island and see the Creative Hub, it's an amazing ecosystem—full of events, communities, and young talent joining the industry.

I strongly encourage global gaming companies to come and see what's happening in the region.

Talent development is another major focus area. Universities across the region, including in Jordan, are starting to offer game development and game design programs. In the coming years, we'll see an increase in homegrown talent emerging from these universities, which will be great for the industry.

As for Tamatem, our focus remains on bringing more high-quality games to the region. Payments continue to be a major pain point, and we're working hard to address that with a stronger push in alternative payment solutions.

We're also expanding our internal game development efforts. We now have our own gaming studio, where we're launching multiple in-house games. That's something we're really excited about, and we want to grow it as much as possible.

That's where we're headed.

Do you think publicizing regional startup success stories is an effective way to empower local entrepreneurs?

Absolutely. Having successful case studies is the best way to encourage entrepreneurship.

I always think about the PayPal Mafia—the group of former PayPal employees who went on to start some of the biggest tech companies in the world. Many of the top entrepreneurs in Silicon Valley came from that ecosystem.

We need something similar in the Middle East. Universities here should be teaching these success stories so that young entrepreneurs can see that it's possible to build something big.

One challenge in our region is that many successful entrepreneurs don't openly share their journeys. Some family businesses have fascinating stories, but they are rarely told in a way that new entrepreneurs can learn from. Many of these companies started 60 or 70 years ago with trading or import/export businesses. But how do you replicate that success in the digital age? That's what people need to understand.

———

> ONE CHALLENGE IN OUR REGION IS THAT MANY SUCCESSFUL ENTREPRENEURS DON'T OPENLY SHARE THEIR JOURNEYS.

———

Similarly, startup founders often don't publicly share the details of their success—whether it's raising money, scaling, or exiting their companies. There's a tendency to keep these things private.

Some of this is cultural. People fear being too public about their success due to superstitions like the evil eye or attracting unnecessary attention. Others just prefer to stay humble.

But we need more transparency. If I know exactly how someone built and scaled their business, I have a better chance of following in their footsteps. That's a social responsibility that successful entrepreneurs should embrace.

How has the success of companies like Maktoob inspired more entrepreneurs to share their journeys?

One great example of such story is that of Maktoob. Many of the entrepreneurs who worked at Maktoob went on to start their own companies because they were inspired by its success. They saw that it was possible, and that gave them the motivation to try.

Similarly, Tamatem has produced a lot of entrepreneurs. Many of our former employees have gone on to start their own companies. We've built a culture that encourages that.

Sounds like you're carrying forward the torch of instilling the right ethos at Tamatem, just as Maktoob did back in the day.

Indeed, I look at my own experience for example—leaving Maktoob to start my own company. But I'm not the only one. Many of the most successful startups in the region were founded by people who once worked at Maktoob.

If you look at their resumes, you'll see that many of today's founders spent time there. Maktoob didn't intentionally create this, but it had an open and collaborative culture that encouraged people to think big. That culture made a huge difference.

True. Yahoo's acquisition of Maktoob only included certain parts of the company. That left many other projects free to evolve into independent businesses. Some of the spin-offs included CashU, Souq.com, and others.

Maktoob was ahead of its time in many ways. They had a product called Bint Alhalal—essentially a Muslim-friendly version of Tinder—before Tinder even existed. That was back in 2006 or 2007.

We've always had the ideas and the talent—we just need to believe in ourselves more, and we need investors who are willing to bet on those ideas earlier.

———

ISMAEL BELKHAYAT & SOPHIA ALJ

Powering small businesses

Co-founders of CHARI

chari

Casablanca, Morocco

www.chari.ma

IISMAEL BELKHAYAT is a distinguished serial entrepreneur within the vibrant Moroccan tech landscape. Following a tenure in consulting at the esteemed Boston Consulting Group, Ismael embarked on his entrepreneurial journey, founding two groundbreaking companies that laid the foundation for his entrepreneurial career: Wib.co, a pioneering startup studio, and Chauffeur.ma, a premier ground transportation service in Morocco, subsequently acquired by Avis Car Rental.

With a keen eye for opportunity and a drive for innovation, Ismael ventured into the realm of real estate technology by establishing Sarouty.ma, an intuitive real estate marketplace facilitating property transactions across Morocco. Within a remarkably short span of two years, Sarouty soared to become the nation's premier real estate platform, forging a strategic alliance with Property Finder, LLC to bolster its technological capabilities.

While serving as a Board Member for his prior ventures, Ismael's passion for catalyzing digital transformation led him to co-found his latest venture in 2020 alongside his spouse: Chari, a B2B e-commerce and fintech application tailored for retailers. Leveraging his expertise in logistics and marketplace dynamics, Ismael has propelled Chari to unprecedented growth, garnering accolades such as the prestigious "Disruptor of the Year" award from the Africa CEO Forum and positioning it as a frontrunner for potential unicorn status, a groundbreaking achievement for the Moroccan startup scene.

Backed by substantial investment from renowned entities including Y Combinator, Airbnb, Orange, and even Harvard University, Chari is a testament to Ismael's entrepreneurial vision. Harvard University has written a compelling business case study on Chari, underscoring its transformative impact and industry significance.

Ismael is a graduate of Cornell University and a distinguished member of Y Combinator, Endeavor, and YPO.

―――――

SOPHIA ALJ is a Moroccan entrepreneur and the co-founder and Chief Operating Officer (COO) of Chari, a B2B e-commerce platform with integrated fintech services targeting traditional retail stores in French-speaking African countries. Born and raised in Casablanca, Morocco, Sophia pursued higher education abroad, earning a Bachelor of Engineering in Civil Engineering from McGill University in Canada in 2012. She furthered her studies with a Master in Management from ESCP Business School in France, specializing in consulting, completed in 2015.

Sophia's professional journey began with an apprenticeship as an Innovation Manager at BNP Paribas Corporate and Investment Banking in Paris from January 2014 to August 2015. She then joined McKinsey & Company in October 2015 as an Associate Consultant, where she worked for over four years, focusing on digital transformations across various sectors in Africa.

In November 2019, Sophia co-founded Chari alongside her husband, Ismael Belkhayat, who had previously worked at the Boston Consulting Group and had entrepreneurial experience in Morocco. Chari is a mobile application that enables small retailers to order consumer goods and receive free delivery within 24 hours. The platform also offers financial services, including microloans, payments, and micro-insurance, to support the business needs of these retailers.

Under Sophia's leadership, Chari has experienced rapid growth since its inception. The company participated in Y Combinator's Summer 2021 cohort, becoming the first Moroccan startup to be selected by the renowned accelerator. Chari has expanded its operations beyond Morocco to countries like Tunisia and Côte d'Ivoire, serving over 20,000 customers and employing more than 180 people as of 2022. Additionally, Chari received a payment institution license from the Central Bank of Morocco, enhancing its ability to provide financial services to its clients.

Sophia's entrepreneurial efforts have been recognized regionally; she was featured in Forbes Middle East's list of "20 Women Behind

Middle Eastern Tech Brands 2023," ranking 10th. Before founding Chari, Sophia co-founded Mondentiste.ma, a digital toolkit for dentists, and served as a co-managing partner at Wib.co, a startup studio and web incubator.

Balancing her professional and personal life, Sophia is also a mother of three children: Malyk, Leyla, and Aya. Her journey reflects a commitment to leveraging technology to empower traditional businesses and drive economic growth in Africa.

CHARI is a Morocco-based B2B e-commerce and fintech platform dedicated to empowering traditional retailers across French-speaking Africa. Through its mobile application, Chari enables local businesses to efficiently order consumer goods and access integrated financial services, streamlining operations and fostering growth.

Founded in 2020 by Ismael Belkhayat and Sophia Alj, Chari was created to address the fragmented and informal nature of trade in Morocco. Ismael Belkhayat, who serves as the Chief Executive Officer, brings extensive experience from his time at the Boston Consulting Group and other entrepreneurial ventures. Sophia Alj, the Chief Operating Officer, is a former McKinsey consultant with a strong background in digital transformations.

The mission of Chari is to digitize the supply chain for small retailers by providing a one-stop platform that simplifies product procurement and financial transactions. Retailers can browse and order from a vast selection of fast-moving consumer goods (FMCG) at competitive prices while benefiting from free delivery within 24 hours. Beyond product procurement, Chari offers financial services such as microloans and payment solutions, allowing retailers to better manage and expand their businesses.

Since its inception, Chari has grown rapidly, expanding its operations to multiple countries and serving over 25,000 clients with more than 1,200 products. The company has made strategic acquisitions, such as the purchase of the Ivorian startup Diago in 2022, further strengthening its footprint in Francophone Africa.

Chari's innovative approach has earned international recognition. In June 2021, it became the first Maghreb startup to join the prestigious Y Combinator accelerator program, highlighting its potential in the global startup ecosystem. The company has also secured investments from major players, including Orange Ventures, Endeavor Catalyst, and Plug and Play Tech Center, reflecting strong confidence in Chari's business model and growth potential.

By digitizing the supply chain and providing essential financial services, Chari is transforming the traditional retail sector in Morocco and beyond. The platform's user-friendly application not only simplifies inventory replenishment but also gives small retailers access to financial tools that were previously out of reach. Through its commitment to innovation and digital transformation, Chari is playing a pivotal role in formalizing and supporting small businesses, driving economic growth, and fostering financial inclusion across the region.

———

Give us a brief background about yourselves.

Ismael: Thank you for having us and featuring Chari in your book. Sophia can start.

Sophia: So, very quickly about myself—I am the Co-founder and COO of Chari, and before Chari, let me tell you a little bit about my story.

I was born and raised in Casablanca. So, I am Moroccan, and I studied outside of Morocco. I went abroad to study civil engineering—first at McGill University in Montreal, Canada, where I spent around four and a half years. Then I did an internship in engineering but realized that I didn't want to become an engineer and stay in that field my whole life. So, I decided to pursue my master's degree at a French business school—one of the top three ranked business schools in France—called ESCP Europe, where I spent two years doing my master's in management.

I was working at the same time while studying. I worked at the bank BNP Paribas in the corporate banking sector. When I graduated from ESCP Europe and finished working at BNP Paribas, I decided to go back to Morocco. I had spent almost seven years outside my home country, and I really wanted to return because I believed that the country needed people trained abroad to help with its development.

So, I went back to Morocco and started my career as a strategy consultant at McKinsey. I worked at McKinsey for around four years, traveling extensively across different African countries. In the beginning, I worked on various topics, but by the end of my career at McKinsey, I specialized in digital transformation, mainly in the private sector.

While at McKinsey, I had two kids. I had known Ismael, who is now my Co-founder, before McKinsey, and we got married before I joined. We had our two kids, and I decided to leave McKinsey because I had always wanted to become an entrepreneur. Since I was young, when people asked me what I wanted to do with my life, I would say in French, "Je veux devenir une femme d'affaires," meaning "I want to become a businesswoman" in English—without really knowing what it meant at the time.

But by then, I realized that I didn't want to stay at McKinsey. I wanted to build my own company and become an entrepreneur. Ismael, who became my Co-founder, was already a tech entrepreneur, so I decided to join him in building Chari together.

Ismael: I am the Co-founder and CEO of Chari. My background is quite similar to Sophia's because I was also born and raised in Morocco, but in Rabat, which is the capital. I went to a French school up to high school.

I was born in the 80s and was a teenager in the 90s. At that time, it was the beginning of the Internet. I remember I was the first kid to get, for his birthday—while others were asking for toys—I asked for a CD and DVD maker. I don't know if you remember those things that allowed you to copy music and MP3s. I think you remember those well. I don't think Sophia will know what an MP3 is. But anyway, I remember making my first revenue back when I was a teenager.

After high school, I flew to Paris and did what we call Classe Préparatoire, which is two years of intensive preparation to join the top schools. I ended up joining the school Sophia mentioned—ESCP Europe. That's how Sophia and I ended up meeting. I'm a bit older than her, but when I finished ESCP, she was just joining. She reached out to a few alums, and I used my status as an alum to my advantage—to convince Sophia to become my girlfriend.

After ESCP, I went to the US to Cornell University and started working for BCG as a consultant. I was initially hired by the Paris office but was later sent to Casablanca because they were opening a new office there at the time. I worked for almost three years at BCG before deciding to become an entrepreneur.

One of the people who convinced me to take that step is someone you also feature in your book—Michael Lihyani, the founder of Property Finder. When I met Micahel in Dubai, and he told me he was from Morocco. He said, "Look at what I've done with Property Finder. I've always dreamed of doing something in Morocco because that's where I'm from. Why don't we team up and do something together?"

That's how we built Sarouti.ma, the Moroccan version of Property Finder. That's how I got to know the startup world and participated in the fundraising of Property Finder. Today, Michael is one of my closest friends, and his whole family—from his brother to his father—are very close friends of Sophia and me. We love these guys.

After that, I continued as an entrepreneur. I started a ride-hailing app in Morocco, which quickly became the leading service in the country. It was called Chauffeur Privé.ma, and it was partially acquired by Avis—the rental car company that now operates it.

Then, I built a venture studio, or startup studio, and started a few ventures—mainly in online travel agencies. When COVID hit in 2020, Sophia and I decided to build Chari. Chari was launched in January 2020, just a few months before COVID. And thanks to COVID, well... that's how Chari came to be.

Sophia: Going back to 2019, Ismael was already a tech entrepreneur. He mentioned that he had built a company with Property Finder, then a ride-hailing app, and I was a McKinsey consultant traveling across different French-speaking African countries.

Because Ismael was already working remotely, he used to join me on my trips. During those trips, I typically had 2–3 or even 4-month projects, and during that time, you have to live the way people live in that country. You go to the supermarket, you explore the city as if it were your own, and you get to experience daily life firsthand.

We realized, during those trips, that across African countries, there were a lot of similarities in how people lived and did their grocery shopping.

How did observing global small businesses shape your vision for this company?

Sophia: We noticed that the concept of mom-and-pop shops existed everywhere, though they had different names depending on the country.

In Morocco, for example, they are called hanout in Arabic—I will send you the exact spelling in the chat. In other places, they are called traditional proximity stores, or in the U.S., they are known as bodegas. These small grocery shops are found on the corner of every street, usually near people's homes or workplaces.

When people need to buy groceries, they don't always go to large supermarket chains. Instead, they buy whatever they need for the day or the next two days from these small neighborhood stores. These shop owners play a central role in their communities, whether in Morocco or elsewhere.

Back in Morocco, Ismael and I lived near a grocery shop that we visited regularly. The shopkeeper knew everything about us—who my husband was, where I worked, when I traveled, what coffee brand I liked to buy, and what tea brand my husband preferred. He even allowed us to buy on credit. I could tell him, "Listen, I don't have cash today, but I'll stop by tomorrow and pay you back for what I need now."

Through this concept of mom-and-pop shops, we started brainstorming and identified some key challenges these shop owners faced—especially in procurement and financial inclusion. We saw that they struggled with sourcing their products efficiently and lacked access to proper financial tools.

We realized that we wanted to build a company that would help these shop owners compete with the growing dominance of modern retail chains. Our goal was to help them stay in business, increase their revenues, and ultimately thrive in the evolving market.

———

" WE REALIZED THAT WE WANTED TO BUILD A COMPANY THAT WOULD HELP THESE SHOP OWNERS COMPETE WITH THE GROWING DOMINANCE OF MODERN RETAIL CHAINS. OUR GOAL WAS TO HELP THEM STAY IN BUSINESS, INCREASE THEIR REVENUES, AND ULTIMATELY THRIVE IN THE EVOLVING MARKET.

———

Ismael: Sophia and I were a married couple traveling together, and we saw a lot of similarities in other African countries. We realized how these shopkeepers were essential to their communities.

Back home, we used to do our grocery shopping together at a small shop next to our place. In Morocco and other developing countries, people don't always go to big supermarkets. Instead, they buy from the neighborhood mom-and-pop shops on a daily basis, purchasing only what they need for the day.

We were young professionals, always in a hurry. Sometimes, we would arrive at the shop, and it would be completely empty—so we would just grab what we needed and leave. Other times, the shop would be packed, because the owner was usually a one-man show—a single person behind the counter, handling everything by himself. He had to manage not just his customers but also his suppliers.

There were times when we would visit the shop, and he would be overwhelmed because of the number of people inside. We had to wait, and we could see how stressful it was for him to manage everything alone. At the same time, there were hours during the day when his shop was completely quiet, with no customers at all.

Sophia and I felt that this was a missed opportunity. This shopkeeper had rush hours when he couldn't serve all his customers efficiently, followed by idle periods when he had nothing to do. That's when we thought: Why not solve this procurement problem by providing him with an app?

What specific obstacles did shopkeepers face in transitioning to digital solutions, and how did you address them?

Sophia: With an app, he could place orders for the goods he needed during those quiet hours, without waiting for suppliers to visit or having to close his shop and go to a wholesaler himself. Our idea was simple: optimize the time of these shopkeepers and make their lives easier. This idea came from a real experience—something we personally witnessed—and we wanted to improve the daily lives of shopkeepers like him.

So this is how Chari started. It began as a very simple app—a procurement app where mom-and-pop shop owners could order any consumer goods they sell and receive free next-day delivery.

We were solving a basic procurement issue. Instead of waiting for a large distributor's van to visit once or twice a month, or closing their shop to go to a cash-and-carry or wholesale store, shopkeepers could simply order what they needed through the app and have it delivered to them the next day. It was a fast, easy, and convenient solution.

We launched this in January 2020, and just two months later, COVID hit—by the end of February. At the time, most shopkeepers were still operating in very traditional ways. But because of COVID, they quickly realized that ordering products online was much easier. The shift to digital ordering became normal, and adoption skyrocketed.

For us, this meant our startup gained traction very quickly. Ordering through an app became more convenient, and it was much easier to educate shopkeepers on how to use the platform. Just a few months after launching, we saw great traction—double-digit growth. Everything was going well.

But as we spent more time with mom-and-pop shop owners, listening to them and understanding their challenges, we realized they had another major pain point that we could solve.

What role did the acquisition of Karni play in Chari's transition into fintech?

Sophia: By spending time with and talking to these mom-and-pop shops, we realized that they had another pain point that we could solve—financial inclusion.

A few months after launching Chari and our e-commerce activity, we acquired a small app at the time called Karni. Karni was essentially a credit bookkeeping app that allowed small shop owners to digitally track the money they were lending to their customers.

Imagine yourself in El Jadida back in the day. You go to buy something from the small hanout (corner shop) next to your house. As a kid, you might not have money on you, but the shopkeeper knows your parents will stop by the next day. So, you buy some biscuits and juice, and instead of paying immediately, the shopkeeper takes a small notebook and writes down that you owe him five dirhams. Later, when your dad or mom visits the shop, the shopkeeper reminds them of what you took on credit and asks them to settle the amount.

What Karni did was digitize this pen-and-paper system. It provided mom-and-pop shops with an app where they could record customer loans and track repayments. The app even allowed them to send WhatsApp reminders to customers, letting them know they had an outstanding balance.

Thanks to the data we collected through Karni, we realized that mom-and-pop shops played an even bigger role in their communities than we initially thought. It wasn't just about selling FMCG (fast-moving consumer goods) daily—they were also lending money to people who often didn't even have bank accounts. In many cases, these shopkeepers were lending more money than they were getting back, essentially functioning as small, informal banks within their neighborhoods. They were filling a financial gap by offering credit to people who had no access to traditional banking services.

With this insight, Ismael and I realized that these mom-and-pop shops could greatly benefit from proper financial inclusion—access to essential financial services like payments, microcredit, and microinsurance. This would allow them to be integrated into the formal financial ecosystem.

Ismael: So, when we had the idea, Sophia and I came back to the office. You know in cartoons when a character has a light bulb appear over their head? That was us. We felt like we had found the right model.

We spent three months building an amazing MVP. We focused on great UI/UX, used the best libraries, and developed it for both Apple and Android. After three months, we were super proud of ourselves.

Then, we went back to the shopkeepers to show them our product, and that's when we realized something shocking. Most of these shopkeepers had very old Android phones with no storage space. This was in 2020, and many couldn't even install our app because it was too heavy or built using the latest technologies.

Even for those who could install the app, they struggled to use it. It was too complex, with too many buttons. We had designed it based on our hands, but their fingers were bigger, so they kept pressing the wrong buttons. Some of them didn't even know how to read or write, so they wanted more pictures and fewer words. But our app had long descriptions instead of images.

That's when we realized a crucial lesson. You should never build a product based on what you think your client wants—you should build it based on the time you spend with them and their real needs.

———

> YOU SHOULD NEVER BUILD A PRODUCT BASED ON WHAT YOU THINK YOUR CLIENT WANTS—YOU SHOULD BUILD IT BASED ON THE TIME YOU SPEND WITH THEM AND THEIR REAL NEEDS.

———

What adjustments did you make to your technology and business model to better suit the shopkeepers' actual needs?

Sophia: To avoid wasting time, we quickly adapted. We told shopkeepers that instead of using the app, they could simply send us a WhatsApp message whenever they wanted to order something. Every day, we sent promotions to shopkeepers via WhatsApp, and they responded with voice messages to place their orders. Back at the office, we had a customer support team who would call back the shopkeepers to confirm the orders and make sure everything was correct.

At first, this WhatsApp-based model worked well, but it was expensive. Listening to hundreds of voice messages and manually processing orders took too much time. That's when we started thinking about how to build an easier-to-use app and incentivize shopkeepers to use it instead of calling or messaging us.

This led us to acquire Karni, the credit-book app that Sophia mentioned earlier. Karni was super simple to use, and we started promoting it heavily. As of today, we have around 45,000 monthly active users on Karni. These users come at a low acquisition cost because the app is free. Then, we cross-sell our services by reaching out to these shopkeepers and introducing them to Chari, allowing them to order products with free next-day delivery.

That's how we scaled. Things were going great, our growth was strong, investors were excited, and we raised a lot of money. We got into Y Combinator, became Endeavor Entrepreneurs, and attracted amazing investors, including Harvard University, which even wrote a business case about us. You can check it out at hbs.Chari.com. It might help with your book.

Everything was going well, until mid-2022. That's when the funding crisis hit.

How did you navigate the shift from a growth-at-all-costs mindset to a focus on profitability, and what lessons did you take from that?

Imsael: The same investors who had been telling us to keep growing suddenly changed their tune. They started asking about our path to profitability, a phrase we had never heard before in 2020 or 2021.

Sophia and I had to pivot. We needed to improve our unit economics, so we decided to add fintech services, especially payments.

What challenges did you face in gaining regulatory approval, and how did you overcome them?

Isamel: We approached the Central Bank of Morocco and told them that we already had tens of thousands of active shopkeepers using our services. They trusted us, they shared their data with us, and if the Central Bank granted us a neobank license, we could create a financial solution tailored to shopkeepers, helping them move away from cash-only transactions and become financially included.

———

   WE APPROACHED THE CENTRAL BANK OF MOROCCO AND TOLD THEM THAT WE ALREADY HAD TENS OF THOUSANDS OF ACTIVE SHOPKEEPERS USING OUR SERVICES.

———

After months of hard work, we secured our neobank license and built the Chari Neobank. Today, shopkeepers can not only buy and sell FMCG products but also process bill payments, handle tax payments, offer mobile top-ups, facilitate domestic money transfers, and provide remittance services.

Essentially, we turned corner shops into local banks.

We're proud of this because we're helping mom-and-pop shops fight the rise of big chains like Carrefour and Walmart, using technology as their competitive advantage. We've seen what happened in the US and Europe, where independent shops were replaced by big retailers. But that was in a time when small shopkeepers didn't have access to technology. Today, by providing them with digital tools, we're not only making their daily lives easier but also giving them new ways to generate revenue and sustain their businesses.

That's what keeps us going—knowing that we're making a real impact on these small businesses and helping them stay competitive in an evolving market.

What were the biggest obstacles in securing a reliable supply chain for your business?

Sophia: So, Amir, the first major challenge I want to talk about was the launch of the company. We had a great idea, and we knew it was solving a real problem, but actually making it work in the market came with two big obstacles. The first was sourcing consumer goods at competitive prices because we needed to buy them from existing suppliers. The second was getting our target customers—mom-and-pop shop owners—to change their purchasing habits and adopt a new buying channel.

For the first part of the challenge, we knew that if we were buying goods at a higher price than other distributors, we wouldn't be competitive. Mom-and-pop shop owners are extremely price-sensitive, so even the slightest difference in cost would make them prefer their existing suppliers over us. We needed to buy from major FMCG suppliers at market rates, but getting them to trust us was incredibly difficult.

When we started approaching suppliers, we met with at least ten of them, and all of them shut the door in our faces. They told us we were too small, that we were a new player they didn't trust, and that they didn't want to risk working with us because we might disrupt their carefully controlled pricing policies. The FMCG market is very price-sensitive, and suppliers were afraid we'd introduce instability if we didn't follow their pricing structures.

Since we couldn't buy directly from suppliers, we had to start by purchasing goods from large wholesalers instead. That meant we were essentially an intermediary of the intermediary, which resulted in significantly smaller margins. It was painful because we had to physically go to wholesalers, buy goods in bulk, transport them back to our warehouse, and then resell them with very little room for profit. We operated like this for about three months.

During this period, we focused on gathering data that would help us convince suppliers to work with us. Instead of just going back to them as a new distributor, we wanted to offer something unique—something no other distributor could provide. What we realized was that our app allowed us to track exactly what each shop was buying, how often they were purchasing, and which products were selling the most.

So after three months of struggling with wholesalers, we went back to the suppliers who had originally rejected us. This time, we showed them data that no other distributor had. We could tell them, "Look, we know exactly which shops are buying which products, at what frequency, and what their customers prefer. We can even help you push targeted promotions directly to these shop owners through our app." That was the turning point. With that added value, our first supplier finally agreed to give us a distribution contract, and from there, others started following.

The second major challenge was getting shop owners to trust us and switch to our platform. These small retailers were used to a very traditional way of buying their stock, either waiting for a distributor's van to visit them once or twice a month or physically going to a wholesaler to purchase products. We had to convince them to adopt a digital ordering system, which was a huge behavioral shift.

At first, we thought our beautifully designed app would be enough. We had developed an amazing product with a great user interface, but when we launched it, barely anyone used it. We quickly realized that digital adoption would require a process.

We had to build what we now call the "lifecycle of a mom-and-pop shop" before they start ordering digitally. It wasn't just about providing the app—it was about guiding them through a transition. First, we had to send people on the ground to visit these shopkeepers, introduce them to Chari, and build trust. Then, we got them to place their first few orders over the phone by calling our customer service center. Once they were comfortable doing that, we slowly educated them on how to use the app itself.

This process took about six months before we received our first fully digital orders. Looking back, I realize we could have done this more efficiently. Instead of spending months building the app first, we should have focused on onboarding customers through phone orders and WhatsApp before introducing the app. If we had done that in parallel, we probably would have shaved off four or five months from our go-to-market timeline.

For the supplier challenge, we were also a bit naive in the beginning. We assumed that suppliers would be open to signing distribution contracts with us from the start, without us offering anything truly different from existing distributors. Had we approached them from the beginning with our unique data insights, we could have gained their trust much faster.

What was one misstep you made early on in hindsight?

Sophia: Looking back, I think the biggest mistake we made was underestimating the importance of customer behavior change. We thought launching a great app would be enough, but in reality, adoption required a structured approach. If we had first worked on getting shopkeepers comfortable with phone orders before transitioning them to the app, we could have saved a lot of time.

On the supplier side, our mistake was assuming they would work with us just because we had a good business idea. We didn't realize at first that trust and differentiation were key. If we had gone to them earlier with hard data proving our value, we probably wouldn't have spent those first few months struggling with wholesalers.

Ismael: So while we were doing all of that, of course, as you know, we were a startup that was rapidly acquiring users and educating them, because what Sophia described was essentially an education process. And education is very costly. To finance that education, we had to raise funding.

We went to the market as probably one of, if not the first, Moroccan startups to raise a Series A. Coming from a geography that investors don't necessarily know well made things even more complicated. Typically, when investors consider a startup, they analyze exit opportunities, liquidity events, and benchmarks from similar markets. In our case, we had no real local geographic benchmark. The closest comparisons were in Southeast Asia or South America. So, in addition to explaining our business model and what we were building, we also had the added challenge of convincing investors why Morocco was a stable and promising market for investment.

That was one challenge. The second major challenge was that in 2021, when we raised our seed round, investors were primarily focused on top-line growth. No one was asking about unit economics. It was all about scaling fast and growing revenue. But by the time we raised our Series A in 2022, the conversation had completely shifted. Investors were no longer just looking at the top line; they were scrutinizing the bottom line as well.

We, along with many other startups in our space, realized that the business model we initially pursued was not inherently profitable. The margins from suppliers were extremely low, and logistics costs were high, making it difficult to sustain the business purely on e-commerce.

So, with our existing and potential investors, we had to find ways to bring in additional revenue streams. That's when we started exploring fintech services. Neither Sophia nor I had any background in fintech. In fact, before our investors suggested it, we hadn't even considered it as an option. We had to become fintech experts practically overnight— understanding the best use cases, finding revenue opportunities, and spending time with our customers to uncover their financial pain points.

———

" WE HAD TO BECOME FINTECH EXPERTS PRACTICALLY OVERNIGHT—UNDERSTANDING THE BEST USE CASES, FINDING REVENUE OPPORTUNITIES, AND SPENDING TIME WITH OUR CUSTOMERS TO UNCOVER THEIR FINANCIAL PAIN POINTS.

———

Beyond that, we had to convince the central bank, which was no easy task. And once we got approval, we realized that being a licensed financial entity was an entirely new challenge in itself. We had to comply with strict regulations, including KYC (Know Your

Customer), KYB (Know Your Business), anti-money laundering, terrorism financing controls, continuous compliance audits, and permanent monitoring. The list of regulatory requirements seemed endless.

This was a massive challenge because, at the same time, we were still running our e-commerce business. We had to learn an entirely new industry, convince regulators, meet all legal requirements, and keep investors engaged in what we were building. It was an incredibly difficult period, but we pushed through by staying committed to our mission.

When you asked what advice we would give to other founders, I would say the first thing is to make sure you have patience. Fintech, in particular, is a challenging industry, and if we weren't passionate about what we were doing, we would have given up a long time ago. What kept Sophia and me going was our love for the business we were building.

The second piece of advice is to believe in yourself. If you don't, you'll stop at the first big challenge. The roadblocks are enormous, and self-doubt can be dangerous. Having a strong co-founder makes all the difference. Sophia and I are very complementary—she's an engineer, and I'm a business developer. When I'm down, she's up, and when she's down, I lift her up. The loneliness of being a founder is one of the biggest obstacles, so finding a co-founder who balances you out is essential.

Lastly, expect to fail many times along the way.

Can you share an example of a major failure or setback you faced and how you overcame it?

Sophia: We've had several failures, including attempting to expand into new markets and realizing that some were nearly impossible to crack. Without a mindset of constant iteration and learning from mistakes, we wouldn't have survived.

Going through these challenges made us stronger, and we firmly believe that the best is yet to come. The past few years have been tough, but they've also prepared us for the future. We now have our banking license, our technology is built, and things are going well. We're signing up new clients every hour, and the business is growing steadily.

When we decided to launch our fintech vertical, it wasn't because we initially set out to do it. We heard about fintech opportunities from investors and advisors, but neither Ismael nor I had any prior knowledge of the industry. We had to learn everything from scratch, which made it incredibly difficult.

At the same time, because we were so new to fintech, I think that lack of experience actually allowed us to dream big. We weren't limited by preconceived notions or industry norms.

To build our financial services, we developed all our technology and products internally. Our tech team, just like us, had no fintech experience. We had to find the right technical consultants to guide us, but ultimately, it was a collective learning journey. Together with Ismael, our tech team, and external experts, we built something amazing.

We created a core banking system, a mobile wallet, an infrastructure to manage banking cards, and an online payment gateway. When we first shared our vision with industry experts, I think they were secretly laughing at us. They didn't believe we could actually execute it. But two years later, when we showed them what we had built, people were shocked. They couldn't believe how much we had achieved in such a short time.

Looking back, this was both a challenge and an opportunity. The challenge was that we were entering an industry we knew nothing about, and the learning curve was steep. But the opportunity was that because we didn't know what was "impossible," we built something that many established players wouldn't have even dared to attempt.

This is one of the few challenges where, if I had to do it over again, I wouldn't change anything.

What is it like to be a married couple and co-founders at the same time?

Sophia: We always get that question, by the way. My honest answer is that working together works for Ismael and me for different reasons, but I believe it's not for everyone. If you're a couple or in a relationship and you're thinking about working together, there are a few things you need to consider beforehand.

To be honest, it wasn't something I was completely sure about at first. Ismael was very insistent that we should work together, and I hesitated a lot. I even took a leave of absence from McKinsey, telling them, "Hey, I'm going to try something, but I might come back if it doesn't work out." Thankfully, it did work, but there were things we had to put in place to make sure it functioned well.

The first thing is having a clear organization in place. There needs to be a defined CEO, and the CEO has the final say in company decisions. There should be no ego involved in the relationship within the business. That separation is crucial.

The second thing is that the couple needs to be complementary, meaning they shouldn't have the same skills or interests. If you both like doing the same things and excel at the same tasks, it can become difficult. For example, Ismael is more focused on strategy and development, while I am more operational and detail-oriented. He likes to look at the big picture, while I focus on execution. Our natural separation of tasks makes sense based on our personalities, strengths, and what we enjoy doing. That's very important because if two people in a relationship are working together and they're too similar, it can create conflicts rather than balance.

Lastly, it's essential to have golden rules in place. Work should stop when you go home. That's extremely hard, because as entrepreneurs, you're constantly working—at night, on weekends, even during vacations. But there need to be clear boundaries on when it's the right time to discuss professional matters and when personal time should be prioritized. It's easy to fall into the trap of letting work consume every aspect of your life, so setting these limits is crucial for maintaining a healthy balance.

Ismael: Before answering that question, I just want to add something to what Sophia said. I think we can summarize it by saying that if you want to make a work relationship function within a marriage, you shouldn't talk about work at home.

So, I mean, the rule is simple: you shouldn't talk about work at home, and you shouldn't talk about home at work.

What challenges come with working together as a couple, and how do you manage them?

Ismael: It's important to learn how to mentally separate work from home, and vice versa. You have to develop a sort of split personality, where you behave in a certain way with the same person at home and differently with them at work. And it has to go both ways.

――――

> YOU HAVE TO DEVELOP A SORT OF SPLIT PERSONALITY, WHERE YOU BEHAVE IN A CERTAIN WAY WITH THE SAME PERSON AT HOME AND DIFFERENTLY WITH THEM AT WORK.

――――

For instance, like any couple, we have arguments at home. That's normal. But what happens when you step into the office? Do you stop talking to your co-founder because you had a disagreement at home? And what if something happens at work? If I make a mistake, and Sophia is upset with me at work, what happens when we go home? Do we suddenly act like everything is fine? It's easy to say that you can separate personal and professional matters, but in reality, it's very difficult to do.

We've now been working together for five years, and we've had to learn how to manage each other. Sophia is very patient, and she has figured out how to handle me. Likewise, I've learned what works for her. I know what frustrates her and what makes her happy, and I try to balance between those things. It's all about understanding each other and making sure our relationship doesn't suffer because of work.

Regarding kids, we have three. We just had a five-month-old baby. One thing that's very important to acknowledge is that while I may be the CEO at work, believe me, if you want this setup to succeed, the real Chairman of the Board—not just at work but in life—is Sophia. On paper, I manage the company, but in reality, she manages our lives. She's even more important than I am in that regard. I feel incredibly lucky because having her in my life has significantly improved its quality.

A lot of people ask how we handle running a startup while raising three kids. But honestly, I don't know if you have children, Amir, but for me, I don't think I would have been able to get through the hardest moments of entrepreneurship without my kids. The emotional rollercoaster of building a startup is intense. In the same day, you can feel like you're building the next unicorn, and a few hours later, you might feel like giving up entirely.

For me, my kids provide balance. They bring me joy, energy, and motivation when I need it most. So when people tell me it's impossible to manage a business while raising kids, I tell them the opposite— it's almost impossible without kids because they are the emotional recharge you need to keep going.

Regarding inspiring the next generation of entrepreneurs, Sophia and I are Endeavor Entrepreneurs, and part of our mission is giving back. We feel lucky to be among the first Moroccan entrepreneurs to succeed at this scale, and we believe it's our responsibility to serve as role models.

I personally do a lot of podcasts, but in Moroccan Arabic, because I want to reach as many young people as possible in our country. I truly believe that ambition and the desire to become an entrepreneur only happen when you have relatable role models. Experience, in my opinion, is like a light bulb on your back—it illuminates the path for those who follow behind you. My job now is to carry that light bulb and show others that it's possible to take the risk and become entrepreneurs.

The education system in Morocco is still very theoretical and focused on rote learning. I strongly believe that entrepreneurship should be introduced at a young age. Kids should be learning skills like coding, AI, problem-solving, and independent thinking as early as possible.

As parents and entrepreneurs, how do you approach raising your children?

Ismael: That's a great question. Sophia and I actually have different approaches when it comes to this. She needs a calm environment to sleep, while I can't fall asleep without listening to an audiobook. So every night, I listen to personal development books—specifically about parenting, leadership, and growth.

For me, life is a continuous learning journey. There's so much free knowledge available, especially online. Many parents think of YouTube as a distraction for their kids, but I see it as one of the richest sources of education we have. You can find everything you need to improve yourself.

My mindset shifted completely when I started diving into personal development books. I strongly believe that learning about self-improvement should be encouraged more. The challenge is figuring out how to introduce this mindset to more people. Maybe governments could create incentives for personal development— whether it's classes on financial literacy, meditation, leadership, or soft skills. In more developed countries, initiatives like this already exist. But in Morocco, the government is more focused on fighting inflation than improving people's well-being, so we're still far from that reality.

Sophia: I just want to add one thing. Not everyone is meant to be an entrepreneur. Even though Ismael and I are both entrepreneurs, I would be totally fine if our kids chose a different path.

If you do want to be an entrepreneur, you need to have enough energy to sustain the journey because it's a marathon, not a sprint. That's why I believe passion is critical. If you don't love what you're doing, you won't have the endurance to push through the toughest moments. That's something I want to teach my kids—pursuing what makes them happy is more important than following a predefined path.

Would you say that developing entrepreneurial skills early on is important, regardless of whether someone intends to start their own company?

Sophia: Yes, of course. Being entrepreneurial at work is often referred to as intrapreneurship, and I believe it's an incredibly valuable skill. When I recruit people for our team, the best hires we've made are those who are autonomous and have an entrepreneurial mindset within the company. These are the people who take initiative, solve problems on their own without needing constant supervision, and proactively think about solutions without us having to brainstorm with them every step of the way. So whether someone becomes an entrepreneur or not, having this mindset is a huge advantage in any career. That's why I think entrepreneurial skills should be included in our education system from an early stage.

Any exciting upcoming plans you like to share?

Ismael: The most exciting projects are coming from our fintech division. As I mentioned earlier, we received our banking license from the central bank, and it's a very comprehensive license that allows us to offer a wide range of financial services.

One of the key services we're rolling out is merchant acquiring. We're equipping local shopkeepers with POS terminals, enabling them to accept digital payments from their customers. We're also providing them with payment gateways so they can start accepting online payments if they want to expand their business digitally. Our goal is to digitize shopkeepers' payment flows and help them move away from a cash-only model.

At the same time, we're also operating as an issuer. The money collected by these shopkeepers is settled in a bank account that we open for them within our system. Since we're a neobank, we provide them with an app where they can track all transactions, payments, and earnings.

One of our most recent milestones, which happened just two months ago, is that we became Visa Associates. This means that Visa has given us permission to issue our own Visa cards, using our own Bank Identification Number (BIN). The first four digits of the card belong to Chari Neobank, which is a huge step forward.

Now, shopkeepers who receive digital payments can access that money through their Visa cards, allowing them to make purchases from their own suppliers. So, for example, if a customer pays a shopkeeper digitally, the money is deposited into their Chari account. That account is linked to a Visa card, which they can then use to pay their FMCG suppliers. By doing this, we're creating a fully integrated fintech ecosystem where shopkeepers can both receive and spend digital money seamlessly.

On top of that, we're expanding into additional financial services. We recently became the fourth distributor of Orange in Morocco. Orange is a major French telecom operator that is also one of our investors. Until now, they only had three main distributors in the country, but we've become the fourth. This opens up a world of opportunities for us because we can now distribute mobile top-ups, scratch cards, and airtime.

Beyond telecom services, we've also partnered with various utility companies to offer bill payment services. This means that shopkeepers using Chari can now allow customers to pay their electricity, water, or internet bills directly at their store.

Ultimately, our vision is to transform from a B2B e-commerce platform into a super app that provides financial and commercial services to shopkeepers.

Where do you see Chari in five years, and what's the ultimate vision you're working toward?

Ismael: Instead of just being a place where they buy and sell goods, we want to empower them to become financial service providers in their communities.

Lastly, we've started opening our own B2C retail stores under the Chari brand. The idea is to open a few flagship stores to test and refine our model before expanding through franchising. The long-term plan is to convince existing shopkeepers to rebrand their stores as Chari shops. This would allow them to not only sell everyday consumer goods but also offer financial services such as digital payments, mobile top-ups, gaming and streaming vouchers, bill payments, money transfers, and cash withdrawals from digital wallets.

How do regulatory challenges influence your market expansion plans?

Ismael: Our current neobanking license applies only to Morocco, but we've already applied for additional licenses in other regions. Specifically, we've applied for one license in Ivory Coast and another that covers the entire West African region. However, we haven't received approvals yet, so we're waiting to see how that progresses.

We've also applied for a license in France because we believe there is a strong opportunity to serve the Moroccan diaspora living there. Many Moroccans in France send money home regularly, and we see potential in offering financial services that connect them to merchants in Morocco.

On the e-commerce side, we initially attempted to replicate our model in other countries, mainly Tunisia and Ivory Coast, where we opened branches. However, we quickly realized that expanding e-commerce operations was extremely complex because we had to rebuild the entire logistics infrastructure from scratch. Given the cost and complexity, we decided to pivot our approach.

Instead of focusing on e-commerce expansion, we chose to scale our Karni bookkeeping app because it doesn't require logistics. Today, we've expanded Karni to 12 countries, mainly Francophone African nations where small shopkeepers need better ways to track their finances. I'll let Sophia share more details since she has the exact list of countries.

Sophia: So the bookkeeping app is now available in multiple French-speaking African countries—including Morocco, Tunisia, Algeria, Senegal, Ivory Coast, Mauritania, Gabon, Cameroon, and the Democratic Republic of Congo, among others.

Ismael: Exactly. The idea is to keep Morocco as our main hub while expanding internationally through our bookkeeping and fintech services, which are much easier to scale than logistics-heavy e-commerce operations.

Ismael and Sophia, your journey is truly inspiring—and a great model for married co-founders.

Sophia: Thank you, Amir.

———

FEATURED EXPERT

Philip Bahoshy

Founder and CEO of MAGNITT

∷ⲘⲀⲄⲚⲓⲦⲦ

Dubai, UAE

www.magnitt.com

PHILIP BAHOSHY is the founder and CEO of MAGNiTT, the premier startup data platform serving founders and investors across emerging venture markets. Born in the UK to Iraqi parents, Philip has spent over 13 years in the UAE, dedicating himself to enhancing the entrepreneurial ecosystem in the Middle East, Africa, Turkey, and Pakistan.

Before establishing MAGNiTT in 2015, Philip gained valuable experience at Oliver Wyman in the Financial Services practice and later served as Chief of Staff to the CEO at Barclays Wealth, advising on strategic initiatives. He holds an MBA from INSEAD and a BSc in Economics from the London School of Economics.

MAGNiTT has evolved into a comprehensive enterprise SaaS platform, offering verified data, insights, and analysis on startup venture investments. The platform empowers decision-makers by providing access to extensive information on startups, investors, funding rounds, and industry trends across emerging markets.

Under Philip's leadership, MAGNiTT has expanded its reach, launching in Pakistan and Turkey in 2020 and in Africa in 2021. The company has also secured funding, including a $1 million seed round in 2018, with investors such as 500 Global and Middle East Venture Partners.

Philip's commitment to fostering entrepreneurship is evident through his active involvement in the region's startup ecosystem. He has participated in various events, including speaking engagements at institutions like Hult International Business School, where he shares his insights on connecting entrepreneurs with investors and promoting data-driven decision-making.

Raised in the UK with Iraqi origins, Philip's diverse background has equipped him with a unique perspective on cultural differences and business practices. This perspective has been instrumental in his approach to building and scaling businesses in emerging markets, emphasizing adaptability, humility, and a deep understanding of regional dynamics.

Featured Expert

Through MAGNiTT, Philip Bahoshy continues to bridge gaps in the emerging markets' venture capital landscape, providing stakeholders with the tools and insights needed to drive growth and innovation across these regions.

———

MAGNITT is the premier investment data platform that serves a broad and diverse market, covering the Middle East, Africa, Southeast Asia, Turkey, and Pakistan. Headquartered in the prestigious Dubai International Financial Centre (DIFC), MAGNiTT plays a pivotal role in the venture capital and private equity ecosystem by providing real-time, verified, and comprehensive data to a wide range of stakeholders.

The platform offers an extensive and dynamic analytics system that grants users unparalleled insights into the investment landscape. With a vast database that tracks over 35,000 private companies and 12,000 investment firms across 70 countries, MAGNiTT enables investors, government entities, corporations, and policymakers to access critical market intelligence that drives strategic decision-making. By leveraging its proprietary technology and data-driven methodologies, the platform ensures that all information remains accurate, up-to-date, and reflective of market trends.

MAGNiTT's impact extends beyond just numbers; it acts as a catalyst for innovation and economic growth by facilitating connections between startups, investors, and corporates. Entrepreneurs benefit from visibility on the platform, gaining access to potential investors and funding opportunities, while investment firms and government bodies use MAGNiTT's insights to identify emerging market trends, assess risks, and discover lucrative opportunities.

As a key player in the MENA startup ecosystem, MAGNiTT is instrumental in shaping the region's entrepreneurial landscape. Its extensive research, expert analysis, and thought leadership have positioned it as a trusted authority in the field. By tracking startup funding trends, sector dynamics, and market movements, MAGNiTT enables both investors and entrepreneurs to make well-informed strategic choices. The platform's insights are highly valued by industry leaders, venture capitalists, and policymakers who rely on its accurate data and comprehensive reports to drive economic growth and innovation.

Additionally, the platform provides deep market analysis through its reports, benchmarking tools, and proprietary research, making it a trusted resource for those looking to understand regional investment trends. Whether it is tracking funding rounds, monitoring exits, or analyzing sectoral shifts, MAGNiTT empowers its users with the tools they need to navigate the rapidly evolving startup and investment ecosystem.

By continuously enhancing its capabilities and expanding its reach, MAGNiTT remains at the forefront of transforming how investment decisions are made. Through data transparency, in-depth research, and innovative analytics, it fosters a well-informed, connected, and thriving investment community, ultimately delivering greater value across the financial and business landscape.

––––––

Give us some background on MAGNiTT and your activities.

MAGNiTT is a data research and intelligence platform focused on private capital data, specifically venture capital, private equity, and private credit. We also have plans to expand into infrastructure, real estate, and other private capital areas, with a core focus on emerging markets. Currently, we cover Africa, the Middle East, and Southeast Asia.

We complement, if not add value to, many of the global platforms because we believe there is a lack of comprehensive, accurate data gathering in the emerging market space. To understand that, you need to recognize that in the UK, you have Companies House, and in the US, there are different authorities from which you can pull data. However, in the emerging venture space—and we call it "emerging venture" rather than "emerging markets" because countries like

Singapore and Saudi Arabia are not necessarily emerging markets but are emerging in venture capital—there is a lack of comprehensive and accurate data.

> WE COMPLEMENT, IF NOT ADD VALUE TO, MANY OF THE GLOBAL PLATFORMS BECAUSE WE BELIEVE THERE IS A LACK OF COMPREHENSIVE AND ACCURATE DATA GATHERING IN THE EMERGING MARKET SPACE.

Our goal is to become the unbiased, objective reference for research and intelligence in emerging markets. While there are very strong global players, research reports often focus on the US, Europe, South America, and large parts of Asia, with other regions being lumped together as an afterthought. Our mission is to become the leading private capital data platform for these "other" regions, providing an opportunity to benchmark the markets we cover.

What do I mean by that? If we look at venture capital in emerging markets, we can see trends in different regions. The MENA region is now entering its second decade of venture capital investment, dating back to early VCs like Wamda, Fadi Ghandour, BECO Capital through MEVP. Southeast Asia, on the other hand, has about 17 to 18 years of history in venture capital, with early investors like Vertex Ventures. Africa is at around seven to eight years. These geographies share similarities, differences, and nuances, but they also offer comparables within the emerging venture space. However, they cannot be directly compared to Europe, where venture capital investment has been active since the 1980s and 1990s, or the US, where it has been happening since the 1960s, if not earlier.

At MAGNiTT, we support governments, corporations, big tech, VCs, and service providers—such as consultants and legal firms—by delivering the most comprehensive research and intelligence in this private capital space.

Could you highlight some of your reports and key findings?

We publish in-depth reports on the markets we cover. It's rare to find international platforms that provide dedicated reports on MENA, and even when they do, there is often debate about what MENA includes—sometimes it includes Turkey, sometimes Iran.

Our research is structured into quarterly reports that provide deep dives into emerging venture markets in Africa, the Middle East, and Southeast Asia. We analyze venture capital, private equity, and private credit where possible, and we also focus on specific geographies. For example, we regularly produce reports on Saudi Arabia and the UAE.

In addition, we explore thematic topics in the region, such as investor rankings by activity and capital, as well as exits and IPOs in the markets we cover. We examine international influence on emerging venture markets, using data-driven insights. To enrich our research, we now conduct interviews with key players from different markets, providing an ecosystem perspective.

These reports are published quarterly. One of the key challenges I set for our research manager and team is to focus on the why behind market trends. It's not just about numbers going up or down—we want to understand and explain why these changes are happening. This ensures that both regional and international players can gain deeper insights into the markets we cover.

Let's talk about how the startup ecosystem has evolved since 2018, when *Startup Arabia* was first published.

It's been an interesting period. One thing we strongly believe in is that the region is not immune to global trends. In fact, a lot of what happens here is driven by global trends, especially in emerging markets.

I always quote my good friend Elie Habib from Anghami, who

says that we have a "superpower" in this region: the ability to predict the future. This is because what happens in the US often reaches the local ecosystem with a delay of six to nine, if not 12, months. So whenever we conduct research or analyze trends, we always start by examining global venture capital trends and then assess their impact on the region.

Looking back at 2018 and 2019, there was growing global interest in venture capital as an asset class. We also saw regional success stories like Amazon's acquisition of Souq and Uber's acquisition of Careem. During this time, Saudi Arabia began focusing more on startup growth, the UAE continued its government-led initiatives, and other MENA governments started catching up.

During the period of abundant venture investment and available capital, founders were encouraged to scale aggressively across multiple geographies. Careem, for instance, positioned itself as a leading "MENA player," operating in Egypt, the Levant, Africa, Pakistan, and even planning expansion into Turkey and Bangladesh. The mindset at the time was "scale at all costs," with companies raising funds every 12 to 18 months to fuel growth. This trend was not unique to the region—it mirrored global patterns. Valuations kept rising, and investor appetite grew, partly driven by the fear of missing out (FOMO) on major exits like InstaShop, Amazon-Souq, and Careem.

Then, COVID-19 hit. Initially, there was panic—founders, investors, and governments had to quickly adapt to the new environment. E-commerce and digital services surged, but more importantly, COVID served as a wake-up call for governments regarding the role of technology.

For example, in the UAE, essential services like food delivery, medical supply delivery, and grocery delivery were among the only sectors allowed to operate. Saudi Arabia's Central Monetary Authority made a significant shift by removing the requirement for cash-on-delivery payments and instead mandating cashless transactions. This accelerated the adoption of digital payments in a region where cash was still dominant.

COVID also pushed governments to embrace technology in new ways. Remote work platforms like Zoom, which were previously restricted due to telecom industry regulations, were suddenly allowed in order to support business continuity.

Post-COVID, in an effort to stimulate the economy, the US Federal Reserve slashed interest rates to 0%. This triggered what we call the "Black Swan" period of 2020-2021, where massive amounts of capital were pumped into venture capital markets. Our research—along with CB Insights data—shows a hockey-stick growth in venture investments during this time.

With interest rates near zero, traditional investment options like fixed deposits and bonds became unattractive. As a result, capital allocators—including venture capital firms, private equity funds, hedge funds, and asset managers—had an abundance of liquidity and needed to deploy it. This led to a surge in global venture funding, and the MENA region also benefited from this influx of capital. Sovereign wealth funds and government-backed initiatives in Saudi Arabia, the UAE, and the wider GCC encouraged first-time fund managers, supported existing VCs, and attracted international investors looking for new opportunities.

———

" SOVEREIGN WEALTH FUNDS IN SAUDI ARABIA AND THE UAE HAVE STEPPED IN AS KEY SOURCES OF CAPITAL. THE ABUNDANCE OF LIQUIDITY IN THESE MARKETS, FUELED BY HIGH OIL PRICES, HAS DRAWN FUND MANAGERS FROM AROUND THE WORLD TO SEEK CAPITAL IN THE REGION.

———

This fueled a VC boom from 2020 until the latter half of 2022. However, when global interest rates started rising in 2022 to curb inflation, venture investment began to decline. By 2023, we had already seen two to three consecutive years of declining VC activity, with transaction volumes dropping steadily for eight to nine quarters from their peak.

Our data shows that while global venture investment peaked first, the decline in MENA was delayed by about six to nine months. This lag was partly due to the transparency and efficiency of data reporting in the US, as well as the experience of seasoned investors who had seen previous interest rate cycles. Experts in the US—like those on the All-In podcast or Bill Gurley—were ringing alarm bells long before investors in MENA fully reacted.

As international investors shifted focus back to their home markets, participation in MENA declined. The big names—SoftBank, Tiger Global, NEA—were no longer as active, particularly in late-stage funding.

Another overlooked consequence of COVID was the decline of accelerator programs. These programs—such as Techstars and Plug and Play—are traditionally run in-person over several months, fostering mentorship, networking, and hands-on support. Many of these programs attempted to transition online, but the community-building aspect was lost. This led to a decline in early-stage funding, especially in a region where angel investing is not as prevalent as in the US or Europe.

By 2023, we were facing a tough situation: early-stage investment was slowing, late-stage capital had dried up, and international investors had pulled back. The region, like the rest of the world, was adjusting to a new, more challenging venture capital environment.

From a founder's mindset perspective, the game completely changed between 2018 and 2023. It was initially an environment of scale at all costs. The approach was simple: raise another funding round, focus on expansion, and worry about profitability later. Unit economics was not a priority for VCs or founders.

As I mentioned earlier, the region had only about a decade of venture experience. Most founders and VCs—though there were exceptions—had never operated through a historical economic downturn. In contrast, VCs in the US and Europe had seasoned veterans who had navigated multiple downturns and could offer guidance to founders, governments, and other investors. They knew how to communicate effectively with LPs (limited partners) and adjust their strategies in response to market shifts.

As global sentiment changed, founders in the region were quickly advised—based on international rhetoric—that they needed to cut costs and focus on unit economics. As a result, company failure rates began to rise. Layoffs started in big tech—Google, Facebook, LinkedIn—and eventually trickled into the startup ecosystem. Capital became scarce, forcing companies to either cut their losses or shut down entirely in an effort to become unit-economics efficient.

We are still largely in this environment, but in my opinion, we have plateaued, aligning with global trends. Last year, we saw the early signs of an interest rate decline in the US, which led to a slight global pickup in venture investment. In fact, 2023 marked the first year of global venture capital growth, with total investment increasing by about 5%, even though the number of transactions declined.

However, in the MENA region, capital deployment and transaction activity remain on a downward trajectory. M&A (mergers and acquisitions) activity, which I had anticipated for two years, did begin to rise between 2020 and 2023 as corporates sought entry into the venture space. Big tech acquisitions, like Uber's purchase of Careem, played a significant role in stimulating investor interest. But since 2023, we have now seen three consecutive years of declining M&A activity in MENA. Hopefully, 2025 and 2026 will see a return of investor appetite for acquisitions.

Why is this important? Because the biggest challenge for the region, which we can learn from Southeast Asia's 17-year venture investment journey, is the lack of exits—particularly high-quality exits that generate returns for the ecosystem. Just as sovereign wealth funds and LPs (limited partners) fueled venture growth in the UAE and Saudi Arabia, the same happened in Southeast Asia. However, without exits, the cycle of venture investment is incomplete.

———

> THE BIGGEST CHALLENGE FOR THE REGION, WHICH WE CAN LEARN FROM SOUTHEAST ASIA'S 17-YEAR VENTURE INVESTMENT JOURNEY, IS THE LACK OF EXITS— PARTICULARLY HIGH-QUALITY EXITS THAT GENERATE RETURNS FOR THE ECOSYSTEM.

———

Exits provide liquidity to GPs (general partners), founders, and employees. They also demonstrate returns on investment, helping justify continued LP investments into the asset class. The typical window for a startup exit is around six to seven years. Unfortunately, many of the startups founded between 2015 and 2016—the period discussed in *Startup Arabia*—faced their exit window during the economic downturn of 2022-2024, if not into 2025.

As a result, exit activity has been extremely low. When we analyzed 10 years of startups that had raised capital in MENA, we found that less than 6.5% of those companies had exited. Even then, I can't speak to the quality of those exits—many may have been acqui-hires rather than substantial M&A deals.

What's driving faster startup scaling, and what challenges remain?

Going back to the point I made earlier about Careem—at the time, the focus was purely on user acquisition and growth. Regardless of regulatory challenges, unit economics, or operating at a loss in countries like Egypt, the goal was to expand into as many markets as possible.

During the liquidity boom, Pakistan also experienced a surge in startup activity. Despite the country's infrastructure, political, and economic challenges, the potential for disruption was extremely high.

However, with declining capital availability, reduced interest from international investors, and a slowdown in M&A activity, the startup landscape began to shift. This change disrupted the cycle of incentives that had previously driven aggressive expansion.

As a result, companies had to rethink their priorities and focus on markets where they could achieve unit-economic profitability. Over the past three years, there has been a noticeable migration of startups toward the UAE and Saudi Arabia, which have emerged as the dominant hubs for venture capital. Today, nearly 75% of all capital in the MENA region is concentrated in these two countries.

With this shift, many founders and investors have started questioning whether it makes sense to operate in certain markets, particularly in the Levant and Egypt. The ongoing currency devaluation in Egypt, the economic impact of the Ukraine war on trade, and broader macroeconomic instability have made scaling in Egypt significantly more challenging. At the same time, much of the GCC consists of smaller markets that do not necessarily offer the scale needed for high-growth startups.

As a result, many companies have moved their headquarters and revenue-generating operations to the UAE and Saudi Arabia, where capital is more accessible and profitability is more achievable. This does not mean that startups have completely abandoned other MENA markets. Many still maintain back offices in countries like Egypt and Jordan, where operational costs are lower.

———

> " As a result, many companies have moved their headquarters and revenue-generating operations to the UAE and Saudi Arabia, where capital is more accessible and profitability is more achievable.

———

This shift raises an important question about the true scalability of the MENA startup ecosystem. One perspective we at MAGNiTT find particularly interesting is the increasing focus on cross-continental expansion rather than a purely regional approach.

Looking at Southeast Asia, similar challenges exist. Singapore, despite experiencing a decline in investment activity, still attracts five times more venture capital than Saudi Arabia. However, with a population of just five million, startups in Singapore must expand into larger markets like Indonesia, the Philippines, and Vietnam to achieve scale. The challenge, much like in MENA, is that not all of these markets are equally attractive from a unit economics standpoint. Some companies are reassessing whether it makes sense to operate in Taiwan or the Philippines, while others are questioning whether Indonesia, despite its large market size, offers viable scaling opportunities given that wealth is concentrated among a small portion of the population.

With these dynamics in play, there is now a noticeable shift toward cross-pollination in expansion strategies. Many Singapore-based companies are looking to Saudi Arabia and the UAE as new high-growth markets, while startups in the UAE and Saudi Arabia are exploring opportunities in Indonesia. Shared cultural and economic factors, such as a large Muslim population and an underdeveloped digital ecosystem, make these markets appealing for expansion. Instead of taking a broad regional approach, companies are now selecting specific international markets where they can scale profitably, rather than trying to establish a presence across MENA at all costs.

A key factor driving this shift is the role of sovereign wealth funds in Saudi Arabia and the UAE, which have become the focal point for global fund managers seeking LP funding. The global venture capital slowdown has largely been driven by a scarcity of LP funding. In the US, major LPs such as endowment funds, pension funds, and corporate investors have been restructuring their portfolios, prioritizing domestic markets, and focusing on more stable asset classes. When interest rates were near zero in 2020, venture capital was an attractive investment because risk-free alternatives were not available. However, with interest rates now at 5.5%, investors can earn reliable returns through fixed deposits or corporate bonds. Meanwhile, stock markets have rebounded, with the NASDAQ and S&P 500 posting record highs driven by the AI boom. For venture capital to remain an attractive asset class, investors must now justify minimum returns of 25% annually, a challenging benchmark compared to other available investment opportunities.

With global LPs becoming more risk-averse, sovereign wealth funds in the UAE and Saudi Arabia—such as PIF, Jada, SVC, Mubadala, and ADIA—have stepped in as key sources of capital. The abundance of liquidity in these markets, fueled by high oil prices, has drawn fund managers from around the world to seek capital in the region. Over the past few years, there has been a clear shift in approach. Where sovereign wealth funds once focused mainly on global investments to diversify their economies, they are now requiring that a portion of the capital they deploy into international funds be reinvested locally. This shift has led to a growing number of international investors setting up operations in MENA, bringing with them intellectual capital, portfolio companies, and global expertise.

According to MAGNiTT's latest MENA report, 40% of venture capital deployed in the region last year came from international investors, with 55% of all investors in MENA-based startups coming from outside the region. This shift underscores the increasing influence of sovereign wealth funds in attracting global investors while also ensuring that capital is reinvested locally to drive growth.

————

" 40% OF VENTURE CAPITAL DEPLOYED IN MENA CAME FROM INTERNATIONAL INVESTORS, WITH 55% OF ALL INVESTORS IN MENA-BASED STARTUPS COMING FROM OUTSIDE THE REGION.

————

Despite these positive developments, challenges remain when it comes to scaling startups in the region. Market size limitations, bureaucratic hurdles, political instability, and the availability of talent with experience in scaling technology companies all continue to be obstacles. Most importantly, funding availability remains a key factor in determining how startups will be able to navigate these challenges and sustain long-term growth.

How does Saudi Arabia's venture capital growth compare to other markets, and what factors are driving its expansion?

Right now, nearly 75-80% of all capital being deployed in the MENA region is going to companies based in the UAE and Saudi Arabia. While venture capital in MENA has been developing over the past decade, Saudi Arabia's journey as an asset class is more recent. Based on MAGNiTT's first SVC reports from 2018 and 2019, Saudi Arabia has only about five years of structured venture capital development. Although companies like HungerStation existed earlier, the real push came with concerted government efforts, starting with the establishment of SVC and Jada, which were created to stimulate venture capital investment as part of Saudi Vision 2030.

Since then, Saudi Arabia has seen a surge in venture capital activity. Where it once ranked third or fourth in the region in terms of capital deployment and deal flow, it now ranks first in capital deployment and second in total transaction volume, as reported in MAGNiTT's 2024 MENA report. Previously, Egypt had outpaced Saudi Arabia in transaction count, but now, the UAE leads in total transactions, with the gap between Saudi Arabia and the UAE narrowing from 30% to less than 5%.

———

> SINCE THEN, SAUDI ARABIA HAS SEEN A SURGE IN VENTURE CAPITAL ACTIVITY. WHERE IT ONCE RANKED THIRD OR FOURTH IN THE REGION IN TERMS OF CAPITAL DEPLOYMENT AND DEAL FLOW, IT NOW RANKS FIRST IN CAPITAL DEPLOYMENT AND SECOND IN TOTAL TRANSACTION VOLUME … WITH THE GAP BETWEEN SAUDI ARABIA AND THE UAE NARROWING FROM 30% TO LESS THAN 5%.

———

One of Saudi Arabia's biggest strengths has been its ability to attract global general partners (GPs) and institutional investors. The government has been proactive in ecosystem-building, led by initiatives from entities like MCIT and the leadership of His Excellency Abdullah Al-Swaha. A key differentiator has been Saudi Arabia's strategy of outward engagement—rather than just focusing on attracting investment, it has actively sent delegations to global tech and investment hubs like London, Paris, Silicon Valley, Korea, and Singapore. This willingness to learn from other ecosystems and build international relationships has played a critical role in the country's ability to develop its venture market.

In addition to attracting investors, Saudi Arabia has also focused on strengthening its local ecosystem through programs like NTDP (National Technology Development Program), which supports different stages of the venture capital value chain. It has introduced accelerator programs, fund-matching initiatives, and incentive structures to offset the costs of setting up in the country. Companies relocating to Saudi Arabia can access subsidies for talent acquisition, business incorporation, and ecosystem integration. The government's emphasis has now shifted from simply growing the number of startups to ensuring liquidity within the ecosystem. This is evident in ongoing discussions with the Capital Market Authority (CMA) around increasing exit opportunities through Tadawul and Nomu, the parallel market, allowing wider participation in tech investment.

While Saudi Arabia has gained momentum, the UAE continues to play a central role in the region's startup ecosystem, particularly at the early stage. The UAE's startup landscape has been heavily shaped by expatriates, with over 90% of funded companies founded by non-nationals. Over the past five years, the UAE has successfully positioned itself as the first point of entry for founders, investors, and talent in MENA. This was further reinforced during the COVID-19 pandemic, when the UAE became a global destination for relocation, attracting entrepreneurs from Asia, the UK, and other regions affected by economic or political instability.

Unlike Saudi Arabia, which has recently become a hub for later-stage investments, the UAE has maintained its position as a launchpad for early-stage startups. Many companies first establish themselves in the UAE before scaling into Saudi Arabia and other regional markets. The regulatory framework, ease of doing business, and lifestyle incentives continue to make the UAE an attractive base for startups and investors alike.

In contrast to the rapid growth in Saudi Arabia and the UAE, other MENA markets have faced significant challenges. Egypt, historically a fertile venture market, has been severely impacted by currency devaluation, making it difficult for companies to maintain financial stability. As a result, many startups that were originally based in Egypt have shifted their headquarters to Saudi Arabia and the UAE, leveraging Egypt's talent pool while focusing on revenue generation elsewhere. Similarly, geopolitical instability has hindered the Levant's startup ecosystem, forcing many founders and employees to relocate in search of funding and operational stability. The hesitancy of investors to deploy capital in these regions has further exacerbated this trend.

———

" IN CONTRAST TO THE RAPID GROWTH IN SAUDI ARABIA AND THE UAE, OTHER MENA MARKETS HAVE FACED SIGNIFICANT CHALLENGES. EGYPT, HISTORICALLY A FERTILE VENTURE MARKET, HAS BEEN SEVERELY IMPACTED BY CURRENCY DEVALUATION, MAKING IT DIFFICULT FOR COMPANIES TO MAINTAIN FINANCIAL STABILITY.

———

While much of the GCC has not prioritized venture capital development in recent years, Qatar has emerged as the next standout market. Through initiatives like the QIA-funded investment programs and the introduction of Web Summit in Qatar, the country has actively worked to position itself as a growing hub for early-stage investment. These efforts are beginning to show results, with an increasing number of startups and investors exploring Qatar as a viable ecosystem within the GCC.

The overall regional shift reflects a broader trend where capital and talent are increasingly consolidating in Saudi Arabia and the UAE. As the venture landscape matures, the ability to provide liquidity and create successful exit opportunities will determine the sustainability of the growth seen in these leading markets.

What challenges do laggard ecosystems face, and how can they leapfrog ahead?

The challenges faced by lagging markets in the region are not solely about internal weaknesses but rather about what other countries, particularly Saudi Arabia and the UAE, are doing to accelerate their growth. Both nations have had a strong, concerted government focus on developing their venture ecosystems. Saudi Arabia's Vision 2030 has provided a clear mandate to drive technology growth, supported by MCIT and structured fund-of-fund programs that have fueled venture capital investment. Similarly, the UAE, through various initiatives across Abu Dhabi and Dubai, has actively stimulated its startup landscape through fund-of-fund models.

This trickle-down effect is evident—capital attracts founders, founders create employment, employment fosters scalable products, and successful exits create reinvestment. In contrast, other GCC markets have not had the same structured approach to venture capital. While some, like Oman and Qatar, are beginning to develop fund-of-fund programs through entities like the Oman Investment Authority and Qatar Investment Authority, they are still in the early stages. Bahrain was the first to introduce a fund-of-fund structure through the Al Waha Fund, but there has yet to be a second fund announced, likely due to a wait-and-see approach regarding returns and liquidity.

The absence of a focused government push toward technology and structured investment programs has meant that venture ecosystems in Kuwait, Oman, and Bahrain have lagged behind. Additionally, none of these markets are large enough to be self-sufficient. Even startups that originate in these countries ultimately have to scale into the UAE and Saudi Arabia to achieve meaningful growth.

How have government-backed initiatives like conferences and accelerators influenced startup growth in MENA?

When considering government policies beyond capital deployment, various factors can help catalyze startup ecosystems, including education programs, regulatory support, and tax incentives. One of the most visible government efforts in the region has been the rise of large-scale conferences, which have taken center stage as platforms for ecosystem building.

Historically, between 2016 and 2019, grassroots events such as the STEP Conference, ArabNet, and RiseUp Summit played a critical role in bringing together founders, investors, and government stakeholders. In recent years, these have largely been replaced by government-backed conferences such as LEAP in Saudi Arabia, GITEX in the UAE, and Web Summit in Qatar. Additionally, sector-specific conferences like SuperReturn for private equity and venture capital have entered the scene, along with high-level investment summits such as the Milken Institute events and FII, which bring together global financial leaders.

While these conferences effectively attract international stakeholders, the model could be refined to focus more on long-term value creation rather than just the number of attendees. Beyond networking, the region has also seen increased efforts to enhance educational content. Organizations like MAGNiTT and institutions such as INSEAD, through Claudia Zeisberger, have been working to create more transparency in market data. The Kauffman Fellows program has also gained traction in the region, offering educational pathways for investors and startup founders. Meanwhile, community-driven initiatives like Endeavor have played a significant role in knowledge transfer and late-stage investment through Endeavor Catalyst.

Despite these efforts, the challenge remains in translating educational programs into tangible ecosystem growth. While there is no shortage of initiatives, specific, structured national programs that focus on upskilling and reskilling talent—particularly in emerging areas such as AI, deep tech, and advanced financial services—could accelerate the development of high-impact startups.

Why is international exposure and cross-border collaboration crucial for startup growth?

One of the most effective initiatives that Saudi Arabia has embraced, which other countries could learn from, is its outward-facing approach to global collaboration. Saudi Arabia has been proactive in sending delegation trips to major tech and investment hubs, including London, Paris, Silicon Valley, Singapore, and Korea. This strategy mirrors what countries like Israel have done with their "Startup Nation" model—actively promoting their most promising companies to investors and policymakers in key global markets.

Expanding this approach across other MENA markets could significantly benefit startups by increasing exposure, fostering knowledge transfer, and improving access to international capital. Beyond government-led efforts, corporations that operate across multiple geographies could also play a stronger role in facilitating cross-market learning. Banks, cloud service providers, and social media companies have extensive experience in emerging markets and could serve as valuable bridges between MENA and other global startup ecosystems.

At a regulatory level, there is also a significant opportunity to streamline cross-border business operations. Today, startups looking to scale across the GCC must navigate a complex web of licensing requirements. In the UAE alone, obtaining a license in Abu Dhabi differs from Dubai, and entering Saudi Arabia requires an entirely separate process. Establishing a unified GCC startup licensing framework could dramatically reduce friction and cost, enabling startups to scale faster and more efficiently.

How are sectoral shifts influencing startup investment trends?

In emerging markets, startup investment typically follows a predictable pattern of disruption. The first wave of investment usually targets transport and logistics, with e-commerce being the initial driver of technological adoption. This is because first-time fund managers can reference established case studies from the US and Europe, making it easier to understand investment risks and opportunities. These sectors also solve clear, large-scale inefficiencies, making them attractive to both founders and investors.

Once e-commerce takes hold, transport and logistics naturally follow. Ride-hailing, delivery services, and last-mile logistics solutions often gain traction, leading to further investment in supply chain innovation. After these sectors reach a saturation point, financial services emerge as the next major investment trend.

Currently, MENA is experiencing a fintech boom. For two consecutive years, Fintech has been the most active industry in terms of both total investment and the number of transactions, not just in MENA but across all emerging venture markets. The sector continues to attract investment because it solves a critical scalability problem—financial transactions are universal, and clear regulatory frameworks provide structure for investment. Acquirers in the fintech space are well-defined, and cross-border expansion is more feasible compared to other industries.

Most of the fintech investment in MENA has focused on core financial infrastructure, including buy-now-pay-later services, remittances, payments, and cross-border transfers. Unlike more speculative areas such as blockchain, AI-driven wealth management, or decentralized finance, these financial products address immediate consumer and business needs, making them attractive investment targets.

Looking ahead, the next wave of sectoral growth is likely to come from deep tech. This is already happening in Southeast Asia, particularly in Singapore, where fintech and e-commerce disruptions have paved the way for investments in AI, biotech, and advanced computing. The UAE and Saudi Arabia are now taking similar steps to position themselves as deep-tech hubs, supported by government initiatives through AI ministries, MCIT programs, and national R&D investments. However, deep tech requires patient capital, significant research and development, and highly specialized talent. Unlike traditional venture capital, which operates on shorter timelines, deep-tech investments often take years to mature, requiring a different funding approach.

> LOOKING AHEAD, THE NEXT WAVE OF SECTORAL
> GROWTH IS LIKELY TO COME FROM DEEP TECH. THE UAE
> AND SAUDI ARABIA ARE NOW TAKING SIMILAR STEPS TO
> POSITION THEMSELVES AS DEEP-TECH HUBS, SUPPORTED
> BY GOVERNMENT INITIATIVES THROUGH AI MINISTRIES,
> MCIT PROGRAMS, AND NATIONAL R&D INVESTMENTS.

How does talent migration impact startups, and what challenges exist in retaining skilled workers?

The movement of talent is another critical factor shaping the region's startup ecosystem. Success breeds success, and the rise of major exits—such as Careem, Souq, and Instashop—has helped create a new generation of experienced founders and startup operators. Similar to the "PayPal Mafia" in Silicon Valley, the "Careem Mafia" and other successful startup alumni have begun launching their own ventures, reinvesting their knowledge and capital into the ecosystem.

However, the lack of liquidity and exits remains a major red flag. Many professionals who joined startups in the hope of benefiting from stock options (ESOPs) have not seen those promises materialize. If exits continue to be scarce, the ability to attract and retain top talent within the startup ecosystem will become increasingly difficult.

At the grassroots level, governments have begun investing in coding education and tech upskilling programs, but the challenge remains in keeping this talent in the region. Many skilled workers still see greater opportunities in the US and Europe, leading to brain drain. To counter this, the region needs more long-term incentives—whether through equity participation, R&D grants, or favorable immigration policies—to retain highly skilled workers and ensure they contribute to local ecosystem growth.

What are the key trends and challenges for startups expanding beyond the MENA region?

Expanding beyond MENA into other emerging markets like Africa and Southeast Asia presents a mix of opportunities and challenges. Africa remains a high-potential but difficult market due to persistent issues like limited access to capital, political instability, and economic uncertainty. These factors continue to make Africa attractive for private equity and venture capital investors seeking long-term disruption opportunities, but they also create significant barriers to scaling startups.

Many Egyptian and African startups are looking to Saudi Arabia as a growth destination while maintaining their operations on the continent. This trend is driven by the stronger capital availability and economic stability in Saudi Arabia, which provides a more predictable environment for scaling. However, cross-border expansion into Africa remains challenging due to fragmented markets, currency fluctuations, and inconsistent regulatory environments.

Southeast Asian investors and startups, in contrast, tend to be more risk-averse. Having operated in markets with more mature ecosystems, many Southeast Asian firms have been cautious about entering MENA. However, this is beginning to change. A growing number of Southeast Asian venture capital firms, such as Golden Gate Ventures and Openspace Ventures, are exploring investment opportunities in the region, hiring locally, and assessing potential partnerships.

This increased interaction between Southeast Asia and MENA raises the question of whether strategic mergers, acquisitions, or joint ventures could help startups from both regions achieve better scale. If companies from different regions with complementary strengths combine, they could potentially accelerate growth beyond what either could achieve independently. Some organizations, such as the DIFC, have already started facilitating fintech roadshows in Singapore to build connections, and geopolitical collaborations between Asia and the Middle East are also strengthening economic ties. While this cross-pollination is still in its early stages, the momentum is expected to grow, especially in fintech and tech-enabled services.

At this point, most of the international expansion efforts are concentrated on Southeast Asia and the Middle East rather than Africa. While Africa remains on the long-term horizon, immediate cross-border activities are more likely to happen between MENA and Southeast Asia, where there are stronger economic and regulatory synergies.

What role is generative AI playing in shaping MENA's startup ecosystem?

AI has rapidly become a key focus area in the global startup ecosystem. While AI as a concept has been around for decades, its recent mainstream breakthrough came with advancements in generative AI, led by ChatGPT, and massive investments from major global tech firms.

In MENA, AI adoption is still in its early stages. Currently, AI is being used primarily as an efficiency tool rather than as a foundation for AI-native startup creation. Many startups are integrating AI into their products to enhance automation, streamline operations, and improve customer engagement, but the number of truly AI-native startups remains limited.

Globally, AI accounted for approximately 18% of all venture transactions and 38% of total capital deployed in 2023. In contrast, in MENA, AI-focused investments accounted for less than 4% of total venture funding. The gap highlights that while AI is gaining traction, the region is still at the beginning of its AI-driven transformation.

Governments in the UAE and Saudi Arabia are making significant investments in AI infrastructure. This includes cloud computing infrastructure, data centers, and hardware capabilities that will form the backbone of future AI development. As these foundational investments mature, software and AI solutions will likely follow.

Over the coming years, AI is expected to shift from being a tool for operational efficiency to becoming a core pillar of startup innovation, especially in deep-tech and enterprise applications.

What are some of the untapped opportunities for startups in the MENA region?

The startup landscape in MENA is still ripe for disruption across multiple sectors. While traditional industries like fintech, logistics, and e-commerce have attracted significant investment, several high-impact sectors remain underserved due to investor hesitancy and unclear exit pathways.

Sustainability, for example, has seen minimal investment despite growing global interest. In 2023, MENA received only 1% of global venture capital funding, and sustainability-focused startups accounted for just 1% of MENA's total investment. This reflects a broader challenge—traditional venture capitalists still struggle with liquidity and return on investment. As a result, many investors prefer to focus on sectors with more immediate monetization potential rather than emerging fields like sustainability, healthcare, or education, where acquisition opportunities and IPO pathways are less defined.

This hesitation to enter new sectors slows down innovation in areas that could have significant long-term economic and societal impact. As the ecosystem matures, investors will need to take a more diversified approach to funding, embracing sectors that may require longer growth cycles but offer substantial opportunities for scalable solutions.

How can smaller markets differentiate themselves to attract investment and drive startup growth?

For smaller countries and cities looking to strengthen their startup ecosystems, specialization is key. In the US, Silicon Valley became the epicenter of tech, while cities like New York emerged as fintech hubs due to their proximity to Wall Street. Austin developed a focus on sustainability and agri-tech, while Los Angeles positioned itself as the leader in media and entertainment.

———

> For smaller countries and cities looking to strengthen their startup ecosystems, specialization is key. Mena's smaller markets need to take a similar approach. Instead of trying to compete broadly, each country should identify its niche and build communities around it.

———

MENA's smaller markets need to take a similar approach. Instead of trying to compete broadly, each country should identify its niche and build communities around it. Abu Dhabi, for instance, has an opportunity to position itself as a sustainability hub through initiatives like Masdar. Kuwait had early potential in food tech but did not fully capitalize on it. By creating specialized hubs with dedicated investors, regulatory incentives, and industry partnerships, smaller markets can establish themselves as global leaders in specific sectors rather than trying to be generalists.

Is there an aspect of startup culture in the region that is often overlooked or underappreciated in discussions?

One of the challenges in MENA's startup culture is the reluctance to have open and critical discussions about failures and missteps. Historically, the region has placed a strong emphasis on positive narratives, focusing on opportunity and growth rather than acknowledging mistakes.

Comparing this to Pakistan, when its venture ecosystem faced a downturn, there was an abundance of journalistic analysis critiquing the mismanagement of funds, poor business decisions, and broader structural issues. In MENA, similar discussions remain relatively muted. There is still a hesitation to publicly analyze failures, whether due to cultural norms, business sensitivities, or political considerations.

As MENA enters its second decade of venture capital development, there needs to be a shift toward embracing constructive criticism. Learning from past challenges—whether in fund deployment, startup failures, or regulatory shortcomings—will be essential for building a more resilient ecosystem. Honest discussions about what has worked and what has not will help both founders and investors make better decisions in the future.

What is the future outlook for the MENA startup ecosystem, and how does MAGNiTT contribute to its growth?

The MENA startup ecosystem is at a pivotal moment. While Saudi Arabia and the UAE have solidified their positions as leading venture hubs, other markets still face significant hurdles. The ability to create liquidity, foster cross-border collaboration, and develop deep-tech capabilities will determine the region's long-term competitiveness. With continued investment in talent, infrastructure, and regulatory reform, MENA has the potential to sustain its upward trajectory in the global startup landscape.

———

> THE MENA STARTUP ECOSYSTEM IS AT A PIVOTAL MOMENT. WHILE SAUDI ARABIA AND THE UAE HAVE SOLIDIFIED THEIR POSITIONS AS LEADING VENTURE HUBS, OTHER MARKETS STILL FACE SIGNIFICANT HURDLES. THE ABILITY TO CREATE LIQUIDITY, FOSTER CROSS-BORDER COLLABORATION, AND DEVELOP DEEP-TECH CAPABILITIES WILL DETERMINE THE REGION'S LONG-TERM COMPETITIVENESS.

———

Predicting the future remains difficult, especially in a period of global economic and geopolitical uncertainty. Much of the optimism at the end of 2023 was based on expectations that interest rates would come down, leading to improved liquidity in venture capital markets. While rate cuts are still anticipated, global markets remain volatile, and the impact on venture capital investment will depend on broader macroeconomic trends.

Government focus on venture investment in Saudi Arabia and the UAE remains strong, and as interest rates stabilize, venture capital is expected to grow. One of the biggest challenges in recent years has been the decline in late-stage funding. According to MAGNiTT's 2023 report, 45% of all venture transactions in MENA were between $1 million and $5 million, reflecting a shift toward early-stage investments. Investors have focused more on the early stage, betting that by the time these companies mature in six to seven years, market conditions will be more favorable for exits.

As macroeconomic conditions improve, late-stage funding is likely to pick up, particularly with increased participation from international investors and corporate venture capital. Over the next 12 to 18 months, significant efforts will likely be made in Saudi Arabia and the UAE to facilitate IPOs and secondary markets, addressing the liquidity challenge that has constrained exits in recent years. Additionally, companies will continue exploring cross-border expansion into Southeast Asia, Africa, and even Eastern Europe to achieve scale.

MAGNiTT aims to play a crucial role in this evolving ecosystem by continuing to provide data, research, and intelligence on emerging markets. The goal is to offer accurate and comprehensive insights that help investors, founders, and policymakers make informed decisions. While the platform has historically focused on venture capital and private equity, future plans include expanding coverage into private credit, infrastructure, and real estate, complementing existing public data sources.

Where can readers access MAGNiTT research and reports about the MENA startup ecosystem?

All of MAGNiTT's research and reports are publicly available on its research platform. Anyone interested in accessing market intelligence, data insights, or investment trends can reach out to the team for a free demo and deeper engagement.

Ultimately, MAGNiTT's role is not to push an agenda but to provide an objective, data-driven view of the ecosystem. The platform has consistently highlighted market trends—both positive and negative—without sugarcoating realities. Whether during the peak investment years or the recent downturn, the goal has remained the same: to offer insights that help stakeholders navigate MENA's evolving venture landscape. Top of Form

Much appreciated, Philip—thank you again for your time and valuable insights.

My pleasure, and congrats in advance on another outstanding and timely book.

---

10 SCALEUP TAKEAWAYS

1. Scaling Requires a Shift in Leadership Mindset

- Early-stage founders are hands-on; scaling requires delegation and team trust.

- Founders must transition from problem-solvers to enablers of high-performance teams.

- Leadership is about culture; a great product alone won't sustain long-term growth.

- Decision-making speed must increase, but so should strategic patience.

- Founders must balance visionary thinking with operational discipline.

2. Hiring the Right People is Everything

- The first 50 hires define the DNA of your company's future.

- Hire carefully, fire fast—keeping underperformers too long is costly.

- Invest in people who are "too much"—obsessed, driven, and deeply committed.

- Offer meaningful equity to create alignment between employees and company success.

- Scaling requires different leaders—what works at 10 employees may not work at 1,000.

3. Product-Market Fit Must be Strong Before Scaling

- Scaling a bad product only speeds up failure.
- Customer retention is a better metric than acquisition when assessing fit.
- If you have to rely too much on discounts, your product isn't sticky enough.
- Focus on one core product before expanding into multiple services.
- Early adopters provide the most valuable feedback—listen to them.

4. Funding Should Accelerate Growth, Not Fix Problems

- Raising capital won't solve fundamental product or market issues.
- The best companies raise funding when they don't need it.
- A bad investor can kill your company—choose partners, not just money.
- Maintain financial discipline—scaling requires efficiency, not just expansion.
- Timing matters—funding too early or too late can both be fatal.

5. Expansion Must be Intentional, Not Opportunistic

- Expanding into new markets before mastering one can be a distraction.
- Each country has different regulatory, cultural, and logistical challenges.

- Scaling operations is harder than scaling software—build systems, not just teams.

- Data should drive decisions—expand based on traction, not gut feeling.

- Over-expansion is one of the fastest ways startups burn out.

6. Regulatory Strategy is Key to Long-Term Success

- Don't position yourself as a disruptor—find win-win solutions with regulators.

- Different countries have different policies; one-size-fits-all doesn't work.

- Government partnerships can give you a competitive edge over global competitors.

- A single regulatory misstep can shut down an entire business line.

- Compliance is not optional—plan for it from day one.

7. Brand Loyalty is Built on Trust, Not Discounts

- Long-term customer loyalty is more valuable than short-term acquisition.

- Poor customer experience destroys trust faster than bad marketing.

- Consistency is key—customers should know what to expect every time.

- The best brands create emotional connections with their users.

- Discounts should be a tool, not a strategy—loyalty comes from value.

8. Local Knowledge is a Competitive Advantage

- Global strategies don't always work in local markets.
- Deep understanding of customer behavior beats broad market assumptions.
- Hiring local talent helps avoid costly missteps in new markets.
- Localized pricing, product features, and service models matter.
- What works in Dubai won't necessarily work in Cairo or Riyadh.
- What works in Silicon Valley or U.S. won´t necessarily work in MENA.

9. Culture and Values Drive Long-Term Success

- Culture isn't what you say; it's how decisions get made daily.
- Strong company values help scale decision-making across large teams.
- Toxic hires, even talented ones, can kill company morale.
- Every leader must embody the values they want to see in the team.
- Company mission and purpose should be clear to every employee.

10. Exit Strategy Should Be Considered Early

- Even if you don't plan to sell, prepare for acquisition scenarios.
- Negotiating from a position of strength means building a strong, independent business.
- Founders often overvalue control—sometimes a strategic exit is better.
- Smart exits preserve culture and team rather than just maximizing financial outcomes.
- The best deals are built on trust between founders and acquirers.

10 COMMON SCALEUP MISTAKES

1. Scaling Too Fast, Too Soon

- Expanding before achieving product-market fit.
- Raising too much money and spending inefficiently.
- Hiring too many people before establishing a clear structure.
- Entering new markets without deeply understanding them.
- Launching too many products instead of refining one.

2. Hiring Poorly and Not Firing Fast Enough

- Prioritizing speed over quality in hiring.
- Holding on to underperformers due to loyalty or fear of disruption.
- Over-hiring senior talent without clear roles.
- Hiring friends instead of qualified professionals.
- Not investing in a strong hiring process early.

3. Ignoring Unit Economics and Cash Burn

- Relying on unsustainable discounts to drive growth.
- Expanding without clear profitability on a per-customer basis.

- Assuming funding will always be available.
- Burning too much cash on marketing instead of organic growth.
- Failing to plan for worst-case funding scenarios.

4. Mismanaging Investor Relationships

- Choosing investors based solely on valuation, not alignment.
- Giving up too much control early.
- Raising capital reactively instead of strategically.
- Overpromising and underdelivering to investors.
- Neglecting investor updates until a crisis arises.

5. Losing Focus on the Core Business

- Chasing too many opportunities at once.
- Entering unrelated industries too soon.
- Scaling operations without the right technology infrastructure.
- Prioritizing growth over customer satisfaction.
- Ignoring early signs of operational strain.

6. Not Adapting to Market Changes

- Assuming what worked at launch will work at scale.
- Failing to pivot when customer behavior shifts.
- Ignoring new competitors until it's too late.
- Over-relying on a single revenue stream.
- Being too rigid with the original vision instead of evolving.

7. Underestimating Regulatory Challenges

- Expanding into new markets without regulatory preparation.
- Treating regulations as obstacles instead of strategic priorities.
- Ignoring tax and compliance issues in different countries.
- Failing to build government relationships early.
- Assuming regulators will adapt to your business model instead of the other way around.

8. Letting Culture Erode as the Company Scales

- Hiring for skills without considering cultural fit.
- Allowing toxic behaviors from high performers.
- Losing the startup spirit as the company grows.
- Failing to reinforce company values at scale.
- Not addressing cultural issues until they become unfixable.

9. Overcomplicating the Product Instead of Improving It

- Adding too many features instead of perfecting the core offering.
- Building tech without clear customer demand.
- Prioritizing complexity over usability.
- Ignoring customer feedback in favor of internal ideas.
- Assuming more features equal more value.

10. Failing to Plan for an Exit (Even If You Don't Intend One)

- Ignoring acquisition discussions until too late.
- Not building financial transparency for due diligence.

- Overestimating company valuation without market validation.
- Assuming buyers will come when you need them.
- Not aligning stakeholders on long-term goals.

ARE YOU SCALEUP-READY?

IT DOESN'T MATTER whether you're building a small team in a shared workspace in Cairo, managing your first branch in Jeddah, or running a fast-growing operation in Dubai. It doesn't matter if you started with bootstrapped savings or venture capital. It doesn't matter if your company is rooted in e-commerce, fintech, or cloud kitchens. What matters is whether you're ready to take the next step—the one that transforms a business into a legacy.

Scaling up is not just about growth; it's about evolution. It's about finding the courage to expand beyond your comfort zone, to face the daunting challenges of new markets, and to build something bigger than yourself. It's about creating systems that multiply your impact, empowering teams that can thrive through uncertainty, and staying resilient when the stakes are higher than ever.

Scaling up is where the real test begins. Can you navigate the tangled web of regional regulations and cultural nuances? Can you manage the growing pains that come with expanding teams, operations, and customer bases? Can you transform a vision into a scalable reality, even when the path ahead is uncertain?

In the Middle East and North Africa, scaling up has unique challenges, but also unprecedented opportunities. With surging investments, supportive policies, and a thriving entrepreneurial spirit, the region is poised for transformation. Those who dare to scale are not just growing businesses—they're shaping industries, communities, and the future of the region itself.

This book is your guide to that journey. It's about the grit, strategy, and innovation required to scale in one of the most dynamic markets in the world. It's about turning obstacles into opportunities and local ambitions into regional—and even global—success stories. So, *yalla scaleup!*

HONORABLE MENTIONS

While this book features the stories of 15 exceptional entrepreneurs who have played a pivotal role in shaping the startup and scaleup landscape in the MENA region, I had the privilege of speaking with 19 incredible founders and business leaders. Due to space constraints, I was unable to include all of them in full, but their insights, experiences, and contributions were invaluable in shaping the broader narrative of Scaleup Arabia.

I would like to extend my sincere gratitude to the following visionaries, whose work continues to inspire and impact the region's entrepreneurial ecosystem:

Muhannad Ebwini, HYPERPAY (www.hyperpay.com)

A fintech pioneer, Muhannad Ebwini, Founder & CEO of HyperPay, has revolutionized digital payments in the Middle East. His company provides secure and seamless online payment solutions, empowering businesses to scale and enabling smoother financial transactions across the region.

Jeremy Crane, YELLOW DOOR ENERGY (www.yellowdoorenergy.com)

Co-Founder & CEO of Yellow Door Energy, Jeremy Crane is leading the charge in the renewable energy transition across the MENA region. His company specializes in solar energy solutions, helping businesses reduce costs and lower their carbon footprint through innovative commercial solar leasing models.

Ahmed Hamdan, UNIFONIC (www.unifonic.com)

Founder & CEO of Unifonic, Ahmed Hamdan has built one of MENA's most influential cloud communication platforms. His company enables enterprises to enhance customer engagement through AI-powered messaging and voice solutions, setting a new standard for business communication in the region.

Noor Al Hassan, TARJAMA (www.tarjama.com)

As the Founder & CEO of Tarjama, Noor Al Hassan has transformed the translation and localization industry in the MENA region. Her company leverages AI-driven language solutions and human expertise to provide high-quality content and accessibility in Arabic and beyond, making global communication more seamless.

Though their full stories were not featured in this edition, their contributions to the startup and scaleup ecosystem in the region remain profound. I encourage readers to follow their journeys as they continue to redefine industries and drive innovation.

ACKNOWLEDGEMENTS

Thank you to everyone who contributed to this publication—for your insights, feedback, and support. Your time and efforts are greatly appreciated. Though you may not all be named individually, please know that your influence is felt throughout this book.

Special gratitude to the contributors in this book for your time and input— Mudassir Sheikha, Abdulmajeed Alsukhan, Tomaso Rodriguez, Omar Hagrass, Noureddine Tayebi, Tarneem Saeed, Mohamad Ballout, Abdulaziz B. Al Loughani, Michael Lahyani, Hamdi Tabbaa, Yara Burgan, Mostafa Amin, Ali Hashemi, Hussam Hammo, Ismael Belkhayat, Sophia Alj, Faisal Toukan, Sarah Toukan, Jeremy Crane, Ahmed Hamdan, Noor Al Hassan, Muhannad Ebwini and Ronaldo Mouchawar.

Special thanks to the distinguished individuals who generously provided endorsements for *Scaleup Arabia*—David Cohen, Tim Draper, Christopher M. Schroeder, Michael E. Gerber, Verne Harnish, Strauss Zelnick, Jonathan Ortmans, and Ankur Warikoo. Your kind words and belief in this project added tremendous encouragement and credibility—thank you.

Thank you for your help to—Zadya Dias, Christina Christou, Isra Hassan, Daryl Hardy, May Youssef, Layla Hajjaj, Menna Gamal, Chanelle George, Stacey Pinto, Nai Issa, Natalie Faulkner, Fadwa Torbey, Rawaa Fattouh, Christian Tassin, Swati Trivedi, Nadin Doughem, Habiba Waleed, Mariane Villano, Mariam Aboutaleb, Brian Habibi, Esra Sehweil, Hind Rasheed, and Iman Benomar.

My sincere apologies to those whom I couldn't feature given scope and size limitations of the book.

I would like to extend my deepest gratitude to the remarkable contributors from my previous book, *Startup Arabia*. Their journeys and invaluable advice have resonated with thousands of aspiring and current entrepreneurs, inspiring and empowering a new generation of changemakers. A special thank you to Samih Toukan, Mona Ataya, Mudassir Sheikha, Omar Soudodi, Maaz Sheikh, Delphine Eddé, Idriss Al Rifai, Kunal Kapoor, Bana Shomali, Elie Habib, Omar Gabr, Muhammad Chbib, Sara Alemzadeh, Jon Richards, Fouad Jeryes, Khalil Shadid, Mai Medhat, Amir Barsoum, Abdulaziz B. Al Loughani, Niama El Bassunie, Zain Alabdin Tawfiq, and Philip Bahoshy. Your insights, experiences, and wisdom continue to shape and inspire the entrepreneurial ecosystem, and for that, I am truly grateful.

To Andy Meaden—for your invaluable, timely help and patience.

To Rimy Allam, Erika Vericima, Aysha Espada, and Oreo Juve— for your wonderful encouragement and support through every twist and turn of this journey.

To Rawia Helmy, Ahmed Soudodi, Omar Soudodi, Reem Soudodi, Ranya Naji, Ashraf Naji, Amal Elsayed, Maryam Allam, and Reem Allam—thank you for being an anchor of unwavering support.

To Mariam Allam, Liala El Edwy, and Moustafa El Edwy—this book was written with you in mind.

To Nash Salah—for your priceless friendship and encouragement, both in this project and throughout the years.

Special thanks to Ahmed Rostom, Muhammed Mekki, Heba Badawy, Vera Ilisoi, Amal Dohkkan, Bill Liao, Amr Belal, Sid Slover, Dr. Dariush Zahedi, Dr. Yahya Tabesh, Len Braudis, Mark Driscoll, Dilek Barcin, Kimberley Ong, and Levi Lewandowski.

To the staff at NAC—for your incredible hospitality and accommodation.

Finally, to my mother and father, may they rest in peace—you are my guiding light, and all my achievements are in your honor.

THANK YOU, EVERYONE, for being part of this journey and for helping make this book a reality.

ABOUT AMIR HEGAZI

AMIR HEGAZI is the Managing Director of CapitalDemocracy, a global professional advisory firm specializing in helping founders and startups raise venture capital, where he serves as an advisory board member for multiple startups across diverse sectors and geographies. Additionally, he is an Advisor to the University of California, Berkeley, on its global AI initiative. Prior, Amir was the Co-Founder and Managing Partner at intoMENA Group, a market-entry strategy firm that assists companies in doing business in the MENA region.

Amir also played a key role in launching and managing Souq. com's marketplace. Souq.com, the largest e-commerce platform in the Middle East, was acquired by Amazon. com in one of the region's largest exits to date. Amir is a pioneer in digital media in the Arab world, having launched the region's largest online TV networks at Talfazat and JumpTV. JumpTV raised $150 million and completed a dual listing on the Toronto Stock Exchange and the AIM Market of the London Stock Exchange before being acquired by Neulion.

Amir advises ministers, policymakers, and founders on go-to-market and e-commerce strategies. He is the author of several Amazon.com bestsellers, including *Startup Arabia* and *Ecosystem Arabia*, both recognized among "Best Startup Books to Read of All Time" by Book Authority. Amir has also authored *Venture Adventure*, *ChatGPT for Startups*, and *Discover Your E-Why*.

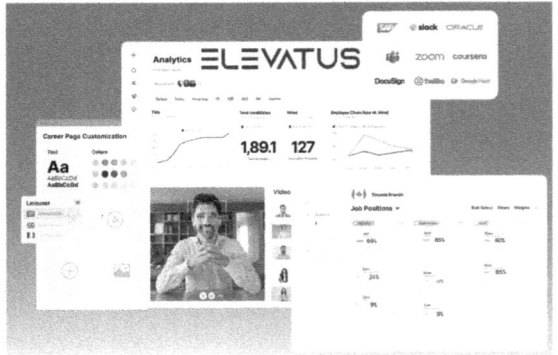

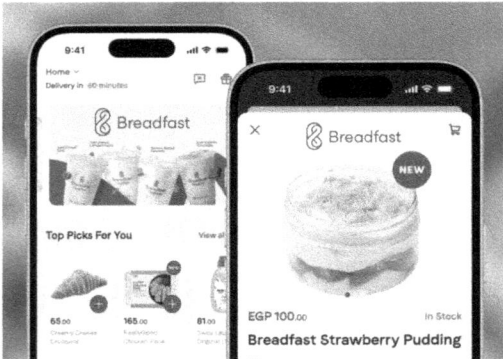

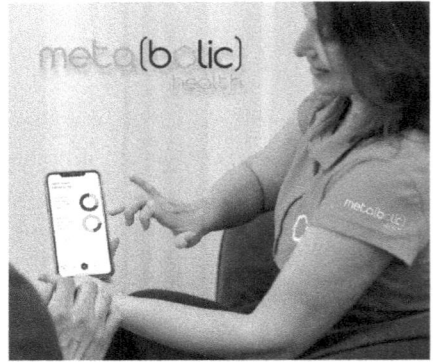